Internationalizing
Media Theory

The Media, Culture & Society Series

Editors: John Corner, Nicholas Garnham, Paddy Scannell,
Philip Schlesinger, Colin Sparks, Nancy Wood

Internationalizing Media Theory

Transition, Power, Culture

Reflections on Media in Russia, Poland and Hungary 1980–95

John D.H. Downing

SAGE Publications
London • Thousand Oaks • New Delhi

First published 1996

 SAGE Publications Ltd
6 Bonhill Street
London EC2A 4PU

SAGE Publications Inc
2455 Teller Road
Thousand Oaks, California 91320

SAGE Publications India Pvt Ltd
32, M-Block Market
Greater Kailash – I
New Delhi 110 048

British Library Cataloguing in Publication data

A catalogue record for this book is
available from the British Library

ISBN 0 8039 8710 2
ISBN 0 8039 8711 0 (pbk)

Library of Congress catalog card number 96–070413

Typeset by Mayhew Typesetting, Rhayader, Powys
Printed in Great Britain by The Cromwell Press Ltd,
Broughton Gifford, Melksham, Wiltshire

Contents

Preface

Many institutions and individuals have made this book possible. Let me name the institutions first. The PSC–CUNY Staff Congress Political Science panel allocated me an award in 1986 to travel to Russia and Czechoslovakia. The Communication Research panel allocated me a further award in 1988 to travel to Eastern Europe over that summer, and renewed it the next year, which enabled me to return in 1990, this time combining it with a semester sabbatical leave from Hunter College over the spring of that year. My John T. Jones Jr Professorship at the University of Texas at Austin and the Center for Post-Soviet and East European Studies there enabled me to make further visits from time to time, and another sabbatical leave granted by the University of Texas in the autumn of 1994 enabled me to complete most of the writing. The *Media, Culture & Society* editorial board were good enough to recommend to Sage Publications that they award me a contract to write the book for this series, and Sage were good enough to comply.

Among the individuals, let me first, and entirely fairly, thank for their challenges, probings and insights the many groups of students over the past twenty years who were on courses I taught on Russia and Eastern Europe, in Greenwich University, London, in Hunter College of the City University of New York, and in The University of Texas at Austin.

Some versions of parts of the text appeared in the *Electronic Journal of Communication/Revue Électronique de la Communication*, 4.1 (1994); in my chapter in Marjorie Ferguson and Peter Golding (eds), *Beyond Cultural Studies* (Sage, forthcoming); and in a paper delivered to the conference on The Restructuring of Broadcasting in East and Central Europe, at Westminster University, London, in October 1993. My thanks to Tom Jacobson of SUNY Buffalo, Marjorie and Peter, and to Colin Sparks and Anna Reading, organizers of the Westminster University conference, for their responses, and to Colin for his reading of this manuscript.

Other individuals are numerous, but let me, perhaps unfairly, single some out for thanks – unfairly because they should not be held responsible for errors of fact or interpretation, and also unfairly because I am sure to have inadvertently forgotten some to whom I owe thanks. Volodia Padunov, Jakab Zoltan, Szekfü András, Karol Jakubowicz, Tadeusz Kowalski, Jerzy Szejnoch, Jerzy Oledski, Marianna Sidoryanskaya, Boris Bagaryatsky and Dina Iordanova particularly stand out as individuals who, some over many many years, have generously tried to help me understand better the many nuances and realities of media, culture and society in Eastern Europe and Russia. To this understanding have also contributed the many media professionals and educators – too numerous to name – whom I interviewed in Russia, Poland and Hungary over a series of years.

Philip Schlesinger of Stirling University, UK, Nancy Wood of Sussex University, UK, John Sinclair of Victoria University, Melbourne, Michael Hanchard of Northwestern University, USA, and Horace Newcomb of my own department, were kind enough to comment upon various drafts, as were Volodia Padunov and Dina Iordanova. Ellen Wartella loaned me her laptop computer for a crucial semester. Jun-hao Hong served as my research assistant for a semester. Eithne Johnson transcribed some interview tapes for me. My faculty colleagues in the Department of Radio–Television–Film have consistently been supportive and stimulating. Special thanks to Tom Schatz, who chaired my department during my semester's leave. My gratitude, too, to Steve Barr and Sophy Craze, who successively oversaw the process at Sage; to Pascale Carrington at Sage for her eagle eye and understanding of what I was (really) intending to say; and to Moondisks for designing an excellent jacket cover.

For whatever shortcomings remain in this text I take full responsibility.

Gratitude is definitely due to my staff colleagues in the department office, namely Susan Dirks, Kathryn Burger, Paul Johnson, Lillian Respress and Cathy Simmons, who have created an environment in which it was possible for me to consider devoting a chunk of my mental energy and time to writing this book while serving as chair – as have Doc Hamilton (who also was ever-helpful with computer problems), Derek Young, Bob Grubbs, Marc Herbst and Peter Bretz in the technical staff.

To Ash Corea, *la imperatriz de las empanadas*, belongs the ultimate accolade, by now impossible to express fully in words after so many delicious years together.

John Downing
June 1996

Introduction

Theories of media communication, acknowledged or unacknowledged, as surely shape our understanding and practice of communication as do economic theories frame our understanding of and involvement in economic practices. John Maynard Keynes' famous remark about the latter sphere of analysis, that people's spontaneous economic common sense usually turns out to be the theory of some long-dead economist,[1] is more than a quip at the expense of the self-satisfied ignoramus. It suggests that theory is much more influential in human affairs, in common sense – for better or worse – than the anti-intellectual current that exists in most cultures is disposed to admit. Even the pragmatism often trumpeted as a reassuring aspect of Anglo-American culture's respect for everyday common sense, is itself the name of a philosophical school.

Thus the understandable opprobrium that scholastics, brahmins, mandarins, rabbinists, mullahs and all species of academic theorist have drawn down upon themselves for their esoteric themes and language, not to mention their airs and graces, cannot hope to exorcize the effects upon the rest of us of their labors in theory. Only understanding their work and exposing its problems, and only developing better theory in the most straightforward yet precise language that can be achieved, together stand any chance of putting us, rather than them, in the driver's seat.

The seemingly most obvious features of our existence are typically among the most complicated. Communication is an activity even worms and fleas may engage in to some rather restricted extent, and so it may not be surprising that in the academic and professional worlds it has long been thought obvious, a rather banal topic of study, a little like the fact that we all, not just Molière's Monsieur Jourdain, speak prose. Communication media, similarly, unless we include 'Literature' (spoken in vibrato, or pronounced LIT-ruh-chuh) and its books under this heading, are claimed to be such commonplaces – the telephone, the soap opera, the rock video, news-on-the-hour – such casual and superficial factors in our lives, that intensive analysis of them is only for the intellectually slipshod, a signal that the academy has lapsed into total trivia and deserted its high and holy calling.

This take on the supposed fatuity of communication research offers more insight by far into the resolute philistinism of the academic mind than it offers illumination of the contemporary human condition. It is indeed paradoxical that the same academic can cite with pleasure the Latin phrase that 'nothing human is foreign to me' (*nihil humanum mihi alienum est*) and simultaneously flush away the ongoing practice of culture (communication) and the hugest feature of modern communication (media).

This paradox shows itself in a variety of situations, one of the key ones for the purposes of this study being the repeated virtual absence – it is tempting to cite the term 'structuring absence', signifying a skewing process rather than simply an omission – of consideration given to communication process in the study of power in political science. There are exceptions, the huge political science literature focusing on the specifics of presidential campaigns and electoral communication being a case in point. Yet as we shall see, questions of the state, of totalitarianism, of political and social movements, of regime transition, have generally been researched without benefit of attention to communication processes, rather as though politics consisted of mute pieces on a chessboard. Hough (1977: 201–2) has been an unusual voice among political scientists in acknowledging that 'it is striking how rarely these concerns [of how horizontal and vertical communication are shaped] are placed at the center of comparative political analysis'.

At the same time, not everything in the garden of communication theory is lovely. Politics and power, as though by some obscure reflex reaction to the lacunae of political science, are often missing, presumed dead – a curious outcome in the case of US communication research, given its substantial initial sponsorship by government agencies intensively involved in shaping and honing Cold War and 'Third World' politico-military strategies (Simpson, 1994).

Furthermore, and equally crucially, the overwhelming body of media communication theory is based upon data from just two spots, Britain and the United States, which have – despite the joke about the dissimilarity of their uses of English – remarkably similar leitmotifs in their cultural, economic and political history that mark them out from most other nations on the planet. They have both (since 1865) been stable capitalist democracies, deeply involved in global affairs as imperial powers, not invaded by other nations, strongly marked by a diffuse Protestant Christian tradition, and highly affluent by planetary standards.

The other nations on whose experience and culture media communication theory has mostly been based have been Germany, France and Italy, although the rapid growth of media studies in the Canadian and Australian academies has recently added those nations to the list. In general, however, we are still dealing with problematics from nations in the same approximate mold as Britain and the United States: stable, affluent capitalist democracies with some form of imperialist history (a rather contradictory one, albeit not identically so, in the cases of Australia and Canada).[2] The experience of fascist rule in Germany from 1933 to 1945 and in Italy from 1922 to 1944 is counter to this general drift, but oddly enough, rather little has been explicitly drawn from that experience into reflection on media communication theory.

It could be argued, to the contrary, that implicitly a core conclusion from the fascist experience was indeed drawn in some governmental quarters in the USA, namely that intelligently organized propaganda communication, the one-way transmission of information to a target audience, was politically highly effective. This would help to explain the very considerable sums of money that Simpson (1994) has indicated were spent on so-called 'psychological warfare' research in the period 1945–60, that in turn he argues were highly constitutive of the parameters of academic communication research in the United States since that time.[3]

None the less, many of these studies, as he notes, were classified until recently and thus unable to be read or cited and so to saturate the intellectual climate as fully as they might otherwise have done. Perhaps even more to the point, these studies did not seek, it would seem, to explore communication within the fascist phenomenon so much as to work with one of the key assumptions in the minds of fascist strategists, namely the potent impact of organized top-down communication for propagandistic ends.

Thus in the absence of much attention to the European fascist phenomenon itself, there has arisen a body of literature that implicitly theorizes media communication as part of a benign societal process – or, in the case of some critical theorists, equally basing their approach on the small group of nations indicated, as *superficially* benign whilst in truth highly problematic for the advancement of a democratic culture. Hence issues of power, the state, endemic conflicts, societal change, the economy, institutionalized racism and ethnic insurgency, secrecy, surveillance, have tended to be marginalized at best in the mainstream literature.[4] In the critical literature, the tendency has been to try to explain why a number of these issues have not been as salient or explicit in the media, and therefore in public debate, as they might be expected to be and need to be.

A second major theme of this book, therefore, is the necessity for communication theorizing to develop itself comparatively, acknowledging in particular that to extrapolate theoretically from such relatively unrepresentative nations as Britain and the United States is both conceptually impoverishing and a peculiarly restricted version of even Eurocentrism. Hence, in part, this book's focus on change and mediatic processes in Russia, Poland and Hungary over the turbulent years from 1980 to 1995.

The former Soviet Union and most of the other twenty-seven contiguous nations at one time within the Soviet bloc, before, during and since the transitions of their regimes at the close of the 1980s and the beginning of the 1990s, evinced every one of those issues and processes typically marginalized in much media communication theory, and did so center stage. They are not alone in this respect: media communication has also centrally exhibited these features in South Africa, in a considerable number of Latin American nations, in South Korea, in Iran, in China, in Taiwan, in varying forms.[5] Indonesia, Thailand, many other African and also Arab nations, the South Asian nations, regardless of their manifold specific differences, equally present a media scenario quite different in many respects from the Anglo-American one, yet comparable with each other at a number of points in terms of the key issues and processes specified above.

This degree of relative commonality does not blot out differences, not least the notable differences between Russia, Poland and Hungary. As will be frequently evident in the chapters that follow, during neither the Soviet nor the post-Soviet period were they simply amalgamated echoes of each other, any more than any other nations in the former Soviet bloc. Thus whereas the primary reason for their selection in this study is that they offer much more characteristic examples of media processes across the planet than do Britain or the USA,[6] a second ground for their selection is precisely the informative contrasts between them. A number of the contrasts and parallels will be explored in some detail in the following chapters, but in essence the choice of these three nations for research was originally based upon the complexity and centrality of Russia, the system-battering insurgency of Polish society, and the – sharply contrasting – 'piano piano' changes by the Hungarian regime from the mid-1960s onwards.[7]

So far, we have referred to media communication theory as a single entity. In reality, currently, media communication theories may be conceptually divided into three categories, namely **segmented**, **fragmented** and **totalist**.

By **segmented** is meant typically US-originated mainstream approaches, which theorize media as discrete entities in society, and in that way suffer from a frequent failure to integrate their findings even with research on communication in educational institutions, family processes, religious bodies, organized 'leisure' activities or everyday interpersonal communication (not to mention a failure to connect up with political or economic research). Examples would include gatekeeper analysis (Snider, 1967); agenda-setting (Protess and McCombs, 1991); cultivation theory (Melischek et al., 1984; Signorielli and Morgan, 1990); and 'uses-and-gratifications' theory (Rosengren et al., 1985).

By **fragmented** is designated authors writing from a great variety of perspectives, much of their work long pre-dating the post-modernist wave of celebration of fragmentation, such as Benjamin, Barthes, Bakhtin, Enzensberger, as well as current cultural studies research. Their work offers a plethora of insights, but is not internally systematic.

By **totalist** are meant marxist approaches, such as Gramsci, Althusser, Williams, Hall, Schiller, but also non-marxist systematists such as Habermas, and functionalists such as Parsons, or media system dependency theorists (DeFleur and Ball-Rokeach, 1990). Unlike the 'segmented' group, neither the 'totalist' nor the 'fragmented' categories include people whose analysis is restricted to media as such, but this arguably strengthens their theoretical contributions rather than somehow invalidating them from consideration under the heading of media theory.

I will not venture a comparable categorization of political science theories, but rather will flag those which have a clear bearing on the empirical subject-matter of this book, namely totalitarianism theory, social movement theory, democratic transition and consolidation theory, civil society theory and public sphere theory. The two latter are also current within critical communication analysis debates in some quarters, as the mention of Habermas above testifies.

This study will therefore seek to reconfigure media communication theories by conducting a triangular analysis. It will assess: (1) linked politico-economic and cultural-mediatic changes in Russia, Poland and Hungary[8] over the period 1980–95, from time to time referencing comparable situations in a few of the other nations just now mentioned; (2) the adequacy or inadequacy of existing media communication theories in relation to these fresh but, I argue, more inclusive foci; and (3) relevant debates within political science (whilst avoiding being hobbled by the bemusing capacity of some political science approaches to handle these transitions without significant reference to key communication processes).

At the same time, the study will seek to avoid being snagged by the opposite snare of marginalizing the USA and the cluster of nations customarily drawn upon by media theorists, and at the close will review how best to advance media communication theory in the light of combining all these empirical foci. Thus in revisiting the standard cluster, it will be proposed that media communication theory should centrally embrace consideration of major features of those 'preferred' nations that it has traditionally tended to leave out of account.[9]

Indeed, a significant thread in the empirical argument of this book is that the difference between the media-power structure relation in authoritarian regimes and contemporary liberal democratic regimes is not of the order of night and day, as per the classical *Four Theories of the Press* approach,[10] but rather night and twilight.[11] That is to say, that the controls characteristic of the latter regimes are more targeted, less blanketed; cheaper, more supple, and more effective in the long run because harder to spot and challenge. On this reading, the process of mediatic change in Russia, Poland and Hungary was a change toward 'business as usual' in the West, not into dazzling daylight. A number of the protagonists of demolishing sovietism undoubtedly thought dazzling daylight would be the consequence of their struggles. Perhaps if they had not, they might not have had the spirit to try so hard as they did to effect change. Perhaps they needed a Sorelian myth. But, all honor due them, they were wrong. The political agenda has had to be reconformed to twilight standards, not junked entirely.

A third central contention of this book is that communication research should be an inherently integrative exercise, and thus one which poses a challenge to the organization of the analysis of society conventional in the academy for well over a century, namely its hacking up into anthropology, economics, geography, history, international relations, linguistics, philosophy, political science, psychology, sociology. Of these disciplines, some have no pretension to integration. Indeed their practitioners rather pride themselves on the solid results they feel they produce from focusing on but one dimension of our social existence. Others sometimes have ambitions toward integration – anthropology, and, in Europe, sociology – and in the hands of their best practitioners, fulfill them. Geography, at the present time, is the only well-established discipline whose practitioners regularly come close to bringing together a full range of foci and methods under one roof.[12]

In the perhaps now waning days of post-modernist analyses, such integration and systematic analysis have been rather suspect activities. When only flux and disconnection whirl about one's head like a wild storm of dust, someone seeking out settled patterns and interrelations and – worst of all – system, could seem intellectually and even politically on the edge of extinction. Interesting insights have been produced within post-modernist discourse, yet its alarming dimension has often been the license provided, in the name of attacking the spurious imposition of a rational grid on discombobulated experience, to casual, ill-thought-out (and still more, clumsily articulated) formulations. It has sometimes felt a little like watching an inexperienced and frustrated poker player dawning to the recognition that the game is unpredictable, and then playing at random as though it were utterly unpredictable and any hand or play worth any other.

Simply because any intellectual system is a construct and thus an artificial imposition on our experience, and simply because it will always be contradicted at a series of points where it does not 'fit', this should not be taken to mean that the search for intellectual coherence and connection is itself fatally flawed and counterproductive – whereas a strong case could be made for the opposite contention, namely that abandoning such a search is to cast off any shackles of intellectual discipline whatever.

Just as over the past thirty years geography has in some sense reinstated the pre-modern assumption that human society and its physical ecology are indissolubly linked, and has done so in concert with the growing recognition that the past five human centuries have violently accelerated the perils of the planet, so it is high time for communication researchers in particular to overflow the dams created by the nineteenth- and twentieth-century academy's spiralling parcelization of knowledge, and to connect up their research foci. This book is intended in part as a contribution to that project of recombining history, political economy, the sociology and geography of culture, the technologies of communication and philosophy.

In this connection, Williams (1982: 208) has such a well-phrased statement of how that recombination should be conceived in relation to signification and culture, that it deserves citation in its entirety:

> the distinction of culture, in the broadest or in the narrowest senses, as a realized signifying system, is meant not only to make room for study of manifestly signifying institutions, practices and works, but by this emphasis to activate study of the relations between these and other institutions, practices and works. The key to these relations turns twice. It activates these relations by insisting that signifying practice is deeply present in all those other activities, while preserving the distinction that in those others quite different human needs and actions are

substantially and irreducibly present: the necessary signification, as it were, more or less completely dissolved into other needs and actions. It then activates the relations in an opposite direction, by insisting that all those other needs and actions are deeply present in all manifest signifying activities, while preserving the distinction that in these practices these other needs and actions are, in their turn, more or less completely dissolved. The metaphor of solution is crucial to this way of looking at culture, and the qualification 'more or less' is not a casual phrase but a way of indicating a true range, in which relatively complete and relatively incomplete degrees of solution, either way, can be practically defined.

Fourthly and finally, the book further argues in favor of the following specific positions.

1   Mainstream media and their cultural expressions are a pivotal dimension of the struggle for power that is muted but ever-present in dictatorial regimes (as in all others), a struggle that then develops between political movements and the authoritarian state in the process of regime transition, and equally in the consolidation period after the transition.

2   Alternative media of numerous kinds are both the interior dialogue and outward self-expression of these movements, and thus are central to any understanding of the movement process itself.[13]

3   Many types of media, not simply broadcasting or print or cinema, but also such forms of expression as graffiti, theater, music, religious observances, need to be incorporated into the analysis.

4   The symbolic and emotive dimensions of media are critically important, not merely their explicit content as typically categorized within a ratiocinative problematic.

5   International[14] dimensions of media communication are also fundamental, as the 'globalization' debate has – sometimes clumsily – underscored (Featherstone 1990; Ferguson 1992; Robertson 1992; Schiller 1989).

6   Finally, the capillary communication that takes place in a variety of settings, whether in the social networks often underlying social movements, or in the very vertices of state power within and between nations, and indeed at all levels, not least including telecommunicated interaction, is also part and parcel of understanding all these situations. To divorce it from mediatic communication as 'merely interpersonal' is idiotic.[15]

The plan of the book is to address in the first chapter the need for political science perspectives in communication research, whilst simultaneously underscoring the communication research lacunae in political science. In the second chapter, written primarily for those unfamiliar with Russia, Poland and Hungary, a brief overview is provided of those nations' twentieth-century developments. (Those familiar with them may wish to read the chapter to ascertain where the author stands in many areas of empirical contention, although there will be no space there to justify the positions adopted.)

Chapters 3–6 will examine, in turn, sovietized media in the post-Stalin era in Russia, Poland and Hungary, especially in the decade leading up to the 1989–91 biennium; the role of culture and communication in the dissolution and collapse of sovietized structures; the role of political and economic factors in conjunction with communication processes in that regard; and, lastly, a number of the main mediatic developments in the years since the biennium up to the close of 1995. Obviously, these chapters represent an outsider's perspective, albeit rather well seasoned with views of those on the spot. At the same time, a careful and sometimes fairly detailed empirical overview is important to serve as a source of illustrations for the book's primary theses concerning communication theories' priorities and problems.

Chapters 7 and 8 will then critically review mainstream and critical media communication theories in the light of the foregoing and their own intrinsic problems. The book ends with a Conclusions chapter, which will seek to reflect critically upon media theory based upon this more inclusive problematic as well as the typical lapses of traditional media theory in considering media communication in stable capitalist nations such as Britain and the United States.

Excluded will be any systematic attention to bio-physical dimensions of media influence (such as notions of persistence of vision), or to what might be termed psycho-cognitive aspects of media (how readers and spectators individually process media texts), or to the details of textualist theories (such as those of Bakhtin or van Dijk). This is not intended to dispute their significance, for indeed at various points the argument will touch upon some of these issues. The primary focus of the book, however, is on the media–society–culture–power relationship at the level of state and economic structures, societal change, institutional and international conflicts, and political and social movements.[16]

It would be as senseless to try to divorce these and other levels of strictly mediatic analysis from each other as it is to separate mediatic considerations from issues of power. The book does not seek to reify any such divide. It simply sets out, within an already very large compass, to be manageable. In that regard, it acknowledges the practical rationale of academic specialization. It persists, however, in rejecting any attempt to settle back stably into specialization's cosy but fissiparous routines as though they were inexorable, or, ultimately, productive of true insight.

Notes

1 '. . . are usually the slaves of some defunct economist'. His next sentence concerning political philosophers is less cited: 'Madmen in authority, who hear voices in the air, are distilling their frenzy from some academic scribbler of a few years back.' John Maynard Keynes, *A General Theory of Employment, Interest and Money*. New York, Harcourt Brace Jovanovich, 1964, p. 383.

2 A rather influential text for many years, Siebert, Peterson and Schramm's *Four Theories*

of the Press (1956), now under major revision by Christians, Nordenstreng and White, did propose a categorization of media structures on a global scale into authoritarian, libertarian, Soviet and social responsibility models. The ultimate purpose of the book, however, appeared to be to highlight the splendors of the media system in the Anglo-American duo, poised a little uncomfortably but still beautifully between freedom and responsibility, as contrasted with repressive systems. It described the models ('theories'), with varying degrees of adequacy, and in a static manner, rather than drawing back and asking the more basic questions addressed here. The distinction it drew between authoritarian and Soviet models is one which will be discussed and critiqued in the first chapter.

3 Simpson does not extend his argument in this direction, but the literature on presidential and other election media campaigns, albeit by definition concerned with democratic and not fascist political strategies, is similarly unilinear in its communication focus. Advertising communication strategies normally fall into the same mold as well.

4 Among the notable exceptions are Cumings (1992), Kellner (1992), Raboy and Dagenais (1992). War is a particularly acute form of crisis, but there are many others less dramatic but equally far-reaching. At the 'undramatic' end of the spectrum Raboy (1992) appropriately draws attention to what he terms 'the invisible crisis of everyday life', in this instance violence against women.

5 For further information see, for example, on South Africa, Louw, 1993a, 1993b, 1994; Tomaselli and Louw, 1991; Waisbord, 1995; on Latin America, Fox, 1988; Kaiser, 1993; Lloréns, 1994; Mattelart and Mattelart, 1974; Skidmore, 1993; Straubhaar, 1989; on South Korea, Kim and Lee, 1994; Aie-Ree Lee, 1993; Lyu, 1994a, 1994b; on Iran, Sreberny-Mohammadi and Mohammadi, 1994; on China, Calhoun, 1991; Schell, 1988: 9–37, 119–76, 193–244; Schell, 1994: chs 5–9, 25–8; Zha, 1995; on Taiwan, Cheng 1989.

6 Again, some commentators would vigorously dispute this judgment on the ground that sovietized nations had totalitarian regimes, different in essence from merely authoritarian ones such as Indonesia from 1966, or Saudi Arabia, or Chile under Pinochet. See Chapter 1.

7 There is no absolute logic claimed for this choice. Attention to nations such as Romania, Czechoslovakia or Albania that had the most Stalinist of the bloc regimes, would have provided informative contrasts as well. So would attention to other multi-ethnic and multi-national states such as Uzbekistan, Tajikistan or Georgia.

8 Clearly, the experiences of yet further societies than Russia, Poland and Hungary over the fifteen-year timespan reviewed here, will be invaluable in pushing this reconfiguration still further.

9 In this regard, the critical analysis of Eurocentrism and the project of a multicultural media studies proposed by Shohat and Stam (1994), the ongoing project of feminist media studies (cf. Van Zoonen, 1994), Martín-Barbero's (1993) recomposition of media research in the light of Latin American realities, and the study of oppositional social movement media (cf. Downing 1984/1996), are all part and parcel of the effort to reconfigure media communication theory in the direction of inclusivity, not simply on political grounds – although there is no shame in that – but on the fundamental scientific premise of examining a variety of situations and manifestations heretofore relegated to the margins of intellectual concern.

10 See note 1 above. Sue Curry Jansen (1988: 29–32) presents an important argument concerning the ideological uses to which the Nazi dictatorship was put since 1945 by both an imperial West and a dictatorial East, to disarm opposition to their own regimes. She writes: 'the winners have also used this history . . . to vindicate their own violence . . . it is just such denials, such refusals to see, which create the conditions that could permit it to happen again . . . It is easy to exorcise aberrations . . . But it is far more difficult to discover ways to restructure social systems and human institutions so that they do not encourage ordinary men to behave like monsters' (pp. 30–1).

11 Properly speaking, the depths of night in this metaphor of media and culture would be fascism, and in the USSR the Stalinist period and the earlier Brezhnev period (1964 to about 1975), by comparison with which the Khrushchev period and the later Brezhnev period to 1982 were already some form of late twilight. In making an important point about the distance

liberal democracies still have to travel, it is not intended to understate the unspeakable horrors of actual totalitarianism.

12 See Giddens (1984: 355–68) for a strong statement in favor of considering sociology, history and geography as a single endeavor.

13 Included in this and the following points should be consideration of the nationalist and ultra-nationalist media that have circulated in most if not all of the post-Soviet lands. Attention should not be so engrossed by the struggle for and against democracy up to the crises of 1989–91 that the succeeding social movements and battles for power are relegated to the rear.

14 Literally, that is, between nations.

15 Giddens (1984: 139–45) provides an excellent statement on the absurdity of dividing micro- from macro-analysis. Unfortunately the typically scientistic tradition of analysing interpersonal communication in the US academy provides little intellectual encouragement to overcome this divorce in the field of communication.

16 My friend and colleague Colin Sparks at Westminster University is preparing an important analysis of the implications of media change in Poland, Czechia, Slovakia and Hungary for understanding the relation between media and democracy.

1

Political Science, Communication Research and the Transition, 1980–95

It is vital to address first some basic conceptual issues in political science concerning the character of sovietized states and their political process, and the changes that took place within them from the 1980s onwards. In societies as top-heavy as these were at the beginning of their decline, clarity on these issues is central to the analysis of culture, communication and media both before and after the transition. The two phases are cemented together, given the patent truth that after the collapse of the Soviet system, none of the nations within it was a *tabula rasa*.

There are two further basic propositions underlying what follows. The first is that the declining decade of the Soviet bloc nations was not radically different from, and therefore is usefully comparable to, the processes and structures, including communication processes and mediatic structures, of other dictatorial regimes. The second is that, as already proposed in the Introduction, the cultural and communication dimension is frequently missing, or minimally present, in analyses of the power processes of Eastern European change, thereby generating an analytical image of mute, if astute, pieces on a chessboard rather than actual societies in flux and movement.

We will begin with the frequently debated – and debased – concept of totalitarianism, and then continue that discussion by specifically focusing on the appropriate characterization of the Soviet state, especially in its final decade. I will then shift to commentary on the relevance of three debates within political science with a clear bearing upon these transitions. One is the debate on **democratic transition and consolidation**. A second is the debate on **social movements**. The third is the debate, spanning communication research and political science, on **civil society and the public sphere**. This is only intended to be commentary, not a systematic literature review.

The Concept of Totalitarianism

In the decade before the transition, including during martial law in Poland from 1981 to 1985, it is analytically unhelpful and indeed fundamentally misleading to describe any of these three regimes as totalitarian.[1] This is not an admirer's bouquet, merely a rejection of conceptual demagogy.

In terms of this book's focus, it therefore follows that the role of media during this transition phase does not constitute an aberrant set of data belonging to a now fossilized, completely *sui generis* social system. On the contrary, with due acknowledgment to post-imperial, national and certain other structural specificities, these societies are more informative about the societal roles of media across the planet than is the Anglo-American focus conventionally dominating the field. Many of their features are replicated elsewhere in one way or another.

Furthermore the Anglo-American focus has typically been a highly selective one, *even in its own terms.*

The term 'totalitarian' has been used intensively since it was first widely diffused by Mussolini (*lo stato totalitariano*), but with many different senses. Even Gramsci, for example, used the term (Femia, 1981: 172ff.), but in his case to refer to any philosophy that seeks to be comprehensive and/ or has a systemic impact on societal organization. In this sense, market liberalism would be the totalitarian philosophy of a developed capitalist society. To this ideological dimension of the term he added two others related to his vision of a post-capitalist order, namely the emergence of a collectively unified rather than a competitive or fragmented society, and of a public consciousness dedicated intensively to building up society in that mold (cf. Adamson, 1987). Just to complicate the picture further, we may note that Arendt (1958: 256–7, 308–9) argued that until 1938 Mussolini's state was not in reality totalitarian, despite his enthusiasm for using the term.

In the 1980s Kirkpatrick (1982), in her dual capacity as political scientist and the Reagan administration's Ambassador to the United Nations, used the distinction between the adjectives 'totalitarian' and 'authoritarian' to argue in favor of a long-standing US foreign policy. She deployed it to defend the fact that monstrously corrupt and brutal dictators who were anti-Communist (e.g. Indonesia's Suharto, Zaire's Mobutu, Argentina's Videla) were continuously supported by the US, on the ground that they were only 'authoritarian', whereas unacceptable but empirically less barbaric Communist regimes had to be confronted and extirpated. Authoritarian regimes, she claimed, had a limited shelf-life; totalitarian regimes, because of their all-embracing ideologies, went on for ever unless overthrown from the outside.

Her argument proved her a far better ambassador than political scientist, as we shall see now when we examine the core literature on totalitarianism. (It would be to descend to her poor terrain to attack her on the ground that the regimes she categorized under this heading all collapsed within a decade of her assertion, since everyone was taken by surprise by the speed of those transitions.)

In a number of key respects the concept of totalitarianism itself is flawed, although even with those flaws it has an ethical integrity absent from Kirkpatrick's Reaganite *raisonnement d'état*. None the less, it would be pointless to investigate Russia, Poland and Hungary further without assessing this concept's applicability to them. No serious analysis of media communication can divorce it from the character and operation of the political regime within which it operates. We will begin with the work of Arendt, the most distinguished single scholar to have deployed the term. We will then review Lefort's position on the subject, representing a later and distinctive approach to totalitarianism with a particular emphasis on sovietism.

In essence, Arendt strove to acknowledge analytically what effectively defeated and still defeats the imagination, let alone the rational intellect, namely the Nazi and the Stalinist destruction of human life: 'What common sense and "normal people" refuse to believe is that everything is possible. We attempt to understand elements in present or recollected experience that simply surpass our powers of understanding . . . there is an inherent tendency to run away from the experience' (Arendt, 1958: 440–1). Earlier, in about 1951, she had written: 'it has brought to light the ruin of our categories of thought and standards of judgement' (Arendt, 1994: 318). This is the core of her position on totalitarianism, its ultimate foundation. It is to her permanent credit that she fought to carve out concepts that would not simply assimilate Nazism and Stalinism to the everyday processes of political repression; that she was determined to pay homage, so to speak, to a 'radical evil [that] has emerged in connection with a system in which all men have become equally superfluous' (1958: 459).

To struggle to express the inexpressible, she dug back into the very foundations of modern European society in order to argue the profound roots as well as the profound newness of the Nazi and Stalinist states. To discuss these foundations and her assessment of them would take us too far afield, but one element in her position requires acknowledging here, namely that totalitarian rule begins with totalitarian movements and therefore comes to power with support from below, not as though it were some pre-dawn coup d'état imposed by stealth on an unwilling populace.

In terms of the growth to ascendancy of totalitarian regimes, that observation is particularly important. It means that the totalitarian ideology (the march of History for Stalinism, the force of Nature for Nazism) which she identifies as a key component of their rise is not simply a regime-sponsored public relations fog, but a vital mobilizing force in the transition from movement to regime and for the inner core of the regime (the SS, the NKVD[2]).

In turn, however, although Arendt does not address this important specific, her emphasis on this paramount role of ideology implicitly underlines the significance of media communication in diffusing and developing such ideologies at every phase in the coming to ascendancy of such regimes. The absence of media communication from her analysis of this issue is a notable lacuna, one which Poulantzas (see Chapter 8) redresses somewhat.

The core of the totalitarian system, she proposes (1958: 437–59), is the concentration camps, both ideologically and organizationally. She describes them (p. 437) as 'the laboratories in which the fundamental belief of totalitarianism that everything is possible is being verified'. One of her strongest observations is that totalitarian domination is not amenable to conventional economic, let alone political, rationality. She harnesses data from both Soviet and Nazi regimes to support this (pp. 410–11, 427; cf. 347–50, 387–8, 444–5), such as the economic and military absurdity of prioritizing the transport and extermination of the Jews in Eastern Europe in the latter stages of the Second World War, and the liquidation of 90 percent of the Soviet officer corps in the 1930s purges. Thus the camps represent the peculiar dynamic of totalitarianism. It is a dynamic beyond the all-too-conventional repression of protest or resistance, common to many regimes throughout history. This can blast all other priorities off the map. The camps in this regard represent that dynamic's perfect realization.

However, in part as if to emphasize the hideous singularity of the totalitarian dynamic, Arendt repeatedly fences off seemingly comparable instances that might be described as 'totalitarian', but which in her view are not. Thus, as we have seen, she refused to describe the Mussolini regime as such until 1938, or even the Nazi regime as such until the beginning of the war,[3] or the Soviet regime as such until 1930 (p. 419). She dismisses Franco's and Salazar's fascism (pp. 308–10) as nontotalitarian dictatorships preceded by totalitarian movements, and indeed asserts that only large countries can 'control enough human material to allow for total domination and its inherent great losses in population' (p. 310) – so that even Germany could not definitively venture down the totalitarian path until it had annexed vast contiguous territories. She actually proceeds on this basis to speculate (p. 311) that India and China have 'frighteningly good' prospects for totalitarian rule, given the size of their population and their traditions of despotic governance.

At this last juncture Arendt appears to be carried away by the apparent logic of her argument. It is cited here, however, to establish a different point, namely the great care with which she tried to differentiate totalitarianism and its genesis from other forms of absolute rule. In practice this precision was hard to sustain. Thus she refers to 'semitotalitarian' movements (p. 308) without ever defining the term, and to 'totalitarian tendencies' in McCarthyism (p. 356, n.36), which may be reasonable acknowledgments of grey areas, but inevitably cloud the precision and clarity she was seeking.

Similarly she proposes (p. 456) that it 'is in the very nature of totalitarian regimes to demand unlimited power. Such power can only be secured if literally all men, without a single exception, are reliably dominated in every aspect of their life.' Is this an implicit theory of the inevitable collapse of totalitarian regimes, inasmuch as the insistence on unconditional power may indeed be their drive and dynamic, but really cannot be 'secured . . . reliably' over the longer term? By her own reckoning this dynamic lasted very few years in the case of the Nazis (overthrown by outside force), if somewhat longer in the case of Stalinism.

She had relatively little to say even in her second edition about the character of these regimes in the post-Stalin era, though given its date this was probably to be expected. Her commentary in that edition upon the 1956 Hungarian revolution was penned before the gradual relaxations implemented by the Kádár regime were remotely visible. What she does propose, however, at the close of the commentary upon Hungary is very interesting in the light of 1989 and 1991, namely that the most likely outcome of the Soviet system is 'a sudden and dramatic collapse of the whole regime [rather] than a gradual normalization' (p. 510).

In a sense that is true, the demolition of the Berlin Wall being its supreme symbol. In another sense, as we shall see when we investigate the role of media in these collapses in more detail, the collapse was dramatic but hardly sudden, if by 'sudden' is meant 'out of the clear blue sky'. These are not meant as cheap shots from hindsight at Arendt's analysis of trends that were yet to evince themselves when she was writing, only observing that probably for this reason she did not have an articulated account of totalitarian decline or collapse, which in turn raises the question rather sharply as to whether these Soviet bloc regimes in the 1970s and 1980s actually fitted her use of the term 'totalitarian'. The argument here is that her use of the concept is not very helpful in analysing that later phase of the development of those regimes,[4] with possible exceptions such as Albania or North Korea.

Before leaving this discussion of Arendt, we need to examine further those few points when she does analyse communication within the totalitarian system. She only ever addresses it in very broad brush-strokes, offering much less empirical detail in this regard than in many others.

We have already noted that her emphasis on the bridging role of totalitarian movements implies but never states the role of media in communicating ideology and propaganda. She defines the typical basic content of these movements' initial propaganda as their claim to expose issues systematically covered up by the regimes then in power, the 'truths' that they refused to acknowledge to the public (e.g. the Versailles Treaty and the 'stab in the back' legend).

At one point (pp. 341–4), now analysing the established totalitarian regime, she proposes a very specific sense for the term 'propaganda', defining it as externally directed communication from the regime, as opposed to 'indoctrination', which at that point she characterizes as domestic propaganda. Elsewhere (pp. 365–7) she discusses the communicative role of the 'fellow-travelers' in other countries in – usually naively – buffering, for those nations' citizens who would greatly prefer not to have to confront such horrors, the monstrosity of what such regimes were doing. This is a further, socio-psychological dimension of Arendt's frequent assertion that the totalitarian experience is almost uncommunicable (pp. 437–41, 445–6).[5]

Arendt does not hold consistently to this external sense of 'propaganda', however. For example she argues a further distinction to have been significant, namely that propaganda to camp inmates was forbidden in the Nazi system, since they were conceived of as 'superfluous' human beings, whereas the SS guards were very thoroughly indoctrinated (p. 438). In turn this statement about the SS also seems to contradict another of her positions, one closely akin to her famous dissection of Eichmann and the banality of evil, concerning the simple, straightforward 'philistinism' of administrators and guards on which Himmler's camp organization depended (p. 308). If that depiction were accurate and sufficient, then indoctrination would hardly be needed.

She has other observations on the cocooning of the regime's public 'in the gruesome[6] quiet of an entirely imaginary world' (p. 353), and on the key realm of secrecy in such regimes, namely the operations of the secret police at the heart of the control system (pp. 435–7). There is, she argues, a necessary relation between the publicity for creating the new Soviet man or for global Aryan leadership, blazoned everywhere, and the deathly secrecy of the ruthless, violent organization adopted to achieve that end.

The Frankfurt School's 'mass society' definition of communication in a totalitarian regime (see Chapter 8) is expressed by Arendt in limpid terms: 'Total domination succeeds to the extent that it succeeds in interrupting all channels of communication, those from person to person inside the four walls of privacy no less than the public ones.' Interestingly, however, she immediately offers qualifications:

> Whether this process of making every person incommunicado succeeds except in the extreme situations of solitary confinement and of torture is hard to say; in any event, it takes time, and it is obvious that it is far from completed in the satellite countries [i.e. Eastern Europe]. So long as terror is not supplemented by the ideological compulsion from within, so hideously manifest in the self-denunciations of the show trials, the ability of people to distinguish between truth and lies on the elementary factual level remains unimpaired. (p. 495)

This qualification is important for present purposes, because it shows once more Arendt's readiness to qualify and express caution, her alertness to the national and developmental specifics of this form of domination, rather than – as some of those who have used the term 'totalitarianism' since – simply squashing together all Soviet bloc regimes into a unitary procrustean mold from the date of their inception onwards.[7]

Her remarks on communication, though fragmentary and sometimes contradictory, are often rich in implication for the roles of communication media under dictatorship. Like much in political science literature, however, Arendt's analysis falls short of explaining, and limits itself to asserting, the effective operation of the propaganda and ideology integral to dictatorial – and in her focus, to totalitarian – regimes.[8]

Lefort (1986: 273–319) concentrates his analysis of totalitarianism strictly on sovietized regimes. Within this frame, his overriding concern is less with the specifics of how such regimes operate than with the 'phantasy' of the project that the system sets itself: 'we would be victims of the phantasy which inhabits this system if we imagined that it actually realized itself, that it could ever succeed in realizing itself, even in the heyday of Stalinism' (p. 316). This is important to establish at the outset, since many analyses using the concept of totalitarianism have explicitly or implicitly portrayed extreme and absolute power in action. Lefort's agenda is different.

For Lefort, the essence of the totalitarian phantasy is to collapse all distinct levels of social functioning – law, science, aesthetics, economics – and to try to make the phantasy actually happen: 'to efface social division, to absorb all processes of socialization into the process of state control, to push the symbolic into the real' (p. 317). This includes the attempt at dissolution of the individual subjective consciousness. Elsewhere he writes: 'Anyone who does not pay attention to the immense apparatus constructed to dissolve the subject, wherever it can express itself, into an "us", to agglomerate, to melt these various forms of "us" into the great communist "us", to produce the People-as-One, will fail to understand how the logic of totalitarianism operates' (p. 290).

This observation directs our attention in principle to the communicative logic of the system, although Lefort does not expand on it further beyond, on the same page, listing the supposedly special interest organizations set up by such regimes (such as Youth Fronts, women's organizations and the like) as communication microcosms of the whole system. Thus in his argument the very appearance of diversity conceals the strategy of ideological unification.

Lefort identifies certain other specifics as peculiar to the system (pp. 286–9). One is the image of 'Power-as-One', paralleling that of the 'People-as-One', and ultimately expressed as faith invited in a single supreme leader. A second is the assumption that enemies and parasites constantly threaten the project and must be searched out and destroyed. A third is that society can recreate itself totally according to an already understood definition of where it will end up at the close of the process (the five-year plans would be a major instance). A fourth is that 'total knowledge of the detail of social reality' (p. 288) is available to the power structure. And a fifth is that the project addresses 'the most secret, the most spontaneous, the most ungraspable element of social life: . . . customs . . . tastes and . . . ideas' (p. 285).

In some ways, Lefort's analysis offers more scope for understanding the way in which the Soviet system began to crumble than does Arendt's. With the impact of *Solidarnosc* much in mind, and acknowledging the erosion of totalitarianism since the death of Stalin, he writes:

> The power which dissimulates itself runs the risk of reappearing as the organ of oppression, towering over the whole of society and becoming the common target of all contestation. The party, which penetrates every milieu and exercises control over all activities, runs the risk of being seen everywhere as a parasite. The distance between those above and those below, and, more generally, inequality, runs the risk of being exposed. Finally, the all-pervading ideology runs the risk of provoking a generalized refusal to believe, a radical mode of disaffection which relegates it to the status of a pure political lie; the power of discourse collapses, leaving the image of the oppressive power without a protective screen. (p. 317)

This represents a rather effective summary of some key dimensions of the final decline of Stalinism, with the exception that the different nations in the Soviet bloc saw 'the generalized refusal to believe' in the system emerge and grow, including within the *nomenklaturas*, at varying points in time, and not simultaneously in a rush (despite the telescoped final enactments in 1989). A further exception needs making, namely that declining living standards generated a further ever-widening and unsuturable tear in the already threadbare ideological fabric. The *nomenklaturas'* and some post-Soviet political parties' increasing recourse to nationalist symbols and appeals in order to sustain their faltering hegemony is a phenomenon noted in the next chapter as being a consequence of these developments.

However, it is clear that for Lefort too the latter stages of the Soviet regimes represented a clear if slow – too slow by far – retreat from the original 'totalitarian' project. The extent to which the regimes in that period can be described as totalitarian in Lefort's terms is therefore somewhat akin to pinning down the point at which the Cheshire Cat in *Alice in Wonderland* is still present when only its smile remains. And this question is still posed within Lefort's framework, where actual practice is not to be confused with the totalitarian project: how many people were left in Poland, Hungary or even the Soviet *nomenklatura* in the 1980s who still accepted the totalitarian project as something which could and should be realized? Political control strategies to secure the well-being of the then-ruling *nomenklaturas* were in no way the same as commitment to the original totalitarian project.

Thus the casual application of the term 'totalitarian' to the final period of the sovietized regimes is either to dilute the term to a point of vacuity, or alternatively to issue empirically unsustainable claims about such regimes (cf. the discussion in Goldfarb, 1989: 3–29). Van Atta (1989: 149) makes the very important observation that

> totalitarian theorists tended to assume that the regime's decisions were carried out once made . . . [yet] the Soviet state has historically been able to exert many more negative sanctions on people's behavior (to prevent undesired activity) than positive sanctions (to reward desired actions). This weakness in the state's implementation capacity has emerged more and more glaringly as the tasks of administering Soviet society have become more complex. In this respect the Soviet Union is often a very weak state.

Van Atta's point was demonstrated throughout the Khrushchev and Brezhnev eras by the perpetual pronouncements that the Plan would shift resources from heavy to light and consumer industry, which were scarcely ever realized (Asselain, 1981: chs 4–5; Radvanyi, 1982: chs. 3–6; Schroeder, 1979; 1982).

None the less, let it be clearly restated: this book's entire critical project could itself be argued to be vacuous, on the ground that the political system and political transition in the former Soviet bloc nations was unprecedented and thus entirely *sui generis*. Not only those who use the term 'totalitarian' sloppily would argue this. As some people said to me in Poland in 1990, 'What are we supposed to do now, read *Das Kapital* backwards?'

There is a clear element of truth in this position, in that the Soviet system should not be identified in all particulars with any and all dictatorships, economically, ideologically or politically, any more than those others should be regarded as detailed equivalents of each other.

All the same, to inflate these obvious truths into an absolute theory of 'Soviet exceptionalism' would be to join hands with a particularly weird *de facto* alliance, consisting of former apologists for the so-called socialist camp on the one hand, and on the other of Cold War essentialists and Russophobes[9] for whom the combined brains of an 'émigré German-Jewish librarian' and an 'obscure Russian political pamphleteer' (Brzezinski, 1989: 3) mysteriously and miraculously created the *Ungeheuerlichkeit* of Communism, to be radically distinguished, as Kirkpatrick sought to claim, from mere authoritarianism of an anti-Communist stripe. In terms of repression and terror, the essays in Corradi, Fagen and Garretón's *Fear at the Edge: State Terror and Resistance in Latin America* (1992; cf. Merrett and Gravil, 1991), are sadly more than sufficient to dispel that distinction.

Let us take this issue of the appropriate use of the concept of totalitarianism, and the question of the legitimate comparability of the terminal decade of many sovietized regimes with other dictatorships, into some specific observations about the later Soviet state. These will be extended to review cultural and mediatic dimensions in more detail in Chapter 3.

The Later Soviet State: a General Characterization

Perceptions and theories of the character of the state in the Soviet bloc nations up till 1989 and 1991 vary widely – including within those nations themselves. While rather few would apply the adjective 'democratic' to the regimes in question, there is still a basic split between what I shall call the fundamentalists, who, as we have seen, typically[10] espouse the term 'totalitarian' when defining the Soviet-type state structure, and the pragmatists, who focus more on its unwieldy mechanisms, lack of coordination, internal contradictions, and functional equivalents to the inputs and outputs of Western political systems.[11]

Rather as one pair of English humorists[12] once described the contending forces in the English Civil War as 'Wrong But Wromantic' (the Cavaliers) and as 'Right But Repulsive' (the Roundheads), one may feel a certain emotional affinity with the fundamentalists' radical revulsion against the Soviet state's attempt to squelch people's freedoms – even if often the fundamentalists' moral outrage did not extend to the cause of the dispossessed in non-sovietized lands, including their own. One may also experience a degree of irritation with those who phlegmatically, almost amorally, seem to be temporizing with tyranny by pointing out the Soviet state's limits and the full complexity of everyday existence and power relations in that system.[13]

None the less, this conceptual and moral nettle, the question of the character of the later Soviet state, has to be grasped, since understanding media power without understanding state power is impossible – and, in modern societies, vice versa, *pace* many prominent communication researchers and political scientists. If we can answer that question, then we can begin to identify in which ways these sovietized states' relation with their media system differed from or resembled those of a variety of forms of state control, whether military dictatorships, the South African apartheid regime, the British government's media policies regarding Northern Ireland from 1969 onwards, or the Reagan administration's attempts to restrict the free flow of information to its own public.[14] The contrasts and parallels illuminate each individual media–state relation more exactly, and in turn may allow us workable and illuminating generalizations on certain levels concerning that interrelation. Simultaneously, the important post-transition relation between state and media communication is illuminated.

There follows a five-point bare-outline proposal for understanding the character of the Soviet state in what we now know to have been its declining years. It will be illustrated with symptomatic observations. (Some more detail, especially on the Polish and Hungarian states, will be provided in the following chapter for those wishing it.)

The first *aperçu*, denoting the core of the original Stalinist state, is the horrified reaction of Bukharin[15] in the late 1920s, anticipating what Stalin's policies for rural Russia and Ukraine – peasants then comprising the vast majority of the Soviet population – would bring about, namely 'military-feudal exploitation' (Cohen, 1971: 320ff.). This was no Marxist jargon, but a very precise, concentrated forecast of exactly what transpired: (1) the dominance of the military on many levels of Soviet society; (2) feudalism, (a) in the exact sense of the permanent quasi-corvée mode of extracting an agricultural surplus, and (b) in the wider sense of the extension of clientilistic power relations to every sphere of society (Kennedy, 1991: 216–21; Lampert, 1985: ch. 2; Willerton, 1979, 1987), and (c) in the general meaning of economic backwardness.

Bukharin's pithy phrase conveys the everyday political and especially economic reality of the Stalinist state more accurately than 'totalitarianism', which at best – as we have seen – signifies an attempt rather than a finished achievement, and which in some uses ultimately implies a drive for power derived from a psychic charge abstracted from any specific history, rather than as integrally related to a political economy and culture (neither Arendt nor Lefort can be accused of this debased use). The economic dimension, in particular, is important to understand.[16] As is argued in the next chapter, in the Soviet case the roots of this political economy are precisely in the Civil War, its genesis the policies of 'War Communism', readopted and made permanent at the close of the 1920s with the official turn to state planning and rural 'collectivization'. These policies were first the test-site and then the crucible of the Stalinist state. They generated its core, which then took about four decades following Stalin's demise in 1953 to disintegrate sufficiently to collapse.

The second source is James Millar's characterization of the Brezhnev regime's policy as 'The Little Deal' (Millar, 1988). The term is derived from

Dunham's (1976) term 'The Big Deal' (adapted in turn from FDR's New Deal), which she used to characterize the gradual relaxation, beginning over the last eight years of Stalin's life, of certain extreme levels of behavioral restriction. Millar in turn pinpoints the further decay, first under Khrushchev and then in Brezhnev's latter years, of the furious and hideous dynamic of Stalinism into a set of structures from which a keystone of the original driving impetus had gone, namely the fear of extreme, instantaneous and unpredictable repression, to be replaced by a series of unofficial piecemeal concessions to those who were not aiming at any of the nerve-centers of the inherited system.[17] Similarly, Shlapentokh (1986: 137ff.) wrote of 'the gradual extinction of fear' among the younger generation, leading ultimately to their 'loss' to the system.[18]

One could roughly describe this general mutation as a kind of feudalism in simultaneous reform and decay.[19] In an essay first published in 1981, Ruble (1984: 912–13) perceptively observed that 'muddling through . . . *is* the system', and added that 'the Soviet threshold of pain is, like the sloth's, far higher than we might expect'. Breslauer (1984: 239) coined the term 'welfare-state authoritarianism' to characterize the late Soviet state, by which he meant 'providing a less austere and repressive daily life for the masses, while cracking down on the dissenters'. Millar, Shlapentokh, Ruble and Breslauer render the actual flavor of the late Soviet state's overall form of domination infinitely better than the simplistic nostrums of the totalitarian label.

The third source is Shlapentokh's immensely perceptive, if somewhat unorganized, monograph (1986) on the dual 'pragmatic' and 'mythological' levels of mentality common in the latter decades of the Soviet Union. By these terms he refers to the everyday activity of the society, as opposed to the regime's mythological definition of that reality:

> the leading role of the working class, internationalism, social and national equality, and socialist democracy make up the mythological part of the official ideology. Planning, socialist property, Russian patriotism, science, education and the family represent values that are part of the pragmatic level of ideology. (1986: 37)

This is not in the first instance an analysis of the Soviet state's organization, but dissecting that state's dual hegemonic communicative processes helps to illuminate its degree of effective daily functioning.

Shlapentokh distinguishes this dual level of ideology and communication both from Orwell's 'double-think' and from Freud's concept of rationalization (pp. 183–4, n.11). 'Double-think' implies a simultaneous adhesion to two contradictory ideas, whereas in Soviet society there was, rather, a permanent conscious discord between mythological ideas/words and pragmatic deeds. For Freud, rationalization obscures the truth, whereas in Soviet citizens' awareness the truth did not normally evaporate, except in the case of a small minority of true believers, the 'self-satisfied slaves' in Sinyavsky's phrase (Sinyavsky, 1990: 145ff.). The permanent disjunction

Shlapentokh identifies offers us an important insight into how the Soviet state maintained itself for as long as it did, but also why it teetered to a fall (see Chapter 4). Its contradictory character also challenges concepts such as 'legitimacy' (Weber), 'totalitarianism', and 'hegemony' (Gramsci),[20] which in the case of sovietized societies do not penetrate sufficiently some of the key elements of communication in regime maintenance and decay.

The fourth source, a very important balancing element in relation to the last two, is Amalrik's (1982: 246–7) account[21] of how the KGB major who had been sent to arrest him suddenly quietened and froze as he saw for the first time how the abyss could open up and swallow someone if that person were actually deemed guilty of aiming at a nerve-center of the system. The episode perfectly reveals the continuing ultimate basis of the system, namely repression, but acknowledges that for most people this reality was no longer staring them in the face, was no longer so supremely capricious as in earlier decades – always provided they avoided predictable minefields.

The fifth and final source for this interpretation of the late Soviet state is Dusko Doder's analysis (1986; cf. Albats, 1994) of the forces behind the rise of Gorbachev, in particular Doder's recognition that the last Soviet leader owed his rise and eventual promotion to Party chief to the KGB and the patronage of Andropov, long the KGB Director.

The role of the KGB as king-maker – not a lone role, to be sure – and as protagonist of limited reform, is one that accounts of its repressive and spying mission have hardly prepared us to expect. Yet while the omnipresent KGB was not composed of totally like-minded, let alone reform-minded, individuals, its hierarchy may well have had the most accurate and comprehensive picture of Soviet and global realities of any institution, Soviet or non-Soviet. A sense of the urgency for economic rejuvenation was probably better represented there than in the Party, the government bureaucracy, or even the military (which depended on technological innovation to continue to compete in war). At the same time, this dimension of Gorbachev's rise to power underscores the continuing massive power of the police state apparatus in determining policy at the highest and most strategic level (cf. Rahr, 1994: 19–21; Albats, 1994: chs. 4–5). And this apparatus showed few signs of dissolving in Russia in the post-Soviet period: quite the reverse.

These five observations do not exhaustively delineate, let alone explain, the character of the late-era Soviet state – how could they? – but they will serve as highly suggestive combined indices of what that state had become by the early 1980s so far as the general Russian[22] public was concerned. In other words, the state's original draconian and totalitarian character, but not its core economic structure, had become transmuted for the general population into an agency that could turn a blind eye to a number of infractions of the code, to petty graft, even major graft at the top, but retained as rigid a clamp as it could muster on oppositional activity or communication. The pragmatic level of the state's ideology continued to function alongside simultaneous public lip-service to its mythological level. Its political police 'wing' continued in force, backing Brezhnev's long-term successor, the reformer Gorbachev (two successors, Andropov and Chernenko, each took office and then shortly afterwards died). And the KGB easily outlasted both Gorbachev and the collapse of the Union.

This has deliberately not been a structural description of the main agencies and institutions of the Soviet state, but rather an attempt to characterize its formative genesis and the later development of its methodology of power, that could be regarded as having been gradually grafted on to that original core, thereby modifying it in a number of significant ways.

The client-states' modes of operation were in turn officially modeled upon the Soviet exemplar, although as we will see in the next chapter and will note again at intervals throughout, their similarities in a number of very significant respects should not blind us to a number of noteworthy differences.

The role of communication in this delineation and in the process of decay and change is barely stated above, but will be addressed in Chapters 3 and 4. A prime aim in drawing this brush-stroke characterization of the late Soviet state is to dislodge the false expectations and premises set up by the concept of 'totalitarianism' for understanding the states, economies, cultures and media communication processes of the former Soviet bloc during the period under review in this analysis. The realities were a great deal more complicated than common uses of the concept, or Arendt's or Lefort's more measured uses, would lead us to suppose (cf. Goldfarb, 1989).

How should then the processes of decline and reconfiguration of sovietized regimes be conceptualized, and the role of media within those processes? To address this question, it is necessary first to respond to the literature on regime transition and consolidation, on social movements, and on the much-debated concepts of 'civil society' and the 'public sphere'.

Regime Transition and Consolidation: Comparative Analyses

Theories and analyses of regime transition have been intensively developed in recent years, mostly based on the experiences of Southern Europe and Latin America, from the post-Mussolini period in Italy through the transitions from fascism in Portugal, Greece and Italy in the 1970s, but mainly concentrating on the emergence of democratic national governments in Latin America in the 1980s (Di Palma, 1990; O'Donnell, 1993; O'Donnell et al., 1986; Stepan, 1988, 1989). The initial formulations dealt simply with the transition from authoritarian rule, the breakdown and collapse of military regimes. Later these researchers came to focus on the consolidation process of democratic regimes as well (Mainwaring et al., 1992), and on attempts to categorize democracies and thereby clarify the notion of transition to 'democracy' (O'Donnell, 1992b, 1993).

One caveat is immediately in order concerning the applicability of their studies to Eastern Europe, namely the assumption that the political transitions in that region would automatically be to some form of democracy. A number of East European countries may have at best a very long, even stalled transition in that direction, notably Serbia, Croatia, Romania, Slovakia, Ukraine, the Transcaucasian and Central Asian republics of the former Union, and not least Russia itself.[23] This consideration does indeed force us to define more carefully what is meant by the term 'democracy', and perhaps to join O'Donnell (1992b) in exploring the notion of 'delegative' democracy, which he proposes as a potentially enduring regime-type, with its own particular features, midway between dictatorial rule and representative democracy.

Amongst these he lists the endowment of the presidency with more and more formal powers in order to be able to address ever-worsening economic crisis, but leading in practice to 'a curious mixture of Presidential omnipotence and impotence' (p. 14). Although he has Peru, Brazil and Argentina in mind, this is highly reminiscent of Russia under Gorbachev from 1988 onwards, and under Yeltsin thereafter. In a second essay, O'Donnell (1993: 18) writes of the short-term *sauve qui peut* culture that emerges, of the 'angry atomization' of society and the consequent continuing crisis of the state – again, highly reminiscent of many of the CIS states, and to some degree of Poland and Hungary in the first half of the 1990s.

There are obvious differences, however, between the Latin American and Eastern European situations. The main ones are as follows.

In the Latin American situation, the public forces for change had and have to confront the military, often with major sections of agrarian, industrial and financial capital behind it, and with the US government often behind those. In Eastern Europe, the prime visible enemy was the Party, with the military–industrial complex and the secret police playing a rather complicated role, often internally split for periods of time, but in this region with the Soviet government acting as ultimate prop in East-Central Europe up until 1988,[24] and directly in the former Union until 1991.

The economic structure of sovietized nations is another difference that many analysts have foregrounded, and indeed the absence of market forces – outside the second economy – did differentiate the sovietized nations from even the most statized economies of the dictatorships. None the less, there are some interesting parallels to be traced between *nomenklatura*[25] economic control and patronage structures, and similar military-bureaucratic power-positions in a number of Latin American countries at the point of transition.

Indeed, Walder (1994), basing his argument mostly on data from the People's Republic of China, has proposed that the intra-bureaucratic deal-making necessitated by this emerging economic pattern in late sovietized nations was a potent factor in detaching local elites from the power of the center, since the latter was less and less the source of all economic advantage. The unparalleled size of China, demographically speaking, may make his point moot for smaller nations. None the less, his observation underlines the importance of digging below ideological rhetoric concerning state and private ownership when making comparisons between sovietized and other nations.

In support of this argument, let us recall that the second economy in sovietized nations may have been the only economic sector subject to market forces, but it was never segregated from the main economy. It generally operated precisely to relieve some of the rigidities of the latter. The post-transition phenomenon of ex-*nomenklatura* capitalists, and of some criminal mafias, did not emerge from a pure blue sky or a pure Red State.

A further difference, however, is the international dimension of sovietized regimes' collapse (cf. Grilli di Cortona, 1991).[26] Sometimes this is read the wrong way (cf. Di Palma 1991), and each regime is implied to be a carbon copy of all the others. There is a further proclivity to read the DDR, Czechoslovakia and Romania, the 'tighter' examples, as especially emblematic of the Soviet bloc. The very tightest of all (Albania) and the ones that do not quite 'fit' (Bulgaria, Yugoslavia) are not used in this way. Yet as the next chapter will make clear, without the interaction of Russia, Poland and Hungary, the 'tighter' examples might still be extant. This homogenization, selective or general, is highly unproductive.

The difference that a number of analysts, not simply Kirkpatrick, would immediately cite is of course the totalitarian character of the regimes. Máckow (1994: 329) asserts that the transitions to democracy would surely have been complete by the time he wrote his article if the regimes had merely been authoritarian. In an interesting twist to this approach, Karklins (1994: 30) proposes that totalitarianism, i.e. the Soviet bloc, was an integrated system such that if one piece fell out the whole machine would collapse. That piece, she states, was 'the underpinning of the monopoly over the media and ideology . . . [which underwent] such a complete transformation, setting off a chain reaction'.

Despite the fact that she joins the meager ranks of those who underscore the role of communication in these processes, she and Máckow are wrong. He never defines either democratic or economic 'success', which enables him to assert that Russia and the rest have failed, whereas 'authoritarian' transitions have succeeded already. Karklins errs in seeking a sole cause, prompted to do so by the simplistic nature of the totalitarian model, and is inevitably unable to explain why that piece 'fell out' of the machine. She just asserts it was pulled out by Gorbachev. If so, why?

The number of empirical studies of the transitions is vast and continues to grow, but no attempt will be made here to evaluate them systematically. Perhaps the purest of them is Marcin Król, at the time editor of the then-permitted independent Polish journal *Res Publica*, who dismissed any attempt at sociological complexity out of hand:

> What happened was that (1) ideology disappeared; (2) fear disappeared. And that
> was the end of it. There is nothing more. It is not really so complicated, not so
> sophisticated, as the pseudoscientists imagined. (Król, 1990: 159)

This is not, of course, purely empirical. It is founded on a very basic set
of ethical tenets, in the same way that other commentators such as
Solzhenitsyn have spoken of 'the Big Lie'. Yet while it is vital not to lose a
moment's connection with the ethical dimension of dictatorship, these
positions still do not explain very much. They are poetic headlines.

Studies with some conceptual orientation are fewer,[27] but often omit
entirely the dimension of communication or media. Karklins is an exception; Remington, Chirot, Tismaneanu and Molnár lay varying degrees of
stress on civil society and public sphere issues, with some emphasis on
questions of alternative media (see below in this chapter for a further
discussion of the concepts 'civil society' and 'public sphere').

The nearest approach the Latin Americanist transition researchers make
to an analysis of communication or media in regime breakdowns is couched
in terms of highly general statements about legitimacy and hegemony and
the role of the diffusion of fear in repressive political climates. Equally,
when they turn their attention to consolidation, their focus is rather
exclusively on such topics as the quality of the new political leadership, the
attitudes of the former military rulers to their appropriate role in government, the role of continuing economic problems in fostering the public's
growing *desencanto* with the new regime, the continuing public fear of a
reversion to dictatorship, the importance of generating a political culture of
compromise between previously polar political forces.

They make good liberal nods in the direction of freedom of expression
and association, of the opportunity to have one's political views institutionally represented during the consolidation process: 'democratic actors
must go on creating a fabric of institutions which can carry out the
mediation of the interests, identities and conflict mobilized in a given
period. This . . . is the crucial thread which leads to a consolidated democracy' (O'Donnell, 1992a: 22). But they do not even note how media would
be pivotal to that mediating fabric. They are obsessed with the political,
strictly conceived, tightly wrapped.

An exception to their virtual silence are some very interesting comments
on the social mechanisms of awakening change at the dawn of regime
breakdown – referred to by O'Donnell et al. (1986) as the 'resurrection of
civil society' – which do have a strong communicative dimension even
though they do not trace it out in much detail. The authors refer to the
importance of public political gestures by exemplary individuals – Walesa,
Sakharov, Havel, are names which come to mind in our region – in testing
the limits of the possible. They note the impact of satire and ridicule by
artists and intellectuals in small settings such as cafés, classrooms, book-
stores, apartments. They emphasize the importance of informal activity and
discussion in universities, literary journals, unofficial research groups. They
stress the potential effectiveness of dress and gesture as signals of dissent.

All these are significant topics. But the mediatic dimension is essentially treated *en passant*.

The strength of the literature cited is in its focus on the perspectives and strategic behavior of various, mostly elite, political actors. They focus on such issues as the important difference between 'liberalization' instituted from on high, and democratization implying power from below (e.g. the difference between Russia and Hungary, and Poland, in the *Solidarnosc* era); on how far hard-liners in the elite are risk-insensitive, and doves, risk-aware (i.e. rational souls rather than gentle ones); on the customary military, bureaucratic and police detestation of uncertainty and disorder, leading to instinctive support on their part for a strict regime; on the role of conspicuous elite corruption in alienating the public; and on the conditions under which a section of the elite may 'secede' from the regime and form a coalition with some oppositional forces. They nicely describe the tense period after the collapse of military regimes, where a reversion to military control is always on the table and the new democracy may die a slow death, pushed back step by step to what O'Donnell terms a *democradura*, a sad fusion of *dictadura* and surface democratic forms (O'Donnell, 1992a: 19).

It is strange: their remarks on the effect of the culture of fear in deterring hope for change, on the excitement of the mutual discovery of shared ideals (cf. Alberoni, below) among the atomized, repressed public at the dawn of change, and on the tense climate in the pre-consolidation period, all cry out for an analysis of communication processes. So-called 'rational choice theory' is part of the bedrock of these analyses, of some in particular (e.g. Przeworski, 1992), but the role of communication of any kind in the process of strategizing choices, even within the elite, is only hinted at or implied, never examined.[28] Whether rational choice theory gives sufficient space to expressive dimensions of society and politics is also one of its major problems, a problem from which communication and cultural analysis, by virtue of its normal lens, is considerably less likely to suffer.

Thus the democratic transition and consolidation literature offers necessary but only partial insight into the themes of this book. Ultimately, as already remarked, it is in serious danger of treating political actors as mute, albeit astute, pieces on a chessboard, and thus of producing a very curious abstraction from societal reality. It also tends to concentrate on the apex of power. These deficiencies rather naturally prompt an examination of certain other political science literatures which explore (1) social and political movements, contesting the political order, that surely do communicate in numerous ways both within their own ranks and to the rest of society, and (2) the associated concepts of civil society and the public sphere. Let us first examine the relevance of social movements for understanding the multiple relations between media communication and the state in the era of regime change in Russia, Poland and Hungary.

Social and Political Movements and Communication

The impact of popular movements varied considerably between Russia, Poland and Hungary. Poland's *Solidarnosc* clearly exerted the most impact by far, having arguably been, along with the Afghan resistance movement, the slow detonator of the entire Soviet bloc's dissolution (see Chapters 2 and 4). Notwithstanding the great insurrection of 1956, Hungary's overt oppositional movements in the 1970s and 1980s were miniscule by comparison with Poland's (Ramet, 1991: 100, 113–21), though it could also be argued that their undramatic, almost capillary character set up an amazing level of dialogue between Party reformists and dissidents that unobtrusively but permanently altered the political topography inside Hungary (cf. Seleny, 1994), and by their very uneventfulness made change seem feasible to tentative reformers in other bloc countries.

The Soviet Union's movements were primarily ethnic and/or religious (Tökés, 1975), though with an additional very powerful environmental component during the 1980s, which emerged into greater, if selective (Orechkine, 1993) force once the Gorbachev regime's *glasnost* policies had lifted the lid on public expression (Babkhina, 1991; Helsinki Watch, 1990; Sedaitis and Butterfield, 1991; Tolz, 1990; White, 1995). In Chapter 4 we will also examine youth movements and musical formations, which arguably were significant over the longer term in precipitating regime change.

Interestingly, workers' movements, although intense at certain moments, such as the Tyumen' oil field workers' or the Russian and Ukrainian miners' militancy in 1989–90 (Bova, 1991b; Crowley, 1994; Rutland, 1991; Sedaitis, 1991), made far less of a dent on the dissolution of the regime in the USSR (or Hungary), than in Poland. This may have been partly a product of the sheer physical expanse of the USSR and the geographical distance between the centers of agitation and Moscow, the concentrated center of state power, which reduced the immediate visibility and communicative capacity of the strikers.[29]

Taking a longer view across the 1980s as a whole, Migranyan (1991) has argued that in the specific conditions of the Soviet Union, unleashing freedom of communication in the *glasnost* era before making headway in solving economic problems was a recipe for the chauvinist social movements and the ethnic and nationality confrontations which scarred the former Union and Eastern Europe thereafter (cf. Butterfield and Weigle, 1991; Goble, 1991; Hockenos, 1993). Despite Migranyan's known statist bias, the point is important: in the USA, especially, there is a powerful long-standing cultural optimism about the instantaneous benefits of free speech. The 'public sphere', in other words, is thought to be automatically a space for positive and constructive communication, and negative, poisonous speech will be purged of its effects by fresh doses of the former organically erupting in response. As Georgii Kuznetsov, cited in Chapter 3, put it: 'It's all very well to talk about freedom of speech in the

West where differences are minimal. But in Russia . . . freedom of speech can lead to tanks on the streets again.'[30]

Particularly in Central and Eastern Europe, cultural expectations of open communication are considerably more cautious, not necessarily as a result of elitist prejudices, but rather because of tragic historical – and now contemporary – experience. At all events, Migranyan's perspective acts as a brake on false optimism concerning the automatic benefits of all popular movements and the public communication in which they engage. While the nationalist movements were often the most powerful of all opposition currents in dislodging the old regimes, they did not cease operation once the old regimes had collapsed. Their reformulation into political parties, their prior presence in and penetration of various branches of the state, including the military and police forces, all combined to shape the initial post-Soviet era very substantially, especially in the former Union itself.

What, given this diversity, do we mean by a 'movement'? Arato and Cohen (1992: ch. 10) have argued that social movement research has gone through three phases. Initially it was heavily influenced by traditional notions of the crowd or the mob, a sea of irrational human beings swept up in a fit of passion communicated from one to the other almost via naked nerve endings, instinctually, hysterically and dangerously. The second model, in conscious opposition to the first, defined social movements as composed of sentient and reflective beings seeking to maximize their influence by choosing the available methods of protest and communication at their disposal (the 'resource-mobilization' and 'rational-actor' model).

The third and most recent model, 'New Social Movement' research, examines the collective identity of the participants and tries by this to establish what the factors are which lead people to define themselves as, and to continue to participate as, members of a given social movement. This literature on social movements particularly seeks to establish their typical forms, phases and modes of self-constitution (Alberoni, 1984; Dalton and Kuechler, 1990; Melucci, 1989; Touraine, 1981[31]). Contemporary social movements are conceptualized as an ongoing, almost cyclical phenomenon, and as an expression of sectoral, pragmatic discontent, by contrast with what are defined as earlier movements (typically, labor movements) that, in this view, typically set themselves a revolutionary target, or pinned their hopes on harnessing state power to their goals, or demanded global and rapid industrial growth for wage-betterment without regard to its ecological implications.[32] Habermas (1987: 391–6; cf. Ray, 1993: ch. 4) defines such movements as a continuing dimension of the contemporary scene, in his analysis striving to challenge and resist the encroachments of the economy and the state into our 'lifeworld'.

Regrettably for our purposes, the empirical focus of this third type of research is almost exclusively on recent Western European movements, that is to say on peace, ecological, anti-nuclear and feminist movements. However, their aims, character and trajectories were radically different from Eastern European movements, or for that matter from the civil rights movement in the USA or the anti-apartheid movement in South Africa. The insights of this research need rather carefully sifting before they can be applied outside their culture zone.[33]

Each of the three approaches has a different implication in regard to communication and media. For example, the traditional 'collective behavior' approach to political movements derives from earlier definitions of the 'mob', and leaves us to infer an almost animalistic mode of communication, either within the 'mob' or from it to its intended and accidental targets. The resource-mobilization model tends to be as hyper-rational as the collective behavior model is hyper-instinctual. It implies a political chessboard on which social movements are typically lacking a number of their opponents' chesspieces. In this view, the capacity to mobilize news media attention is a cheap resource, if it can be successfully realized. The quality and tenor of the attention may be poor or negative, but mention may at least bestow public existence on an otherwise barely known movement. In line with its rationalistic bias, however, complete clarity about both resources and the consequences of action is often assumed to be a part of a social movement's communication process, indeed its foundation.

The 'New Social Movement' (NSM) approach tends more to imply a view of communication as a process of subcultural exploration and of reaffirming and expressing a collective awareness. Alberoni (1984) has some interesting comments on the phenomenological drama of becoming aware of oneself in a new way as a result of being in communication with an active social movement. He coins the term 'the nascent state' to denote the transitional condition in which individuals redefine themselves as members of a social movement, and discusses the importance both of the rediscovery of previously hidden, denied history for social movements, and of 'the overpowering experience that a new beginning is possible where truth is predominant rather than falsehood' (pp. 55–7).

These insights have considerable resonance in the East European situation in the build-up to the regime changes, especially in the initial period of opening up of media and public debate (see Chapter 3; Ash, 1990; Goodwyn, 1991) and in the rediscovery of suppressed history (Eisen, 1990; Melville and Lapidus, 1990, chs. 2, 4; Nove, 1989). They also dovetail suggestively with analyses of the 'culture of fear' in the Latin American context (Corradi et al., 1992): both its atomizing, paralyzing impact, and the colossal sense of release when the movement at last bids fair to burst its bounds and engage society in a major transformation of the former regime.

On the other hand, Alberoni's discussion of the 'paradox of incommunicability' (1984: 82–3) of social movements, namely the difficulty their members have in explaining their commitment to those outside the movement in question, is only relevant to feminist or religious movements, for example, not to Eastern Europe. Tarrow (1989), writing out of the same Italian context in the same period, contradicts Alberoni by stressing the processes, some communicative, that amplified what he terms the 'cycle of protest' to the point where for a while in the 1970s it seemed 'that the entire system was under siege' (p. 117). Incommunicability, *pace* Alberoni, was hardly the issue in that case. But Tarrow acknowledges rather than analyses the communication dimension, as for example when he discusses the interaction between long-organized political organizations and new spontaneous activists (pp. 82, 90–1, 129ff., 166–7), or between substantive and expressive protest demands (pp. 124–7), or even the competition among different groups to be seen as more militant and thus – not least – more effective in devising fresh communication strategies (p. 221).

Attention to communication in interpersonal networks – on which, after all, they are significantly built and sustained – is to be found among some social movement analysts, especially in some recent feminist writing and writing on Latin American social movements. Álvarez (1990: 59–75), for example, strongly emphasizes their key role in her discussion of the 'base christian communities' in the developing social movements in Brazil during the 1970s. She cites the term *trabalho de formaginha* (ants' labor, p. 74) as used by activists to describe their activity. Di Palma (1991: 70–2) suggests that social networks may likely have been very important in Eastern Europe as the infrastructure for movements, as they developed their battles against the sovietized regimes. It certainly was the case that such networks of former school friends and others functioned as very important resources through which to soften the rigidities of sovietized distribution and service systems.

Burdick's research on such networks in Brazilian social movements (1992) sets up an excellent framework for research, drawing on the strengths of both the resource mobilization and the cultural identity approaches. Yet although what he sets out implies communication issues at every single step, in his chapter he never explores them (beyond contrasting the communicative expression of status dynamics in meetings of Catholic groups as opposed to Pentecostalist ones):

> processes of connecting, relating, and distancing people from movements; insidership and outsidership; boundary-marking; access, socialization, and recruitment; rites of initiation . . . the way in which all these processes articulate with local social differentiation along lines of gender, race, class, age, literacy . . . In order to understand these processes we must begin to look at social movements as existing not just within a given place but within complex fields of competing and overlapping practices and discourses – including households, families, television, churches, the male prestige sphere . . . (Burdick, 1992: 193)

Hanchard (1994) closely analyses how the overall political development of Afro-Brazilian social movements has to date been stymied by a consensual cultural terrain, namely the presumption that, all evidence to the contrary, racism is not a structurally embedded feature of Brazilian life. His focus on the politics of culture and the realities of racism puts us in a different zone altogether from the standard 'NSM' approach. Berger (1990)[34] is one of very few published sources on the significant role of alternative newspapers, video, clandestine radio, theatre, in the developing resistance against the Brazilian dictatorship.

It is very rare, however, for 'NSM' analysts to incorporate media communication into their framework.[35] Yet for political movements, although the research literature frequently neglects this obvious reality, communication and media are their life-blood. Typically they must create their own communication strategies and radical media against the silence or hostility of official media and repressive organs of the state. Raboy (1984: 125) comments very well on this[36] dimension:

> The typical opposition social movement is born with no particular concern for communication strategies, but new forms of social action inevitably bring with them innovations in communication.
>
> As they evolve, social movements become critically aware of dominant communication institutions and practices as reflected in the mass media. The evolution of this critical awareness takes place not only in the action of the movements, but also in the social relations inside the media themselves.
>
> Depending on their position of relative strength, social movements may take concrete steps to influence the situation by developing a coherent communications strategy and practice . . . They may choose to launch independent means of communication, or even try to establish direct communication with society as a whole.

Western sociological research on social movements has additionally been criticized, correctly in my view, for having little or no sense for the role of the state in the play of forces (Butterfield and Weigle, 1991: 184), for implicitly integrating the pressures exerted by social movements into a pluralist model, as though they were interest groups negotiating with a state structure, itself presumed to be ultimately benign. As Butterfield and Weigle point out, this optimistic view of the state was much harder to find plausible in the East than it has been in the West (except for members of an excluded group in the latter region, such as people of color). Thus the twin tendencies to ignore or downplay communication and/or the character of the state are both drawbacks of much of the social movement literature.

Nevertheless, it would be totally implausible to depict the regime transitions in the period under discussion without major reference to social movements, their varying geneses, florescence and decline. They have been, and are, highly influential, though not always immediately visible as such. Simply put, that research focus has to be widened to include all aspects of communication, mediatic or otherwise.

Civil Society and the Public Sphere

Despite or perhaps in part because of being considerably vague in meaning – the academy feeds on imprecision[37] – the terms 'civil society' and 'public sphere' were in considerable vogue in and out of the region in the latter 1970s and during the 1980s. I will argue here that they are in essence simply a pair of abstract nouns denoting collective activity, albeit, once carefully defined, with some heuristic value. They are not, however, explanatory concepts in their own right. At the close of this section I will comment on their relation to social movements.

As Norberto Bobbio (1988) has demonstrated, historically the term 'civil society' has frequently changed its meaning, from signifying the antithesis of the state of nature (Hobbes through Locke); the antithesis of the despotic state (Kant); economic, judicial and administrative structures intermediate between family and the state (Hegel); capitalist economic relations (Marx); or the arena of societal and cultural interaction outside the realm of the state, the economic order and the family (Gramsci).

In the period of regime change in Eastern Europe, 'civil society' and 'pluralism' were terms often used by the region's dissident intellectuals as a kind of mantra, signifying both a highly idealized view of pluralistic democracy in Western countries, and a normative commitment to fostering that idealized model within and against the sovietized regimes (Curry, 1993; Graziano, 1993; Mische, 1993; Reidy, 1992: 172–4). Some commentators on Eastern Europe (e.g. Habermas, 1993: 454–5; Helsinki Watch, 1986; Molnár, 1990; Rau, 1991; Starr, 1990) have similarly used the former term to refer to the growing vigor of public dissent in the latter years of the Soviet system, as in the phrase 'the rebirth of civil society'.[38]

A conceptually related term deployed by some East-Central European writers was 'anti-politics' (cf. Konrád, 1984), to denote the spaces they were attempting to open up within and against the Communist regimes. 'Anti-politics' signified in the first place the refusal to engage any longer in 'coquettish' (Ost, 1990: 39) negotiations for reform with regimes that had repeatedly shown that they would never undertake serious steps to reform; and consequently, to begin living civic life so far as possible as though the regime's ideology and restrictions were non-existent, to carve out a space of honest public interaction between citizens untainted by the debased politics of the regimes. The formation of small political and literary discussion groups meeting initially in each others' homes was an initial expression of this initiative. KOR in Warsaw or Charter 77 in Czechoslovakia were among the most distinguished examples. Adam Michnik described the strategy as 'anticipatory democracy' (Ost, 1990: 67; cf. Downing, 1984/ 1996: 23–4). 'It was not a program to seize power, but *to eliminate it*' (Bozoki and Sükösd, 1993: 227).

The problem is that the term 'civil society' is a descriptive category, not an explanation, and moreover a category with multiple definitions, its use as almost a mobilizing rhetoric[39] in Eastern Europe or Latin America being only the most recent definition-shift. In no case does the term explain the genesis or impact of what is being described. There is always a positive ring to it, similar to the benign glow shed by de Tocqueville's famous comments about informal associations in the United States and their underpinning of democratic politics. A certain patriotic (or envious) nostalgia often under-lies the use of de Tocqueville's observations, subtly but powerfully steering attention away from precisely what the enthusiasm for public associations may or may not contribute in plain reality to a national democratic culture. Let us not forget the traditions of the old Russian village community (*mir*), with its septennial assembly (the *skhod*) to redistribute land according to need and ability to work it. This practice – admittedly dominated by the village's male elders – quite easily co-existed with Tsarist despotism.

The discussion of civil society needs to become much more ruthless in separating out the analytical from the wishful. Putnam's (1993) analysis of the role in northern regions of Italy of what he terms 'civic engagement' represented a welcome step forward in this direction. He does not use the term 'civil society', but his discussion effectively takes that fuzzy term and gives it a defined and dynamic meaning. He defines civic engagement as consisting of long-standing horizontal networks of support, negotiation and exchange, and argues these networks demonstrably generate 'social capital' in the form of economic progress and political solidity in the northern Italian regions where they are historically strong. The communicative tissue of these networks over their centuries-long existence has necessarily been a core ingredient of their operation (cf. the remarks by Raymond Williams cited in the Introduction), although true to the sad traditions of political science Putnam does not explore this dimension.

None the less, his work has very interesting implications for post-sovietized nations and the role of media within them. It suggests that the temporary assertion of civic initiative in the oppositional movements against sovietism, however courageous, was not the same as a historically grounded structure of civic engagement. Thus the recreation of 'civil society' within and despite the structures of sovietized regimes needed, in the aftermath of the latter's collapse, to continue to forge itself anew and thereby to extend its roots. On such a reading, pre-soviet cultural traditions of Eastern Europe may in some cases have also been a quite substantial impediment to this happening.[40] The difficulties that dedicated journalists often faced in the post-Soviet public arena were probable testimony to this issue (see Chapter 6).

The 'public sphere' or 'public realm' are terms which have also quite often been used as a close equivalent to 'civil society' in its Gramscian sense. Calhoun (1993: 268–9) has criticized this conflation rather vigorously, insisting that civil society is a condition for the operation of a public sphere. 'There is a strong temptation,' he writes, referring to both Eastern Europe and China, 'to leap from the presence of business institutions, free housing markets, newspapers, and telephones to the presumption that civil society prospers and democracy will inevitably follow' (p. 276). He further observes, correctly in my view, that the growth of private business should not be conflated with the growth of democracy: 'the crucial early contribution of markets to the idea of civil society was as a *demonstration* of the possibility of self-organization' (p. 271, original emphasis). In this light, a public sphere is something which may or may not be developed by a citizenry, and at all events should not be trivialized by being applied to cover any and all private forms of association.

Thus in Calhoun's view the term 'public sphere' should be restricted to Habermas' use of the term *Öffentlichkeit*, namely a socially organized rational-critical discourse targeted on influencing state power. This is derived from Habermas' idealized extrapolation from the initial processes of public opinion formation in early modern England, France and Germany, in his *Strukturwandel der Öffentlichkeit* (1962/1989). Subsequently the kernel of this notion resurfaced in Habermas' concept of the 'ideal speech situation' (1984, 1987), which in his later work functions as a normative-goal-cum-yardstick for democratic structures and procedures. Whereas in his early study he wrote of the 'refeudalization' of public life in the later twentieth century that was shrinking the public sphere back down again, in his later work he wrote of the 'colonization of the life-world' of the public by both corporate and governmental forces, against which the public has come to react by organizing various types of oppositional social movements.

However, as Calhoun (1993), Fraser (1993), Hanchard (1995) and Landes (1988) have argued, Habermas and many of his epigones have been culpably silent or vague about the conditions which historically excluded women, Africans in the New World, and many other groups from this *Öffentlichkeit*.[41] Their different realities were not admitted into the supposedly universal 'rational-critical' discourse as perspectives that could be part of acceptable public communication.

Linked directly to that critique is the fact that the concept of *Öffentlichkeit* can be attacked for its overwhelmingly ratiocinative character, a kind of macro-socratic vision of the operation of public debate.[42] There is no intention here to offload the importance of reason in democratic procedure, but rather to underscore the absolute necessity of acknowledging that imagination, emotion, fantasy, drama, comedy are inevitably part and parcel of societal life and public debate as well.[43] As Young (1990: 103) observes:

> Feelings, desires, and commitments do not cease to exist and motivate just because they have been excluded from the definition of moral reason. They lurk as inarticulate shadows, belying the claim to comprehensiveness of moral reason.

The two issues, ratiocination and exclusion, are conjoined, because as she further (1990: ch. 4) notes, it has been precisely this ratiocinative abstraction that has helped to exclude at least one half of the public from *Öffentlichkeit*, given that males have historically argued themselves to be virtually the sole proud possessors of impartial reasoning faculties. Their continuing massive over-representation in 'democratic' legislatures and in the upper echelons of civil service departments around the world indicates that this history is far from merely historical. Ethnic minority men and at an earlier stage non-bourgeois men of the ethnic majority have typically been lumped with women in this regard.

Thus the notions of 'ideal speech situation' and *Öffentlichkeit* can be critiqued, the one for its overwhelmingly normative character, the other for its ahistorical refusal to acknowledge the exclusion of other social actors apart from bourgeois white males. Furthermore, and paradoxically – although perhaps not so, given the consistent lacunae this chapter has already pointed to – in Habermas' use the term also more or less excludes communication media from any roles in the authentic discursive process, which leaves incredibly vague the actual forum or fora in which rational-critical public debate may be expected to take place, especially in the contemporary world. Garnham (1993a), Benjamin Lee (1993) and Warner (1993) variously observe that Habermas' singular enthronement of the dyadic speech-act seriously distorts communication analysis, omitting as it does intertextual, multi-media and genre dimensions.[44]

Maybe it is more productive, therefore, to shed *Öffentlichkeit* and Habermas, and revert to 'public sphere', even if we are bastardizing the concept, and simply fly the bend sinister without apology. I have argued elsewhere (Downing, 1988a; Hansen, 1993; cf. Negt and Kluge, 1972) in favor of two steps being taken in this regard.

The first is to take Habermas' gloss out of the term *Öffentlichkeit*, and to define it simply as 'public forum' or 'public stage' (although these English terms are overly spatial and do not convey the sense of communicative activity, movement or exchange suggested by the German word). The second is to extend the term to include 'alternative public sphere', as a way of understanding the alternative media of social and political movements, and the new spaces those media open up for debate, reflection and organization around crucial issues neglected or distorted by mainstream media, the official public sphere.[45] My original examples were antinuclear movement media in the Federal German Republic and Britain in the mid-1980s. Fraser (1993: 123ff.) independently makes the same basic point in her discussion of 'subaltern counterpublics', although she appears to envisage multiple separated counterpublics as typical whereas my implicit conceptualization was more directed to their interconnections, actual or potential.

A third step would be to acknowledge the strength of Young's observations noted above, and to incorporate affective and imaginative communication into the concept, sloughing off its strictly ratiocinative skin.

Left unexplored by myself or Fraser were the forms of interaction between official and alternative public spheres. It would, however, be a patent nonsense to see them as tightly insulated from each other. Rather, the two terms are a way of capturing the reality and significance of different and generally competing zones of public communication, perhaps including in particular the refusal within alternative public fora to accept the very parameters of debate, not merely the topics or the priorities, sanctioned by the official realm. (There are considerably more issues to explore in the interaction between these official and alternative fora than can be dealt with here.)

Let us draw upon a proposal by Arato and Cohen (1992: ch. 10) to begin to pull all these threads together on social movements, civil society and public spheres. They argue that the term 'civil society' would most productively be used to refer to the combination of the public and the private (i.e. familial) spheres of life, namely those two dimensions of our contemporary existence not primarily dominated by the logic and procedures of the state or of the corporate world. Further, they argue that the public sphere today is primarily constituted in practice by social movements of various kinds.

So far, so good. This at least provides some clearly stated definitions that can be worked with, and the fuzziness of much of the civil society/public sphere debate can be reduced. However, there are some continuing shortcomings in their presentation. Arato and Cohen seem content to define social movements very much in the terms of the NSM literature, which above has been argued to have some serious limitations of its own, whatever its merits *vis-à-vis* mob and resource-mobilization models of social movements. These include a certain fixation on the supposedly 'new' dimensions of these movements, a seeming disinterest in social movements outside feminist and ecological currents in metropolitan nations, and rather little to say about, for instance, nationalist and separatist movements.

Furthermore – for reasons obscure to this writer – they too scarcely even allude to communication processes or institutions in relation to social movements, except by defining the public sphere in a sweeping gesture as empirically constituted by them.[46] We are still rather stuck on our mute chessboard, it seems.

A Note on the Question of Political Economy

Political economy is not political science as generally practiced, although some political scientists deploy its paradigms. To say 'its' is already to confuse the issue between marxist and non-marxist political economy, never mind their respective variants. None the less, there is a common core in all versions which acknowledges the necessity of incorporating economic forces and processes into social analysis. The exact character of the interconnections between economic and political power is hotly debated within as well as without the borders of political economy, and at the present time it cannot be said that any of these debates have reached anywhere near a consensual resolution. Thus for many purposes political economy is more a question of insistence on the impact of economic vectors as a matter of empirical observation than of having a developed and generally acknowledged theory which illuminates their interaction with other sets of factors. On this basic premise it is hard to disagree.

When it comes to media communication and culture, the role of the economic forces in play is variously handled. On the simplest level, media corporations, or corporations with substantial media interests, are simply analysed as any major corporation might be in conventional microeconomic analysis, or in terms of a given industrial sector. The analysis may equally be from a pro-business or a critical perspective. On another fairly simple level, they are analysed by financial journalists interested in digging up the usual skullduggery their profession allows them to observe in the corporate world, with the added twist that in this case the 'product' tangibly affects huge sections of the society, unlike some of the more recondite aspects of financial transaction whose ramifications pass through numerous and often obscure transformations before their general impact can be specified.

On another level, this interrelation is posited again almost as a matter of common sense: the powers that be in the economic sphere do wield enormous influence over government and society, and why should we assume media and culture are somehow 'clean' and insulated from that general process? Sensible as this observation is, it does not advance our understanding much further of how the process actually works, and particularly what snags and slips-between-cup-and-lip and even structural contradictions may be involved.

Also, what constitutes 'influence'? Getting favorable legislation passed, heading off unfavorable legislation, attracting huge advertising budgets, corralling the news, marginalizing media competitors, depoliticizing the public, plugging the virtues of particular candidates for public office, vilifying others, producing a steady drip-drip of racist and sexist content? Finally, what is meant by economic power? For some writers the answer seems to lie mostly within accountancy – who in the short term gained and how much?[47] For others the answer is more relational – what are the long-term connections between dominant economic institutions and the rest of society?

In the Soviet context, some of these relationships were easier to pin down, inasmuch as economic and political power were largely conjoined, and no secret was made of it. The political economy of sovietized media was not a matter of overly great mystery. During and after the transitions of 1989–91, however, the situation began to become much more compli-cated, for very gradually media institutions began to develop a separate, non-state economic base. At the same time, major areas of the economy remained under state ownership, foreign corporations began to buy up media properties, and the independent private business sector flourished only in certain initially rather restricted areas of economic life. At the time of writing, although it is possible to specify certain endemic – and quite often conflictual – relationships between state and media (see Chapter 6), and while it is possible to describe the main economic dimensions (e.g. Jakab and Gálik, 1991), the full dynamic remains as hard to pin down as in the consideration of much more established capitalist economies. The continuing movement of consolidation does not assist in this regard.

In Chapter 5 some of these politico-economic issues are raised in relation to the collapse of the Soviet bloc system. Even there, however, many observations must remain tentative. In Chapter 8 there is a brief discussion of Herman and Chomsky's 'propaganda model' (1988) of media, which sets out to be a political economy model. However, there is a very long way still to go in establishing more clearly the interconnections between economy and media. Currently, many attempts to do so read more like denunciations and exposés than analyses. X corporation makes money by showing pictures of naked women in its newspapers. Y corporation under-cuts its competitors and buys them up. Z corporation has a sweetheart relationship with the government party in power. All these may be entirely true, but they still fall far short of a connected, conceptually based demonstration of an argument. This is not to contest such an argument, merely to observe that it is too seldom made.

Conclusions

The objectives of this chapter have been to clarify a series of political and conceptual issues centrally related to the overall goal of the book. A number of these will be addressed again, often with more empirical detail, in later chapters. Here, the nature of the concepts themselves has been the prime focus.

Stripping away the accretions of the 'totalitarianism' discourse in order the better to perceive the character of sovietized states in their final decade of existence has been one such objective. The ability to acknowledge the substantial commonalities of the late Soviet state with other dictatorial regimes, as opposed to the deepest abysses of the Stalin-era Soviet state, also underscores the relevance of this study to understanding the media-state-politics-change relationship in many nations, not merely sovietized nations. Furthermore, this refocusing of the question away from the Anglo-American 'data-dyad' is a first step towards a more comprehensive media communication theory (one which, it is argued in the Conclusions chapter, will make sense of aspects of the Anglo-American situation that have customarily been downplayed).

To achieve these goals, communication research must be dovetailed with a number of concepts and their accompanying literatures in political science. The insouciance of many communication researchers toward these is extremely troubling. At the same time, we have seen a parallel 'know-nothingism' among political scientists about the very communication pro-cesses by which authoritarian rule, regime transition and contestatory political movements develop or decline. These failures to connect are a victory for the typical university departmental structure, not for under-standing. And paradoxically, even those who deploy concepts such as civil society, *Öffentlichkeit* or public sphere, are remarkably timid when con-sidering the communication and mediatic dimensions of the phenomena to which they apply them. When mentioned, it is almost in passing, so that communication becomes a pathetically shrunken dimension of the processes they analyse.

Here by contrast, as proposed in the Introduction, it is asserted that mainstream media are a pivotal dimension of the struggle for power that is muted but present in dictatorial regimes, that then develops between political movements and the state in the process of transition from dictatorship (though perhaps only into some form of 'delegative' democracy). This equally applies in the consolidation period after the transition. Alternative media of numerous kinds should be seen as both the interior dialogue and outward self-expression of political movements engaged in the transition and consolidation processes, and thus as central to any understanding of the movement process itself. Numerous media, not simply broadcasting or print or cinema, but also such forms of expression as graffiti, theatre, music, religious observances, should be incorporated into the analysis. Symbolic dimensions of communication, and international dimensions, should also be included as major elements. Finally capillary communication, whether in the social networks often underlying social movements, or in the very vertices of state power within and between nations, or in a variety of other settings, is also part and parcel of understanding all these situations.

In Chapters 3–6 we will particularly survey leading elements of media communication activity before and after the transitions in Russia, Poland and Hungary. Their contribution at the moment of transition is also of interest, but has been rendered as overly decisive in the total process by some (e.g. Brinton, 1990; Turnley and Turnley, 1990), and not least by Habermas who, perhaps to make up for lost time in this neglected area of his research, has described the regime collapses in the DDR, Czechoslovakia and Romania as not just 'a historical process that happened to be shown on television but one whose very *mode of occurrence* was televisional' (1993: 456, original emphasis). The communication question is far deeper and more extensive than this formulation allows.

First, however, let us survey the leading elements of the three nations selected for particular emphasis. Those unfamiliar with them will need this basic background before proceeding further. Those who know them well may either skip the ensuing chapter, or read it to ascertain the author's interpretive position on a mass of historically and politically contested issues in the narratives of those nations in the twentieth century.

Notes

1 For a brief but excellent history of the concept 'totalitarian', see Lipset and Bence (1994: 180–93).

2 There are empirical doubts about the NKVD's ideological fervor (cf. Knight, 1993). Perhaps the top Party bureaucracy of that era would be a more exact illustration of such commitment.

3 She even says that in Germany it 'was not until 1942 that the rules of totalitarian domination began to outweigh all other considerations' (1958: 410).

4 In Chapters 3–5 evidence will be provided in support of this position, focusing primarily upon media.

5 A frightening reality that in some measure perhaps explains, and excuses, the contradictory statements she makes from time to time.

6 The German word *grausam* can be translated thus, but more usually means 'terrible' or 'hideous', more abstract adjectives than 'gruesome'. Perhaps Arendt's sense would be better thus rendered.

7 In an essay dated approximately 1951 she made a further observation concerning other dictatorial regimes around the world, namely that they had often learned new devices from observation of Nazi and Soviet practices. She went on to speak in terms that might have been framed with Kirkpatrick's vulgarizations in mind: 'The natural conclusion from true insight into a century so fraught with danger of the greatest evil in politics should be a radical negation of the whole concept of the lesser evil in politics, because so far from protecting us against the greater ones, the lesser evils have invariably led us into them. The greatest danger of recognizing totalitarianism as the curse of the century would be an obsession with it to the extent of being blind to the numerous small and not so small evils with which the road to hell is paved' (Arendt, 1994: 271–2).

8 Friedrich and Brzezinski (1966) offer many perceptive observations on totalitarianism, including forms of resistance to it, its capacity for ideological change, its degree of success in getting its preferred thought-patterns internalized, the differences and similarities between sovietism and fascism. Total control of communications media is one of six required features that for them, if all present, actually constitute totalitarianism. Mass media, they propose, are precisely one of the features that make totalitarianism modern and different from earlier forms of despotism. On the other hand, the date of their work considerably preceded the beginning of the decline of sovietism, so that their media analysis only partially captures the later realities that are this book's primary focus. The complete 'vacuum' they argue (pp. 136–43) exists in the heart of the totalitarian communication process, namely the absence of any real information from top down or bottom up, was substantially challenged during the 1980s by both underground media, including music, and by foreign radio stations (which considerably reinforced the roles of unofficial media). (See chapters 3 and 4.) On the other hand, there were many mechanisms for the top to gauge the opinions on the bottom, from readers' letters to the press to police informers.

9 Dallin (1992) nicely skewers the obfuscations of these two latter positions in handling the regime transition.

10 Naturally, there are exceptions. Motyl (1992: 261–3) argues that despite the attacks on the term, it at least sought to provide a comprehensive account of the Soviet Union, as opposed to the mass of disconnected empirical comment that often constituted sovietology.

11 It would be interesting at this point to pursue the debate among advocates of the concept of 'political system' as preferable to the concept of the state, counter-advocates for 'bringing the state back in' (Evans et al., 1985), and some critics of both positions (cf. Mitchell, 1991). On the one hand the seemingly hyperactive Soviet state would seem a perfect case in point for the 'statists'. Recognizing its actual limitations, however, should be grist to the mill of the 'political system' theorists such as Almond and Easton were it not for the fact, underscored by Mitchell, that in using the term they were often pursuing a Cold War agenda in which US political structures were regarded as a panacea for the rest of the globe to adopt (under US economic hegemony). Unfortunately Mitchell, having dispersed a considerable amount of fog produced by these rival camps, proceeds to produce some foucauldian fog of his own, arguing that 'the producing and reproducing of this line of difference [between state and society]' is 'the essence of modern politics' (p. 95). Certainly not so for sovietized regimes, nor for others, in my view.

12 R.J. Sellars and P. Yeatman's mock primer of British history, *1066 And All That* (London, Methuen, 1930).

13 Hough (1977: ch. 8), a leading voice among the pragmatists, has attacked functionalist theorists in political science, not for the adequacy of their concepts, but for what he considers their inexplicable inability to apply them to Soviet realities. In particular, he argued that the Soviet state's regional, city and district entities were just as much processors of bread-and-butter demands as was any Western polity: they were not simply organizations for the perfection of repression. Complementarily, Benn (1989: 124) has observed of claims that the Soviet regime was totally in control of its public: 'Effective control presupposes effective

feedback. How, for instance, can a regime control public opinion if it has no reliable way of finding out what the public really thinks?' Both analysts have a different empirical focus, but combine in demythologizing the notion of absolute Soviet power. Hough, however, in the text above veers polemically to the point of virtually evacuating any repressive content to Soviet state policies, rather as the political scientists upon whose work he depends (Easton, Almond) do for the Western polities they theorize.

14 Curtis, 1984; Demac, 1990; Downing, 1986; Schlesinger, 1987.

15 Leading Bolshevik intellectual, systematically marginalized by Stalin from the end of the 1920s, and eventually executed in 1938 in the show-trials that finally cemented Stalin's power.

16 One of the problems with Arendt's assertion that totalitarianism evacuates normal economic or military rationality – the examples of Jewish deportation and mass genocide in the latter stages of the Second World War, the liquidation of the Soviet officer corps – is that these strong instances in support of her case seem to ignore counter-instances such as the generation of mass slave-labor in the gulag and near-slave-labor on the collective farms, or Albert Speer's extremely effective Nazi war economy and use of slave-labor to that end. The economics of totalitarianism proper was an extremely important component of the system, and contained a tragic and hideous rationality, as pointed out in a memorable essay by Herbert Marcuse in his *Negations* (Boston, Beacon Press, 1968), ch. 4.

17 Hough (1977: ch. 9) reports from his comparative study of *Pravda* and *Izvestiya* contents in 1951 and 1971 that in the latter period positions on regime policies had come to be supported by evidence rather than mere assertion. He also found that problems were much more likely to be traced to general causes rather than to individual failures. What he terms the 'dramatization of protest' (e.g. picketing or leafletting) was banned still, but the circulation of some critical commentary was possible so long as it avoided the known nerve-centers of the system. He adds that 'one of the most useful ways of visualizing the changes in communication policy is in terms of a greater breadth in audience to which and within which a freer flow of policy-relevant information was permitted' (p. 201). One might contest his argument as unduly vague about exactly what constituted 'policy-relevant information', and also his failure to address the problem of secrecy within the scientific-military-industrial sector (Cockburn, 1983: ch. 5). None the less, his emphasis on the fact of change in state communication policy since Stalin, glacial in pace though it may have felt within the USSR, is an important one if we are to understand the processes by which these regimes eventually subsided.

18 See further the discussion of youth cultures and rock music formations in Chapter 4.

19 The term 'decay' is not only meant to designate key political structures or public ideological convictions. Under Brezhnev various forms of corruption became institutionalized throughout the apparatus. These practices and networks were the ultimate roots of the rise of organized crime in the period after 1991, assisted in the latter period by the forms in which privatization was often implemented.

20 We shall return in more detail to Gramsci in Chapter 8, but the point here is that although he had a much stronger sense of the frequent tension between different class and political values within working class individuals' consciousness than many social analysts, he saw it more as an intermittent, situationally determined see-saw between these values than as a permanently conscious dualism (Gramsci, 1971: 327, 333).

21 'Later, one officer told me that my trial had reversed his attitude toward the regime, and that he no longer felt himself to be a believing "Soviet man". This kind of thing is well understood by the authorities, who see to it that even the best-prepared political trials are not open to the public. "Soviet man" possesses, in regard to politics, something like the human body's innate feeling for space. Just as instinct keeps a person away from the edge of the abyss, so instinct (and not reason) keeps "Soviet man" at a distance from words and deeds that have a political coloration. And the fact that this is a matter of instinct, and not of reason, has two consequences. On the one hand, "Soviet man" exaggerates what is forbidden to him; on the other, he is amazed by the harshness with which the system reacts to any "violation". He stays as far away as possible from the edge of the abyss. But when someone falls into it, he gasps: "Is it really that deep?"'

22 In the republics, nationalist movements were gathering increasing momentum below the surface.

23 With the transitions in Eastern Europe, some of these authors touched upon this new source of data as well (Di Palma, 1991; Karl and Schmitter, 1991; O'Donnell, 1993; Przeworski, 1992).

24 In a July 1988 conversation with Stefan Bratkowski, leader of the pro-*Solidarnosc* Polish Journalists Union officially dissolved by the martial law regime in 1981, but himself still highly active in oppositional circles, he observed to me that the regime was no longer getting any signals from Moscow as to what was expected of them. Cf. Pravda (1992b: 17); Sanford (1992: 99). In Hungary it was leaked that discussions were taking place between the government and Moscow concerning the phased withdrawal of Soviet troops from Hungarian soil (Partos, 1992: 135ff.).

25 The term often used to denote the governing class in sovietized societies. It is derived from the files, originally established by Stalin during the first years of the revolution, that indicated the career and regime loyalty of individuals available for appointment to major office in the government or party.

26 Its interactive character is underscored in Chapters 2 and 5.

27 For example, Bova, 1991a; Chirot, 1991b; Dallin, 1992; Di Palma, 1991; Grilli Di Cortona, 1991; Karklins, 1994; Kuron, 1991; Lynn and Schmitter, 1991; Molnár, 1990; Pravda, 1992b; Ramet, 1991; Remington, 1990; Tismaneanu, 1992; Walder, 1994.

28 The tendency of this school to focus on elite actors may be a factor here. Once given that focus, the role of communicative interaction between elite and society, or among the public, rather naturally slips into the shadows. A major empirical and intellectual push in that direction was provided by Stepan's (1988) absorbing analysis of the role of the military in the long Brazilian transition. His research was in part prompted by his sense that too much analytical attention was paid to popular movements there, and far too little to the complex roles played by and within the military. In making this argument, he indeed established that the *genesis* of political liberalization in Brazil was in one wing of the military establishment. Álvarez (1990: 15), however, has countered a common over-reading of his finding, with her observation that the subsequent long-drawn-out shift (1974–85) from liberalization to democratization there had everything to do with a dialectic between popular social movements and the military leadership, and in no way was just the product of the military's initiatives. In turn, her analysis of women's social movements – although equally lacking in media or communication analysis – opens up a series of issues directly bearing upon media. Undoubtedly, feminist research by very dint of its focus is more prone to investigate social movements as a whole, not just their leadership or its relation with the power structure. The discussion below on social movements, civil society and public sphere will further illustrate the importance of her emphasis.

29 Attempts by the Soviet regime in 1989–90 to cling on to power through mobilizing so-called 'workers' front' movements were analogous only in name, and rather quickly withered on the vine (Sedaitis, 1991: 13–19; Tolz, 1990: 60–8).

30 There was also a longstanding Cold-War-induced optimism in the USA about the character of nationalist movements in the so-called 'captive nations' of the Soviet bloc, some of which had historically been overtly sympathetic to Nazism, and a number of which were not simply yearning to shake off the Soviet yoke but had vengeful agendas for their neighbors and domestic minorities. Kuznetsov is cited in Post-Soviet Media Law and Policy Newsletter, 29 (30 April 1996), pp. 1–2.

31 Touraine's approach is distinct from, though connected to, the main body of 'NSM' research. For him, social movements are not simply significant moments of societal turbulence, but rather 'lie permanently at the heart of social life' (Touraine, 1981: 29) in the modern era. They represent contemporary strivings for self-management of our lives, as opposed to becoming an element in what he terms the 'programmed' society (pp. 7–9, 22, 80).

32 Whether these characterizations in 'NSM' research offer an adequate description of any of these movements, 'old' or 'new', is another matter entirely. Pragmatism is not the universal hallmark of these movements' strategies (for example, the women's sustained anti-nuclear

protest at Greenham Common in England in 1983–5), nor was a totalizing ideology necessarily the hallmark of socialist movements earlier this century (cf. Lidtke, 1985, on a key instance, the socialist labor movement in Germany up to 1933). Furthermore, NSM studies' identification of contemporary movements as 'single-issue' is very problematic, seemingly equating a challenge to the nuclear arms race or to the roles of women in society with the demand of a group of parents for a new traffic light on their street.

33 Ray (1993) argues this case in relation to Eastern Europe, South Africa and Iran. Éscobar and Álvarez (1992: 15) propose that 'NSM' should be used simply as a temporary analytical construct, not as a seasoned concept.

34 My thanks to José Marques de Melo of the Universidade Metodista, São Paulo, for drawing my attention to this reference.

35 For a partial exception see Thomas Rochon's study of the British anti-nuclear movement (Dalton and Kuechler, 1990: ch. 6).

36 The empirical literature is very considerable: cf. Dowmunt, 1993; Downing, 1984/1996; Gitlin, 1981; Mattelart and Siegelaub, 1983; Sreberny-Mohammadi and Mohammadi, 1994.

37 Since the later 1960s, these have been some of the other terms academics have bandied about with abandon precisely because of their striking imprecision: deep structure, ideology, discourse, hegemony, cultural studies, deconstruction, feminism, post-colonial studies, post-modernism, post-industrial society, the information society, multiculturalism, globalization. The perfect Ur-theorist is one who leaves meanings fuzzy, giving scope for endless seminars where participants are using the same term in different senses.

38 And in some nations of Latin America, especially Brazil, although there rarely if ever with the contrast with a supposedly splendid Western standard incorporated into the model.

39 Katznelson (1990: 565) observes that although in their opposition to sovietized regimes these circles defiantly proclaimed themselves 'ideology-free', their maintenance of such a claim after the collapse of the regimes was purely mystificatory. The statement only made sense as an absolute rhetorical negation of regime-speak.

40 Molnár (1990: 45–55) offers a mixed and uncertain assessment of the degree of strength of the civic tradition in Hungary and Poland. Mische (1993), by contrast, focuses more on the dynamics of the transition itself, especially as they brought about the intensified exclusion of women from the official public sphere and the tendential relapse of the private sphere of the family into its customary Western form, i.e. an extruded sphere reserved especially for women and small children, as opposed to its frequent location in the final decades of sovietism as a zone of critique and partial autonomy.

41 Insofar as it may be said to have existed: Arato and Cohen (1992: 316–19) argue that his historical support for the concept is only really convincing for England, not for France or Germany. Schudson (1993) makes a similar point regarding the United States. On the other hand, for a very productive deployment of the concept in relation to the Russian press before 1917, see McReynolds (1991). Postone (1993: 167) proposes that Habermas 'seeks to elucidate the . . . conditions for an effective public sphere and hence democracy'. On his reading, then, the public sphere is an analytical project of enduring validity, whatever its current degree of success in being applied historically. This has the flavor of a last-ditch rescue attempt.

42 If university department meetings, for instance, are the slightest guide – constituting as they do a gathering of informed minds – to the rational-critical timbre of *Öffentlichkeit* in action, then I think we must regretfully acknowledge that the normative vision of the concept has all but drowned out the verbal viciousness, not to mention tedium, of at least this segment of a potential public realm, although by instancing everyday academic folk in action I may have chosen a particularly inapposite and even unfair example. I am happy to report that my current department at the University of Texas was neither source nor target of this observation.

43 A very strong empirical example is to be found in M. Susana Kaiser's (1993) analysis of the communication strategies of the Mothers of the Plaza de Mayo, the mothers of 'disappeared' young people during the era of extreme military repression in the period 1976–83 in Argentina. At a time when protest was exceedingly dangerous, and also when many Argentines as a consequence did not want to get involved in any acknowledgment of the

vicious persecution of political dissent, when therefore the public sphere had effectively been strangled, the Mothers used a plethora of emotive and imaginative devices to force open the public sphere once more, centimetre by centimetre.

44 Habermas (1993: 438–9, 454–7) eventually acknowledged the validity of some of these criticisms, claiming that communication research was undeveloped when he wrote *Strukturwandel* in 1961.

45 In the second volume of his *The Theory of Communicative Action* (1987: 391), he devotes a single half-sentence to what he terms the 'anarchist visions' of 'video pluralism' and 'television democracy', thus casually dismissing all forms of alternative democratic media as pie-in-the-sky.

46 Their two main communication-related observations are as follows (Arato and Cohen, 1992): 'the mere existence (however inadequate) of parliaments and of forms of workshop self-management, codetermination, and collective bargaining, indicates that publics can be constructed even within institutions that are primarily system-steered (p. 479) . . . the political issue is how to introduce public spaces into state and economic institutions . . . by establishing continuity with a network of societal communication consisting of public spheres, associations and movements' (p. 480).

47 This is what Gramsci (1971: 163), carefully putting quotation-marks around the racist term, called the false equation of a political economy critique with identifying 'the self-interest of an individual or small group, in an immediate and 'dirty-Jewish' sense . . . [which] is content to assume motives of mean and usurious self-interest, especially when it takes forms which the law defines as criminal'. This kind of quasi-leftism does indeed lend itself, amongst other things, to anti-semitism.

2

Russia, Poland and Hungary in the Soviet and Post-Soviet Era: a Preliminary Overview

The chapter will begin by offering a series of basic dates and names referred to in the rest of the book, in chronological order. Then will follow an account of the bare-bones elements in the development of the Soviet Union, Poland and Hungary since 1917.[1] The chapter concludes with two sections that encapsulate (a) changes in politics and state structures, and (b) developments in nationalism, ethnic relations and the economy, between the transition biennium of 1989–91 and the close of 1995. Those unfamiliar with the region and its history should read what follows aware that almost each and every statement is part of contentious intellectual terrain.

These three nations,[2] sharply different as they are from each other, offer a myriad illuminating contrasts once the telescope is held the correct way, rather than the way in which we are forced to commence here. Although the experience of some other comparable societies will be referred to at times, there is enough diversity and to spare amongst and within these three nations to sustain a potentially inexhaustible analysis.

In essence, in terms of the build-up to the transitions of 1989–91, Russia represented the keystone of the system's arch whose own changes, initiated from its elite, began finally to dissolve the system, although it was the very last unit of the system to change; Poland represented the most doggedly, albeit non-violently, disruptive element in the system,[3] where changes were perpetually being pushed from below rather than from above; Hungary represented a case of very gradual, almost imperceptible changes from above and in its quiet way acted as a stimulus to other bloc regimes to experiment with seemingly safe modifications of the Soviet system.

Dates and Names[4]

1917   The Russian February Revolution overthrows the Tsar and the imperial dynasty.

The October Revolution – November in the Western calendar – installs the Bolsheviks in power.

1918   May: the Civil War begins for control of Russia between the old regime's forces (the Whites), supported by fourteen nations, including Britain and the USA, and the Bolsheviks (the Reds). It finally ends in November 1920. At certain points, it is fought over three fronts, together measuring 8,000 kilometres.

July: 'War Communism' – the Bolsheviks' slogan/title for rapidly developing war-related policies of government-mandated allocations, including forcibly requisitioning farmers' foodstuffs, direction of labor, cancelling commercial transaction, rendering money worthless.

1921
March: at the beginning of the month the naval garrison at Kronstadt, very close to the capital, St Petersburg, and hitherto a bastion of the revolution, revolts and is bloodily suppressed; famine begins throughout Soviet territory and claims between 5 and 9 million victims over the twelve months that follow.

15 March: The 'War Communism' policy is abruptly reversed in favor of the 'New Economic Policy', which reinstitutes markets, money and certain levels of freedom to trade. At the same Party Congress it is decided to ban organized groups ('factions') within the Communist Party, thus cancelling any remaining fora for effective public debate on controversial political issues.

1928
December: the policy abruptly begins of forcing each village to combine its farms into large units whose policies will be determined by the government. By the time the policy is fully operational in 1933, many millions have been deliberately starved to death to crush their resistance or have died in the process of compulsory relocation to completely undeveloped zones in harsh climates. The purpose is to secure economic and political control over the majority of the population, i.e. the farming classes. In the same year is begun the first Five-Year Plan for the crash industrialization of the economy, utilizing the labor of millions of farmers pushed out of the countryside, and subjecting them to intensely harsh working conditions and draconian controls. By now Stalin and his lieutenants are in control of most policy.

1928–38
Stalin and his many appointees in the Party and state system institute a reign of terror against artists, writers, journalists, scientists, professors, the military hierarchy and experienced members of the Party and the government. A vast archipelago of forced labor camps is set up in which untold numbers slave and die. The camp system continues in absolute force until after Stalin's death in 1953, when probably a majority of prisoners are released.

1939
In the infamous Nazi–Soviet pact, Poland is partitioned by the two dictators, and the three Baltic republics are annexed by the USSR.

1941
Nazi Germany invades the USSR, until then non-combatant in the Second World War, and rapidly seizes most of its western

territory. The USSR bears the brunt of the war and loses about 25 million citizens in the next four years. Russian nationalism and Orthodox religion are allowed easier expression so as to assist Russian national morale.

1945   Victorious Soviet troops enter East-Central Europe and kilometre by kilometre expel the Nazi invaders. They are first among the Allies into Berlin, prompting the suicide of Hitler and Goebbels, and the collapse of the Nazi war machine.

1948   By the end of this year, by differing methods in differing countries, the USSR establishes Stalin-style regimes from Estonia to Albania with the single exception of Yugoslavia, but including the eastern portion of Germany.

1948–53 The full resumption of Stalinist terror, more marked in some bloc nations than others.

1948   In Poland, the USSR installs Bierut in power; in Hungary, Rákosi. The latter's repression is even worse than the former's.

1953   Stalin dies; first major anti-Stalinist demonstration in the newly conquered territories, in Eastern Germany; hundreds are killed; in the USSR, Khrushchev begins his slow ascent to power, pushing first Malenkov and then Bulganin aside.

1955   First 'thaw', minimal liberalization in Soviet literary and artistic world.

1956   January: Khrushchev delivers unheralded midnight 'secret speech' to the 20th Soviet Communist Party Congress, with delegations present from Communist parties the world over in Moscow (some of whose members receive leaked copies and leak them in turn), in which he denounces a number of the Stalin regime's atrocities.

June: there are major labor disturbances in Poznan, Poland; Bierut dies; Gomulka, already publicly identified as pro-Polish rather than pro-Soviet, is brought out of political disgrace and made leader by the Polish regime with the reluctant acceptance of the Soviet leadership.

July: in Hungary Rákosi, by now a source of growing political instability, is replaced by Gerö, less known, although more or less his clone.

October: after loosening of some repression in Poland, Hungarians begin to demonstrate against Soviet control. Gerö steps down in favor of Kádár, who in turn, in a popular upswell, is almost immediately sidelined by Nagy, a strongly reformist Communist; Soviet troops are pushed out, but soon return and crush the revolution in blood.

1958   Nagy is executed and secretly interred.

1962   Second literary 'thaw' in the USSR; Solzhenitsyn's *Ivan Denisovich* is published, publicly exposing for the first time aspects of life in forced labor camps; Khrushchev makes another major speech against Stalin at the 22nd Soviet Party Congress, with still more details.

1964 Khrushchev is pushed out of office by Brezhnev and his co-conspirators. His 'offences' included his attacks on the Stalinist era, together with a series of policies that threatened to unsettle the Soviet order, such as limiting the tenure of Party and state officials.

1965 Measures of repression are instituted against dissident Soviet writers Daniel and Sinyavsky, heralding the reimposition of harsh controls on all oppositional voices; *samizdat* publication begins in the USSR.

1968 March: student uprisings in Poland are violently suppressed, and an officially sponsored anti-semitic campaign is mobilized to deflect student and public dissent.

April: a new leadership comes to power in Czechoslovakia, dedicated to 'socialism with a human face'; in August its leaders are removed by a Soviet military invasion, supported by the Polish, East German, Hungarian and Bulgarian military.

September: in Hungary the New Economic Mechanism is introduced, offering an initial measure of independence to firms to make and implement their own decisions; it will be modified backwards and forwards many times over the succeeding twenty years.

1970 December: after many demonstrating workers are killed and wounded by the police in the Polish port cities of Gdansk, Gdynia and Sczeczin, the Polish politburo forces Gomulka to resign, with Soviet acquiescence, and Gierek succeeds him as Polish leader. Gierek proceeds to attract large quantities of petrodollars recycled as loans through Western banks in the aftermath of the 1973 oil shock, but only a small proportion fuels economic growth, and giant debts build up rapidly.

1976 More workers' uprisings in Poland; the anti-system Committee for Workers' Defense (KOR) is formed in Warsaw.

1980 August: a major strike in the Gdansk shipyards. A Catholic mass is celebrated actually in the shipyards, with almost universal striker participation. The Prime Minister comes to negotiate personally with Lech Walesa and the strikers. Polish Baltic port and shipyard workers unite to form the first independent labor union in the Soviet bloc, *Solidarnosc* (Solidarity). Over the next sixteen months *Solidarnosc* comes to have 10 million members, and many turn in their Communist Party cards.

1981 December: following the staggering growth of *Solidarnosc*, and amidst repeated expressions of alarm from Moscow, Berlin and Prague, Polish President General Jaruzelski declares martial law, which stays in force until 1985; dissident leaders who do not manage to escape underground are interned.

1982–5 When Brezhnev dies, he is succeeded at short intervals by the ailing Andropov, former KGB Director, and then the ailing Chernenko, and finally by Mikhail Gorbachev, a new generation reformist, who pioneers policies of a certain degree of openness in public debate (*glasnost*), restructuring of the government and economy (*perestroika*), and acceleration of technological advances (*uskoreniye*), of which only the first achieves any marked success. However, as *glasnost* expands step by step, mounting excitement, anticipation and genuine amazement grip the public. The genie seems to be escaping from the bottle.

1988 May: Kádár is forced by the Party to resign as Hungarian leader, and a more active reformist leadership takes his place.

1989 February–April: the Polish government holds extensive Round Table talks with *Solidarnosc* on Poland's future course.

April: Soviet troops violently suppress a peaceful demonstration in Tbilisi, capital of Soviet Georgia.

May: Yeltsin, Gorbachev's arch-foe, is elected President of the Russian Republic by four parliamentary votes in the third round. He proceeds to utilize the position energetically to contest Gorbachev's authority.

June: parliamentary elections are held in Poland, and *Solidarnosc* candidates sweep the board; Mazowiecki is installed as the first non-Communist prime minister since 1948, though Jaruzelski remains for the time being as President; in Budapest the remains of Hungarian former Premier Nagy are solemnly reinterred, with non-stop TV coverage all day.

November–December: the regimes in East Germany, Czechoslovakia, Bulgaria and Romania collapse.

1990 January: in Baku, the Azerbaijan capital, hundreds are killed by Soviet Interior Ministry troops in response to public unrest and anti-Armenian pogroms.

March: there are national elections to about two-thirds of the seats in the new Soviet parliament, and the debates are televised, arousing enormous initial interest. Lithuania's parliament unilaterally declares independence, the first of the fifteen Soviet republics to do so.

April: in the first free elections in Hungary since 1947, the conservative nationalist Magyar[5] Democratic Forum is the main winner in the second round.

1991 January: in an attempt to crush nationalist secession among the Soviet republics, Soviet special forces violently occupy the TV tower in Vilnius, capital of Lithuania, and fourteen Lithuanians are killed; in a similar action in Riga, Latvia, six Latvians are killed, and the main newspaper printing plant is seized.

August: an attempted coup in Moscow lasts three days; Gorbachev's role in the proceedings continues to be murky and contested for many years to come; the coup is defeated with the loss of only three lives, and Yeltsin emerges as the dominant political figure in Russia.

December: Gorbachev resigns as Soviet President and the Soviet Union is officially dissolved as a political institution; it is formally replaced by a notional body named the Commonwealth of Independent States, whose role is very obscure and whose powers are non-existent.

1993 October: Yeltsin officially dissolves the Russian parliament, and there follows a confrontation which ends with the military firing heavy artillery at the parliament building (the White House), and with the parliamentarians being forced to surrender; simultaneously there is a pitched battle outside Ostankino, the Moscow TV headquarters.

1994 November: Russian troops are sent to crush a secessionist rebellion in the quasi-autonomous ethnic republic of Chechnya in the south; after massive destruction of life and property the conflict was still raging at the close of 1995.

1995 Yeltsin's and his government's standing slide faster and faster downhill. Meanwhile the Russian Communist Party experiences a strong revival.

For further events and individuals in the period 1991–5, see below.

Brief Commentary

There is a key dimension to these histories that demands recognition, and there is a decisive moment in their interrelated histories that requires acknowledgment. The key dimension is that the sequences were never smooth nor simply evolutionary. The Soviet system was not a fixed fact from its birth to its death, despite its face of monolithic power. The single, supremely decisive moment in the constitution of the former Soviet Union, and therefore of the Soviet period in the life of the nations who modeled their politico-economic systems on it – whether with the prompt of Red Army bayonets (East-Central Europe) or without (China, Cuba) – was not Lenin's and the Bolsheviks' dedication to achieving and holding power. It was not Russia's crushing rural economic backwardness. It was not the fourteen nations arrayed militarily against the new republic. It was not the historical dead weight of Tsarism's political culture. It was not the war weariness and chaos of 1917 that gave the Bolsheviks their opportunity to seize power. Nor was it even the indescribable repressions organized by Jozef Stalin's apparatus. All these had their place. But they were not the cornerstone.

That constitutive moment was in the Civil War of 1918–20, and yet not even in the terrible rigors of the Civil War itself. The fatal threshold was ultimately in the *response* of the new Soviet leadership to the Civil War.

These leaders equated a minutely state-directed wartime economy and society with the structures of successful economic planning in peacetime and with the movement towards a rational, just and effective future society ('War Communism'). Militaristic methods, such as food requisitions, were defined as fully politically acceptable as well as supremely effective. Furthermore, they were the sole detailed experience anyone possessed of a non-capitalist economy, since the Bolsheviks had no detailed economic policies upon coming to power.[6]

One of the constituent ironies of Soviet planning was that so far from working on a smooth, predictable five-year basis, not subject to irrational market vagaries, it was in practice conducted on an annual and even monthly basis. It was repeatedly being amended and revised quite chaotically as it went along. Just as might be expected in wartime. Thus the so-called 'command' economy was not rationally directed from above rather than by some supposed 'invisible hand', but was intensively and continuously steered from above on a daily basis via the 'audible telephone'. Yet the issue is far more than ironic: the draconian micromanagement of society in the Soviet Union, its unprecedented repression, symbolized but not explained by the figure of Stalin, had its origins in wartime, in what the Bolsheviks at first propagandistically named 'War Communism' to try to put a positive gloss on the equality of misery imposed by the Civil War.

After the brief interlude of the 1920s and the 'New Economic Policy', and consequent upon some of the dislocations and crises of that decade, economic and state policy swung back sharply and massively to the Civil War model at the close of 1928, and effectively a new and even more far-reaching civil war was declared (the onset of what Bukharin named as 'military-feudal exploitation'). This struggle would initially engulf millions of farmers from 1929 onwards, together with dissident and non-dissident intellectuals and professionals. Then, from December 1934, it stretched out to the state bureaucracy, the Communist Party, the original core of the Bolshevik leadership, the military command, and even the secret police itself. The industrial working class, officially the pivot and beneficiary of the revolution, was pinioned ever more tightly with bands of stronger and stronger steel from the beginning of the 1930s onward. The vast expansion of forced camp labor was the harshest but far from the only manifestation of their repression.

The Great Patriotic War (the Russian term for the years of its involvement in the Second World War, from 1941 to 1945) threw the USSR into a gigantic new crisis – this time originating from outside. Yet paradoxically the war ended by appearing to legitimate the effectiveness of the Soviet system, which had been finally able to repulse the invaders and then lead their defeat through its military-technical strength. The senseless slaughter of millions through Stalin's and the Soviet high command's military errors, over and above the Nazis' colossal carnage, was very successfully and carefully redirected into Soviet and Russian patriotism, and blame for losses into rage against the Germans. It was also a period of high national unity, when in addition patriotism was not politically suspect and the Orthodox Christian religion could be practiced without penalty, which many survivors looked back upon with warmth, not only with sadness for those lost. Stalin's role as military leader of genius was pumped out and very widely accepted, even for those who took their distances from him on other grounds.

Moreover, as much later events showed when the Soviet bloc was collapsing, the creation of a colonized *cordon sanitaire* of East European countries, especially including the division of Germany, was widely supported in Soviet society on defense grounds. The experience of 25 million lost to battle, an experience that totally dwarfed the historic invasions of Napoleon or the Teutonic knights or the Mongols, was successfully redeployed against the Soviet population as a legitimation of 'their' state. However, by the 1980s endless Soviet movie spectaculars about the Great Patriotic War only appealed to the elderly. The ideological medicine was losing its effect.

For East-Central Europe, the ravages and chaos of war combined with the Nazis' genocidal liquidations generated despair in many at the imposition of another dictatorial rule. Others, however, were optimistic at what they hoped would be not merely physical and economic reconstruction under Soviet tutelage, but also political and moral renovation. As one Jewish Czech, a teen-survivor of the camps, related to me thirty-five years later: 'My father said to me, "Look I'm not a Communist and I'm not going to be, but half our Czech party's Politburo are Jews, so the party can't be that bad." So I joined.' Then he added sadly, 'How wrong he *was!*' In like vein a few years later a Pole showed me a school exercise book in which, at the age of nine in 1950, he had written a two-page essay on how Comrade Stalin was the best friend Poland had.

Both in the Soviet Union and the newly colonized band of nations at its western frontier, the years up until 1954 were particularly harsh in terms of state repression. After Stalin's death in 1953, repression began gradually and very fitfully to ease, if not in relation to civilized standards, at least in relation to what had just passed. None the less, even at the height of Bierut's and Rákosi's rule in Poland and Hungary respectively, the scale of repression – though fierce – never reached the unimaginable proportions of either Stalinism or Nazism.

The ascent of Khrushchev to power by 1956, the rehabilitation and ascent of Gomulka following the upsurges of protest in Poland in 1956, and from the close of the 1950s Kádár's millimetre-by-millimetre softening of repression in Hungary, following the bloodbath of the 1956 revolution, all signalled a relenting of the inconceivable to the frightening. As noted at the outset, however, in this history, the sequences were never smooth or simply evolutionary: the 'milder' Khrushchev's Hungarian bloodbath in 1956, his regime's shooting down of hundreds of unarmed protesting workers in Novocherkassk in 1962, the 'gradualist' Kádár's execution of Nagy in

1958, the 'nationalist' Gomulka's slaughter of protesting Baltic seaport workers in 1970, the 'reformer' Gorbachev's bloody suppressions in Tbilisi 1989, Baku 1990, Vilnius 1991, are cases in point.

The sharp difference between Khrushchev and Stalin was that the former did not pursue political objectives or battles via systematic extermination of real or claimed opponents. He thereby released the upper echelons of the branches of the Soviet state from their ever-present fear of being redefined as an enemy of the state and shot or enslaved.[7] At the same time, he retained in many respects Stalin's capacity for sudden, arbitrary policies that generated immense social upheaval. He became caught up in the contradiction of his own strategy because repeatedly his policies threatened the Party and state bureaucracy with upheaval in their own power and procedures, yet he patently did not intend to back up the threat with extermination.

In his attempts to generate support against the old guard and also to put the most appalling traits of Stalinism to rest, Khrushchev adopted inter-mittent policies of slightly relaxed control over cultural and media policy, allowing for example the first Soviet account of Stalin's camps to be published in the book-sized leading literary monthly, *Novy Mir* (New World): Solzhenitsyn's *Ivan Denisovich*. News of these developments began to reach East-Central Europe, where in any case there was a little more air to breathe.

However, following (a) Khrushchev's ousting in 1964 and then (b) student revolts in Poland in 1968, and especially (c) the peaceful 1968 'Prague Spring' Czech experiment in developing a non-repressive state socialism, ideological and cultural clamps were very aggressively reimposed in the Soviet Union.

The Brezhnev era style can be characterized in the same rapid way as the Khrushchev era style. It was a combination of three dimensions (until the very last years): (a) strict persecution of the expression of dissent, but generally short of direct execution (people died or had their lives shortened in harsh camp conditions); (b) guarantees of stability and more autonomy for Party and state officials, as opposed to the frequent upheavals under Khrushchev; (c) attempts to provide butter as well as guns to the Soviet populace, which became more and more possible following the rise in world oil prices after 1973 (the USSR actually had the largest known reserves in the world, although it was usually left out of the reckoning in international comparisons).

Meanwhile, in Poland and Hungary very different routes were being followed. Following the police slaughter of hundreds of demonstrating workers in the Baltic ports of Gdynia, Gdansk and Szczecin in 1970, there was yet another regime change, with Gomulka ceding under Soviet pressure to new leader Gierek. The same kind of laxer, tendentially corrupt scenario began to develop under Gierek that was emerging at the same time under Brezhnev in the USSR – the 'Little Deal' as Millar (1988) described it.

However, by now, as we will see in more detail in Chapter 4, auton-omous labor organization in the Baltic ports was painfully beginning to develop. Significant worker turbulence in 1976 at two major sites was followed by the momentous development of *Solidarnosc*, the first-ever successful independent labor union in the Soviet bloc, in 1980.

The intense drama continued with the December 1981 imposition of martial law in Poland and the forcing of *Solidarnosc* underground until 1985. Effectively the years from 1985 to 1989 were a stalemate between state power and *Solidarnosc*. In 1989 came an official Round Table – implying no one had precedence – set of discussions between state authorities and representatives of the opposition, dominated by *Solidarnosc*. This extraordinary breakthrough, from imprisoning the opposition to discussing with it on symbolically equal terms, was definitively made possible by simultaneous developments in the Soviet Union, to which we shall turn in a moment.

Hungary, meanwhile, was having no such *Sturm und Drang*. Kádár's snail-like reforms, sometimes reversed for a while and then picked up later, were such that although some influential Soviets tut-tutted, no one policy was ever large enough to seem to justify drastic reaction, nor did it ever appear of such import that it could not be reversed. The problem was that Hungary's foreign bank debt during the 1980s was beginning to rise to the high per capita level of Poland's generated under the Gierek regime, and then to exceed it. Economic austerity policies began to be imposed one after the other, and the slow but at least steady increment in general living standards over the previous generation was frozen and then reversed step after step. The January 1988 imposition of a very stiff income tax was the most painful and unprecedented of these steps, and more than any of them signalled a regime which in the economic sphere could not deliver the goods and did not know where it was headed.

Meanwhile, in the Soviet Union, beginning in 1985, three interlinked developments were in process.

1　In the interests of modernizing and cleansing Soviet economic and public life, the Gorbachev regime was gradually opening up its public sphere (the so-called *glasnost* policy) to measured doses of honesty, whether about the Soviet past under Stalin, or its true economic situation, or levels of public corruption under Brezhnev.

2　Half-hearted and poorly conceived attempts at radical economic reform, along with a sharp reduction in the USSR's hard currency earnings (see Chapter 5), were producing a more and more disorganized economy and general standard of living.

3　Long-suppressed and festering ethnic antagonisms of numerous kinds, whether nationalist as in the Baltics and the Caucasus, or ethnic minority as throughout the Union in numerous forms, were beginning to assert themselves simultaneously, to the point where even the repressive Soviet state could not control them all at once. Ultimately the most corrosive of these was the rebellion of Russians against the Soviet state, which Yeltsin very effectively harnessed to his own ends. As noted in Chapter 1, *glasnost* policies put wind in the sails of these antagonisms.

With these pressures absorbing attention in the USSR, and with the decision of the Gorbachev administration to respond only occasionally with lethal armed force to nationalist self-assertion within the Union (Tbilisi April 1989, Baku January 1990, Vilnius January 1991), the silence on the telephone circuits from Moscow became louder and louder in Warsaw and Budapest. In turn, these two nations, Hungary by November 1988 (with the publication of a draft law on independent public associations), and Poland by June 1989 (permitting a one-third non-Party presence in the lower house and 100 percent in the upper house of parliament), were setting the pace for the rest of the bloc. The stage was set to relinquish the unique role of the Communist Party, which along with the political police was a cornerstone of sovietism. The leaders of the other East-Central European Soviet bloc nations were aghast, but then in very short order and remarkably peacefully except in Romania were swept away by the end of 1989.

Thus the outer Soviet empire disintegrated, and was followed within less than two years by the inner empire, the fourteen republics of the USSR. Already in the spring of 1990 the Soviet Congress of Deputies had followed the lead of Poland and Hungary and shed the Soviet Constitution's Article 6 on the Party's leading role. The process overall grew very rapidly in momentum towards the end, and consisted, needless to say, of many more specific interacting dynamics within and between the nations concerned than would be appropriate to include in this kind of overview. Some are reviewed in the next three chapters.

Subsequent Changes in the State and Political Life

A paradox grappled with by Bozoki and Sükösd (1993) and also by Mische (1993), amongst many others, is the distinctly depressing quality of political life in the years immediately succeeding the change. Perhaps we always hope for painless miracles, and everyone's 1989–91 euphoria was mainly charged with the energy generated by that chimera. Also, the pain was infinitely greater in some places – former Yugoslavia, Tajikistan, Nagorno-Karabakh – than in many others. None the less, the gap between what Bozoki and Sükösd (p. 237) define as the societal emphasis of the earlier movements for change as opposed to the state-centered focus of the populist movements that supplanted them, and the further political marginalization of women noted by Mische among others, reinforces what above I have described as a transition from night to twilight, rather than to anything resembling daylight. They are referring mainly to East-Central European experience, especially to Hungary and former Czechoslovakia, but their observations unfortunately have resonance elsewhere.

Delpeuch (1995: 53) also noted how throughout the former bloc the image of power characteristic of the past continued to dominate people's thinking after the transition. The entrenched tradition of a single party and a single truth gave no guidance or encouragement for people to learn to accept conflicts of interest or disputes of opinion as typical of democracy. Rather, they were often interpreted as evidence of its failure. The very fact of different interpretations of constitutional provisions was often read as dangerous, the inevitable ambiguities of the law as matters of great regret, and constitutional courts were often dragged into support of presidents insisting on their absolute rights against parliaments, or vice versa, rather than being left to adjudicate properly legal issues. Adding to this broth was the profound and widely held assumption, in the earlier post-transition years, that 'democracy' was a codeword for western affluence, not a variable set of rules for managing conflicts in society. When affluence was not immediate, faith in 'democracy' took a severe beating, especially in Russia.

Russia

The changes in the state in Russia have been the most sweeping of all, given that not only was the Communist Party dislodged as one of the pillars of power, but so was the imperial character of the Soviet state. It was a paradoxical imperialism. In the peripheral colonies it was often seen as a Russified apparatus purporting to be generically 'Soviet' and multi-national. But in Russia itself it was frequently seen, especially in the latter 1980s, as an anti-Russian excrescence helping to bleed away the system's scarce and precarious wealth on to the peripheral republics and away from the Russian heartland.[8] Not all who held the latter view thought the republics should be shed, simply preferring that they should be less cosseted and more grateful.

That periphery was but one of four layers of imperial influence, three of which had dissolved by the end of 1991. The six East-Central European states were one layer, the fourteen Soviet republics another. Beyond them, the far outer layer was constituted at various points in time and under different modes by India, Cuba, Vietnam, Ethiopia, Angola, South Yemen, Egypt, Libya, and some other states, none of them contiguous with the Soviet Union. The deep inner layer was composed within Russia itself by Chechnya, Tatarstan, Sakha (formerly Yakutia), North Ossetia, Dagestan and other ethnic zones, often would-be nation-states. Although within Russian borders, these zones had been victims of Tsarist colonialism just as much as Georgia or Kyrgyzstan.

When the dust had settled in 1991, only this last, often restive layer remained. At the same time, the contiguous periphery of former Soviet republics that came to be referred to in Russia as the 'near-abroad', had not cast their moorings and sailed away. The ensuing years saw most of them engaged in a variety of negotiations, often to recategorize rather than radically to reconstruct, their still typically dependent relationship with Russia. The post-colonial relation of Britain and France to their former colonies in Africa offered a loose parallel, though contiguity was a major difference in this instance.

The other pillars of the former Soviet state, its departments of domestic government, its military–industrial complex and its political police force, effectively continued in operation, albeit buffeted about at intervals by severe political and economic winds.

The central government departments continued, with the exception of such entities as the once powerful Gosplan, the central planning agency. However, with the demise of Soviet planning many of their nationwide control functions became seriously atrophied. Local regions and industrial complexes began to assert themselves more and more, partly in line with developments that had even begun under Brezhnev and partly in response to the collapse of effective central direction and previous economic contracts. Aside from the ethnic-based autonomous republics, of which some were listed above, other regional movements began to gather force, whether for Siberian self-rule, or even pushing for a single province such as Sverdlovsk to be assigned an autonomous status.[9] These regionalist assertions, however, did not typically evince any strong new drive for internal democracy, so the power structure was not scheduled for any rapid change in its procedures.

The military–industrial complex was severely shrunken in terms of soldiers under arms, being reduced to well under 2 million[10] by early 1995 as opposed to the nearly 6 million of a decade or so earlier. However, the military in general continued to wield very considerable political power both in foreign and domestic policy. An instance of the former would be the Russian government's ongoing suspicion of NATO and hostility to its admission of East-Central European states. Of the latter, the chief examples would be Yeltsin's dependence on the military for his survival both at the time of the attempted putsch in 1991 and during the sieges of Parliament and Ostankino Television in October 1993.

Indeed the military was deeply riven, as was the nation as a whole, by the 1993 events. Reports that were inevitably unverifiable in detail because of military discipline, but none the less very widespread, suggested that in the elections of November 1993 a very substantial proportion of votes by military personnel went to the ultra-nationalist Liberal Democratic Party headed by Vladimir Zhirinovsky.[11]

The industrial wing of the military–industrial complex continued to exert very substantial influence over economic policy. Arkady Volsky, president of the Union of Industrialists and Entrepreneurs, was the chief spokesman for this powerful sector of leading state enterprises, and was widely seen as influential in obtaining continuing state bank credits for the sector. This could be justified on one level as enabling economic units to survive during a chaotic period of transition to capitalism, but at the same time necessitated printing huge volumes of rubles, thus accelerating inflation at a giddy pace.

The remaining pillar-agency, the KGB, was inherited by the Russian state from the former Soviet state. Historically divided into foreign and domestic sections, the foreign section was preserved virtually intact. Yeltsin fired 400 senior officials in 1992 from the 135,000-strong domestic section, but at the same time left the rest of it untouched and simultaneously expanded internal surveillance authority to a number of additional agencies (Albats, 1994; Yasmann 1993). It went through a variety of name-changes but continued to be referred to as the KGB in general conversation.

We shall examine further the relation between the post-Soviet Russian state and the media in Chapter 6, but this section would be radically incomplete without noting the extraordinary turbulence of Russian central government in these years. The 1991 putsch, the bloody October 1993 confrontations, and the Chechnya war have already been mentioned. In spite of these upheavals, however, for some observers the continuation firstly of Gorbachev in power until the end of 1991, and then of Yeltsin as Russian President over the next four years, still implied a certain stability. This was very far from the case. Not only did the economy go through a series of wrenching spasms, as we will note below, but government ministers came and went with extraordinary frequency (and sometimes came back again). Political parties and groups formed, split, reconstituted. And in the meantime a steady stream of public policy ukases issued from President Yeltsin's pen, bypassing parliament altogether, but none the less often honored in their breach as much or more than in their observance.

By the latter half of 1995, no party and no presidential candidate seemed to be able to garner any significant public enthusiasm. For the younger generation in particular, the political process seemed utterly irrelevant and absurd, and even nauseating. Vainshtein (1994), however, offered some interesting reflections on the effective convergence of statist attitudes in Russian political culture during this period, even from rather opposite ideological corners. Thus those who wanted a strong state to modernize the economy, and those who wanted a strong state to preserve people's Soviet-era economic entitlements, both saw the state as a necessary instrument to their ends. He too (p. 256) underscored the way 'ordinary Russian citizens perceive[d] the absurdities and defects of the current political system as characteristic of genuine democracy [so that] the democratic idea turns out to be increasingly discredited'.

Poland

The post-Soviet Polish state began its life in the February–April 1989 round-table talks between the Jaruzelski regime and *Solidarnosc*, and in the compromise national elections of June that year when *Solidarnosc* candidates won all but one of the seats in parliament which they were permitted to contest (they could run for all upper house seats and 35 percent of lower house seats). With the exception of some activist grass-roots groups such as *Fighting Solidarnosc* who condemned and boycotted the talks, the Round Table negotiations and the ensuing election result generated very considerable euphoria in many circles across the nation. There was great anticipation that Poland was going to vault in one tremendous bound into a new era, an era when it would rapidly be reintegrated culturally and economically into Western Europe and resume its supposedly normal and authentic evolutionary path.

What actually transpired was a long way from that vision. It had a great deal to do with economic forces whose role was grossly underestimated initially by many Poles, and which will be briefly reviewed later in this chapter. There was a very rapid turnover in administrations, although Walesa, having succeeded Jaruzelski as president in November 1990, continued in office throughout the period under review. The first post-Soviet government, albeit initially with Jaruzelski still as president, was that of Tadeusz Mazowiecki, the long-term *Solidarnosc* advisor and editor of its weekly paper (*Tygodnik Solidarnosc*). This first administration lasted from August 1989 to November 1990.

It was succeeded by the Bielecki administration, the new premier being leader of the tiny Liberal Democratic Congress Party. Almost immediately however, in January 1991, this administration was replaced with a five-party conservative coalition headed by Jan Olszewski, who publicly proclaimed in his first speech as premier: 'If I'd known . . . I would not have accepted this position. It's a catastrophe' (Lewicka, 1992: 46). In June 1992 his government was in turn replaced by the first Pawlak administration, which then in August ceded to the Suchocka administration, until the September 1993 elections, at which point Pawlak returned to office a second time at the head of a new coalition. Some Poles referred to these last events as the 'Jurassic Park' elections, inasmuch as the leading party in the new coalition administration was the re-formed and re-named Communist Party, the SLD. Then in March 1995, after Pawlak had finally lost almost universal confidence, and after much haggling, Jozef Oleksy formed a new administration.

President Walesa's powers included appointing the prime minister, and to some degree this constant chopping and changing of administrations reflected his numerous interventions, as well as the problems of the turbulent economy, and intermittent national elections. Like President Yeltsin, Mr Walesa was an advocate of government by presidential decree and issued many such. 'Today decrees are necessary,' he stated in 1990. 'And they will be necessary for a long time to come. Decrees in the cause of democracy, as an effective response to the gaps that Parliament won't fill in on time' (cited in Feffer, 1992: 119). A considerable dimension of 'politics' in this period in Poland consisted of larger or smaller tussles between president and government on a whole range of issues, not least the media.

However, the confused condition of the electorate in the first years of the new regime did not help the situation. For example, Tyminski, the demagogic and unscrupulous Polish-Canadian who 'parachuted' back into

Poland to run for office, actually came in second to Walesa in the 1990 presidential contest (echoes of Zhirinovsky). The many dozens of political parties that formed almost overnight – some Poles at the time referred to them as 'taxi-parties', inasmuch as their total membership could fit into a single taxi – added to the confusion. The harsh public impact of the Mazowiecki administration's economic policies for the transition (the Balcerowicz plan, named after the Minister of Finance who spearheaded it), also had a major role in disillusioning voters from the very first.

As Jacek Kuron, long-term oppositionist and first Labor Minister in the post-Communist period put it in a review of his experience in office (Kuron, 1991: 7), people in *Solidarnosc* fought for the fictive ideals of the Communist regime to be real, for the slogans to come off the walls and be realized. They never anticipated for a moment things would actually get worse. One comic signal of all this political disarray was the success of the Friends of Polish Beer party in November 1990. They won sixteen parliamentary seats.

Electoral turnout continued low, at about the rate in the USA, that is, about 50 percent in presidential elections. This surprised many observers outside and inside Poland who had expected a more vibrant embrace of electoral life. Within the country, different interpretations were offered for this rather depressing phenomenon so soon into a new era, some pessimistic, some the reverse.

Letowska (1992) suggested that Polish political culture was still passive, tending simply to demand that the state intervene to provide solutions, and pinpointed a series of then-recent examples of inexperience with a functioning democracy in Poland – albeit focusing mostly on unprofessionalism at the top. Echoing one of her observations, namely that Poles this century had only had twenty years' experience of any form of democracy – the interwar Pilsudski regime having been only marginally democratic, more a *democradura* – Zawadzki (1991) offered some sober historical context, critiquing strongly the romanticization and myth-making then current in national debate concerning Poland's supposedly profound democratic traditions.[12] Rychard (1992), in like vein, suggested that even the democracy represented by *Solidarnosc* had been, if for no fault of its own, a contestative rather than participative version of the democratic process. At the most negative end, Warszawski (1991) proposed that politics in the new regime was indeed reminiscent, in its irrelevance to public needs, of politics in the old – and hence the public apathy.

As against these views, another observer suggested hopefully that the low turnout reflected the tradition of abstention in the sovietized regime where it served as a signal of deep opposition, rather than total apathy (Kulakowska, 1991). Rychard (1992), taking a slightly longer view, argued that the situation was not as negative as some feared, in that the initial blind and passive faith of many in Mazowiecki had acted as anaesthetic for the Balcerowicz plan, which had initially been necessary simply to break the old economic system quickly and for good. He went on to draw attention to the steady emergence of small-scale enterprise and of local political initiative. This, he argued, should be seen as a more important index of healthy political development in a Poland that had been taught to be passive and to focus on centralized power, than the confused and sometimes absurd dramas then running in the national political arena.

It was certainly the case that the endless running battles during the first half of the 1990s between President Walesa and successive national administrations presented democratic procedures at their least inspiring, and generated frequent political cynicism among the public concerning their national leadership.

Hungary

The Hungarian political dynamic during these years of transition in the state was partly akin to the Polish and Russian situations, but also very distinct in other ways. The first free elections in March 1990 issued in a coalition government led by the Magyar Democratic Forum (MDF), the largest initially (Kende, 1988) of the unofficial groups that had been forming during the latter 1980s. The Alliance of Free Democrats and the Young Democrats (Fidesz), whose formation dated from the same period, found themselves in opposition. The former Communists, now re-named Socialists, received just 11 percent. However, the presidency of the new republic went in a later election to a Free Democrat, Göncz Árpád.

The MDF governed in coalition with two small conservative parties revived from the pre-Communist era and influential in the interwar period, the Smallholders Party and the Popular Christian Democrats. The MDF's deputies rather soon revealed themselves to be a coalition between nationalist conservatives and ultra-nationalists, the latter wing led by the rabidly xenophobic and authoritarian Csurka István, who was eventually expelled in 1993 and formed his own party. The Free Democrats' and the Young Democrats' public platforms called for aggressive moves toward a free market, whereas the MDF coalition preferred to move much more cautiously in that direction. The MDF was the only party to assert that the former government bureaucracy was a fully viable instrument of post-sovietized power, and in the event retained twenty-nine out of fifty-four department heads in post (Gradvohl, 1990). As in all these transitions, the lower civil service continued largely intact, but the MDF's conservatism was striking in regard to the old civil service leadership.[13]

In local elections in September and October the same year, the MDF's national position already began to erode, although with overall voter turnout at under 50 percent, it was hard to assess how far.[14] A significant index of the public mood was that 83 percent of mayors were elected as independents, a phenomenon repeated almost exactly in the 1994 local elections (82 percent). The signs clearly were that Hungarian voters were joining Poles and Russians in an increasing mood of alienation from the official party political process.

However, the political situation remained stable, if sometimes tense and anxiety-provoking, through the national elections of the spring of 1994. This was despite the constantly declining economic situation, despite many bitter verbal confrontations between government and opposition, not least over media policy as we shall note in Chapter 6, and despite a huge taxi-drivers' strike – over a sudden edict sharply raising fuel prices – that paralyzed Budapest and the country for three days in October 1990. It led to a serious confrontation between the President and the MDF Premier over whether to use the army to crush the strike.[15] The government eventually climbed down on both that proposal and the price-hike.

The 1994 elections resulted in a new coalition government a little reminiscent of the Polish one elected in 1993. It comprised the Socialist Party, the reform wing of the old Communist Party, that had gained the largest number of votes of any party (54 percent), and the Free Democrats, with 18 percent. In coalition negotiations, however, the Free Democrats were permitted a nearly equal say over the assignment of cabinet posts in order to allay public anxiety concerning a revival of the old regime.

Thus it might be argued that the very gradual democratization of Hungary over the previous thirty years had helped to produce a political culture in which dialogue, however vituperative or reluctant, was none the less seen as the norm. Conversely, the 'brink' was very widely recognized as a fearful political location, to be avoided if at all possible. The process was successfully played by the rules in the end.

At the same time, the resurgence of reform-minded Communists, as in Poland, Lithuania and elsewhere, lent particular emphasis to the public's urgent demand that economic problems should be solved. In Hungary and Poland the reform Communists' revived popularity had much to do with the public's economic grievances and fears, and the re-titled parties' strong ties to labor unions. It remained for the while unclear how far Hungarian, Russian or Polish voters were basically hoping to restore a providential state machine, a womb-to-tomb welfare system, without the repression that had gone hand in hand with it before. Furthermore, as Guetta remarks (1995: 12), after forty, even seventy years in power, 'only the communists know the machinery of power and have extensive professional experience'.

Moreover, differences between the parties should not be minimized. There is credible evidence (Drweski, 1995b) that from the mid-1980s the Polish Communist leadership had consistently converted to pro-market convictions; there really were no believing Communists left anywhere in Poland. The Hungarian party, once elected, soon established its distance from the trade unions, and its parliamentary rank and file were mostly drawn from a younger generation with no attachment to the old regime (Gradvohl, 1995). The Russian party's resurgence fed directly on the failures of the Yeltsin regime. It also brandished the nationalist flag harder than any other element in its platform. Its resemblance to its past, none the less, was far stronger than in the case of the other two parties, and fears were rife among media professionals in the period leading up to the June 1996 presidential elections that if Communists gained the presidency, there would ensue stronger media interference than even under Yeltsin.

National Identity, Ethnic Relations, Economic Transition

In all three nations, there were nationalist currents strongly at work preceding the transition, albeit of different types in each country, and quite differently handled by the regimes. The core reason for the sovietized regimes' recourse to support of these currents (earlier in the case of Russia, later in the case of Hungary, in a convoluted form in Poland[16]), was the accelerating collapse of any significant public interest in Communist political beliefs and the consequent need to encourage alternative sources of regime legitimacy. The surprise some observers expressed concerning the vigorous emergence of nationalism in Eastern Europe since the regime changes always seems oblivious of the prior history and significance of its tolerated expression.

The very shaky and anxious post-transition regimes were just as concerned with legitimacy as their predecessors, especially given the chaotic and worsening conditions of the economy in each and every case. Resonating to nationalist themes therefore continued to offer a shared discourse between the authorities and the public, otherwise hard to find. It was a period when economic policies and hardships merely provoked bitterness and massive public disillusionment with politics and politicians (some of whose antics, as might be predicted from the long and colorful story of parliamentary cretinism, did provide rich grist to this mill).

Russia

Post-imperial blues are a familiar dimension of political culture in all former colonizing powers. Britain, arguably, has yet to find its way out of them, and in large part the United States twice elected Reagan as president because he was root-and-branch committed to US global pre-eminence, and to recuperating the humiliation of its military impotence in Indochina, Afghanistan, and Iran (1975, 1979 and 1980). Steele (1994) has argued that by contrast, the loss of empire in Russia went remarkably smoothly and without seeming pain for the majority of Russians. He has a strong point in regard to a comparison with, say, the protracted and bloody Algerian war of independence and France's bitter turmoil consequent upon its defeat, but the judgment needs qualifying.

Firstly, as noted already, many Russians saw their empire as a burden, just as many Portuguese saw their African colonies in the period before the 1974 overthrow of fascism. A divided Germany was important to the older generation, and probably to the majority of Russian foreign policy strategists, but far less so to the younger generations. There was a sense among Russians that the Baltic countries, especially Lithuania, since it was taking the lead in demanding independence, were ungrateful for the economic blessings showered upon them by Russia since the Second World War and probably should indemnify Russia for them, but no stronger feeling was widespread than that.

Thus the point is that Russian national identity was not overwhelmingly bound up with retaining Eastern Europe or the other Soviet republics through sovietized mechanisms. Indeed the more racist wing of public opinion was glad to see the Central Asian and Transcaucasian republics shaken loose, simply because of who for the most part lived there. It is not that Russians felt they had no rights to politico-economic pre-eminence and indeed dominance in those areas, but that Soviet mechanisms did not and maybe now could not guarantee them.

Secondly, the whole process happened in such a telescoped fashion, and generally with such tolerance from the Gorbachev regime, that mustering mass opposition was excessively difficult. And thus Russians almost 'woke up one morning' without an empire, and nothing much had changed – least of all their daily economic discontents, which loomed very much larger in their consciousness at the time.

Thirdly, there was a strongly rooted wing of opinion, perhaps relatively small in numbers in the early 1990s, but often very well placed in the military, the KGB and in significant media and publishing institutions such as the Russian Union of Writers, that may without fear of exaggeration be described as ultra-rightist and ultra-nationalist (Brudny, 1991; Laqueur, 1993). Laqueur has described in detail how this official deviation from Communist orthodoxy was tolerated and grew under Brezhnev. Their opponents in the 1990s began referring to them as the 'Red-Browns', but like most political epithets the words disguised as much as they revealed. The epithet was supposed to poke bitter irony at the seemingly weird coalition between never-say-die Communists and admirers of Adolf Hitler, who often appeared to find themselves demonstrating against the same things in the same place, typically over instances of the loss of Russian global power, its humiliation by and kow-towing to the United States, and the need for a strong and resolute state power to restore the situation to where it should rightfully be for Great Russia.

For such as these, the loss of empire was signally important, and it remained to be seen whether they would constitute a permanent fringe minority like similar wings of opinion in some other countries, or would manage to get themselves into the political mainstream through successful pressure on the mainstream to try to adopt their causes. As always, that latter process depended in part upon events and political crises not necessarily under their control, but which if they arose could readily be translated and milked to that end. At such points, definitions of national identity could mutate quite rapidly.

One such issue was perfect for the purpose: the existence of about 25 million Russians, or a sixth of the Russian population of Russia itself, living in the fourteen peripheral republics and now suddenly marooned as a once-protected minority (not always a privileged minority overall). In the resurrection of Russia out of the ashes of the alien Soviet structure, these individuals became important both for themselves and as emblems of the trampled rights of Russians in the world at large. Especially when they were caught up in some violent civil strife, or when they were required to learn little-used and very difficult languages, like Estonian, before they were permitted to be considered for citizenship in the suddenly declared new states, many people in Russia felt strong bonds of sympathy and experienced a desire to support them in some way. No Zhirinovsky or clone could possibly resist exploiting this situation.

Thus decolonization did indeed pass off uneventfully. Where Steele's analysis arguably falls short is that decolonization did not signify the demise of Russian imperial pretensions, pretensions of centuries' standing, pretensions integrated with ties of economy and proximity, and pretensions given a particular twist by the large Russian diaspora that had found itself overnight to be a series of national minorities set adrift. Events in Crimea, where there was a Russian secessionist movement against Ukraine, in Moldova, where a Transdniestr Russian republic was announced, in the Baltic states, where citizenship laws seemed set to give many Russian residents second-class status, in Tajikistan and Georgia, where civil wars raged, were among the leading sources of angst for many Russians that could easily be exploited by ultra-nationalists.

National cultural identity is never a static phenomenon, but is always in the process of being defined in relation to the forces at work at the time. Russian identity during this period was in part being recomposed, in part reaffirmed, often in the form of wondering and planning how to reassert Russia's appropriate global standing and mission.[17] Even for those who found that traditional self-understanding a straitjacket, this agenda was still one they could not bypass. Beginning with the recovery of historical memory of the Stalin years under Gorbachev, national attention then rather rapidly accelerated backwards in time beyond the Lenin years, which became effectively conflated in character with Stalinism (an 'imperfect Stalinism'), and so back into a glorious Russian past, freed of any memory of pain since there were virtually no survivors to tell their tales.

Inescapably, this dilemma of national self-understanding interacted with the extraordinarily painful experience of economic transition. The Brezhnev years appeared by that standard to have been a halcyon era. Kopeks, which up to the end of the 1980s could be used for public telephones, the metro, a newspaper, good bread, disappeared from view as the ruble's value sank through floor after floor. Pensioners suffered atrociously, but they were far from alone. Side by side with sharp increases in poverty and its usual concomitants in sickness and premature death, there arose a highly visible class of entrepreneurs who revelled in conspicuous consumption, thus harshly highlighting the deprivation of the poor. The State Statistics Committee reported in January 1995[18] that two-thirds of the country was living below the mean income, and that the top 10 percent's income was fifteen times higher than the bottom 10 percent's (just three years before the ratio had been a little less than five times higher). Life expectancy for Russian males fell to fifty-seven, the lowest since before the Second World War, and epidemics of cholera and diphtheria were sharply evident.[19]

The sense of impotence and frustration in the face of economic drift and declining living standards, already tangible by the end of the 1980s, had now become a widespread national mood.[20] An Academy of Sciences poll in 1995 reported that only 5 percent believed talent and hard work could bring wealth, 44 percent claimed speculation was much more effective in that regard and 20 percent signalled money-laundering as the best route.[21] Both sources of anxiety and frustration about the negative prospects for economic well-being and about Russia's imperilled status in world affairs fed on each other.

Poland

Kubik (1994) has argued that the Communist regime very consciously avoided public discourse concerning Polish national identity, preferring always to stress the interconnections between Russians, Poles and other peoples within the Soviet bloc. Given the unusual historical strength of Polish nationalism, he however suggests that the official media silence on the subject had the unintended impact of actually intensifying the nation as an object of cathexis precisely because the silence was readily perceived as a direct refusal to address this key question. The lack of cathexis for the sovietized Polish state at national or local level meant that there was no institutionalized focus with which Poles would consider identifying, outside their families and friends, aside from the nation. He further proposes that the vacuum in public ethical values and national sense of direction that characterized the period both before and after 1989 was an additional stimulus to discovering meaning and purpose in the nation.

The role of the Catholic Church in Poland in sustaining national identity among the public, at least through its own interpretation of that identity, was of great importance during the four or so decades of the regime. Given the adhesion to the Church both by intellectuals, including college students, and the industrial working class,[22] its role in fertilizing nationalist consciousness should not be underestimated.

Since 1989, however, the Church's interpretation – or at least, the dominant interpretation within the Catholic Church – of the interconnection between Catholicism and Polish nationalism has been subject to very considerable attacks in Poland. The questions of whether Christian values should be defined as national values, especially on sensitive issues of personal ethics such as contraception and abortion, and how far Catholic Christian tenets should be promulgated in the school system, were hotly debated and the Church hierarchy's positions often defeated in legislative debates. The proposed Concordat with the Vatican was successfully challenged and delayed during the second Pawlak administration. None the less, the argument that to be a real Pole you must be a practicing Catholic – and not, for instance, a Jew or an unbeliever – was alive and well in Poland throughout the period after 1989, even if far from uncontested.

A case could be made for saying that the most powerful catalyst for the definition of Polish national identity, today and yesterday, has in reality been Russia, in that if national identity is in substantial measure a process of defining the collective in opposition to neighboring collectives, then Russia and Ukraine easily outstripped Germany as the chief such stimuli. Although its vigor has sometimes been overstated, anti-Semitism certainly operates in Poland, even virtually without a Jewish community to target, as does bitter and violent anti-Romani sentiment. These are obviously part of the definition of Polish identity for some sectors of the population, but the opposition 'Polish vs. Russian/Ukrainian' might as well have generated the expression 'polar extremes' as the geographical poles themselves.[23]

The problem was to know what to do with this national identity now that it had finally been won on the political and constitutional levels. Western Europeans, supposedly the Poles' natural kinsfolk, turned out not to be especially interested in their return to political normalcy or their economic plight. The sudden lifting of economic sanctions did not generate massive loans to pull the Polish economy out of its dire straits.

After this became abundantly clear, a new mood set in that was some-what xenophobic, for example actively distrusting foreign investors. As in Russia, mythic versions of past paradises began to become popular, some touting the interwar Pilsudski *democradura*, others the vision of his ultra-nationalist and anti-semitic adversary Dmowski, still others digging further back into the Jagiellonian Golden Age (cf. Zawadzki, 1991). With the economic present and future seeming so bleak to so many, with the gulf between the new rich (quite often canny members of the old *nomenklatura*) and the new poor that has already been noted for Russia, with the increasingly out-of-touch ambitions for political and constitutional influ-ence on the part of the Catholic hierarchy, these attachments to national symbols and motifs perhaps represented the only seemingly functioning creed on the market.[24]

The economic situation was indeed drastic for many Poles (Drweski, 1992; Halamska, 1992; Kulakowska, 1991; Naskowska, 1992; Patynski, 1991). In the early 1990s, the gap between rich and poor yawned wider and wider. Small farms, especially in the North-East, were in worse and worse condition and with no realistic prospect of improvement. At the same time, 60 percent of the average household budget of city-dwellers was going on food, with the result that relations between farmers and people in towns became quite sharply hostile for a period. There were quite widespread reports of children coming to school without having eaten in the previous twenty-four hours. Unemployment rose, especially among miners in Silesia and in transfer industries. In general women were fired first. Job-prospects for school-leavers were very poor, and once middle managers lost their job it was virtually impossible to find another. Around 70 percent of the employed actively feared being thrown out of work at any time. Some commentators even linked a rise in the suicide rate to these dire conditions.

As the decade wore on, not much changed in this picture.[25] The inflation rate was nearly 40 percent in 1993, and over 30 percent in 1994, while the unemployment rate stayed at around 16 percent. Simultaneously in 1994 the new Polish stock market enjoyed a huge initial boom, being touted as the best performing stock market in the world. Its performance showed little sign of 'trickling down' to the average Pole, however. Polish workers often seemed skeptical of pluralist institutions, such as parties or media, and exceptionally nervous about losing their jobs, while seeming to define democracy as akin to the chance for prosperity rather than freedom or grass-roots influence (Gardawski and Zukowski, 1993).

Hungary

Some analogous processes to the Polish situation, but seemingly with less widespread impact, could be seen at work in the Hungarian debate about national identity. To understand the debate, it is necessary first to recall the punitive Trianon treaty of 1920 that redrew Hungary's frontiers. It took away a full third of its territory and 40 percent of its population (Wandycz, 1992: 204), with the result that substantial Hungarian minorities are today to be found in Slovakia, in the Transylvanian region of Romania, and in the Voivodina region of Serbia. A smaller minority is also to be found in Carpathian Ukraine. Hungarian politics in the interwar years was obsessed with this settlement, but during most of the Communist period the Trianon treaty was not a permitted topic for public discourse, nor was the situation of Hungarian minorities in neighboring states.[26] It was a major signal of political change when the former regime began in the later 1980s to permit open discussion of the plight of Hungarians in Ceauşescu's Romania.[27]

The MDF and all parties with the exception of Fidesz made the Trianon treaty an item in their 1990 election manifestos. However, the Csurka wing of the MDF put it center stage, and their statements on occasion concerning Hungarian minorities in neighboring countries verged on the mystical and the irredentist. Kenedi and Mihancsik[28] cite their assertion that Hungarians in rural Romania were in some sense pure, true Magyars untouched by nefarious cosmopolitan influences. Admittedly there were some grounds for concern: Slovakia's government began insisting on street signs in Slovak only in the Hungarian region of the country; the new Gabcikovo-Nagymoros dam[29] appeared to be a plus for Slovakia but a clear negative for Hungary; the demise of Ceauşescu halted the worst Romanian abuses of Hungarians but far from all; and it seemed that young Hungarians in Voivodina were more liable to be drafted into the Serbian military than their Serb peers.

However, despite the MDF's best efforts to milk these problems, despite its trumpeting of Christian values as a part of the Hungarian way of life, despite its identification of countryside culture as the true Hungary, despite its assertion that Hungary's wartime alliance with Nazi Germany was justifiable as an anti-Communist defensive measure, despite the diatribes of the Csurka wing against cosmopolitans, foreigners, Bolsheviks and liberals (all of whom being tendentially Jews, and very likely Budapest intellectuals), these attempts to recuperate the past in the service of the present ended by exerting only partial political appeal.[30] At the same time, a very real level of hostility grew explicit on all levels of society concerning Romanis (Gradvohl, 1990; Kis, 1986; Tamás, 1991). Although there was seemingly a more open attitude towards Jews as compared to Poland, none the less Hungarian Jews commonly experienced the paradox that they were made more aware of their Jewish status by gentile Hungarians than by their own families (Szabó and Wald, 1992).

These last two authors make the interesting point that the debate over the significance of the 'Trianon minorities' and internal minorities were all a part of the never-ending process of self-redefinition by Hungarians, the fourth this century (the earlier ones being the post-war years of 1918–19 and 1945–7, and 1948, the year the Rákósi regime took power). Half a decade into the new era, however, it provisionally seemed as though practical and secular priorities were winning out over intensely ideological ones – with the definite exception of Romanis' status, and the ambiguous exception of Jewish status.

The Hungarian economy had been in bad shape since well before the regime changed, with foreign debt per head actually higher than in Poland. Hungarians typically survived by holding two and three jobs, usually involving them in exceptionally long hours at work. (This was not unusual in other bloc countries at the time.) Their welfare provisions, however, were generally very reasonable and these made for levels of expectation of social and health services budgets that were increasingly difficult to fulfill.

In the post-transition period Hungarians' reasons for alienation typically appeared to be economic. One survey found 58 percent thought they had lived better under the Communist regime (Tamás, 1991). Another found 80–90 percent agreeing with propositions that the state should ensure full employment, pensions, protective policies toward industry and suppression of inequality (Toth, 1991). A popular joke went the rounds that Antall, the MDF Premier, had done more in two years to convince people of the merits of Communism than had Kádár in over thirty (Bognár, 1992). A 1994 study surveying political attitudes since 1992 found only 17 percent who disagreed that capitalism in Hungary was doing more harm than good, and its conclusions noted the following widely held opinion:

> the majority of the people do not see real performance behind the enrichment of the entrepreneurial layer. It is an almost generally accepted opinion that in present circumstances it is those who speculate or have good informal connections, who can get ahead. (cited in Andor, 1994: 65–7)

The uncertainty that remained was that the reform Hungarian Socialist Party's economic policies entailed swingeing austerity measures. Its initial Finance Minister was described as a Thatcherite by the *Financial Times*, and the welfare cuts the government announced as part of an IMF package in February 1995 produced 66 percent of voters who described themselves in an opinion poll as 'outraged' (Roe, 1995).

There was therefore a rather murky path ahead at that point in time in Hungary, as in Poland and Russia.

Conclusions

The temptation to anchor oneself to forecasts proved particularly idiotic in the nations of the former Soviet bloc during this fifteen-year period, and so any attempt to predict the latter half of the 1990s will be resisted here. Furthermore, the objective of this chapter is to provide a basic road-map with which to follow the more specific mediatic and cultural route that is this book's focus, in its attempt to reconstitute and internationalize media theory.

Notes

1 It is impossible to list, let alone evaluate critically, all the sources used. Readers may find the following helpful in the first instance, together with the more specific sources cited at intervals in the text: J.F. Brown, 1991; Feffer, 1992; Held, 1992; Heller and Nekrich, 1986; Hosking, 1985; Köves, 1992; Mason, 1992; Nove, 1987; Rakowska-Harmstone, 1984, 2nd edn; Rothschild, 1977; Sugar et al., 1990, chs 13ff.; Wandycz, 1992, chs. 7–8.

2 The discussion will be of Soviet Russia, and only occasionally of the whole Union of Soviet Socialist Republics.

3 This is not to dismiss the tenacity or sacrifice of the Afghan resistance, which also played a key role in disrupting Soviet power. But direct control of Afghanistan was never equivalent to control over Poland in terms of the Soviet system's bedrock foreign interests.

4 These will begin for Poland and Hungary from 1945. This is not to imply their history commenced with Soviet invasion, but simply to reduce the volume of data confronting the reader unfamiliar with the region.

5 Magyar = Hungarian. MDF will be used as the abbreviation here, but HDF is often used outside Hungary.

6 Lenin once argued that the key difference between War Communism and the 1914–18 imperial German economy in wartime was that the latter was much better organized. So much for a superior socialist model. For a detailed description of War Communism policies and policy debates see Carr (1952: 147–279). For the argument that they were the primitive nucleus of Soviet economic and political policies under Stalin, see for example Sapir (1990), and cf. Bordyugov (1995).

7 Even so, as Brezhnev plotted with others to oust Khrushchev in 1964, he was in mortal panic that they would all be shot for their actions. Yet Khrushchev had expelled other challengers from power in 1957 without having them executed.

8 The 1990 re-naming of the former Program Two Soviet Union channel as 'Russian Television' is an interesting case in point. All the Soviet republics but Russia had a second TV channel for local republic programming in the language or languages of the republic in question. In that sense, Russia was simply coming into line with the other fourteen republics.

However, the former Program Two was one of many expressions of the curious duality of the Soviet imperial system – its content was in Russian, its reach was across the entire Union, and yet Russia itself was not availed of its own republic TV channel. The demand that it should be was itself reflective of the growing public assertiveness of Russo-centrism, utilized (and thereby further reinforced) by Yeltsin's successful campaign for power as President of the Russian republic against Soviet President Gorbachev from 1989.

9 Hughes, 1994.

10 *Izvestiya* 17 June 1994 and International Institute of Strategic Studies *1994–95 Annual Report*, cited respectively in *RFE/RL Daily Report*, 116, 21 June 1994 and 194, 12 October 1994.

11 A multitude of factors would have to be taken into account to explain Zhirinovsky's degree of popularity and credibility at that point as a potential head of the Russian state, whether among the military or the public at large. His buffoon qualities, his wild and unpredictable threats, his constant changes of mind, his playing to the stereotype of the menacing Russian bear, his un-nuanced clumsy English, were usually the only aspects of his political persona given play in Western interpretations.

Perhaps a personal experience may help to redress the balance and illuminate the dynamics at work. Sailing in on a small Finnish steamer in August 1993 to the old naval garrison city of Kronstadt, some fifteen kilometres west of St Petersburg across the water at the far end of the Gulf of Finland, our ship was greeted by a 'welcoming' military band playing various tunes as we docked and were processed on deck by Russian customs and immigration officials. As we then descended the gangplank, a military hat to collect our tips was placed on the ground where we had to walk past it.

This example of the humiliation of the military, be it the band or fighting troops, having to beg for its supper from foreigners, stood in for a great deal else by way of illustrating the sources of deeply injured national pride in Russia at that time and gives some sense of the grounds for an ultra-nationalist's appeal. Gorbachev's and then Yeltsin's profound un-popularity, their seeming inability to get the economy back even to the level of the Brezhnev era, and their constant feting by Western governments while they stood before those govern-ments or their IMF representatives as supplicants, cap in hand, also had much to do with it. See the further discussion of Russian nationalism below.

12 An article of faith for seemingly most Poles is that 'Asia' begins at the Belarusian/Ukrainian/Russian frontier, and that Poland's high destiny is to cleave to its European cultural essence, usurped at the state level by its repeated colonization in this and previous centuries. On some lips this is even linked to Poland's supposedly glorious imperial past, when for a while it stretched from the Baltic to the Black Sea. It is hard to know where to begin with this mishmash of ethnocentrism, colonialist nostalgia and *folie de grandeur*. Its absurdity is only to be compared to the retention of the word 'Great' applied to Britain. Its historical basis (the 'Tatar yoke') is highly disputable. Halperin (1985) has presented considerable evidence to suggest that the Russian despotism which is the understandable target of Polish historical memory was at least as much a product of Byzantine Christian culture as it was of Tatar culture, let alone some supposedly Asian enthusiasm for political repression.

13 Kende (1991a: 14–15) suggests, however, that there was a particular historical context to that policy which made it both feasible and reasonable in the eyes of many Hungarians. The feasibility was derived from the Kádár regime's latter-era policy of appointing the competent rather than the merely reliable to positions of authority. The reasonableness issued from the bitter experience of savage purges following the Bela Kun Soviet in 1919, the immediate post-Nazi years in 1945–6, the Rákósi terror after 1948, and the post-1956 reprisals. A similar dynamic did not appear to be at work in the Czech Republic or Eastern Germany, where purges of suspected former Communists were relentlessly pursued, although perhaps the much more repressive regimes there may have accounted for the difference.

14 It gained just 18 percent of the votes cast, whereas the opposition Free Democrats and Fidesz received 36 percent between them.

15 Kenedi János and Mihancsik Zsófia ('The mass media war in Hungary', unpublished article, 1993), suggest that the combination of the taxi drivers' very effective use of CB radios

to coordinate their strategy and tactics, and the honest reporting of the strike in broadcast media, effectively brought the question of media 'political reliability' to the forefront of the governing coalition's agenda.

16 From the Second World War onwards, many Russians (even if anti-Soviet) conceded a certain legitimacy to their military as agents of national defense and world power. The military hierarchy increasingly saw itself as the successor of the imperial Russian army's achievements. Some analysts suggest that even before this the Stalin industrial and agricultural revolution held a Russian nationalist appeal for the *nomenklatura* (Bettelheim, 1983: 30–40). At the same time, any nationalist expression in the other republics was repressed, under Stalin with extreme violence, later harshly. It still grew apace during the 1980s, often initially concerning itself with questions of ancient history or linguistics issues, though these obscure topics always turned out to hold a pivotal symbolic significance for ideological zealots. Part of the Brezhnev regime's decay, in ideological terms, was its concession of more autonomy to the regions and republics and a laxer oversight of these emergent tendencies among the republics' *nomenklaturas*. By 'convoluted' support for nationalism in the case of Poland is meant that the Polish leadership's typical rationale for their repressive actions was that if the Russians took over, they would be worse (Rosenberg 1995: 125–258; Toranska, 1987, *passim*).

17 Public political assertion of these issues reached something of a crescendo by the second half of 1994. It was particularly noticeable that politicians and media typically associated with liberal political positions (in the US sense of the term 'liberal') were part of the chorus. Oleg Rumyantsev, Chairman of the Fund for Constitutional Reforms, called for the CIS to be turned into the 'Russian Union'. Ultra-nationalist demagogue Aleksandr Lebed, the Lieutenant-Colonel heading the Russian forces in the Transdniestr region of Moldova, was strongly supported by liberal newspapers and TV. Yeltsin's foreign policy advisor Dmitrii Ryurikov proposed that ethnic Russians in CIS states should retain dual citizenship for their protection. Yeltsin and his foreign minister Kozyrev publicly proclaimed the need to acknowledge Russia's rightful sphere of influence, i.e. in the former Union territories. A number of leading newspapers argued along the same lines for the recognition of what they termed 'post-Soviet space'. A number of political parties and leading individuals including Arkady Volsky announced a coalition, Third Force, in December 1994, and called for a new Eurasian Community, a successor to the Russian Empire 'in which we all lived for 300 to 500 years'. An interesting instance was official Russian insistence in October 1994 that the Caspian Sea was actually a lake, and therefore that international maritime law did not apply; the further consequence being that Russia could establish a claim over its oil resources, and not simply Azerbaijan. Sources: *RFE/RL Daily Report* 163, 29 August 1994; 165, 31 August 1994; 166, 1 September 1994; 186, 29 September 1994; 189, 5 October 1994; 190, 6 October 1994; 191, 7 October 1994; 192, 10 October 1994; 194, 12 October 1994; 195, 13 October 1994; 229, 6 December 1994. See also Chapter 6, n. 41.

18 *OMRI Report* I.5, 6 January 1995.

19 *Prism* (Jamestown Foundation), 14 July 1995.

20 As early as 1990, the many Muscovites whom the writer asked 'How soon do you think the economy will improve? In seven years?' were already answering with a snort, 'Never!' 'Not in my lifetime!' Even the more optimistic said 'Seven? More like thirty!' or 'More like seventy!'

21 *Monitor* (Jamestown Foundation), 14 June 1995.

22 Interestingly, by the 1990s there were strong signs of only nominal adhesion to religious practice among rural youth (personal communication from Jerzy and Waisza Szejnoch).

23 It is not, by contrast, a theme in Russian nationalism, which does not return the compliment of prime foe to the Poles, even though the Russian Army in 1994 reconsecrated 7 November from Revolution Day to Victory Against Poland Day, harking back to the 1621 Polish invasion of Russia.

24 Interestingly, however, a major survey of nearly 5,000 workers in 461 firms found they rarely mentioned the recovery of national independence as a benefit of the new order (Gardawski and Zukowski, 1993).

25 *RFE/RL Daily Report*, 12, 19 January 1994; 17, 26 January 1994; 140, 26 July 1994.

26 In a Budapest restaurant in December 1978, a somewhat inebriated diner approached

our table and began to explain in Hungarian to my wife, who is black, that however bad the situation might be for black Americans (of whom he evidently assumed she was one), it could not compare with the situation of Hungarians in Romania. Our hosts translated for us. An instance of *in vino veritas*, at least so far as deeply felt public sentiment went. In May ten years later, the biggest demonstration since 1956, permitted by the regime, met in Martyrs' Square to protest silently about the treatment of Hungarians in Romania.

27 In a 1986 interview, Kis János equally observed that in Hungary the only force then filling the cultural and ethical gap that had been left by sovietism, was nationalism (Kis, 1986: 38). In 1986, that same year, a 2,000-page two-volume history of Hungarian Transylvania was published, edited by the then Minister of Culture (Matei Cazacu, 'Manoeuvres dérisoires: histoire de la Transylvanie publié à Budapest,' *La Nouvelle Alternative*, 7 (9/87), 10). Obscure and academic an action as this may have seemed, it was part and parcel of the regime's struggle for legitimacy, which in turn helped to intensify the nationalist impulse. Having said that, the research did endeavor to emphasize the historical roles of Romanians, Magyars and Germans, and their periods of cooperation as well as of strife, in order to get away from the notion of 'eternal confrontation' between Romanians and Hungarians (Köpeczi, 1993).

28 Kenedi and Mihancsik, unpublished paper cited in note 15 above.

29 A Slovak-Hungarian Danube project, originally with Austria involved as well, that was a lightning rod for anti-regime organization in the later 1980s (see Chapter 3). At one point cancelled, it was later reinstated and became a nationalist cause in Hungary, rather than a strictly ecological issue.

30 Kende (1991b) warned that the issue of the non-Magyar ethnic origins of the Budapest bourgeoisie was bound to resurface, since it had been put on ice during the Communist regime, but had never been resolved. In 1995 the rural Smallholders Party, a small conservative party with a significant pre-Communist history, took up the cudgels yet again on this issue. For a dissection of the development of different strands in Hungarian nationalist thinking over the 1980s, based on surveys conducted in 1983 and 1989, see Csepeli (1991). For an account of fascist and racist movements in post-transition Hungary, including Csurka's circle, see Hockenos (1993: 105–65).

3

Media and Communication:
the Post-Stalin Era

In the discussion so far it has repeatedly been emphasized that the last decade or so of the Soviet bloc was a decade of change and development. At the time, those who perceived almost any changes to be under way were often accused of naiveté, either in making the assertion in the first place, or in implying that the perceived changes might be in the process of becoming irreversible. Analytically speaking, however, it is essential at least with hindsight to acknowledge that in point of fact the underlying trends of change were not significantly deflected, even though the decade's outset, with the declaration of martial law in Poland and the apparent crushing of *Solidarnosc*, seemed to reveal an unyielding system. Specifying such trends is a most important task in any nation or region in which there is taking place (or might take or has taken place) a transition from dictatorial rule. Our task here is to focus on mediatic and cultural trends, though always in interconnection with political and economic processes.

Historically speaking, for most writers on sovietized media there has been but one theme: the mechanisms by which those states dominated their media. Equally, for most, this could flatly be reduced to the question of censorship, presuming all viewpoints and information to have been filtered through a Party cell mesh, present in every media institution, that strained out every political heresy. Accidental transgression could then be left to the official censorship body, Glavlit, to deal with, or on a more everyday level, to the KGB. The Propaganda Department of the Communist Party's Central Committee had the leading task of formulating policy to suit particular or changing circumstances.

This was all true, at least by intent of the *verkhushka*,[1] the apex of power. If Mikhail Suslov – in the Brezhnev era the Politburo's Grand Vizier and Highest Eunuch of sterilized, brutalized marxism, apostolic heir of Stalin's and Beria's designated culture tsar, Andrei Zhdanov – had been asked the question, it is safe to say he would have replied in terms such as these.[2]

In other words, there was a tendency among sovietologists to take at face value the admittedly chilling descriptions of the system offered by its most senior advocates. Not only so, but to read the system as being as unchanging and untroubled ('totalitarian') as its propagandists proposed. It is no wonder that its collapse came as such a surprise, almost as a disproof of cherished convictions, to some commentators. Not that the present author, even as of early spring 1989, would ever have predicted the helter-skelter collapse that ensued from the Polish Round Table talks onwards. But there were a series of changes in the wind that considerably pre-dated 1989 and 1991, including in the media and cultural sphere, that implied an ongoing process of redirection in these nations that was not necessarily under the absolute and sovereign control of the *verkhushki* in the Soviet Union, Poland or Hungary.

This chapter will outline a more nuanced account of the media and cultural scenario during the last decade or so of the Soviet system than has customarily been offered; and then in the two following chapters some of the interacting communicative, cultural and societal forces will be reviewed that arguably engendered the collapse of the bloc. The more nuanced account of the media build-up to the transition biennium is offered here in the interests of a more precise understanding of what may be entailed in mediatic terms when regimes founder and are replaced.

Thus rather than relying on the simplified 'set-in-concrete' accounts of sovietized media characteristic of the period before the last years of the Brezhnev regime (e.g. Hollander, 1972; Hopkins, 1970), it is much more productive to see how dissenting communication was managed, and was on occasion unmanageable rather than simply expunged, especially in the final Brezhnev years and the Gorbachev period in Russia, and during the final decade of Communist rule in Poland and Hungary.[3] Part of the argument will be, both in this chapter and in the following two, that as with the emergence of Brazil, South Africa, South Korea and other nations from military or racial dictatorship, the most accurate analysis will need to focus on the interrelation between the intent to liberalize within one wing of the regime and the pressure from underneath for wider freedoms than those envisaged by almost anyone within the power structure. What role did media play within this process?

Let us first of all examine the question of censorship and state control mechanisms governing public communication and culture in the later post-Stalin era. Subsequently we will note in outline three sources of alternative communication during that period, some of which will be discussed at greater length in Chapter 4: underground media; international radio broadcasts; and 'everyday' media, such as lapel-buttons, graffiti and even postage stamps, that also served to contest the regimes' credibility. In conclusion, we will offer a summary characterization of the Gorbachev era's *glasnost* policy, including its relation to simultaneous developments in Poland and Hungary.

These topics are dealt with in much more detail in the published sources cited than they can be allowed here. What is offered in this chapter is an interpretation of those sources as a whole rather than fresh information or original research.

Censorship and Sovietized Cultural Production

The concept of cultural production is drawn here particularly from the work of Hall et al. (1980: 27–8, 128–38), as well as from empirical studies by Elliott (1972), Schlesinger (1987) and Schlesinger et al. (1983). In essence, the concept focuses on the mechanisms, large and small, by which given contemporary cultures are generated, sustained or subjected to decline, with particular attention to the role of media and other communication institutions. Rather, therefore, than looking at culture purely as perspective, this approach seeks to ground the sources of cultural perspectives and their durability or otherwise, in a social, economic and political matrix, and in the very social organization of cultural activity.

As with 'totalitarianism' so with the simplistic analogue concept in the sphere of cultural production, namely 'censorship': the term in its general use narrows our attention to specific actions by state authorities, either to punish people for what they have communicated, or to prevent them from communicating it in the first place. In sovietological discourse, academic and popular, it was also generally implied that such controls were pretty well perfect. Yet in so far as they were effective for so many years, their operation depended fundamentally not on their frequent activation, but on the acquired talents of media professionals, artists and other communicators in the habit of **self-censorship**.

This was the prime factor, the daily cement – or better, in some ways, oil – of the system of control over cultural production. Neither censors nor journalists nor film-makers nor cultural administrators were perpetually making decisions about what to do or allow and what to avoid. Just as in the West, but on a much greater range of issues, media professionals primarily operated by long-ingrained procedures – learned in university, from their colleagues, and by reviewing the output of their own publication or channel. The process of cultural production on the state level was not a jerky, crisis-ridden, confrontational epic. It was simple, strong and smooth, because just as in corporate media, the rules of the game were very well understood, to the point of untroubled, 'instinctive' compliance.

A perfect example is the fact that many critically minded people would consciously avoid careers in the arts or journalism, precisely because they were aware of the restraints they would inevitably have to ingest as their very own in those professions. Science or engineering did not carry the same constraints on research or inquiry, and cultural issues could thus be explored in one's private life. Almost as strong an example is the problem many journalists described to me in all three countries as the changes were developing, and after the regimes had changed, namely how to get the mental censor out of their own heads, even though the restrictions they had so long internalized were no longer in force. 'Because of our history,' TV newsman Aleksandr Tikhomirov concluded, 'most journalists have fear built into their genes.'[4]

However, it is important even so not to take this realization to the extreme and to homogenize journalists into an assembly of *Brave New World* zombies. As Iosip Paperno, by the time of my interview with him in 1990 the start-up publisher-editor of a private South West Moscow monthly newspaper,[5] and no friend of the then-regime, put it:

It's only fair to say though that in spite of Stalinism and in spite of the stagnation under Brezhnev, there were always people working as journalists who had a great potential that was never tapped. They have been in the forefront of the move to *glasnost*, and I think it is pretty obvious that *glasnost* itself has been a great deal more successful than *perestroika*.

Indeed, many of the most active reformers elected to office in the legislative elections of 1989 and 1990 were journalists.[6]

The question of censorship must also be periodized in assessing these nations' communication history. From the death of Stalin to the Gorbachev regime Soviet censorship went through a series of thaws and freezes. Labor camps continued to operate in the USSR, though not nearly on the same scale, but psycho-prisons were added to them under Brezhnev (Fireside, 1979; Grigorenko, 1982: ch. 26; Plyushch, 1979: chs 19–20), where political dissent was redefined as psychiatric illness and 'treated' with stupefying narcotics. Meanwhile Poland too went through a series of temporary thaws of different levels of intensity, following Gomulka's accession to power in 1956, Gierek's in 1970, and then through subsequent freezes. Later openings from 1976 onwards were made from below in Poland rather than from above.[7] In Hungary, as noted already, controls were lifted a little piece at a time, without the jerkiness or the upsurges of Poland. Eventually under Gorbachev censorship was gradually and spottily reduced in the direction only of the degree of liberalization that had been achieved in Poland and Hungary without – at that time – appearing to threaten the pillars of those regimes.[8]

We should also bear in mind that the censorship applied might easily be more personal than political. Tikhomirov, in the interview cited above, made the following observation:

> To be 'undesirable' was a relatively simple matter: the perfect illustration was the playwright Anatoly Efros, who had his plays barred from performance in every single theatre. He went to the then Minister of Culture and asked him, 'Why are you doing this to me? I'm not attacking the Soviet system. Every single play of mine supports it.' He was told, 'We know that. It's not because of that. But you don't like *us*.

Censorship and self-censorship must also be specified by nation as well as periodized. Here the Hungarian case is particularly instructive because the regime there went furthest in lifting controls (Kende, 1985), which in turn displaced them into the minds of the communicators, actually thereby even intensifying self-censorship. As Kende puts it (pp. 44–5):

> This, then, is the first and most important – and invisible – facet of censorship: the consciousness of journalists and editors. A consciousness which in most cases is coupled with professional vigilance and a subtle political instinct. A cultural official *even with minimum experience* knows which style or message, what words or types of arguments, specific references or hidden implications he is free to tolerate without any problem, and which, on the other hand, are those on which he must at least engage in some 'consultations'. (emphasis added)

Similarly, writing in 1977, Krakovoy (in Hárászti, 1979: 155) put it thus:

The poet senses in advance that, innocent as it might seem, the use of such and such an adjective might put the continuance of his creative work in danger; in order to avoid his entire work being defined as foreign to reality, the novelist will proceed to a detailed selection of the background to his stories and of his heroes' character traits; the advertising designer will make his own the notion that in practice there are no impartial forms or colors; the gifted director will instantly sense the moment when the ambiance of such and such a sequence is becoming unacceptably pessimistic.

Given this subtle but powerful process, Hárászti argues that we need to consider

not only . . . the outer regulations . . . but also – and primarily – the inner gravitation, the downward pull, of the artist's imagination . . . where censorship . . . is not the simple oppressor of those who create culture but is their natural home. (1987: 8)

He especially emphasizes how for artists, within a modified censorship process, where they receive the traditional state stipends and privileges of the sovietized system,

the state represents not a monolithic body of rules but rather a live network of lobbies. We play with it, we know how to use it, and we have allies and enemies at the controls . . . Generosity from above will be matched by docility from below . . . It is like an empty sack that artists with a secure existence fill with anything that will not burst it. (1987: 78–9)

These considerations help to de-heroize the David-and-Goliath model of sovietized censorship popular among Western commentators.[9] The range and type of issues that were accepted as off-limits varied, as I have said, very considerably, from what was off-limits in the West. So did the aesthetic quality of print and broadcast media – though here again, Western analysts tended to take their own best examples as the yardstick, such as *The Economist* or *El País*, rather than the *National Enquirer* or *Bildzeitung*. So, tremendously, did the penalties differ for non-compliance, though execution was not among them after Stalin's demise. But the basic professional sociology – not the economics – of cultural production was remarkably analogous in both systems. It depended for its daily functioning on internalized norms of what was appropriate to cover or produce, and what was not, so avoiding predictable, career-threatening confrontation with media executives. In other words, official cultural production ran on routinized self-censorship, structurally similar at *this* point to the process in the West.

An interesting comparison/contrast, for example, is elite sources of information. In the Soviet system, the top elite received accurate, up-to-the-minute, uncensored information, in the USSR via White Tass and especially Red Tass (Antonkin, 1983; Smith, 1976: ch. 14), and through being permitted to read the quality foreign press. The TASS news agency's primary function was in fact to organize and translate such information for the elite, not for the general public as per the Western news agency model. Journalists working in the Polish version of this service regarded their work as carrying particularly high status and interest, and of course they were especially trusted, unlike their confrères in the rest of the profession. In Hungary, to provide a further contrast, already by the late 1970s it was actually possible, without being a Party member, to subscribe to the rather reliable special newspaper *World Economy*, if you were ready and willing to pay the high subscription price.[10]

Thus the mechanisms for restricting the flow of uncensored information varied a little between bloc countries in the later Soviet period. The Western filters have always been more porous, but even so this does not in and of itself suffice to produce widespread effective demand for quality information.[11]

One control mechanism that did not exist in most Western states, but was certainly well used in some (e.g. Mexico right up to the early 1990s), was state control over paper and newsprint supply. All the sovietized regimes in the final decade used their monopoly over paper production to limit, rather than entirely suppress, the diffusion of materials of which they disapproved (Kowalski, 1988; McNair, 1991; Pittman, 1990: 116–17; Vatchnadze, 1991: 32–3), reducing the paper supply to media that challenged the status quo. For example, in interviews in Hungary in 1988 with *Elet Es Irodalom*, the leading political and cultural weekly much in demand among critical intellectuals, it was made clear that twice or even much more the number of copies could be sold if the state would only agree to increase the paper supply.

None the less, this was a half-way mechanism, designed to balance the desire for control against the need to be seen as reasonable, as not stifling thought altogether. Insufferable as it was, it was a very large step forward from Stalinism. It is one of many pieces of evidence that the sovietized regimes in that final period were trying to develop more targeted, less blanket, forms of repression, moving themselves – as proposed in the Introduction – from night towards twilight. It was also a counterproductive device in the longer term, since it permitted the appetites of critical intellectuals and other opponents of the regimes to enjoy a little satisfaction, but only with the effect of whetting those same appetites and thus provoking deeper and deeper irritation at the blatant, almost childish tricks of the regimes to try to hold on to their power in a simultaneously juvenile and nannying fashion.

The most distinctive contrast between sovietized and non-sovietized means of cultural control was to be seen in the vast public lecture system, a parallel provision of political lectures in the workplace and elsewhere by Party, civil defense and anti-religious activists (Remington, 1988: chs. 2–3; White, 1979). These had no analogue in the 'West', but typically played a continuing part of people's lives within the Soviet bloc. Attendance in the workplace was more or less mandatory, and there lasted around thirty minutes. In other settings, such as the House of Culture, or labor union premises, the sessions would be in the evening and might be longer. The lecturers were quite often individuals who knew that offering to do such work would be regarded as solid evidence of the right attitude if they were applying for Communist Party membership, the normal route for upward mobility.

This massive lecture program was then part general ideological reinforcement, part cadre recruitment. It could also be used to communicate issues that the *verkhushka* did not want foreign analysts to spot as they surveyed the Soviet press.[12] However, as Chapter 4 shows, it became a hollower and hollower set of activities as the end drew near.

We have already seen that the term censorship, in its habitual sense, gives too vague a notion of the actual process of control over cultural production in sovietized societies. Let us conclude this section with some considerations which may help to give a still more precise sense of how Soviet bloc media actually worked, especially in the final decade or so of the system. The examples, dealt with rather briefly, will be investigative reporting and the role of readers' letters; the development of television; and the role of marginal media (not underground media, which will be reviewed in the section following).

Investigative reporting in the West is generally honored more in the breach than in the observance, with rather few editorial funds assigned in that direction. In the Soviet bloc, it fulfilled typically a different function altogether: it was there to provide the final seal on a *nomenklatura* decision already carefully planned out in detail. If a given factory, or city Party Secretary, had been identified as a problem, and if the decision had already been taken to clean up the situation – and by 'clean up' I am not proposing an ethical judgment on the matter, for the decision might be to remove someone who was simply making waves, or had personally provoked a powerful individual – then at that point one or more journalists would be assigned to amass negative 'investigative' details on the situation and write them up for their newspaper. The authorities in question would then take 'prompt' action and a day or so later it would be announced that the factory director or the Party official had been removed from their duties.[13]

Readers' letters were a major feature of the sovietized press (cf. Cerf and Albee, 1990; Di Leo, 1973; Revuz, 1980). Not that they were all published, but they were all answered, and their volume was much greater than in the West. Each newspaper had a whole department dedicated to reading and answering them. Needless to say, certain topics were self-censored. People would not write criticizing the Soviet system or its leaders or praising capitalism. None the less, a number of criticisms, nearly always of specific local issues, were regularly ventilated and published. In 1986–8, at the outset of the *glasnost* period, there was a real explosion in public letter-writing of this kind.

This mechanism provided the *nomenklatura* with advance warning of certain problems that might be arising. It also gave people the sense that at least some grievances could be aired, that the system was not totally deaf.

At the same time, the letters department was the Cinderella department[14] of any newspaper, the section to which interns from journalism departments most complained at being sent. It was also a department whose function drained away to nothing after *glasnost* policies had become fully established, and especially (Karklins, 1994: 34) after the Soviet Congress of Deputies began to be televised live in 1989. At those points, exciting new channels had opened up to the public.

The development of television in the Soviet bloc was given very high priority by the *verkhushka* (Downing, 1985; Mickiewicz, 1988). Rather as Kenez (1985) has argued concerning the Bolsheviks' early enthusiasm for film as a medium, so television was seen as possessing three very desirable attributes. It was a one-way channel of communication from top to bottom, and the message was uniform. The third, superior to film, was that like radio, it penetrated people's homes. Western advertisers could not have been more thrilled than was the *verkhushka* at such a prospect. Thus from early on in the development of satellites, their potential as national communication instruments for television and radio was immediately plain to the Soviet authorities. Indeed the first Union-wide satellite television broadcasts were set for 1967, the fiftieth anniversary of the revolution.

As I have argued elsewhere (Downing, 1985), with the deterioration of official political culture in the USSR the *verkhushka* looked increasingly to television for its contribution to propping up social morale. Huge efforts were made to ensure nationwide distribution of at least Channels One and Two (from the 1990s known under their new names as Ostankino and Russian Television), partly to reach mining and petroleum settlements in the North and Far East that were vital for future economic development, partly to combat widespread alienation among huge sectors of the very numerous Soviet armed forces (cf. Gross, 1990), stationed in such inhospitable surroundings as the Chinese frontier, or Murmansk, north of the Arctic Circle. Televised sport also became very important, a form of action-television without noxious political consequences (from the official viewpoint). At the same time, new audience studies indicated that women watched half as much TV as men, no doubt because of their double shift at paid work and maintaining the home, including lengthy periods spent shopping for groceries (Mickiewicz, 1981). The regime's strategy looked likely to be more successful with one gender than the other.

We also need to consider marginal media. By the term 'marginal' media, I have in mind not alternative, but small-scale official media, such as monthly and quarterly periodicals, minor specialized radio programs, a few provincial publications, plays in small theaters, film in some of the Soviet republics, especially Georgia (e.g. Condee and Padunov, 1984–6; Goldfarb, 1981; Markwick, 1994). Demszky (1988) noted how in Hungary by the time he was writing the smaller the outlet the more interesting it would be likely to be. The full story of all these in the process of regime change has still to be told. Let me then give two brief examples, one from the USSR and the other from Hungary.

The Soviet example comes from a monthly magazine, *Chemistry Today* (literally 'Chemistry and Life', *Khimiya I Zhizn*).[15] It enjoyed at its height a circulation of 200,000, quite small relative to the gigantic circulation figures of required newspapers such as *Pravda*, but none the less significant in that its readership generally read it (which quite often could not be said for *Pravda*). This little outlet took a major risk in 1961 and published the full text of the Lysenko Commission report.

The significance of doing so takes a little explaining to those unfamiliar with the region and its history. Lysenko was the spurious genetics researcher canonized by the Stalin regime in the 1930s as the emblem of its self-propagandizing claim to be the most advanced scientific culture – because proletarian-based – on the planet. His 'solutions' to grain-yield problems also promised a technical-fix way out of the feeble productivity of the draconican collective farm system. Perhaps needless to say, scientists who disputed Lysenko found themselves without jobs, imprisoned, and much worse still. This was no typical feud between academics.

Lysenko was finally exposed and demoted only much later, in the early 1960s, but because so many careers had been made on his coat-tails, and so many destroyed through his readiness to denounce those who defended non-Soviet genetics, the public acknowledgment of his exposure was handled with tongs. The Commission report was only planned to be distributed to the select 6,000 members of the Soviet Academy of Sciences. Hence, its unauthorized publication by *Chemistry Today* was a major breach of the political rules. Indeed, the magazine was only able to survive such risky actions because it had one very powerful protector within the Soviet hierarchy. Without that shield, or godfather, its staff would likely have been dismissed and possibly some of them jailed.

The Hungarian example[16] is a Friday evening radio program of the earlier 1980s on economic policy called *Ballpark* (*Dühöngö*), which attracted a mere 1–2 percent of the station's audience. Within this weekly half-hour, the producers set themselves the task of pushing at the limits of what could be broadcast. They took current regime slogans such as 'political reform' and publicly queried what they actually meant, or questioned whether simply repaying foreign banks was the only way to deal with Hungary's debt problem. Again, this would be accounted very mild material by some standards, but it implicitly disputed the regime's competence in political or economic policy. They discovered the limits of the ballpark in 1986 when they allowed a university professor to assert that the whole basis of the new five-year plan was flawed. On meeting the director of radio broadcasting on their way out of the building, the producers were told 'That's the last program you make.' None the less, in the duration of the program series, they felt they had managed to stretch the limits of what could be said over the air, despite many forced compromises that either nauseated them, or generated a cynical protective hide around them.

I have included these last examples of cultural production in order to indicate that there were grey areas at the margins of official media, even in the USSR and even in the period before *glasnost*. The point is also that journalists and media professionals of that period cannot be homogenized either as heroes or as hacks. The further point is that in the Soviet era there was a plethora of publications, many of which came to an abrupt halt when the prices of paper soared out of sight at the time of the transition. In the context of an emerging transition, it thus became more and more possible to begin to experiment at these margins with a small-scale magazine or theater precisely because the *verkhushka*'s attention was anxiously absorbed with the mainstream media, especially television.[17]

Sources of Alternative Communication

Hough proposes (1977: 201) that both the Stalin and the Brezhnev regimes were 'more preoccupied with regulating horizontal communication among the citizenry than with communications between the citizens and the political authorities'. Starr (1990: 30) similarly argues that 'Soviet communications policy under Stalin was aimed at suppressing data judged harmful rather than effectively disseminating positive messages'.[18]

However, Melucci (1989: 208) complementarily observes of social movements and their lateral communications, though in his case focusing on Western Europe, that

> a great deal of activity continues to take place during the invisibility phase. The submerged networks of social movements are laboratories of experience. New problems and questions are posed. New answers are invented and tested, and reality is perceived and named in different ways.

Taking the regimes' preoccupations into account as summarized by Hough, and the essential importance Melucci acknowledges of the groundwork laid by political movements long before they explode into prominence, it is reasonable to recognize *samizdat*[19] media as indeed the stirrings of an alternative public sphere. They were certainly instantly perceived as such by Soviet bloc regimes, which lost no opportunity to suppress them.

In the early days, *samizdat* publication meant typed single-spaced sheets, without margins, often blurry carbon copies rather than the original. The topics might be anything from lists and details of individuals fined or imprisoned for politically dissident activities, to political essays, poetry, novels or short stories refused for publication or that their authors knew it would be pointless to try to get published. Analyses of Soviet era history from a perspective other than the regime's was another genre. As in other spheres of insurgency, the Polish *samizdat* were outstandingly successful, perhaps building upon the long tradition of underground publishing in that nation. (Polish activists willingly acknowledged that their Russian counterparts were the first to engage in this communication strategy in this era.) Later, especially in Poland, the physical quality of the publications came to approach that of official media.

Quite stiff sanctions applied to producing, circulating, reading or possessing such manuscripts, but a major index of the decay of the regimes could be found in the progressive openness with which citizens would initially display a *samizdat* text on their bookshelf, then be seen buying it, then be seen reading it in public. Historically, Soviet *samizdat* began to be an active media sphere following the post-Khrushchev repression of literary expression; Polish and Hungarian *samizdat* became active following the passage of the so-called 'Basket III' clauses of the Helsinki Agreement of 1975, guaranteeing among other things freedom of expression, to which the Soviet bloc regimes were signatories.

To understand the impact of these media, given their very narrow early distribution – with the signal exception of *magnitizdat*, which spread like wild fire – we need to take two factors into account. One is the nervousness of the regimes, whatever the secret police powers at their beck and call, and whatever their disinterest in inhibitions based on human rights considerations. The ghosts of Lenin and the Bolsheviks were always near at hand to remind them of the massive power of insurgent movements at times of regime disarray and weakness, whatever the public bluster of invincibility and rectitude.

Secondly, we must recall the high estimation of the 'writer' as prophet and luminary, especially in traditional Russian and Polish culture, and the long list of seemingly isolated literary figures who eventually wrought considerable impact upon national consciousness. This has historically allocated to writers a weight in the formation of public opinion usually reserved for mass media in the 'West' – even though an audience could barely be seen to exist as such (Kagarlitsky, 1988: ch. 1). Words could seem to possess pungency, almost an extra-terrestrial significance – so different from contemporary Western discourse where their devaluation in the slurry of advertising and public relations copy that drowns us daily has deprived them of at least half their potential sinews. It should, though, be recalled as well that bloc citizens were also deluged with regime woodenspeak, so that fresh writing was like a reviving shower of rain on a dusty summer's day.

In addition, with the availability of reel-to-reel audiotape, followed by proliferating audio-cassettes, *magnitizdat* began to circulate, making available both Russian guitar-poetry with an alternative political edge, and pirated Western rock music (Ramet, 1991: ch. 9; Ryback, 1989; Smith, 1984). Once the easily transportable audio-cassette was available, there emerged virtually a parallel recording industry side by side with the state company, Melodiya. Half a dozen immensely popular record albums were only to be obtained on that circuit. Finally, with the arrival of the video-cassette, this process expanded still further (Boyd, 1989; Mattelart, 1992b). *Tamizdat* media, meaning 'published there' (i.e. in the West) and smuggled back in, consisted initially of print, and later of electronic media. They represented a further dimension of unofficial and underground communication.

I will not proceed further with commentary upon *samizdat* media, except to underline that very well-known figures in the West, such as Sakharov, were only one element in the total *samizdat* picture. As we shall explore in Chapter 4, a whole variety of concerns – religious, ethnic and nationalist, young people's, environmental, peace-oriented – slowly began to be expressed by these means (see also Alexeyeva, 1985; Helsinki Watch, 1987; Tökes, 1975). But their small number and circulation in the USSR and Hungary should not blind us to their long-term cumulative significance: every political movement has to begin from its specific context, with its specific resources and self-understanding. *Samizdat* media had no dramatic, instant impact: they represented a gradual burn into the deep fabric of power. Given the speed with which during the *glasnost* era people seized upon hitherto banned communications, we may infer that *samizdat* reflected a much wider public opinion, even if they did not physically reach it except perhaps by word of mouth.

To *samizdat* media we should add what I will call 'everyday' media, i.e communications of dissent of a more ephemeral kind, such as graffiti (Bushnell, 1990), and the outpouring of lapel-badges and tee-shirts with politically pointed slogans (a cow's face with the words 'No AIDS on our collective farm!', another one with 'Tell them, Boris!'[20]); politically satirical Russian dolls lampooning first Brezhnev, then Stalin, then moving in one breath backwards and forwards to both Lenin and Gorbachev (one showing Gorbachev with a forked tongue) – even a piggy-bank with Brezhnev's face and the money-slit in his throat (Condee and Padunov, 1991a).

In Wroclaw, Poland, on International Children's Day, 1988, twelve students dressed in little red dwarf's caps and dark glasses marched through the streets, singing children's songs, handing out candies and carrying a giant toy bear (Goban-Klas, 1994: 197–8; cf. Misztal, 1992). Their performance art was laden with political satire: the portrayal of adults as children and dwarfs, infantilized and reduced in stature by the regime; the hats they wore were red, the color of colors of Communist banners; their dark glasses, rarely needed in the Polish climate, spoofed General Jaruzelski, the president, whose trademark they were (like so many military dictators[21]); the songs they were singing had the same rhythmic intonation as *Solidarnosc* chants; and the giant toy bear they were carrying was a message to Mother Russia to get off their backs. Yet not a single subversive word was spoken.

This was one of many such activities of the self-styled Orange Alternative, student activists drawing on Poland's lively tradition of student theater, performance art and poster art. They organized street happenings mocking the regime's secular rituals, such as International Secret Policeman's Day, and lampooning its everyday economic failures by setting up a demonstration entitled 'Who's Afraid of Toilet Paper?'[22] Other groups invented political stamps, which they would fix to the envelopes along with regular stamps (Kobylinski, 1989). Favorite emblems were Father

Popieluszko, the pro-Solidarity priest murdered by a vengeful secret police detachment, the Pope, and Jozef Pilsudski, the De Gaulle-style president of interwar Poland. One rather sophisticated stamp showed the *Solidarnosc* emblem on three sides of a sphere, with the words 'eppur si muove'[23] on it. Existing stamps were also overprinted with dissident messages. Many of the stamps were produced in internment camps.

Such dimensions of cultural protest deserve a more extended treatment than they are given here. It is always easier to analyse the impact of ongoing media, especially when they can be stored in print or electronic or film form, than of pungent and acerbic ephemera such as these. Yet these ephemera may often stick in people's memories like a burr under the saddle, one part of their impact being precisely that they manage to be politically sassy and (sometimes) get away with it because the forces of law and order are too stupid to grasp straightaway what is being communicated.

The third aspect of alternative communication, and one which often succeeded in amplifying the impact of *samizdat* media by broadcasting the text of hard-to-find underground pamphlets and essays (especially if the listeners lived in small towns or the countryside), was foreign radio services such as the BBC World Service, Deutsche Welle, Radio Liberty, Radio Free Europe and the Voice of America (Shanor, 1985). Each had its own style: the BBC, Deutsche Welle and the Voice of America tended to be more reserved, the other two more overtly partisan. The rationale for the former style was in part the need to demonstrate the appropriate approach of serious journalism, unlike Soviet propagandistic writing, and also the attempt at various points in time to avoid being jammed by the Soviet authorities (better some communication than none). The latter style was driven by the understandable logic of such situations the world over: how is it possible to be balanced about an unbalanced reality?

It was paradoxical, because admitting to anyone else that you listened to 'the voices' as they were sometimes called, could get a person in trouble, especially at some periods. Thus the normal consequence of media communication did not usually ensue, namely that one or more aspects of the broadcast or newspaper report will be discussed with people who have already been exposed to it, or who have the habit of being. The communication tended to remain atomized, unless there was a close and trusty friend or relative with whom to share it. Revelations after the collapse of Communism about the informer-networks set up by the secret police in sovietized states show just how widespread suspicion of one's associates needed to be – and was encouraged to be as a matter of policy.

None the less, as the years gathered momentum toward the collapse, listening to these stations became more overt and more widespread. One of the many surprise signals of major change in the transition biennium was the way that even Radio Free Europe and Radio Liberty were invited to set up bureaux in capital city after capital city in the nations where they had so often had their broadcasts jammed and had been denounced as agents of imperialism rather than voices of critique and alternative information. Not to overstate: sometimes their programs were colonized by émigré representatives of weird and not so wonderful viewpoints (Alexeyeva, 1987). None the less, the amplification they provided for dissident political movements was of the greatest importance in the process building towards regime transition.

The *Glasnost* Era: an Initial Characterization

In Chapter 4 there will be a more detailed account of the communicative and cultural build-up toward regime transition in Russia, Poland and Hungary. Here I simply wish to set the stage by some preliminary remarks on the *glasnost* period in the three countries.

They were moving at very different rhythms and speeds at the beginning of the final decade. *Solidarnosc* was creating conditions in Poland from August 1980 through to December 1981 that were completely exceptional for the rest of the bloc, and that tremendously alarmed the other sovietized regimes in Eastern Europe, not to mention the Kremlin. A major dimension of that period was the explosion in alternative publications in Poland, and increasingly insistent demands from *Solidarnosc* toward its close for access to national radio and television (always refused). With the imposition of martial law, alternative publishing was forced underground again, but still continued to be remarkably vigorous none the less, and was added to on a major scale by the underground distribution of video-cassettes from about 1985 (Blumsztajn, 1988; Warszawski, 1989; X.Y. (Varsovie), 1986).

In the USSR there were much more muted and delphic signals of change during the final years of the Brezhnev regime and the tragicomic succession of the sere (Andropov and Chernenko). With the accession of Gorbachev in 1985, and his initiation of *glasnost* and *perestroika* policies, the signals became progressively less muted and delphic. The initial excitement was principally among the Soviet intelligentsia[24] at the prospect of still long-suppressed truths being opened up for public debate concerning the horrors of the Stalin era. The recovery of obliterated history for general scrutiny led, however, to a wider and wider debate about the present, stretching ever further beyond the Moscow and Leningrad intelligentsia. Certain newspapers, especially the weeklies *Ogonyok* and *Moscow News*, were given editors charged with opening up certain debates. Later the weekly *Argumenty I Fakty* – at its zenith selling 33 million copies – became a further flagship of *glasnost*, offering a style of unadorned, straight-to-the-point news totally unprecedented in Soviet journalism.

Such signals were greeted with even more alarm than the earlier Polish events by most of the sovietized regimes in Eastern Europe, to the point where some Soviet publications and films were denied circulation in East Germany (Brown, 1990: 141–2). For those without that stake in the status quo, however, the signals coming from Moscow were an immense boost to their spirits to be venturesome. If it was happening in the imperial center, it must be permissible. Hungarian journalists, for example, used to cite *Moscow News* and *Ogonyok* at that juncture to allay the censors' fears they were going too far too fast (Varró, 1989).

In Hungary, meanwhile, the steady drip-drip continued, the situation being characterized very often by a kind of unseen minuet between reformists within the system and dissidents outside it (Frentzel-Zagorska, 1990). It had a very different feel from the highly dramatic Polish situation, and the increasingly dramatic Soviet one. Rather than key events we should note a constellation of smaller ones. They would include the increasing assertiveness of radio journalists, especially in the program *168 Hours*; the *Danube Circle* ecological initiative opposing the Gabcikovo-Nagymoros dam (Feffer 1992: 151–6; Vavrousek, 1989); the alternative publication *Beszelö* (Conversation); the emerging popularity of satellite and cable TV (Szekfü, 1989); and the increasingly open character of the weekly *Elet Es Irödalom* (Life and Literature), the approximate equivalent of *Literaturnaya Gazeta* in the USSR or *Polityka* in Poland, namely a sanctioned forum for somewhat more open coverage and debate of political issues.

Having sketched the different cycles and noted their points of interconnection, let us now focus particularly for a moment on the Soviet situation in the middle and late 1980s.

Condee and Padunov (1987) and Vatchnadze (1991) offer excellent empirical commentary on the Soviet Russian cultural and media scenarios during that period, the former writers surveying such themes as the recuperation of the émigré heritage, rescripting history, attention to contemporary problems, the unseating of the old leaders in the cultural establishment, and related issues. Vatchnadze concentrates on strictly mediatic and journalistic dimensions, whether the persistence of forms of censorship, the new business press, or the emergence of cable TV.

The first reality which requires recognition, however, is how spottily reformed media policies were actually enacted in Russia or the USSR as a whole. *Glasnost* was generally conspicuous by its rarity outside Moscow, Leningrad and the Baltic republics, and was a fairly rare commodity even in Moscow city localities.[25] The regimes' control over the importation of foreign media included even[26] books (e.g. Remmer, 1989). The first more or less complete relinquishment of control was not until the Polish Round Table negotiations in the spring of 1989, when underground media – in that nation alone – were permitted to be circulated without interference.

The communication policy hallmark of the 1980s, then, in the USSR, Poland and Hungary, was the initially very gradual relaxation of censorship enforcement. This always depended upon prominence of the given media outlet, the particular administrative entity involved, the juncture, and the given topic.

For example, the seeming explosion of ecological critique in the late Soviet era press was interpreted by many at the time as an unambiguous instance of *glasnost* at full blast. In reality (Orechkine, 1993), the focus was carefully narrowed to soil, air, water, forests, bio-diversity, and away from 'important people'. For instance, when the Central Committee canceled the projected diversion of the Ob River in Siberia to the Central Asian republics, there was a rush of media coverage of water pollution. Yet the roles in polluting the environment of the chemical and nuclear industries, and of the military–industrial complex, were barely touched. Very severe ongoing regional radiation issues following the 1986 Chernobyl disaster were not ventilated until 1990.

Furthermore, just as in the Khrushchev era, when *Novii Mir* was Khrushchev's outlet, and *Oktyabr'* was his opposition's, but on a much larger scale in the Gorbachev era, certain media were deployed from on high in a bitter ideological war. *Ogonyok* and *Moscow News* were key instances of Gorbachev's media, but conservative and extremist nationalists of various ilks controlled *Sovietskaya Rossiya*, *Literaturnaya Rossiya*, *Nash Sovremennik* (Brudny, 1991).

Television, before as after the transition biennium, was the most strictly under surveillance. An example from Soviet Russia in the spring of 1990, during the crisis set in motion by Lithuania's declaration of independence, was that television news each night on the 100 million audience *Vremya* program began to display the words 'TASS communiqué' (*TASS soobshchayet*) on the screen once the topic was Lithuania. In other words, TV news bureaux were not being trusted to write 'reliable' news: they were compelled to read the state's bulletins word for word as news. Critical TV news magazine programs such as *Syem' Dnyei* (Seven Days), *Vzglyad* (Perspective), *Pyatoye Kol'tso* (Fifth Wheel), *Dvenadtsatii Etazh* (12th Storey), were perpetually under threat of closure, or eventually closed.

Radio usually had more license. Small circulation monthlies or quarterlies had still more. Two examples of what was possible in this area are as follows, the first from Moscow (from a slightly earlier epoch), the second from Hungary.

In Moscow, as veteran radio journalist Georgii Kuznetsov told the author, once they had run a satirical humor program on the radio in the mornings, called *Twenty-Five Again*. 'Well it had to be moved to two hours earlier in the day, because it turned out that government ministers and party bosses' chauffeurs were listening to it on the car radio as they drove their employers to work, and so ministers ended up hearing it as well. And were not pleased with what they heard in a number of cases. But once it was shifted to the earlier slot, everything was back to "normal".' The same proposal was on the table in 1990 at the time of this interview, this time to put Tikhomirov's Sunday TV news magazine *Seven Days* two hours later in the evening, rather than to close it outright (Tikhomirov had already been fired). 'Just what has changed?' Kuznetsov asked.

A different example of a cautious move in this area would be Radio Danubius in Budapest, set up in early 1988 to provide a German-language service to summer tourists from Austria and the German Federal Republic.

From the beginning, Danubius had considerably more free play than other radio channels, made possible by the fact it was not broadcasting in Hungarian, and that it was commercially structured. The fact remains that it was a type of wedge into the system. Similarly the foreign language weekly *Moscow News*, though barely available in Russian, was immensely influential once Yegor Yakovlev was made editor in 1986.

In the terms of the regime transition literature examined in the previous chapter, *glasnost* in the USSR could easily be claimed to be analogous to the Brazilian military regime's *distensão* (usually translated 'decompression') policy of 1975, and thus to be another instance of liberalization induced from above rather than democratization from below. Many analysts have so defined the USSR in that period, including Gorbachev himself, who repeatedly insisted that he was reforming the system, not overthrowing it. To take him at his word, however, is to fall into kremlinological elitism, to presume that because the leader says it, that is how it actually was.

While it is true to say that Gorbachev and those in his immediate circles did not plan democratization, the matter is more complex than that. First, it omits the communicative impact of a whole variety of dissident movements and a whole series of other politico-economic pressures that will be reviewed in the next two chapters. Second, it disregards the fact that an increasing number of key journalists were perpetually pushing at the limits of the possible. Third, the USSR was a part of the bloc, with the result that events in Poland especially, but also in Hungary in less dramatic ways, were part of a continually interactive system. This latter dimension was indeed peculiar to the transition in sovietized nations, but given its presence, and once the quite often febrile Polish situation is taken into account, the argument is virtually impossible to sustain that the motor of change was the regimes' initiatives. What happened was the result of a very multi-level, multi-factor interaction.[27]

We shall return to that theme, and especially to the role of communication, culture and media in the transition, in Chapter 4. In the mean time it is important to end this brief review of *glasnost* by re-emphasizing what an extraordinarily exciting and dynamic period it was. Even if those most dynamized were mainly the intelligentsia, even if it was extremely spotty in its expression, and even if it eventually ceded ground to extremely pressing daily concerns such as feeding oneself and unemployment and the growth of organized crime, it stands as one of the most intense mediatic dramas of the latter twentieth century.

Appendix: Some Short 'War Stories' Illustrating the Patchy Character of the *Glasnost* Era in Russia

In a series of interviews conducted during 1990 in Moscow, with both journalists working in the capital and others who had recently worked in the provinces, it was very evident that *glasnost*, contrary to Western reports, was a very patchy phenomenon indeed. Whether in local boroughs within Moscow itself, supposedly the beacon of *glasnost*, or in districts not fifty miles outside Moscow, the old guard was definitely active in trying to cage media freedoms supposedly permitted in the new dispensation. It was interesting though that they were having to find new, more indirect methods than the tried and tested 'No' or the presumption that people would not be so silly as to try to assert editorial independence of the authorities. One case was told me by Aidar Kokhakhmetov, a young Kazakh journalist who had worked in the provinces in the late 1980s:

> I worked on *Molodoi Leninyets* in Stavropol' District for a while at the end of the 1980s. To give you an immediate idea of the absurd level of some of the situations we faced, let me begin by telling you that one young woman was barred from the District Party Committee because she was wearing trousers and not a skirt. They actually told her she couldn't enter the meeting dressed in trousers or jeans, so she then rang our deputy editor and told him about it. He spoke to them and tried to make them see how ridiculous they were being, by reminding them that when he had been a member of the Party committee, they'd let *him* come in wearing trousers. But as you would expect, that was totally lost on them.
>
> Well, the whole thing took off from there, because a number of the local Party people disliked the newspaper to start with, which was beginning to give them a hard time, and they knew she had a good working relationship with the deputy editor. The editor-in-chief was in their camp, and a really stupid character. So they asked him to torpedo her. He couldn't find anything against her, so he concocted a charge that she was having an affair with the deputy editor, a married man. It was a particularly crude and gross accusation because she was a person of strict morals, and unmarried. So she decided to go to the local hospital and have them produce a certificate attesting that she had never had sexual relations. Which they did, and she promptly took it around to all the editor's cronies and shoved it in their faces.
>
> Well, it was one in the eye for the editor and his cronies, but it shows the degree of degradation at work in people's everyday lives, all the same.

Another young journalist, Aleksandr Kokotkin, who had worked in the small town of Ruza in Ruzkii County, which is in Moscow province, not many miles from the capital, told me the following episode in his career from 1987, a year after the announcement of *glasnost*. A sturdy and calm young man, as he told the story his voice started to shake a little, and toward the close he began to hyperventilate.

> Four years ago I wanted to start a local Communist Youth Organization newspaper, with the intention that it would be an open, pluralistic outlet for younger people in the District. And then the KGB stepped in and squashed the idea.
>
> You want to know how they did it? Well, I had worked out an arrangement with a printshop to bring the paper out. I had a core of myself and four other full-time people to get it off the ground, and of course I'd managed to get the approval of the local Communist Youth Organization to do it, plus the necessary funds for the initial period. Then I got a phone call from the printshop.

'I'm sorry,' the man told me, 'but we can't do your paper after all.' 'What?' I said, 'why ever not? What's the problem?' 'You'll have to ask Big Brother that one,' he told me.

So the first person I went to to find out what was going on was the local Communist Youth Organization leader who'd given permission for the project initially. He told me he'd had a visit from the KGB who'd asked him what this new project was that they had been hearing about. 'We're starting a newspaper,' he told them. 'Who's going to be the editor?' they asked. So he told them it was going to be me.

At that point one of them opened up a file from his briefcase. 'You know this fellow was identified as a dissident ten years ago? We've got to tell you to cut off contact with him. He's a very bad influence.' The Communist Youth leader was furious. 'I'm not going to do any such thing!' he told them. 'Well, you'd better consider your and his position,' the KGB guy told him, 'or something could happen to him.'

Shortly after that, the District Party Committee began to attack me by name, smearing me as being a drunk and a junkie. It also began to issue stern warnings that the Communist Youth Organization wasn't supposed to go its own way but to be subject to the guidance and dictates of the Party. Needless to say, our newspaper project never got off the ground after that.

The thing which really got to me was that the information they had on my views they had gotten from someone I'd worked with closely and regarded as my good friend and ally over a number of years. This still makes me breathe hard and feel really churned up telling you. This was the bitterest pill to swallow. But this is our life here.

Notes

1 As distinct from the *nomenklatura*, the *verkhushka* (vyerKHOOSHka) signified the very pinnacle of power.

2 Suslov finally had the grace to die, his mental faculties having shut down almost completely, in January 1982. It is said that late in his life he walked out to his car to go to his office one morning wearing carpet slippers rather than shoes. His driver opened the door, Suslov slipped off his footwear and stepped into the car, leaving the slippers on the sidewalk. A KGB officer was assigned to stand guard over them there on the sidewalk all day, pending Suslov's return, since no instructions had been received as to what to do with them. Suslov seemed happily insouciant of his behavior. Such stories – true or false – are a weak but necessary – the only available – form of revenge on someone with arch-responsibility for distorting the lives and careers of so many people, countless in number.

3 If space permitted, a particularly interesting exercise of that kind would be to review the famous cultural 'thaw' after Stalin's death up to the supplanting of Khrushchev in 1964 – a thaw which in fact refroze and melted again at least twice during that decade (cf. Priscilla Johnson, 1965; Michael Scammell, 1984, chs 19–38; Dina Spechler, 1982). The decade is not only interesting in its own right as a window on the Soviet cultural system, but also because it was from some of the young activists of that decade that were drawn the major protagonists of *glasnost* policies twenty years later, the so-called *dyesyatilyetniki*, the 'Sixties Guys'. See Stephen Cohen and Katrina vanden Heuvel, 1989.

4 Interview with the author, spring 1990.

5 *Chto U Nas Na Yugozapade* ('What's Up South West').

6 Compare the leading role of journalists in the 1956 Hungarian revolution (Lomax, 1976: 20–6, 40–1, 143–4, 179–81).

7 A nice example of the 'dialectic' was the decision to allow Lech Walesa to debate with the regime's trade union head on television in November 1988. It was indeed an initiative from

on high, launched on the presumption that Walesa was by then virtually unknown, having been barred from the media for seven years, that he was not especially well educated, and that he would be made to look foolish by the labor bureaucrat, who was possessed of considerable verbal adroitness. However, Walesa trounced his opponent and thereby forcefully sprang back into public view (Goban-Klas, 1994: 199–201). The attempted burial became actual resurrection.

8 See below for further comment on the realities and myths of *glasnost* policies.

9 The reaction of many Western commentators to this description of self-censorship as the glue of cultural production is 'thought control – totalitarianism!' But it is distinctly unsociological to produce on the one hand a virtual metaphysics of sovietized media, while still continuing to talk in secular categories about 'trained media professionals' in the West. The comparison suggests the need for a serious reconsideration of how censorship is customarily perceived in Western democracies. See further the discussion of Herman and Chomsky (1988) in Chapter 8.

10 Dzirkals et al. (1982: 65), with the later 1970s in mind, stress how then those in top positions typically professed total contempt for public media as information-sources, preferring always 'the knowledge available to insiders from direct contacts, closed meetings, or internal bulletins or memoranda'.

11 In the 'West' such information is often available to a wider circle, always provided its members have the education, desire and income to consume it. The high-priced specialist corporate bulletins, financial reports, data-base services or remote-sensing images, are not limited to a *nomenklatura*, merely to those who can afford them and have the necessary instruction to make use of them. Yet as Hough (1977: 202) has argued, 'Given the very low level of political policy information of the mass of the population in all countries, the processes by which ideas penetrate to politically relevant elements of the population and especially the processes by which ideas and policies are changed, are enormously more complex than any facile statements about the autonomy of the media of communication would indicate.'

12 The classic instance was the circulation of Khrushchev's historic 1956 four-hour speech denouncing Stalin. Up and down the land there were myriad meetings in which the speech was read to those present, who were barred from taking anything into or out of the gathering.

13 One young trainee journalist I spoke to had been working in a medium-sized town in southern Russia, and had wanted to write a genuine 'investigative' report on a local burns hospital, where conditions were so bad that less than 50 percent of those entering the hospital left it alive. Her story was promptly suppressed by a single conversation between the hospital director and the town's Party secretary, then relayed to her editor. The date was January 1990, five years into *glasnost*. Dzirkals et al. (1982: 69–72) also note, however, that a journalist who exposed one official miscreant might have to contend with later retribution from that person's cronies in the power structure.

14 By contrast the high status department in any of the media was the foreign section. Many journalists in that section went straight in from language school, bypassing journalism departments altogether, which were conceived of largely for domestic reporting purposes. They were averagely better educated, better connected, more trusted, permitted to travel abroad, and had a potentially interesting career ahead of them.

15 Through a 1990 interview with Mikhail Borisovich Chernenko, formerly an editorial writer with the magazine.

16 From a 1990 interview with Dr Gálik Mihály, an experienced radio journalist.

17 Dzirkals et al. (1982: 69) put forward a different position, namely that 'Our respondents were quite emphatic on this point: the local press has very little latitude; the all-Union press has a great deal more.' It may be that the discrepancy originates in the emphasis on 'local' rather than 'marginal', and in their focus on the 1970s rather than the 1980s. None the less, this difference of interpretation is worth bearing in mind.

18 Benn (1989: 42, 84, 172) points out rather soberly how little interest the Soviet regime ever displayed in the psychology of effective manipulation, and how it preferred to confront, exhort or mobilize supposedly socially malleable human beings ('existence determines consciousness . . .').

19 'Self-published', as opposed to state-published; by analogy (see below), *tamizdat* – published 'there', i.e. abroad and perhaps smuggled in – and *magnitizdat* – published on audiotape, often pirated, and always without state permission. See Blumsztajn, 1988; Downing, 1984/96: Part III; Hárászti 1979; Helsinki Watch, 1986; Helsinki Watch, 1990; Hopkins, 1983; Skilling, 1989.

20 A reference to Yeltsin in his later 1980s days as political challenger to the status quo.

21 It is only fair to note that in his case his eyelids had cracked permanently through constant exposure without eye-protection against the sun in the frozen wastes of Siberia, when he was a teenager incarcerated with his family in a Soviet forced labor camp from 1941 to 1943.

22 Toilet paper was such a rare commodity in the stores that when it was available for sale people would buy massive amounts and stockpile it in their homes. Since the state was responsible for industrial production, it followed in the Orange Alternative's ironic imagination that some economic planners somewhere must presumably have an unreasoning terror of toilet paper, otherwise it would be in the Five-Year Plan and available. The imagination then rolls on, suggesting that state bureaucrats prefer to play around with their own excrement rather than wipe it off and clean up like normal people.

23 The words said to have been muttered by Galileo *sotto voce* at his forced public recantation of his opinion that the earth moved around the sun: 'it still moves anyway'. So did *Solidarnosc*, despite being banned.

24 'Intelligentsia' or 'intellectuals' are often used to translate *intelligenty*, a more generic term in Russian than 'intellectuals' in English, signifying people with good education and usually an occupation to match, even if the occupation were poorly paid. Perhaps the very core of the term, however, was the notion of a generalist, for example of a physicist who enjoyed poetry, who was at home in many realms of the life of the mind. Within this more generic category, however, there was a very entrenched pecking order, at the top of which the Moscow set considered itself securely established. Even within the Moscow set, however, there was important stratification, distinguishing members of the Academy of Sciences from mere university instructors, or still more so, mere media professionals from researchers, or mere research secretaries from their bosses. The issue was still further complicated by issues of gender and ethnicity, and by the competing values of the Communist establishment versus more universal intellectual or creative priorities. These observations hold for this stratum throughout the former Soviet bloc countries.

25 See the two interview excerpts in the appendix to this chapter for illustrations of this point.

26 The 'even' is entirely otiose in the heavily writerly traditions of Eastern Europe, but is needed to alert Western readers to the scope of control, since in contemporary Western culture books are less potent than TV. One of the sharpest cultural switches in the former Soviet bloc in the first half-decade after the transitions was the decline of writerly in favor of visual culture (Condee and Padunov, 1995).

27 Again, see Condee and Padunov (1987) and Vatchnadze (1991), who well capture the flux and clashes, four years apart, of that astonishing period in Moscow.

4

Eastern European Transitions: the Communico-Cultural Dimension

There are very few works that have explicitly adopted any communication or cultural studies framework for the analysis of the Russian, Polish, Hungarian or other bloc nation transitions.[1] This is especially true if the later waves of cultural studies that deploy concepts from Gramsci, Benjamin, Bakhtin, Barthes, and feminist approaches, among others, are taken as the litmus test.

In part, this lacuna writes a very scathing obituary on the character of Cold War research on the region. 'Politburo' research, supplemented from the 1970s onwards by research into Soviet bloc economies, dominated the analytical scene completely, reflecting indeed in part the top-heavy character of those polities but in at least equal measure the instinctively elitist sympathies of the mass of sovietologists. If the vigor of conceptual discourse is a yardstick of a field, sovietology was akin to a virgin desert.

The practical effect was indeed to privilege either the Soviet bloc elites, or Western elites, as virtually sole agents in the maintenance or the dissolution of the Soviet structure of power. Of this tendency there are many examples. Some of the most distinguished – this is not meant as irony – are the study by Michael Beschloss and Strobe Talbott (1993) of the leading diplomatic interactions in Soviet–US relations in the period 1988–91; the study by Timothy Garton Ash (1993) of the roles of German state leaders in the reunification of Europe; and the study by Peter Schweizer (1994) of the Reagan and Bush administrations' covert and carefully interlocking strategies to subvert, rather than contain, the Soviet system.[2]

In each instance, we are introduced to the absorbing and intricate story of social agents, enjoying certainly a disproportionate measure of power and engaged (often to their surprise) in the conclusion of the Cold War and the dismantling of the Soviet empire. The role of communication and cultural processes, although untapped by these authors in any systematic analytic or conceptual fashion, is plainly central in their narratives, which repeatedly stress the multiple communicative interactions – actual, anticipated or avoided – between elite actors and factions, their[3] media agencies and the publics on both sides. In this way they mirror the division between political science and communication research already flagged and denounced in Chapter 1.

Very interesting exceptions to this rule among the major accounts by journalists are especially Shane (1994), who explicitly foregrounds issues of culture and communication and thus represents a position very close to the one argued here, and Remnick (1993), whose treatment of the issues is also broader than that of the conventional approaches. In this category also belong the book by Martin Walker (1986) on the earliest phase of change in the Soviet Union, and the reporting by Bill Keller and Serge Schmemann for *The New York Times* at the outset of the 1990s.

Although we shall return to the important contributions of Beschloss, Talbott, Ash, and Schweizer in the next chapter, our focus here is principally the force of popular culture and communication in the period of build-up to the transitions, and its neglect in these writers' *verkhushka* heavy, pinnacle-heavy analyses. Naturally, a single account cannot cover every dimension of reality in the same detail, but this neglect is symptomatic of an implicit and widely held elitist theory of – or at least assumption about – social power.

The nearest any of the three accounts get to acknowledging the power of other agents than the elite ones they hold in view is when they discuss the deteriorating Soviet bloc economies and the attempts by bloc regimes to win investment and credits from the West. There is an underlying assumption that at an undetermined but finally inelastic point the Soviet bloc regimes would be compelled to take serious account of massive public discontent. There is no acknowledgment of popular culture as a steady ongoing internal pressure for substantive change, rather there is a covert presumption that political anger at economic deprivation[4] would spark some kind of jacquerie that might destabilize, perhaps terminally, through some undefinable miracle, one or more of the regimes in question.

It is at this point that the few studies that concentrate on popular culture in this period, whether or not they do so under the explicit aegis of communication or cultural studies, have a major contribution to make to our understanding of how those changes finally came about – and equally, what they entailed. Let us then go back over the period of the build-up toward the biennium,[5] and examine in more detail certain of its communico-cultural dimensions, some of which the previous chapter touched upon. This will be important for those habituated to glide noiselessly and effortlessly past such considerations in their analyses of major political and societal change.

By contrast, in the next chapter we shall examine some of the key issues in these processes to which communication and cultural studies researchers would typically be blind. The objective of the book continues to be to emphasize the urgent mutual intellectual need that specialists in these various fields have – and therefore should constantly recognize – for each others' analytical perspectives.

Culture, Communication and Collapse

The first point is a paradoxical one, a point of silence, of inactivity, almost of communication through non-communication. White (1990) studied the House of Culture phenomenon in Russia, Poland and Hungary. The Houses of Culture – in English they would probably be called 'cultural centers' – were institutions set up in Russia under Stalinism, and then transplanted into other East European nations as part of their sovietization. Their prescribed role was politico-cultural mass enlightenment, as defined and strategized by the Communist Party authorities. White studied the operation of six such agencies during the earlier 1980s in Moscow, St Petersburg, Warsaw, Poznan, Budapest and Debrecen.

What was striking, to summarize her study, was that the closer these organizations came to fulfilling their official role, the less they were utilized. Conversely, the more open they became to local community initiatives, the more likely they were to be frequented. This would not have been known from the official figures of participation, which were as mendacious as other published statistics in the Brezhnev era (White, 1990: 44, 135–6).

This pattern should not be ascribed solely to political alienation, since the advent of television and so of home-based sources of leisure recreation certainly also helped to draw people away from them. None the less, the content of television was as capable of producing political alienation as a rote political lecture in the House of Culture, so that the key issue to keep in mind in this situation is the popularity enjoyed by community-originated activities. And in a curiously powerful albeit indirect fashion, by the end of the Brezhnev era the Soviet Party itself acknowledged the futility of these institutions for its purposes by primarily putting women, often very young women, in charge of their programs (pp. 103, 117, 121–2). This was a dismissive, not a progressive, gesture.

Thus the Party appeared to have given up on the Houses of Culture, albeit without fanfare. Even during the Brezhnev period, they tended to be designed more as locales to crowd out the potential emergence of countercultural activities than as places where people's minds could be seduced into Soviet loyalism.[6] In other words, they were there to try to stop the slide rather than to promote the ideal.

The cultural 'slide' in question took a variety of forms. Here we will concentrate on four of them, sometimes interrelated: young people's dissent; popular music; social movements; religious expression. The primary aspect of their interrelation was probably the energetic involvement of young people in each one of them, so we will begin with a brief assessment of the cultural and ideological location of youth in late sovietized society. It was a location with profound political implications for these regimes, as was briefly observed in Chapter 1 when characterizing the later Soviet state (Shlapentokh, 1986: 137ff.). The earlier discussion of social movements in Chapter 1 should also be borne in mind at this juncture, especially the observations there on the cultural and mediatic dimensions of such movements.

Before we do so, however, let us first pause for a moment to examine an essay by S. Frederick Starr (1990), 'New communications technologies and civil society', for its contribution to this discussion. His detailed and abundantly referenced analysis is one of the few to have proceeded along the analytical path proposed in this book.

Starr's basic argument was that over the twenty years or so before his essay, 'a horizontal information culture' (p. 40) had greatly increased throughout the former USSR. One of the major aspects and, simultaneously, sources of evidence of this trend, was what he termed the 'small technologies of communication': VCRs, ham radio stations, audio-cassettes, home photographic labs, video-dubbers, photocopiers (pp. 35–9). He also argued, however, that the expansion in more conventional media such as domestic telephones, international calling, mail transported by air, personal ads in local newspapers, radio call-in programs, transistorized short-wave radios, periodical titles, and even cars and television sets, were also evidence for his thesis (pp. 31–4).

Starr was careful to qualify some of these judgments, noting that cable television was rare, telephone demand and car demand still far outstripped supply, and that modems, printers and diskettes were rare or of very poor quality (he might have added in, too, the abysmal quality of telecommunications lines and switches). He also acknowledged that television was a one-way communication instrument, and that small technologies were still diffused rather sparsely over the nation as a whole, only conspicuous by contrast with their previous absence altogether. None the less, his argument very much bears the stamp of Ithiel de Sola Pool's contention in his *Technologies of Freedom* (1983) that contemporary communication technologies have an inherently liberatory character, presumably in the Soviet bloc outperforming their capacity to be deployed for surveillance and control purposes by the state – though Starr barely (p. 20) engaged with this question.

One flaw in Starr's argument is that even when he notes the limitations of some of his evidence, he still drafts almost anything to bolster his case. The most extreme example is his citation of an increase in mail theft as somehow constituting an index of growth in a horizontal information culture (p. 32), but he also referenced the privately owned car, international telephone circuits (infinitesimal in number, and all carefully monitored), and even unsatisfied demand for cars, telephones and personal computers, as indices of change in lateral communication. This is much too wide a trawl and weakens his case.

The other flaw is that even though he acknowledged that 'many forces besides communications are fostering political change in the USSR' (p. 20), he offered no clear pointers as to how these technologies might be dovetailing with such forces. Thus despite his caveat, the gist of his essay tends to enthrone the expansion of communication technologies as a generative force in their own right, harking back to de Sola Pool and even to Marshall McLuhan.

These criticisms aside, Starr's essay deserves respect as one of the few systematic attempts to try to collate detailed evidence for the importance of communication in the dissolution of Soviet power.[7] Together with White's study of the decay of official institutions of culture and communication, it nicely prepares the ground for the argument that follows, focusing on youth, musical culture, religion and social movements.

Youth

In most cultures, except the most gerontocratic, the future of the society is taken for granted as being bound up with its young people. Within Soviet ideology, given its overwhelming emphasis on the future construction of a utopian society, the official status of young people was especially enhanced. Consequently, their enthusiasm and loyalty were of the essence of the Soviet project. Without those qualities, the Soviet experiment was doomed.

The reality, as is well known, was widely different from the ideology. The main youth organization, the Komsomol, was legendary for the corruption and arrogance of its leading officials (Pilkington, 1994: 126ff.; Riordan, 1989), which were vividly depicted in the 1989 film *Che Pe*, a Russian acronymic version of the full title which was *Extraordinary Occurrence at Local Headquarters*.[8] The growing disaffection of Soviet youth was acknowledged as a major problem by no less than Marshal Ogarkov, at that point chief of the Soviet general staff, in a book published in 1982, *Always Ready to Defend the Motherland*, in which he vigorously attacked the creeping pacifism, disinclination for military service and pervasive disinterest in the history of the Second World War among the young (Ogarkov, 1982: ch. 3). This anti-militarism was even more unnerving for the *verkhushka* than anti-Communism, representing a second phase in which disinterest in Soviet ideals was being joined by a collapse in basic patriotism. As noted in Chapter 2, nationalism was one of the few remaining discourses on which the regime could draw for legitimacy.

Whatever might be said of this ideological decay among youth in the Soviet context could be multiplied many times over in the Polish and Hungarian contexts. To take the single issue of housing as a pointer, the failure of all the East European regimes to provide sufficient housing for their growing populations – especially in Poland, with its high birth rate – meant that young couples were often forced after marriage to continue living with the bride's or the bridegroom's family, typically in an already cramped apartment. That led to a high early marital breakdown rate and to endless tensions within the primary unit.[9] In the Soviet Union, many young people were compelled by these circumstances to live in extremely unpleasant hostels (Pilkington, 1994: 189–90). Nor was there any relief in sight, so that belief in inexorable progress really was an affliction only of the purblind among young people. To that decay was typically added in Poland and Hungary a comprehensively anti-Soviet nationalism, yet another voracious worm in the bud of the bright Soviet future.

Bachkatov and Wilson (1988) have described in some detail the experiences of many young people in the USSR in the 1980s: disenchantment with the work ethic, involvement with the illegal second economy, a turn to prostitution, petty theft, drugs, gangs, a fascination with the fantastic, whether a mirage version of everyday life in Western societies or even some version of the paranormal. Pilkington (1994: 216–307), one of the very few researchers employing cultural studies concepts to analyse youth cultures, has offered a very nuanced account of the fast-changing currents among young Russians and their shifting identifications at the close of the 1980s. She suggests, interestingly, that a number of these cultural expressions were not nearly as negative a commentary upon some traditional values as the older generation perceived them to be, and argues against the terminology of subculture and counterculture, often used in sociological discussions of youth, as portraying the links between mainstream and official cultures, and youth cultures, as overly insulated from each other.

Correct though she may well be, for the ever more remote *verkhushki* of these regimes, news of these developments was continually more frustrating and perplexing. They had forged their careers in the 1930s and 1940s, when the dramas of collectivization, the anti-Nazi war or of post-war reconstruction had especially harnessed their cohort's energy and vision, more so than any other sector of society at that time. Despite the grimness and the state repression of those decades, at least among their generation there had been at the time a significant number of 'true believers' like the young Lev Kopelev (1980: ch. 2) or the young Petro Grigorenko (1982: ch. 6). The attraction of the Cuban revolution to some members of the Soviet leadership during the 1960s and 1970s was due in part to their sense that the revolution they had once committed themselves to in the springtime of their youth was not growing old or out of date, but was springing up elsewhere.

Yet sooner or later, even some of these dyed-in-the-wool ossified leaders would find themselves surrounded by dissent, not merely among the would-be hippies or heavy metal rockers or religious converts 'out there', but also in their own homes, voiced by their children or grandchildren. Stites (1992: 209) notes how 'the "gilded youth" – or children of the leaders . . . often felt a particular grievance against state culture which they lived so near'. Hoffman (1993: 50–1) makes a similar observation: 'the number of leading Polish dissidents whose fathers and mothers were among the early, leading Communists is quite striking: the crème de la crème giving rise to a sort of anti-crème – or vice versa.'

Stefan Staszewski, a former high-ranking member of the Polish Politburo, recalled how this intra-familial communication worked at times of crisis:

> For the fact is that a party member sees and understands practically nothing of the circles in which he normally lives. I say practically, because it would be hard not to see his children, his family, his colleagues from work; but these surroundings do not trouble him. A party member knows what is being said when the party is criticized, but he can always say: it wasn't me, it was the party. But when the mistakes and absurdities pile up and grow to a stage where they

reach the limit of society's tolerance, then the party member's circle of family and friends will no longer ask him the reasons for this and that, but will instead start jabbing at him and pointing out specific cases of nonsense and idiocy, so that he can no longer defend himself in a rational or effective way. The profundity of the party's crisis is measured by the level of acuteness of the jabs that are made at him. (Toranska, 1987: 159)

To sum up on the question of the younger generation during the 1980s, it is vital to recognize that the customary Western diagnosis of youth in society – transitional alienation and rebelliousness, combined with energy and creativity – worked neither for the elite nor for youth in late sovietized societies. The only youthful transition process which was imaginable and viable for the elite was equal or greater dedication to the Soviet system. Since this was implausible in any of these nations, the only avenue open to young people was increasing alienation and even rebelliousness, the latter taking many different forms. This rang the tocsin for the system even to the elite, for more and more they were hearing it sounding out from their very own children and grandchildren. As Pilkington (1994: 193) notes, for some commentators at the outset of the 1990s, Russian young people were being defined as a lost generation, not any more as the key link to a better future.

It is against this background that Gorbachev's notable summons should be read at the 27th Party Congress in 1986 in favor of openness, restructuring and speeding up of technological development (*glasnost, perestroika, uskoreniye*), especially his call for an end to the dual reality of Soviet life, the one public and swathed in meaningless self-congratulation, the other private and cynically honest (cf. Shlapentokh, 1986). Indeed, he spent some considerable time in his address discussing the deterioration of human relationships in Soviet society and what needed to be done about them. In this sense, it is now clear that he was an incurable optimist in thinking it was still possible to rescue the project. As Bachkatov and Wilson put it (1988: 240), 'the parents lost their faith, but the children never had it'.

Yet the point at issue is this: the impasse reached was such that the solution proposed by antique purist traditionalists in the Politburo such as Mikhail Suslov or Yegor Ligachev, namely the purification and intensive re-ideologization of the society, had zero chance of success with young people. A prime motivating force in the drive for *glasnost* and *perestroika* was then that they represented the last and only chance for success in recuperating the Soviet project, for the younger generation simply had to be the target of targets in that drive.[10] In fact, as we now know, but because of the communicative atomization of sovietized societies (cf. Bahro, 1978: 300–3) neither we nor they were then able to know, the game was already over.

Music

It is at this juncture that it becomes possible to appreciate the significance of new musical movements and expressions as the most tangible of all manifestations of the alienation of youth in sovietized societies at that time. The first and very powerful underground expression of dissent in musical form came from the so-called guitar-poets or bards, notably Bulat Okudzhava and Vladimir Vysotskii (Ryback, 1989, ch. 3; Smith, 1984). In some sense they paved the way for the later proliferation of musical styles, many of the latter initially borrowed from Western sources, unlike the bards whose themes and musical style were deeply Russian. Another such expression was the tenacious persistence against all odds of jazz (Starr, 1983), which finally received official approval almost exactly at the moment when large sections of the younger generation were embracing rock music for the self-same reasons an earlier generation had embraced jazz.

As Ryback underlines, however, rock was much more of a generational expression. As a native phenomenon it developed later in Russia than in Poland, Hungary or other East-Central European countries. Even more so than in the latter region, the cultural bureaucracy in the Soviet Union was very deeply entrenched in the past. Knee-jerk denunciations of subversive Western strategies in the musical arena came easily to it, though in turn this was made easier by the generally greater isolation of Russian (though not Baltic) society from its Western neighbors. Whether as a native phenomenon or as an import, however, Ryback recounts instance after instance in almost every Soviet bloc nation of young people battling with the police, sometimes violently, in order to secure or defend their rights to rock concerts. The right to free musical self-expression was an issue of passionate moment for very many young people.

However, aside from generational clashes of taste on the actual music and its instrumentation, there were profound political divergences between the Party and Komsomol authorities on the lyrics of many rock numbers and on the life-styles associated with rock music. In essence, both sides appeared often to agree on one central point: rock music was globally inspired, not Soviet-inspired.

Bushnell (1990: 53–4, 97ff., ch. 4), in his study of graffiti in Moscow around this period, observed how often even Soviet rock groups were generally honored by having graffiti written about them in English, rather than in Russian: 'English words and symbols enjoy prestige and auto-matically – irrespective of their precise meaning – do the emblem honor' (p. 54). He cites the Burgess novel and the film based upon it, *A Clockwork Orange*, as correctly intuiting 'the key role that the language of the ideological and cultural enemy plays in the Soviet subculture', and connects the prestige of English to 'an image of the West as an affluent, energetic and colorful world the opposite of Soviet society in every respect' (pp. 240–1).

Not unnaturally, the more the Komsomol bureaucracy and its Eastern European clones inveighed against rock as a decadent imperialist plot, the young discovered there was an ideological Achilles heel, a point at which they could challenge the system and see it compulsively react. When the same musical moment, a rock concert, was one which, as it did for many people, also meant a moment of positive mental liberation and psychic intensity, then two values fused together into a very powerful commitment. To capture the latter aspect of this reality conceptually, Pilkington (1994: 239–43) draws on Roland Barthes' use of the word *jouissance* (literally, orgasm) to denote cultural moments 'of pleasure when the body breaks free from social and cultural control'.

Interestingly, toward the end of the 1980s, even the Soviet system began trying to co-opt rock groups and give them official space, though at the cost to the groups of having them censor their own lyrics (Easton, 1989). By then other groups, especially punk rockers and heavy metal bands, had sped past more traditional and melodic rock music, and were the new targets of cultural conservatives and Party officials. In Russia, Poland and Hungary during the 1980s, cultural bureaucrats veered back and forth between allowing punk rockers and others space for concerts and recordings, and trying to rein them in (Ryback, 1989: 11–12, 14). It has to be said that in a few instances the lyrics were of a kind that would draw almost universal repugnance, as in the case of one Hungarian group that called for the extermination of Romanies, or the banner unfurled by Latvian punks at a concert that read 'Latvian punks will finish what the Germans began', i.e. the slaughter of Russians in tens of millions (Ryback, 1989: 215, 275). Heroizing or homogenizing the opposition is a perilous proposition.

None the less, these forms of popular music effectively became an alternative public sphere (Downing, 1988a) for many members of the younger generation in Soviet bloc countries. It must be recalled, in context, that this was the decade of the second Cold War, a period of very pronounced nuclear tension, a period in which the aggressive militarism of the Reagan administration and the Reagan–Thatcher–Kohl 'front' were endlessly highlighted in Soviet bloc media. Yet not even the existence of an external enemy armed to the teeth and rattling nuclear sabres was able to be used to deflect the dissident culture and commitments of many young people. Their insistence on honoring and following Western musical forms was not to be interpreted, as did the official press, simply as slavish imitation of a hollow and frenetic commercialism. It was a constant reminder to the authorities that the younger generation neither believed in nor cared about a single word they were being fed from on high.

This musically delivered message from below was able eventually to reverberate in the ears of even the most hard of hearing in the *verkhushki*.

Religion

The discussion here will be very brief, but two points are of considerable importance. First, that if dissidents in the Soviet Union are to be measured by numbers, then religious dissent was infinitely more significant than those secular figures best known in the West – such as Solzhenitsyn and Sakharov – who were known to and represented only a very tiny constituency up until the late 1980s. Whether considering the Baptist churches, the Ukrainian Uniate church, or a variety of other religious bodies, this form of dissidence was the oldest and most widespread (Alexeyeva, 1985, chs. 11–14; Jancar, 1975). Judgments vary on the large Muslim populations of the Central Asian republics and Azerbaijan, with some claiming the existence of massive underground dissidence and others arguing that the traditional clans of those regions had effectively colonized the formally Soviet power-structure in their republics, and ironically had developed thereby a more stable version of Soviet power than in the non-Muslim republics.[11]

However, religious dissidence in principle was a primary zone of principled opposition, since it drew its inspiration from ethical absolutes that simply could not co-exist with the Soviet claim to have a lock on the future – a much more significant point of conflict than simply the question of the state's self-designation as 'atheist'. The latter could, in the case of many states, be effectively the same as the United States government's self-designation, at least up until the time of writing this book, as constitutionally neutral on the question of religious expression. It was the rival claims to effective total knowledge and ideological supremacy that were irreconcilable, and thus a permanent disturbance of the Soviet cultural project.

The second point is really an extension of the first in a particularly sensitive zone of the bloc. The Polish Catholic Church, by virtue of the cultural homogeneity of Poland in its post-Second World War borders, and by virtue of its own extremely traditionalist intransigence, was never forced underground. Thus Poland was the only bloc nation with a major nationally organized and tolerated – however reluctantly – autonomous entity all through the last years of Stalinism and since. The role of religious bodies elsewhere in the bloc bore no real comparison. The importance of this entity in sustaining some sense of the possibility of an alternative mode of social life is hard to overestimate. Of course the Catholic Church had its own survival at heart, which dominated its strategy in Poland as elsewhere throughout history. It was certainly not anxiously beating at the gates of democracy. But it was there, the only organized counterforce to a regime which insisted by force on its own all-sufficiency.

Catholic churches were the only public location where the language was still used unmarred by obfuscation and jargon, a condition hard to imagine for those who have never lived in such a linguistically oppressive situation.[12]

Thus during the 1980s, as Jakubowicz (1990) has demonstrated, there were actually three public spheres in Poland: those of the official government, of *Solidarnosc* and of the Catholic Church. While predictably there was considerable friction of various kinds between these zones of public debate, the very fact of having three such meant that in the continuing instability of the Polish situation from early in 1988 onwards, the role of the two oppositional spheres was correspondingly enhanced, and even compelled the official sphere's media to open up their doors to intermittent critique and commentary that would have been difficult to imagine at an earlier date.

Hungary was a far more secular society than Poland. The arrest and imprisonment of Cardinal Mindszenty after the crushing of the 1956 revolution, and his later long sojourn in the US embassy (he effectively refused to leave), had nothing of the impact of the incarceration of Poland's Cardinal Wyszynski, nor of the latter's role subsequent to his release. Indeed, the impact seemed to be rather on the Catholic hierarchy in Hungary, which had been intimidated to the point that when Christian base-communities – very roughly on the Brazilian and Central American model – began to spring up at the close of the 1970s, they were severely discountenanced by the hierarchy. When a number of them, inspired by a courageous priest, Fr Bulanyi, began to argue on pacifist grounds against military conscription, they found themselves facing a welded opposition from the state and the hierarchy.[13]

At the same time, it is important not to overstate the 'island of autonomy' view of the Polish Catholic Church. Jozef Tischner (1989), who had been the chief celebrant at the famous *Solidarnosc* mass in Gdansk shipyards in 1980, and was rector of Krakow's Papal Academy of Theology, commented on the way in which the crassness and harshness of the sovietized system had also influenced everyday behavior by clergy. He instanced a priest haranguing his congregation in a sermon, saying 'When I look at all of you I want to throw up', and another one singling out the daughter of a well-known village drunk and asking her to testify then and there as to what kind of father she had. She stood up and remained standing, not saying a word, crying silently. Such behavior in Tischner's view was redolent of the political culture in which Poles had been nurtured. It might be added, on a different note, that Poles were generally very insouciant of their hierarchy's positions on sexual ethics, especially as regarded contraception. On that level, they and the regime shared a certain common position.

The issue of religion is considerably more complicated than can be properly handled here, and would have to include such issues as the deep complicity of leading members of the Russian Orthodox hierarchy with the KGB (Dunlop, 1992), the explosion of publications from the end of the 1980s in Russia dealing with psychic and mystical aspects of religion, including Eastern religions (or versions of them), and the self-defined mission of the Polish Catholic hierarchy in relation to Poland's national future. However, it is important to recognize that one major component in the cultural resistance against sovietism was religious, vary as it might from nation to nation. We shall note below its significance in the development of *Solidarnosc*.

Social Movements

Butterfield and Weigle (1991: 184), as we observed in the discussion in Chapter 1, make the important observation that the Western study of social movements has typically focused on the movements themselves, fundamentally treating them as a form of lobbying in a stable liberal democracy, as social agents facing a presumptively non-malign state apparatus, or more recently, in the so-called New Social Movements, as efforts to reclaim a certain social identity. As a result, there has been a strange vacuum in analysis of the role and character of the state itself in the development or collapse of social movements. While this is distinctly inappropriate conceptually, not least when analysing movements inside authoritarian regimes, and would even lead to gross confusion in understanding, say, the US Civil Rights movement or the Black Power movement, it also illustrates once more the continuing tendency in social analysis to privilege the pinnacle *or* the crowd.

Although focusing at this point in this essay on the impact of certain social movements in both subverting and reconstructing the political culture and communication processes of Soviet bloc nations, it is essential to begin with the recognition that for the bloc regimes autonomous social movements were by definition to be excluded from the spectrum of public activities. In Hungary in 1978, for example, supposedly 'the easiest barracks in the socialist camp' as the local saying went, when I asked a feminist (Veres Julia) about the current condition of the Hungarian women's movement she explained to me that 50 percent of the movement had recently emigrated to Paris. Which left only her . . . And went on to point out that any autonomous movement, not a women's movement as such, was intolerable for the party-state.

Recognition of this political communicative reality helps to place in proper focus the extraordinary achievement of the *Solidarnosc* movement in Poland, not only for Poland but also for the whole Soviet bloc. The Russian scenario has already been addressed in Chapters 1 and 3, so here we shall address the Polish and Hungarian situations.

A variety of accounts of *Solidarnosc* have touched upon the significance of communication in its genesis and development. Kubik (1994), especially, examined the role of symbolic communication in both the sovietized regime's power, and in the growth of *Solidarnosc*. Bernhard (1993: 102–8, 143–50, 159–70, 185–6) devoted considerable space to media and communication activities by a variety of opposition currents in the later 1970s. Lipski[14] presented a detailed empirical description of a variety of the media generated by opposition movements in the late 1970s. Blumsztajn (1988) performed the same task, but for the first half of the 1980s.

Both Goodwyn (1991) and Laba (1991) proposed a particular argument, vigorously attacked by both Bernhard (1991) and Kubik (1994: 230–8), namely that the communicative dimension of the genesis of *Solidarnosc* has often been framed in terms of the 'outside agitator' theory of communication, a position – curiously enough – shared both by the Polish *verkhushka* and by many Western commentators. Both by many Western analysts and the Polish regime, *Solidarnosc* was claimed to be the product of one or more of the following: Pope John Paul II's tumultuous visit to

Poland in 1979; Radio Free Europe broadcasts; and the advice and leadership for Gdansk shipyard workers from a small knot of courageous Warsaw intellectuals such as Adam Michnik and Jacek Kuron, leading activists in the organization KOR. KOR was the Polish acronym for the Committee for Workers' Self-Defense, founded in 1976 in the wake of the extensive labor disturbances of that year, initially to provide information relevant to fighting the repression of activists that followed the upsurge. Some KOR members were prominent as *Solidarnosc* advisors.

Goodwyn and Laba do not deny the involvement or partial influence of any of these factors in the process as a whole. But in their view no one of them, and no combination of them, actually created or enabled the emergence of *Solidarnosc*. In their analysis, the roots of the movement and of its concept of the need for independent unions, are within the accumulated experience of the Polish working class, especially on the Baltic Coast.[15] The role of outside intellectuals was either secondary, or even harmful.

For a full analysis, readers are directed to all the works cited, as well as to Ost (1990). Here it is enough to acknowledge the way in which this very slowly growing movement on the Baltic coast, coming together over decades, did indeed gradually develop its own culture and internal communicative links. Goodwyn in particular traces the transition from endless kitchen-table conversations about the realities people faced – 'we weren't building socialism; we were building shit' (1991: 105) – through to the formation of the Inter-Factory Strike Committee that mobilized the Baltic Coast seaport workers and was the cradle of the 1980 strikes and the formation of *Solidarnosc*. At every point, the struggle over the right to communicate freely was a crucial dimension of the movement, not least during the great 1980 strike:

> Properly understood, the [Gdansk] workers' preconditions that their 'helpers' [leaflet printers, couriers, traffic coordinators] be freed both from prison and from further repression constituted more than half the battle. (p. 57)

Laba (1991) also concentrates on some of the symbolic communications of the movement. He comments on the role of the strike as a rite of passage in which 'individuals rejected social masks' (p. 132) that they wore in public on a routine basis under the regime (compare Shlapentokh's and Gorbachev's comments on the dual reality of Soviet life, noted in Chapter 2). Laba stresses the powerful fusion of religious, nationalist and egalitarian symbols developed by *Solidarnosc*. He also offers a telling contrast between the typical underpinnings of both fascist and Soviet symbols, which relied on images of macho sexuality, aggression, charismatic leadership and dehumanization of enemies, with the leitmotifs of the *Solidarnosc* message that portrayed Walesa as everyman, as a trickster, as an anti-hero (pp. 140–53).

Kubik (1994) offers a sustained analysis from an anthropological perspective of symbolic communication by all the main actors in the Polish drama: the regime, the Catholic Church and *Solidarnosc*. He also reviews a major theatrical treatment of Polish history that was staged every year in Krakow's Wawel Castle from 1972 to 1980. A major strength of his argument is his emphasis on the power of what might be called memorable moments of communication, the lasting symbolic charge of such moments.[16]

His discussion is thus much less concerned with ongoing media communication, representing regime, Church or labor opposition, and far more with such events as the contested 1978 celebration of Polish Independence Day: 11 November 1978 was the sixtieth anniversary of the re-establishment of Poland as a nation after its 123 years of annexation and dismemberment by Germany, Russia and Austria; 11 November was a day that the sovietized regime had consistently refused to mark,[17] but in 1978 found itself compelled to acknowledge it in order not to leave its celebration solely to the Catholic Church and other opposition currents. Kubik discusses (pp. 168–78) the immense lasting impact of celebratory masses attended by many thousands in Warsaw, Gdansk, Krakow, Czestochowa and elsewhere, and how the unofficial celebrations, asserting in public long-suppressed issues in Polish history, succeeded in overshadowing the official ones.[18]

Kubik assembles an accumulated array of such symbolic happenings as a way of tracking 'the formation of [a] public counterhegemony . . . [with] a significant impact on the process of the regime's demise and the shape of the sociopolitical order that emerges afterwards' (p. 265). He notes in particular the significance of the simple wooden cross at the outdoor masses at the Gdansk shipyard, placed on the spot where workers had been shot down in 1970. It was a sign of defiance against the regime, and a long-established metaphor of both national martyrdom (Poland as the suffering Christ of nations during its 123 years of occupation, that role now renewed under Soviet rule), and of Poland as the messiah of nations, at that moment the leader in the struggle against Soviet empire (Kubik, 1994: 189). He cites a Gdansk worker who wrote:

> Outdoor masses . . . made an indelible impression upon us. They were experiences which no Shakespeare and no Goethe could produce by his magic . . . I dare say it was because even the finest theatrical performances lack that supernatural power which emanates from the simple wooden cross . . . For the onlookers the cross was merely a relic two thousand years old and nothing more. For us, strikers, it was something much more . . . We were ready to take the cross upon our own shoulders, the cross in the form of the caterpillar tracks of the tanks, if it came to an assault on us. (p. 189)

Later that year, after numerous tussles with the authorities, a permanent memorial was erected, consisting of three metal crosses 130 feet high, anchors and an eternal flame. Kubik (1994: 196–206) analyses the rich symbolism of these emblems, and equally the monumental importance for people's consciousness of the fact that the memorial was constructed, paid for, and publicly dedicated by the society, not by the regime.

Ost (1990) focuses upon the determination of the Polish oppositional movement, especially KOR, to create an alternative public sphere outside and against the state. They effectively thereby treated the state as irrelevant, either as the source of possible benefits or as the source of fear of repression. Within this tiny incipient alternative sphere, step by step they began to learn to communicate again as free citizens, practicing as we saw in Chapter 1 what some intellectuals involved in such strategies came to describe as 'antipolitics' (Konrád, 1984; Ash, 1990: 170–8). As Ost observes (p. 57), the approach made no sense at all as a clear-headed analysis of practical realities, given the massive power of the Polish state and the overwhelming military power of the Soviet state behind it. It was, however, rhetorically immensely appealing as a strategy of mobilization within the self-same sovietized context, bearing some of the same stamp of quiet, unshakeable confidence in ultimate ethical principle as Martin Luther King Jr and the US Civil Rights movement in the teeth of a corrupt and often violent power structure.[19]

It is important, however, notwithstanding the impact of *Solidarnosc*, to avoid an overly polarized or simplified picture of Poland at this, or any, juncture. Misztal (1992: 57–8) emphasizes this point in his discussion of the provocative surrealist street communications of the Orange Alternative movement commented upon in Chapter 3, which fitted none of the political or cultural styles of either the regime, the Catholic Church, or *Solidarnosc*. Much of what has been written about Poland in this period is – sometimes understandably given its undeniable impact on the collapse of the Soviet system – seduced by the stark and dramatic interpretations of Polish reality that are a traditional current in Polish culture. (A reading of Witold Gombrowicz's novels is a useful corrective.)

The significance of *Solidarnosc*, however, lies not simply in its claim to our admiration for the tenacity and courage of many of its standard-bearers, mostly unknown except to their immediate circles. It lies also in the fact that it forged a popular cultural movement with intense internal and external communication that effectively paralyzed the capacity of the Polish state to govern, even despite that state's 1981 declaration of martial law – for as Gramsci tirelessly pointed out, simply to repress is not to govern. For that state to be able to govern, it had to be able to have some dialogue with society, a reality very clearly perceived by General Jaruzelski despite his inevitable image as Soviet Gauleiter. *Solidarnosc* was that dialogic partner, for it had set out markers in many people's minds that the regime was powerless to obliterate.

As a social movement *Solidarnosc* was never again the huge force it was in the last months of 1981. It was actually caught off guard by the major labor unrest of 1988 that drastically unsettled the regime. By then it barely existed in Polish workplaces. Indeed 'all it still had consisted only of its leaders, its legend and its press . . . a gigantic enterprise [to which] according to official figures three and a half million Poles have regular access . . . the only proof of *Solidarnosc*'s existence was its public utterances, and it was with those who produced them that the government finally had to negotiate a sharing of its powers' (Warszawski, 1989: 12). This strange blend of underground media power with movement weakness, of regime weakness with its need for a partner within society with whom to confer, and of Gorbachev's approval signals for the Polish regime's stance in this respect, made for a particularly unheralded communicative cocktail.

For although Soviet media regularly lambasted *Solidarnosc* and fed popular Russian stereotypes of the Poles as lazy Russophobes, Gorbachev and Jaruzelski – and the teams around them – had a much stronger affinity and communication with each other than was the case with any other East-Central European regime and the Soviet leadership. A revitalized Soviet Union and bloc, purified of many of their inherited negative dimensions, and living in peace with the West, were their shared goals. For Gorbachev, still confident that he could handle change – his conservative opponents were more realistic on this score, despite the bankuptcy of their own solutions – the Polish situation was one more demonstration of the urgency of managed change. Jaruzelski completely concurred. And, finally, Poland was easily the largest nation in the bloc, and was the territorial link to East Germany, itself long seen as the key guarantee of a weakened and therefore less threatening Central Europe. It also bordered the restive Baltic republics whose alienation from Soviet rule was intense.[20] The significance of Poland's stability for the Soviet *verkhushka* was axiomatic.

Thus it was not that *Solidarnosc* directly inspired labor or other movements in Soviet Russia or Ukraine or Hungary, of which there were a variety (e.g. Helsinki Watch, 1987, 1990), albeit of much lesser scope. As a result of media blackouts on Polish realities elsewhere in the Soviet bloc, most people outside the western borderland zone were ignorant of the true situation in Poland. (Lithuania, over time and with the Round Table negotiations before it as well as the earlier history of *Solidarnosc*, was the exception that proved the rule.)

Solidarnosc's impact on the bloc was at a totally different level, precisely through the interpretation of its policy-implications by the reform wings in both Soviet and Polish leaderships. These latter concurred that although limited military actions against civil disobedience were appropriate to retain control, sustained and widespread violence to subdue opposition was indeed impossible on both ethical and practical grounds. If further evidence were needed to support this argument, the war in Afghanistan had supplied it in abundance. So the Polish movement, at its height in 1981 numbering ten million members, as contrasted with 2.5 million for the Party and a million in official trade unions (Ost, 1990: 138), was constantly cited by the reform faction in Moscow as prime evidence of the need for managed change in the soviet system if more such mass movements were to be avoided.[21]

If further evidence of the practicality of managed change were needed, then the superficially calm situation in Hungary, where a centimetre-by-centimetre relaxation of controls had been in force for over twenty years without the collapse of the system, appeared to provide it. Space forbids a deeper analysis, but Konrád has offered some very suggestive comments on the characteristically Hungarian dynamic of the development of an alternative public sphere, sharply different from Poland's. I include it here to underscore, however briefly, the impact of cultural process, the role of its very specificity and of the communication of its implications, on all the regime changes in question. Konrád says of historical and modern Hungarian culture:

> Our people fought against and lived with Turks, Germans and Russians – more than that, they conquered them, conquered them from below even while the Hungarians themselves lay conquered and supine. They had, as it were, a dual consciousness: that of the warrior who scorns all negotiation, and that of the negotiator who shies away from the warrior and tries to get by on his wits . . .
> Our mode of expression is marked by a sentimental and humorous worldly wisdom, by a knowing archness, by jokes, by sly exchanges of winks: 'I know what you know and you know what I know.' Looking at them from a distance, I find considerable resemblance between my progovernment and opposition friends; Budapest is written all over them. (Konrád, 1984: 131)

The 1956 revolution represented what Konrád terms the warrior consciousness, but the decades of the Kádár regime since then represented the other mode, the negotiator using his wits. In identifying that mode specifically with Budapest, he acknowledges the pre-eminent place of the capital in the shaping of the modern Hungarian nation (Lukács, 1988), akin to that of Paris for France.[22] It is not without significance in this context that long-term intellectual dissident Miklós Hárászti entitled his book on artistic censorship *The Velvet Prison* (1987), and that it offers one of the most precise and agonized dissections of the process of *self*-censorship available in the literature. Eva Hoffman (1993: 209), similarly, has commented on the way

> the refined Hungarian scruples turn out to reflect the complex circumstances in which people lived – how the structures of the macro situation become inscribed and repeated in the microcosm of the psyche, as, in a fractal series, the whorls of the leaf repeat the leaf.

None the less, within the dialectic of intra-bloc relations, the Hungarian social movement played its own significant role. That role, to repeat my argument, cannot be understood outside of its cultural and communicative dimensions, which were both intrinsic to Hungary and yet influential beyond its borders, in the manner indicated above, at a key point in the unfolding drama.[23]

Conclusions

In this chapter, the argument has been made that the major regime transitions in Eastern Europe are only to be understood fully with the aid of a communication focus, including a cultural studies focus, rather than a concentration on the *verkhushki*. In the course of the argument, however, it has been clear that not only is this a realm of research rather thinly populated by scholars operating within such a framework,[24] but also that those working within the framework have typically not addressed certain major issues that might be expected to fit closely with their concerns, such as social movements or religion.

At the same time we also need to note that the cultural studies literature has generally not engaged with the Habermas-derived notion of the public sphere. Despite the latter's problematic dimensions already noted in Chapter 1, it offers interesting scope for conceptual and analytical cross-fertilization, especially in its alternative media communication implications (Downing, 1988a; Fraser, 1993). These so far still wait to be properly realized by cultural studies and communication researchers.

We now turn in the next chapter to the implications of these regime changes for criticizing communication and cultural studies approaches and will propose that they suggest certain typical deficiencies within those discourses. It is now the turn of politico-economic analysis.

Notes

1 Bushnell (1990), Condee and Padunov (1987, 1991a, b, 1994, 1995), Pilkington (1994), Shane (1994), Starr (1990), are the main exceptions. A partial exception is Kubik's (1994) anthropological study of regime and opposition symbols and ceremonies in Poland up to 1981.

2 All three books are authored by journalists, not by academic social scientists, but especially in the analysis of changes in Eastern Europe, serious journalism has to date made at least as informative a contribution as the academy, if not more so. Whilst Schweizer's study is not helped by the author's cheerleading for the Reagan and Bush administrations, its data and argument are extremely important.

3 The 'their' being at times perceived and at times real.

4 Maybe if the economic hardships of the initial post-transition years had been experienced pre-transition this might have been the case. There certainly was deep economic dissatisfaction, but there was also deep fatalism in Russia about the prospects for any change for the better. See Chapter 2, note 20. Poles I spoke with that spring tended to the contrary, an uncritically optimistic view of the instant benefits of capitalism (a hope soon dashed). Hungarians I spoke with tended to gloom, an intermittent national characteristic.

5 Neither here nor in the next chapter do we offer similar analyses of the post-transitional situation, the consolidation process, not because such a task is irrelevant, but because at the time of writing the necessary empirical research foundation is missing.

6 White, 1990: ch. 3; cf. Chapter 3 above, note 18.

7 However, Ganley's study (1996) of the explosion of new media outlets in what I have termed the biennium, and published just as this book was going to press, goes some way to qualifying this judgment. Her findings suggest that Starr's position, if reshaped to focus on those two years, would be less open to critique than I have proposed.

8 A rising star in the Leningrad Komsomol, whom we see enjoying the high life with his cronies, has his career threatened. In the course of trying to save it, he sexually brutalizes his girlfriend and terrorizes other ordinary citizens. See Lawton, 1992: 198–200, and more generally on the Soviet cinematic depiction of youth issues at that point, pp. 175–95.

9 A graphic Russian portrayal of these domestic realities was provided in the 1988 film *Little Vera* (Lawton, 1992: 192–4).

10 Ost (1990: 39) puts it rather well: 'although totalitarianism is a necessary *tendency* of a

Leninist party state, it cannot be achieved. And so the Party continually swings between a totalitarian tendency and a reform tendency, which recognizes that the state must *interact* with civil society rather than try to extinguish it.'

11 See Rywkin, 1982: 149–53, for a summary of the debate on this issue.

12 For example, the withering up of public communication was felt so intensely by one woman intellectual, an atheist of Jewish descent, that she regularly attended Catholic mass simply to hear a Polish spoken that was unpoisoned by regime-speak (Panel, Center for Communication, New York City, 1982).

13 'Être chrétien et désobéissant', *La Nouvelle Alternative*, 15, September 1989, 26–8.

14 Jan Józef Lipski, *KOR: a History of the Workers' Defense Committee in Poland, 1976–81*. Berkeley, University of California Press, 1985, pp. 60–2, 109–13, 178–83, 226–31, 300–5, 359–63, 395–9, 447–8.

15 The controversy between Goodwyn and Laba on the one hand, and Bernhard and Kubik on the other, is not one into which we can enter in detail here. In essence I would suggest that the two former were so concerned to dispute the sometimes exaggerated claims of Western commentators concerning the Pope's visit or Radio Free Europe, or in particular for Goodwyn the hauteur of Polish sociologist Staniszkis (1984) in dismissing the communicative and organizational abilities of Polish workers, that they quite unnecessarily allowed themselves to downplay the influential role of KOR from 1976 to 1981 in setting up totally new communication networks between labor opposition groups in a number of cities. Through these horizontal networks it was suddenly possible, despite energetic efforts by the regime to repress them, for information to flow through the society in a manner unprecedented in decades.

16 An absorbing account of the deep symbolic status of Tiananmen Square in Beijing and its relation to the 1989 rebellion and its repression is provided by Schell (1994: 15–30).

17 See the remarks in Chapter 2 on the sovietized regime's consistent attempt to downplay Polish nationalism.

18 The latter were scheduled by the regime to end well before 11, on 6 November, as a way of trying to tie the commemoration to the 7 November commemoration of the Bolshevik revolution. The regime's version was that the Bolshevik revolution had accelerated the end of the First World War and so enabled Polish independence from its imperial possessors.

19 This chapter focuses on the communicative and cultural dimensions of these transitions. Bernhard (1993: 46–75, 151–9), Kaminski (1991) and the next chapter examine a number of the economic and political dimensions. This book's basic purpose is to argue for their conceptual integration (not fusion).

20 It will be recalled that in March 1990 the first Soviet republic to declare its independence was Lithuania, directly on Poland's frontier and with a centuries-long common history. The utter shock and consternation on the faces of the Supreme Soviet deputies when the leader of the Lithuanian deputies announced in the Chamber that from then on his group would not be voting, but would be present merely as observers, is etched in my memory. The fierce but failed struggle to force Lithuania back into submission was a key vector in the dissolution of the Soviet Union some sixteen months later.

21 Teague (1988; cf. also Ruble, 1983) traces a division in regime thinking on the implications of the Polish crisis going back to 1980–1. It is very clear from her research that the Soviet regime was acutely conscious and troubled about the possible spillover of *Solidarnosc* into the Soviet Union, especially into the neighboring Baltic, Byelorussian and Ukrainian SSRs. Chernenko, briefly Soviet leader before Gorbachev, consistently argued before and after his accession that Soviet workers must be listened to and their needs better met if similar crises were not to occur in the Union itself. Suslov equally consistently argued in favor of more discipline. Each position and individual had considerable support, rather evenly balanced as shown by the systematic initial drive in 1980 and through into early 1981 to publicize that the regime wanted the official Soviet labor unions to be much more effective in representing workers' concerns, which was then succeeded further into 1981 by a sharp switch of direction, namely a tightening up of labor discipline and severing of a number of international communication channels. The advent of Gorbachev heralded a gradual swing

back to attempts to reform and so to save the Soviet system from more crises. Given the intensity of these debates and policy divisions, it is hard to overestimate the role of *Solidarnosc* in its first phase in setting in motion the belated attempts by Brezhnev's successors to return the Soviet system to health by one means or another. *Solidarnosc* focused the minds of the *verkhushka*, whatever media silence they imposed for their public on actual events and issues in Poland.

22 Except that we also need to bear in mind the long-standing frictions between 'cosmopolitan' Budapest and the traditional rural elites.

23 Indeed, the decision by the Hungarian authorities on 10 September 1989 to allow East Germans to proceed through Hungary and via Austria to the German Federal Republic could be argued to have been the point at which, metaphorically, the little Dutch boy removed his fist from the hole in the dike and the bloc finally gave way as an international system. Border guards snipping the barbed wire on the Austrian frontier were only the news-photographic symbol of the pivotal signal that had been sent. Romania's long refusal to take part in Warsaw Pact maneuvers had never had such an impact, presumably because it never challenged the principle of a heavily militarized frontier to enforce residence within bloc countries.

24 The studies by Condee and Padunov already referred to are a major exception to this rule. Their array of specifics and their tracing of shifts and eddies in the process, however, are so detailed that it is hard to address them within the confines of a single essay.

5

Eastern European Transitions: the Politico-Economic Dimension

In this chapter I will explore the leading state- and economy-based factors in the regime transitions. On the one hand, this exercise is designed to illustrate the necessity for communication researchers to bring these dimensions of societal reality into play in their analyses, and not simply leave them to others in an explicit or tacit division of intellectual labor. On the other hand, as we proceed, the material will often illustrate a second conceptual premise, enunciated by the citation from Williams in the Introduction, namely that even these seemingly 'structural', 'take-it-or-leave-it' dimensions of the situation typically contain important communicative, cultural and interpretive dimensions.

We will begin then by reviewing some key studies of the transitions for gaps they indicate in standard communication and cultural studies research, the reverse side of the coin that we examined in the last chapter where the utility of a communico-cultural analysis was demonstrated. We will then explore how the internal crisis of Soviet economic decline was publicly communicated within the USSR – paradoxically, given an official media structure which offered that decline little or no coverage or even acknowledgment until toward the close of the 1980s.[1] Finally we will look at the impact of the external crisis, namely the Soviet bloc's declining power in international affairs – equally passed over or distorted by major Soviet media until 1988–9 – on public consciousness within the Soviet *nomenklatura*.

Eastern European Transitions and Communication Research

Three texts on the collapse of the Soviet bloc system direct our attention to a variety of considerations normally off the conceptual radar screens of communication and cultural studies researchers.

Beschloss and Talbott (1993) describe the often intricate negotiations between President Bush, Secretary of State James Baker, CIA Director Robert Gates, US Ambassador Jack Matlock and other leading individuals on the US side, and President Gorbachev, Foreign Secretary Eduard Shevardnadze, Field Marshal Akhromeyev, Russian Republic President Yeltsin, and leading actors on the Soviet side, during the period from shortly before Bush's election in 1988 through to the conclusion of the failed putsch of August 1991 – in other words, the final period of the dismantling of the Cold War.

Ash (1993) recounts the much longer history of the gradual movement toward German reunification, and its constitutive role in the evaporation of the Cold War and the end of the division of Europe. He traces the steps from Adenauer's administration onwards, but especially from the key policy speech given by Egon Bahr, Willi Brandt's chief foreign policy specialist, in 1963, in which he urged increased trade and flow of consumer goods to East-Central Europe as a strategy to avoid crises and so to encourage the regimes to relax and thus make Soviet intervention less likely. Ash indeed argues that German *Ostpolitik* and *Osthandel* were policies initially conceived in the highly specific and extremely local situation of Berlin, especially after the 1961 construction of the Wall (pp. 65–7).

Schweizer (1994) argues, based on a number of hitherto undisclosed National Security Decision Directives from 1982 – numbers 32, 66 and 75 – that under the Reagan Administration there was a foreign policy team (the National Security Planning Group[2]) separate from both the State Department and the National Security Council, that set its explicit mission to engage in economic warfare with the USSR in order to force its collapse and the disintegration of the Yalta Agreement. Its cutting edge, Schweizer claims (1994: 2–3 *et passim*), was William Casey, CIA Director from 1981 to 1987, invested by Reagan with close to plenipotentiary authority.

These accounts largely complement each other, although Schweizer's effectively asserts that the negotiations described in the other two – actually he barely mentions Germany – were only viable because of the prior vision and aggressive strategy of the National Security Planning Group. It is very noticeable how intensively Beschloss and Talbott cite Secretary of State Baker and his pivotal role, but how he practically might never have existed according to the Schweizer version (he is not even cited as a source). Such, perhaps, are inevitable vagaries of such ethnographers of the American *verkhushka*. Let us not impute anything so gross as political bias to them, but nor let us be caught up behind their – methodological – blind-spots.

The essence of what these accounts have in common consists in their focus on (1) the role of certain political agents enjoying a disproportionate measure of power in the international arena, and (2) the extent to which their efforts and schemes were regularly thwarted or were attempted to be out-maneuvered by other highly placed individuals in their own camp ('on their own side' seems sometimes an overstatement). However, there is also in each of them (3) a largely unexplored communico-cultural dimension that will be noted from time to time.

Now although in Chapter 4 I have argued strongly that *verkhushka-*heavy explanations of events are radically incomplete, it is none the less the case that these agents of power played an irreplaceable role in the process. Drawing on the data in the three texts cited, let us dwell specifically on how this was so.

It is evident that bedrock reality so far as Gorbachev and Shevardnadze were concerned signified that the Soviet system could be reformed without risking disintegration. They were convinced that the real threat of disintegration lay in the refusal to reform and to dispel *zastoi* (stagnation). From Andropov's[3] brief period at the helm onwards this basic orientation enjoyed the strong and crucial support of major sections of the KGB (cf. Albats, 1994; Doder, 1986; Rahr, 1993; Shane, 1994: ch. 4; Yasmann, 1993), which support was fundamental in giving Gorbachev and Shevardnadze both their initial access to the positions of power they achieved and their subsequent tenure in office.

Simultaneously US President Bush was intent on building on the later (post-Reykjavik) legacy of Reagan, with Secretary of State Baker acting as his chosen instrument. (In turn Baker saw this process as a perfect platform for his own presidential ambition.) What was decisive at that point was that Baker and Shevardnadze succeeded slowly and in fits and starts in building a rapport of trust and effective communication with each other, which put the interpersonal communication circuitry in place to enable a serious accommodation between the superpowers to be successfully generated.

Thus the decision to avoid any official US comment upon the Soviet Army's massacre of unarmed demonstrators in Tbilisi in April 1989, and the decision in 1990 to act as behind-the-scenes mediator between Gorbachev and Landsbergis, Lithuanian independence leader during the protracted stand-off between Vilnius and the Kremlin (Beschloss and Talbott, 1993: 51, 196ff.) – both decisions calculated with a keen sense of the long-term stakes in a stable and uninterrupted transitional process – were but some instances of this circuitry and its importance.

These factors were, however, only one dimension of the process. For almost two generations, political leadership in the Federal German Republic, despite sometimes sharp conflicts of emphasis between Christian Democrats and Social Democrats, was essentially united in using Germany's medium of power – the Deutschmark – to encourage detente through intensified economic ties, with a view to fostering eventual reunification of Germany. With this as the leitmotif of foreign policy toward the Soviet bloc, there was a fundamental basis for communication and dialogue between the blocs, that operated partly independently of the trajectory of the Cold War stand-off between the Soviet Union and the USA.

An example of this somewhat autonomous German–Soviet communication process is the recognition of urgent Soviet bloc need for extra finance, which began its official policy-life as a carrot for peaceful co-existence under the heading of Basket 2 of the 1975 Helsinki Agreement. The Federal Republic implemented Basket 2[4] far more than any other nation.

However, of all possible illustrations of the strength of this German–Soviet process, perhaps the most striking is the 1983 negotiation by none other than Franz-Josef Strauss, Bavarian Christian Social Union leader and fierce anti-Communist, of a DM1 billion credit for the DDR that made the

DDR internationally creditworthy. This was *at the precise moment* of the greatest tension over the siting of new, intermediate-range nuclear missiles in West Germany.

As Ash notes (1993: 104),

While Soviet negotiators walked out of the Geneva arms control talks and Soviet propaganda stormed, the GDR (joined in this by Hungary) continued to urge the need for dialogue and practical (above all, economic!) co-operation with the West.

Later, summarizing the twenty years of West German policy toward the Soviet bloc prior to its dissolution, he stresses how

From 1969–70 to 1989–90 the bankers and industrialists preceded and accompanied the diplomats and politicians on their way to Moscow, underpinning and facilitating their work. (p. 365)

In the end, he concludes, it was a mixture of Bonn's carrots and Washington's sticks, 'partly intentional and co-ordinated but also partly unintentional and conflictual, which produced the necessary mixture of incentive and deterrent, punishment and reward' (p. 374). On occasion even, what began as a carrot – loans to the Polish State – ended up as a stick in the form of insistence on full and timely repayment during the martial law period 1981–5.

It was at times a truly strange scenario, with Communist leaders running as hard as they could behind the scenes after FRG finance (Ash, 1993: 105, 118, 246–7, 306), while simultaneously leaning with all their might in their media on the revanchist German bogey as a device to try to scare their publics. To an important degree, however, this duality was also the product of different wings of opinion within the Soviet bloc hierarchy, with German reunification being the halt-or-die issue for Soviet hardliners (Beschloss and Talbott, 1993: 239–40).

The interaction between all these factors from a communication perspective would make a fascinating study. To date, sadly, it is a study that neither those who generally focus on *verkhushka* issues, nor those who focus on communication and culture, appear to have considered.

Schweizer effectively disregards all these elements in the process of regime change in the Soviet bloc. None the less, his analysis is of very considerable interest. It effectively confirms the claims of the Soviet *verkhushka* at that time that there was indeed a US master-strategy not simply to contain or roll back certain increases in Soviet power (e.g. Afghanistan, Angola), which had been the leitmotif of US policy since the 1940s. The intent was actually to dissolve the Soviet system altogether (Schweizer, 1994: 136, 201–2, 240). If the National Security Decision Directives, issuing from the National Security Planning Group, were indeed as influential as he argues, and if Casey in his tenure as CIA Director was indeed 'the most powerful director of central intelligence in American history . . . a key figure in the emerging US foreign policy' (Schweizer,

1994: 14; cf. Woodward, 1987: 287), then it is clear that these policies did much to confine the options of the Soviet bloc.

Schweizer concentrates on four key points in NSPG strategy: the Soviet Union's need for hard currency from oil and gas sales; the weakness of Soviet advanced technologies in certain key fields, especially in the informatics sector; and the threats to Soviet power from the very different insurgencies in Poland and Afghanistan. He argues that Casey's supreme achievement was gradually to persuade the Saudi government to lower its oil prices and thereby world oil prices. When they eventually did so in August 1985, cutting the price by two-thirds over the ensuing eight months (pp. 242, 256, 261), this had six simultaneous effects.

The four directly relevant to Soviet power were as follows. First, the USSR's hard currency earnings from its oil sales – it was the leading world oil producer in absolute volume, but was not an OPEC member – immediately plummeted. According to a 1983 US Treasury report cited by Schweizer (pp. 141–2), a single US dollar-per-barrel change in the world price of oil equalled between a half-billion and a billion dollars a year in Soviet hard currency earnings. Schweizer cites calculations that the USSR lost US$13 billion a year as a result (p. 262; cf. Smith, 1992: 90).

Secondly, the lower cost of oil meant that West European nations no longer had the same financial pressure to buy cheap Soviet natural gas. Oil and natural gas together represented 60–80 percent of Soviet hard currency earnings (Schweizer, 1994: 103). It also therefore meant that the Soviet negotiations with West European governments to help them build the necessary pipelines to deliver the gas from Siberia were no longer on the front burner. Future earnings from Siberian natural gas were now not easily utilizable in loan-negotiations with Western banks.

Thirdly, squeezed by this drop in world oil revenues, Iraq, Iran and Libya curtailed their Soviet arms purchases, the weapons sector being one of the USSR's few other money-spinning hard currency enterprises on the world market. That is estimated to have lost the Soviet economy another US$2 billion a year (p. 262).

Fourthly, as early as 1982 the USSR had cut its oil deliveries to East-Central Europe by 10 percent, and this drop in oil prices forced them to cut still further – in turn putting severe economic pressure on its client-states, which had to find the hard currency to make up the difference by buying on the world market.[5]

For the USSR, which had managed to give the illusion of slow but steady economic progress to its citizens during the Brezhnev era, much less because of internal economic performance than because of hard currency earnings from oil-sales, this was an abrupt policy shock that began to ramify through rather soon into everyday living standards. It was one key factor, along with the characteristic internal systemic and policy blockages, in the failure of economic *perestroika*.

High technology developments, especially in the computer field, are the second target identified by Schweizer (pp. 135–7, 200). The combination of

SDI ('Star Wars') development with the ban on even minimal computer sales to Soviet bloc nations, was intended more, he argues, as an economic than a military threat.[6] In fact it was both in equal measure, because contemporary warfare is intensively computerized. Averagely 70 percent of the cost of a warplane today, for example, consists of its electronics. If the Soviet military were unable to have the necessary economic and industrial high technology base, then its weapons systems would inexorably and rapidly fall behind (p. 198). Gorbachev's repeated demands that the USA cancel its SDI program represented his military leadership's recognition of precisely this reality, for however fantasy-based President Reagan's claim as to its capacity, it offered multiple military spin-offs. What Schweizer does not mention, however, is that of all the problems posed by the ban on computer sales, the difficulty in accessing all kinds of software was far more crippling even than the ban on hardware.[7]

The remaining elements in the NSPG strategy, namely support to Polish and Afghan opposition movements, were played out as follows. The active support given to *Solidarnosc*, often clandestinely via Sweden, rose sharply from under US$200,000 channeled through the AFL–CIO in 1980 to $2 million in 1984, to $8 million in 1985 (pp. 60, 76, 84–92, 146, 164–5, 184, 225). The amounts, though an infinitesimal proportion of the US budget, represented a newly aggressive – and dollar-for-dollar, very helpful – support of *Solidarnosc*. Much of the money went on communications equipment of one kind or another, from computers and fax machines to a highly sophisticated military-originated C3I (Command, Communications, Control, Information) installation for the movement's leadership.

Similarly in Afghanistan, initial support included sharing satellite reconnaissance information with some of the guerrilla groups for targeting strategy (pp. 118–19), and then culminated in the supply of Stinger missiles, widely credited with intimidating Soviet military aircraft, including helicopters, from flying combat or transport missions (pp. 268–70).[8]

The significance of Poland's political movements for the decline of the Soviet bloc has been argued earlier in this book, and by many others. Equally important in a different way was Afghanistan, not because of any strategic significance (though its natural gas in the north of the country was useful), but because it represented a 'bleeding wound', as Gorbachev put it at the 27th Party Congress in 1986: a source of increasing subterranean anger in the Soviet public, and a monument to the reckless and bloody overconfidence of the Brezhnev regime's last years. It also cemented Gorbachev's and Shevardnadze's recognition that systematic repression would not solve Soviet problems, either internally or in East-Central Europe.

The Polish case, however, raises a key question for this chapter's contention, inasmuch as it presents with particular clarity both a cultural and social movement dimension, and a superpower-struggle dimension. On the one hand, it is evidence for the impact of popular cultural forces and their communication; on the other, those forces were enabled to communicate far more effectively through the intervention of an outside strategy, in this instance originating in an elite fraction inside the *verkhushka* of the US superpower.

For cheer-leaders, these data may alternatively be held to be enlivening or discomforting. For Schweizer, they are enlivening, because they seem to show that *Solidarnosc* moved from acute disorganization under martial law to effective mobilization as a national movement. For others, they may be dispiriting, because they suggest that Soviet and Polish Communist Party claims were in fact correct, namely that there would have been no *Solidarnosc* without substantial and continuing support from the West. For this analysis, all these 'winning-side' conclusions are marginal. The issue of interest is solely the composite – quite probably the necessarily composite – character of *Solidarnosc*. It is futile to examine *Solidarnosc* either purely as Polish heroism, or simply as a shrunken balloon puffed back into shape and flight[9] through the vision and drive of the late William Casey.

From all the foregoing considerations, it is first of all crystal clear that for communication researchers to focus on communication, media and culture alone, as a form of playing to their strengths, is to underscore their weaknesses. Communication research can only operate convincingly if it embraces its focus of study in close relation to such other foci. Its intellectual task is not to justify its existence within the spectrum of university departments, but to generate the most productive and accurate analyses of which its practitioners are capable. Perhaps the transitions within the Soviet bloc demonstrate this truth with particular clarity, but the more general realities of change, power, conflict, the state, economic process in every social formation equally do so if properly conceptualized.

Secondly, however, although it is impossible to do here more than note them, there were numerous communicative dimensions involved in these politico-economic processes. Under this heading we have already noted as important what was described above as the communication circuitry between US and Soviet leaders, and the relation between that interaction and media communication in a variety of the nations most intimately involved. To these issues may be added the whole dimension of informatics, including its key military aspects; the provision of communication technology to *Solidarnosc*; and the communicative interrelation between declining economic function and regime legitimacy, and between decline in global power and regime legitimacy. These last two topics will now be addressed in a little detail.

Communication in Media Silence: Soviet Bloc Economic Decline

We noted above a major external impetus to the disarray and disintegration of Soviet bloc economies, with Poland and Hungary already running giant deficits with Western banks, and with not a single economy evincing the dramatic growth-rates of earlier decades (Köves, 1992: 1–15; Magas, 1990:

66; Ramet, 1991, Tables 1 and 2). The internal causes were multiple, and cannot be solely ascribed to the planning 'system', so called, even though that was the overriding problem of the economic structure. Nor do they ethically vindicate the extremely dangerous confrontational tactics of the Reagan regime and the NSPG in its fierce military build-up.[10] None the less, this economic stagnation, given a major extra twist by NSPG policies, was probably the primary underlying cause of the collapse of the regimes. It was mediated to their publics in numerous ways, but only toward the very end by media.

This mediation/communication is necessarily our focus. How *was* economic stagnation conveyed, given that Soviet bloc media surely did not highlight the problem, embarrassing statistics were either falsified or their publication discontinued altogether, and that real-life comparisons between western and eastern living standards were restricted to the relatively small percentage of trusted Party members, diplomats and trade officials permitted to travel? For sure, the identification of problems in these economies had been relatively normal in the news media from Brezhnev onwards. However, the problems were normally flagged as issues now being grappled with in order to perfect the system, and never as systemic.

Some evidence (e.g. Gregory and Dietz, 1991; McGregor, 1991) indicates that, correspondingly, widespread critique of the economic system itself was unusual even in the latter years, with objections being rather to specific issues such as the lack of incentives or of work-discipline. If there were any suspicion that such responses were bred of political cautiousness, then that suspicion can be laid to rest by examining the responses of a major émigré survey conducted in the early 1980s (Silver, 1987: 114–15). This found that even of those asserting that the USA had *nothing* whatsoever to learn from the USSR, almost 50 percent were strongly in favor of having the state control heavy industry (as opposed to a mere 7 percent who had something positive to say about collective agriculture).

How, moreover, if there really had been intense and universal dissatisfaction with the previous economic system, of a kind fomenting jacqueries and even revolutionary change, should we interpret the cynical and depressed public attitudes to economic reform during the years of transition and since (Gregory, 1991; Urnov, 1991)? What should we conclude from the dismissive attitudes of many Soviet workers to *Solidarnosc* (except in the Baltic republics and western Ukraine), namely that Polish workers' militancy simply risked taking bread from Soviet tables (Teague, 1988)? Did this reaction – accusatory rather than supportive – not have a connection with the sour conviction of many Russians that to their own considerable cost they were massively subsidizing the other Soviet republics, not to mention foreign dependencies such as Cuba and Vietnam?

All these seem better interpreted as indices of allocative or policy perceptions and consequent grievances, rather than necessarily of opposition to the economic system as such. If so, that might tell us that the media's role in the situation was successfully to take economic structures off the public agenda altogether – an inversion of a standard theory of media functioning in which news media are said to set public agendas, but not what people think about the items on the agenda (McCombs and Shaw, 1972).[11] In which case, Moore and Tumin's (1949) classic analysis of the stabilizing social functions of ignorance would need to be brought into play in conjunction with the agenda-setting approach to make sense of these Soviet data.

It may be argued that citizens were too afraid to express systemic opposition, and furthermore that the data above are Soviet rather than Polish or Hungarian. Yet the period we are discussing is the late 1980s, when many of the taboos of an earlier period had been lifted, either through *glasnost* policies in the USSR, or in the typically less constrained polities of Hungary and Poland. It is indeed fair to say that public attitudes to the economic system in the latter nations were more critical than those generally to be found in the Soviet Union, but even in them such criticisms were normally to be found among intellectuals rather than among the general population, which had thoroughly ingested one truth at least, namely that job-security was much higher in the East than in the West. Furthermore, it was well known that one major cause of economic stagnation in those two countries was the need to repay Western banks' loans, a feature of integration into – not separation from – the Western economic system.

The picture we are facing demands that we explain how economic information, despite being restricted and/or distorted, none the less percolated through to the general public. Let me sketch out a plausible analysis of the impact of media in these different nations in not conveying the realities of economic decline and in none the less arguing for economic reform. As we examine this, we need constantly to keep in mind that people in a number of nations may experience economic stagnation in modes that have little or no media echo or amplification. The Bush administration's dogged refusal over 1990–1 to acknowledge that the United States' economy was in serious recession, rarely challenged in earnest at the time by news media analysts, would constitute a loosely parallel instance of denial in the West.

The first reality which demands recognition is that in Soviet bloc countries cash played much less of a role in everyday life than in the West. Savings were very high for a substantial number of people for the simple reason there was nothing much of interest to purchase. Even the old ladies who for a pittance swept the streets or sat 'supervising' metro escalators – a phenomenon often noticed by Western visitors – did so because they were generally guaranteed accommodation as a result. Furthermore, certain basics such as bread, transport and utilities were heavily subsidized. Thus inability to afford many elementary items or to meet credit-payments was not the source of economic discontent. People complained about the quality of shoes or other consumer items, but not particularly about lack of funds. Workers could normally guarantee at least one solid, if unappetizing meal a day at their workplace canteen, without having to buy it, cook it or clean up afterwards. Furthermore the workplace was a service-distribution node, not only for meals, but also for housing and medical care, in a way totally unfamiliar in the West.

This was not totally true across the bloc. The Polish regime's intermittent attempts to impose sharp price rises for food acted as the trigger for significant unrest there in 1970, 1976 and 1980. Furthermore, fast price inflation in Hungary and Poland during the 1980s, which did not really reach Russians until about 1990, did produce economic angst of a type more recognizable in the West. The 1980s Soviet émigré survey already referred to found that 61 percent of the respondents felt real wages had fallen over the previous five years up till they left the USSR, but that shortages – *defitsit* – were what upset people most (Gregory, 1987: 259–60). They had the cash, but could not find the items.

Furthermore, those most likely to be irritated with the slow rate of economic advance and thus with the system, were precisely those who had been most successful within the system (Millar and Clayton, 1987), the greatest beneficiaries in a sense of the historic trends in mass education and urbanization that Lewin (1988) has argued were the undertow of the Gorbachev phenomenon.

Where the declining level of economic growth more generally impacted on public consciousness was in areas of life such as cramped and scarce housing, poor health care and severe environmental pollution, all of which could often be described as 'Victorian' if not even Dickensian in type. The appalling rates of infant mortality and of respiratory disorders in industrial areas were only the most salient indices of the failure of the senior regimes of the socialist bloc to deliver a viable standard of living to their citizens. Such bitter personal experiences, including the need to pay physicians substantial sums under the counter ('on the left') to avoid endless waits for treatment, certainly impacted on people's feelings about their conditions of life (for Soviet data, see Feshbach and Friendly, 1992).

At the same time, there was no comparison possible for the vast majority on these issues. Official media avoided such topics, with Soviet infant mortality statistics even ceasing to be published under the Brezhnev regime, and instead cynically dwelt on such issues as the very real plight of African Americans and Native Americans in order to try to displace attention elsewhere.[12] The alternative sources, *samizdat* media, had a generally weak circulation outside Poland. This is not to deny their significance in the longer process of rebellion, indeed their surprising significance given their size, but their puny voice does highlight the absence of regular doses of comparative information about economic living standards. They also, as might be supposed, had little access to reliable data on the economy as a whole. Foreign radio services, Red and White Tass, foreign newspapers available only to the already trusted, and the tales of a minority of travelers to Western lands, circulating through relatives and friends, were the only other sources.

Thus in everyday life there were harsh economic experiences, as time went by increasingly so, yet without any clear yardsticks to know how to assess them fully. It is plausible that this had two effects. One was to accumulate a sense of frustration and anger, no less real for being diffuse. The second was that the simplest target for this anger consisted of one's fellow-citizens. Hence, arguably, the degradation of relations in public, symbolized perhaps most tangibly by the virtual class war between waiters and patrons in eating establishments, or between store assistants and customers, but at all events corroding any civility or trust between members of the public. Kira Muratova's 1989 film *Astyenicheskii Sindrom* ('The Aesthenic Syndrome') portrayed this degradation in graphic terms for Russia, and indeed it must be said that the syndrome was even more advanced there than in Poland or Hungary.

A chance encounter in Budapest in the mid-1980s tellingly illuminates both this difference between bloc nations, and the absence of yardsticks. A 'believing' Communist couple from Leningrad wandering around a Budapest supermarket expressed to a friend of the writer's their deep perplexity at how, just since 1948, Hungary had managed to vault over the USSR on the path to Communism, because clearly there was more abundance in Hungary than in Russia, and they well knew full Communism promised abundance . . . In their case, the surging frustration and bitterness of which I have spoken were not evident, but confusion as to how to interpret Soviet reality in the absence of yardsticks was present in full measure.

Within this context, the proclamation of economic reforms by these regimes, trumpeted repeatedly in the official media, probably had a counter-effect. As life got progressively tougher during the 1980s, the merits of reforms, the visibility of reforms, the very purpose of reforms, evoked deeper and deeper cynicism. In the USSR for example, from quite different political stances, both the weekly *Ekonomicheskaya Gazeta*, later *Ekonomika I Zhizn'*,[13] and the government daily, *Izvestiia*, ran stories during the late 1980s on initiatives in radical economic reform. For the former, this was simply a nod in the direction of then-current *perestroika* orthodoxy, while for the latter it represented a strong, if conceptually vague commitment to improve the economic condition of the country. Yet the stories in each newspaper actually served to emphasize the rarity, disconnection from mainstream procedures, and thus the virtual irrelevance of the economic changes trumpeted from on high.

Secondly, the emergence of a highly visible class of petty entrepreneurs, stimulated by the state (Avdeenko et al., 1990; Slider, 1991; Zubek, 1991), led to yet further anger, this time directed against the new private firms ('cooperatives') in the USSR and against businessmen driving Mercedes and BMWs and living in fancy villas in Hungary and Poland. The regimes were widely seen as supporting the re-emergence of ostentatious thievery.

Thirdly, the attempt to substitute the economic signals of a command economy – the plan, the telephone calls from above to below – with the price-signals of a capitalist economy, were repeatedly stymied by ineptitude, irresolution and ignorance of the new rules of the game at all levels. The phone calls from above began to dry up, but were not replaced by any other economic signals. Drift, stagnation and waste ensued on an unprecedented scale, even for sovietized economies.

In turn, since the regimes arrogated all power and authority to themselves, they alone could be held responsible for the entire mess and growing unfairness. This concentration of responsibility on a single source, the government, was arguably a potent solvent of those elements of confidence that still persisted in the public mind.

Thus the putative impact of official media silence as the economic decline gathered speed, was actually to open wider the already institutionalized gap between the state and the general public that Gorbachev vainly sought to close with *glasnost* policies and promises of 'radical economic reforms'. After the initial couple of years' heady excitement of revelations, mostly about the Stalinist past of nearly two generations before, the public began to be much hungrier for substantive economic improvement than for *glasnost*. The Brezhnev years began to seem to some to have been tranquil, manageable, in economic terms almost halcyon. In Poland and Hungary, in any case, the quite widespread current of thought that saw their states as client regimes had already served to subvert their legitimacy. Economic hardships there merely intensified the slide.

The widespread conviction in Poland and Hungary at the close of the 1980s that 'the market' would miraculously solve all problems – a kind of junior high school Milton Friedman ra-ra economics – was not at all evident in the USSR. In the two former countries it served simply as a commentary on people's frustrations, not on their informed opinions. In the Soviet Union there was considerable foreboding, a deep fear that yet another gigantic experiment was going to be played out on their backs, a fear which the first half of the 1990s did nothing at all to dispel. There was no going back, the Gorbachev reforms were producing still worse and worse results, and the future was totally murky. The period of intense public exhilaration so visible in East-Central Europe and the Balkans at the time of the regime changes was not replicated in Soviet Russia.

Thus the degree of public alienation engendered by declining economic realities and their confused and misrepresented media definitions created a political climate in the USSR permitting but not at all welcoming radical economic change. In their pessimism, Russian citizens probably had a keener sense for the likely economic realities of the ensuing transitional decade than did many Hungarian or Polish citizens at the time of the change. But average citizens, whether for or against, were not in charge; and as the next section of this chapter shows, it was the recognition dawning upon the *nomenklatura* that there was no way back to international influence or economic prowess that opened up the gates to irrevocable change.

Communication in Media Silence: Soviet Bloc Global Decline

International relations were the other key element in the media non-picture in the Soviet bloc. By 'international relations', I do not mean the exquisitely boring niceties of diplomacy, or of missile-counts. I mean, rather, the powerfully erosive interacting effects of, initially, the long piecemeal slide away from the Stalin model in Hungary, then the *Solidarnosc* movement in Poland and the Afghan resistance, then the sudden virtual cessation of political signals from Moscow to the client regimes from 1988 onwards, then the 0–60 mph ricochet effects of collapse in the DDR, Czechoslovakia, Romania and Bulgaria, and finally the obdurate stance of tiny Lithuania in asserting its independence against Soviet power. In this concatenation of events needs also to be mentioned the long-term erosion over nearly two decades of effective Soviet influence in the lands of Brezhnev's outreach, from Egypt to Chile, and from India to Angola. Even Vietnam and Cuba, whose regimes stayed loyal until they themselves were cut adrift, increasingly functioned as burden rather than as opportunity for the Soviet power structure.

Thus from the apogee of Soviet global influence, reflecting the supposedly inevitable world trend toward Communism, with its implicit boost to the traditional nationalism of Russia – in the form either of being the 'elder brother' and core of the Soviet system, or of being the spiritual heart of the planet, the 'Third Rome'[14] of the future – the final descent was measured but unceasing. What did that signify, over time, to the power structures and the public of the Soviet Union and its bloc? How were these realities represented and mediated?

Furthermore, what were the effects of the 'hard guy/soft guy' stances of Reaganite 'Star Wars' belligerence, and 'helpful' West German *Ostpolitik* and *Osthandel*? As we saw above, these were not tidily coordinated, for German and US interests were different in certain respects, but we should not underestimate their joint influence on fracturing the cohesion, even the morale, of the more perceptive members of the Soviet bloc hierarchy. The question then is how if at all this erosion of morale and growing uncertainty within the apex actually trickled down to the general public, since it was not reflected in Soviet bloc public media. American imperialists and German revanchists were regularly slung into the same pigsty by the Soviet press, and bloc successes and advances around the globe were continually feted. Foreign news was, it should be recalled, rather more credible than domestic news (although in Poland and Hungary this was not necessarily the case).

It is a complicated question to which there are no answers immediately available. We might hazard that a deepening political angst in the power structure was fed by a combination of factors: by select media, such as White and Red Tass (Smith, 1976: ch. 14), by the *nomenklatura*'s privileged access to superior global news sources such as the *Financial Times* or *Der Spiegel*, by the bulletins of foreign broadcast stations (Shanor, 1985), by the stories told to their families by people who had visited the 'outposts', such as Angola or Laos, especially by veterans from Afghanistan as that war dragged on, by returning diplomats and trade delegations, and by the continuing role of rumor as a mode of communication operating at all levels of Soviet bloc life. We might equally note the KGB as a source for those close to its more senior foreign section personnel.

It is also true that there were significant generational splits regarding foreign policy priorities, even in the *verkhushka*. Pravda (1992b: 2–3, 18) notes how for Gorbachev's cohort East-Central Europe was not a post-Nazi *cordon sanitaire*, but 'a badly managed sphere of influence', with events in Poland indicative of 'the fragility of the command system'. Certainly the *verkhushki* talked about it a great deal: at the very end, through 1989 and early 1990, Gorbachev met with various Eastern European leaders 103 times, and Central Committee officials met with each other 147 times (Pravda, 1992b: 32, n.15). Huge numbers of meetings of Warsaw Pact officials also took place at that period (Eyal, 1992: 51–2). Within Comecon, there was a last-minute mad gallop in 1988 to switch bloc trading out of the fictive convertible ruble and into each country's now supposedly convertible currency (Smith, 1992: 78–9), an index of despair and ignorance at the top if ever there was one, given that marketized price mechanisms then barely operated on any level anywhere within the Soviet bloc.

In other words there was a gigantic volume of inter-elite conversation in process, but at the same time to very little effect judged by the rapid collapse of the bloc. Was the primary impact of all this communication the recognition that indeed the dam had given way and was about to burst whatever anyone did?

In the end, it is no doubt true that the full picture was only available to a tiny, trusted minority. Yet especially in a top-heavy power structure, the morale of the apex is likely to be rather determinative of others' morale. The *verkhushka* in the Soviet Union consisted of the military high command, the military industrialists, and the KGB and Party hierarchies. The system worked similarly in the other bloc countries, albeit generally minus the national military as a resolutely pro-Soviet force (Barany, 1992).

So it is hard to suppose that within that apex the evaluation of the following issues had only a slight effect on the disintegration of the system: (a) the outdistancing of the Soviet economy; (b) the consequent threat to military competitiveness, especially in the computer and laser fields; (c) the decline of the Soviet empire; and (d) the possibility of long-term revitalization through foreign capitalist investment (the true promise of *Ostpolitik*).

In other words, we need to diversify our understanding of Soviet bloc 'audiences'. This does not simply mean adding such criteria as gender, ethnicity or age cohort. It means expanding the typical Western focus on the mass audience in order to concentrate equally on the elite audience, and then on its forms of communicative relation with the mass audience. In particular we need to recognize that the focus on the economy and media in the previous section is intimately related to the focus on international relations in this one.

The fact that these processes are even now inaccessible to systematic empirical study does not mean that we should bypass them in our analysis of the role of communication in regime transition in Eastern Europe. They are the obverse, in a sense, of the remarks above on the modes through which economic decline was communicated to and experienced by the general public during the period of transition. Together, I would propose, these modes of representation constituted the partial and contradictory communication of agonizing present problems and slender future options which steadily gnawed away at the Soviet elite's own confidence in its rule, and at its already very limited hegemony (in the Gramscian sense) over the Soviet Union and the Soviet bloc. The impact within the elite may initially have been in the direction of tightening up internal control, as was the case after the Prague Spring (Kagarlitsky, 1988: 198ff.), and similarly in response to *Solidarnosc* (Ruble, 1983). The fact remains that even the Soviet elite was acutely aware of these developments and their portent. No military or repressive actions were capable of solving the problem over the longer term, or even the shorter term, as the instant collapse of the August 1991 putsch finally demonstrated, and as Afghanistan had already demonstrated. Thus they backed into the future.

Conclusions

As already argued at the close of Chapter 1, despite the undeniable importance of politico-economic analysis, and the political economy of media, there remains a great deal to achieve in moving beyond the merely descriptive and sometimes simply denunciatory strategies that often substitute for such research. This chapter, without having been able to develop any such model, has sought both to emphasize that dimension of the changes in Russia, Poland and Hungary from 1980 to 1995, and to suggest a number of specific points at which communico-cultural and politico-economic analysis are necessarily imbricated the one with the other. The particular points raised are not considered exhaustive by any means.

In the succeeding chapter, we will survey a number of the mediatic and cultural changes that have taken place since the biennium. In doing so, we will endeavor to bear in mind both these levels of analysis.

Notes

1 Gorbachev's 1986 calls for reconstruction and acceleration of technical advance (*perestroika* and *uskoreniye*) acknowledged there were problems, but implied that with the usual Soviet remedy of collective voluntarism they could be and would be overcome. The question was not whether but how, and how soon. Soviet voluntarism had a long history, again with its roots in the winning of the Civil War against colossal odds, but visible especially in the farm collectivization policy, in the crash industrialization policy, in Khrushchev's sudden

attempted reforms of economic planning and the Party, in his policy of planting corn in scores of millions of acres of unsuitable soil in Kazakhstan, and in the policy seriously considered under Brezhnev of diverting water from the great Ob river in Siberia all the way to Central Asia. Soviet voluntarism's victims were legion.

2 Also referred to in Woodward (1987: 185), but simply as 'the informal high-level gathering for the important foreign-policy issues'. Its initial members included Reagan, Bush, Weinberger, Haig, McFarlane, Pipes, and Reagan's successive National Security Directors Richard Allen, William Clark, John Poindexter.

3 Andropov was KGB Director for fifteen years until he succeeded Brezhnev. Some of those closest to him (Kaiser, 1991: 54) were precisely the young, energetic 'Sixties guys' (*shestidyesyatilyetniki*) such as Burlatsky and Bovin who as chief editors of the key weekly *Literaturnaya Gazeta* and the government daily *Izvestiia* played such a significant role in supporting Gorbachev's *glasnost* policies. See the fifth point in the brief characterization of the late Soviet state in Chapter 1, and Chapter 8, note 6.

4 The most talked about was Basket 3, which dealt with civil rights and communication issues.

5 The fifth and sixth effects were that US consumers were suddenly paying far less, directly and indirectly, for oil; and that the US shored up its position as protector of the Saudi regime – and its oil-fields – by selling it AWACS-equipped planes as its part of the bargain.

6 Even though Reagan was behind it because he thought it was a perfect military strategy, ethically acceptable because it did not involve the theory of Mutual Assured Destruction (Beschloss and Talbott, 1993: 113).

7 Information given the writer in a personal conversation with Dr Oleg Smirnov, Director of the Institute of Automated Systems of the Soviet Academy of Sciences, during a Moscow research visit in 1986.

8 Jonathan Steele (1994: 172–3) points out, however, that the basic decision to withdraw was taken in March 1986, and that the Stinger missiles were not deployed until the close of that year.

9 In the previous chapter we saw how the Polish strike-wave in the first part of 1988, that deeply unsettled the regime and was a major prod toward the Round Table talks of early 1989, was not organized by *Solidarnosc*, and indeed took its leaders by surprise. Schweizer's strictly external-factor analysis is reminiscent of those who explain the genesis of *Solidarnosc* by reference to the Pope's visit, or to Radio Free Europe.

10 Which practically constituted a Pyrrhic victory for the USA as it struggled with its consequent monumental budget deficit throughout the 1990s, its politicians constantly pretending that guns were not going to cost butter for *its* citizens.

11 See the further discussion of this approach in Chapter 7.

12 The attempt sadly often led to the reverse assumption, namely that such groups were in reality living high off the hog.

13 'Economic Newspaper', later 'The Economy Today' (literally, 'Economy and Life').

14 When Constantinople (the Second Rome) fell into Muslim hands in 1453, Russian Orthodox ideologues soon began to claim the center of world Christianity had now passed to Moscow (the Third Rome), a claim finally ratified within Orthodox Christianity in 1589. Many nations cherish a myth of their unique superiority, and this one played a major role in recent centuries in Russian political as well as religious thought. One of the attractions of Stalin's insistence in the mid-1920s that socialism could be created in a single country, namely Russia – rather than there having to be a group of nations espouse it more or less at the same time – was that it could seem as though Russia was once again bearing the torch for all humanity, albeit a secular and modernizing torch.

6

Media in Post-Sovietized Societies
from 1989–91 to 1995

'How to freeze flux' might be a pithier chapter heading, given the task of this chapter to try to convey the incredibly fast-moving developments in the region during the first half of the 1990s. Only six years after the previous system had disintegrated in East-Central Europe and four years after the disintegration of the former Soviet Union, it was in some ways premature to be characterizing the reconsolidation of the socio-economic and mediatic structure that had taken place. Furthermore, only three out of over twenty post-sovietized nations are under scrutiny here (not counting the constituent segments of former Yugoslavia, which both was and was not sovietized).

Yet, as Hankiss (1994: 1) underlined in an essay on the so-called Hungarian media wars over control of broadcasting of the early 1990s,

> Present day events and developments are questions of life and death for each individual, family, group and class in these societies; it is being decided in these months and years who will be the winners and who will be the losers in the next decades; who will profit from, and who will lose by the transition to a new social and economic model; whose children will be poor and whose will be rich . . . Too much is at stake.

Thus a provisional attempt at summarization and interpretation is important, even though hindsight will inevitably reconfigure some judgments offered here. It is, furthermore, necessary to do so, as this book argues throughout, in order the better to establish the total process of societal change which needs to be engaged with if media communication theory is to advance. Issues and processes must be addressed that go beyond the currently meagre source of perspectives on which that theory's discourses often pivot.

This chapter will therefore focus on certain commonalities and contrasts between Russia, Poland and Hungary in this key period. (Readers rather unfamiliar with the region or the period may find it helpful to glance again at the latter sections of Chapter 2 before proceeding further.) However, before surveying their specifics, certain preliminary observations are necessary regarding the limitations of existing sources:

1   the question of television's pre-eminent position;
2   the proclivity for capital city coverage;
3   the predominance of legal issues in some analyses;

4 the bias toward news rather than entertainment media, or everyday cultural forms;
5 the unresolved question of the performance of media professionals trained under the previous regimes.

(1) By far the most attention has been paid by both journalists and academic researchers to television in the process of transition, much more than to cinema, advertising, radio or even the printed press, let alone music, dress and other 'everyday' media. This is partly because commentators shared today's conventional wisdom concerning the immediacy and reach of television. Admittedly, TV's impact was accentuated in these three nations by the initial near-collapse of newspaper circulations, consequent upon the withdrawal of traditional state subsidies to the press and the simultaneously sky-rocketing costs of newsprint. It was also probably because in a rather uncritical awe of the conventional wisdom, the authorities in all three countries were fixated on TV as the Medium of Mediums, the Shiva who could both create and destroy, in this case create or destroy their hold on power and, as they saw it, either lubricate or trash their uniquely ample talents for guiding their nations through the transition. (And thus too, no doubt, could secure or block their passage to an honored place in the history books.) In the case of the financially corrupt members of the emerging oligarchies, fear of independent media had yet another basis.

Without then wishing to suggest a drastically revisionist account of the role of television in Eastern Europe, it is important at the outset to acknowledge that there has been something of a mild and unplanned consensus that has overpromoted its significance. Political leaders, dazzled by its huge audiences, paid it especially close attention and, thereby, gave a major topic of discourse to journalists in the short term and academic researchers in the longer term – which in turn fed the consensus. TV may not have been so high on the public's agenda as on politicians' and commentators' radar screens.

(2) It is also important to emphasize that in Russia in particular, but also in Poland and Hungary, both reporting and academic media research have been capital-city-intensive. In all three nations the capitals have been of superordinate political significance for as long as anyone can remember, but it is also the case that they are quite deeply resented in the rest of the country for their pretensions to superiority. The *warszawka*, the intellectual-political Warsaw elite, the Budapest 'cosmopolitans', the Moscow *intelligenty*, are all targets of both suspicion and derision in the provinces. Some of this reaction is indeed rural idiocy, but some represents an important assertion of regional power and identity, or at least worth.

Thus the analysis of media communication in the transition is incomplete without appreciation of the situation throughout the country. Some commentators have suggested that the bedrock of a functioning democratic culture is even more what happens locally than what happens in the metropolis (Huelle, 1992; Rychard, 1992). For the large population and vast expanse of Russia, this is axiomatic. It is also problematic for this study, because at the time of writing there was not even a single collection of essays on any of these nations that systematically offered regional perspectives on media at any point before, during or after the transitions. Given the political restiveness of Russian regions in the early 1990s, the sharp decline in Moscow and St Petersburg media circulating to the provinces, and the sudden simultaneous growth in provincial media (that did not generally penetrate beyond their geographical locales), a full understanding of the Russian media scenario at that time is particularly hard to achieve without a regional perspective. All that can be done at this point, therefore, is to note this significant lacuna.

(3) A further problem, closely related to the issue of television's pre-eminent position through its typically being the chief bone of contention, is that many analyses of post-transition media have seemed obsessed with issues of media law. The issues had the virtue of seeming straightforward: would nations that had suffered from a surfeit of official interference in media communication be able to craft laws and even constitutional provisions that would guarantee media independence? And how far would private ownership of media, like private ownership of land or business, be an important structural component of a freer media system and be written into new laws?[1] How far would it be a condition of encouraging private investment in media? Furthermore, in a highly fluctuating situation, media analysts could focus on something specific, the wording of legislative drafts, which were tangible and appeared to promise more structure and predictability in a future when they had perhaps been made into law, than the murk and fog that swirled over the media scene in other respects at that time.

Given these premises, the long-drawn-out agony of media law non-events[2] that will be noted below (though not described on a blow-by-blow basis), has greatly preoccupied some researchers. Perhaps it has overly preoccupied them, especially in listing clauses never even legislated.

In many ways, the key dimension of any of the numerous legislative drafts that were battled over would have to be whatever censorship restrictions the drafts retained from the previous regime, or new ones they invented. In this case, opposition to them was not a non-event. It is very doubtful, however, that legislation in a positive direction, in the direction of freedom for the entire public to create its own realms of communication, could actively generate those realms. Legislation would have to follow the public's demands in order to ratify and secure what had already been achieved.[3] It could not initiate it. It is for these reasons that the focus on media laws has not so much been misplaced, but over-emphasized, especially since in the absence of a media law – or in the presence of conflicting media decrees – the various media went ahead and blazed their own trails, paying sometimes more and sometimes less attention to reactions from the state authorities. Is what they did of no interest? Did it have no implications for the future?

As Price (1996: 128) has observed, 'especially at times of transition, formal statements captured in the words of laws cannot be taken at face value . . . the language of media statutes may have a purpose of camouflage or may be designed to placate an international community rather than serve as the operative guide to conduct.' He goes on, however, to assert (p. 129ff.) that draft approaches and political reactions to them can be as important as the final product, and perhaps from the point of view of a legal or constitutional historian that may be the case. From the perspective of trying to grasp the interaction between media, law, and societal developments within the transition process, however, laws that were never enacted, let alone had their provisions enforced, seem a much less fertile source of insight than media institutions' actual trajectory.

Having issued this caveat, the legal angle of vision does none the less throw up some interesting and important questions in analysing the mediatic process, and that research will be readily drawn upon below at certain points.

(4) Research also concentrated overwhelmingly on news rather than entertainment media, or everyday cultural process. This is understandable given the central role of public information in the democratic process, especially in this key period of transition. At the same time, it may have vastly over-emphasized the interest of the public in news, overlooking the many indices of widespread alienation from and disaffection with governmental political life. Entertainment media also purvey information and education, albeit in different modes and over the longer term. News media are typically chained to crisis, of which there were plenty during this period, but the crises by and large seemed to sputter to a close without resolving most of the painful dilemmas experienced by the public. In such conditions, involvement in various forms of entertainment or in alternative everyday cultural manifestations becomes an especially significant communicative process, and such was often the case in these three nations.

(5) The other general issue across all three was the persistence of the overwhelming majority of the previous media personnel in their original positions, with no new preparation for the new situation. Many critics, internal and external, accused them of simply reproducing traditional styles of processing media communications, albeit with a different content. Others pointed to the role of a number of journalists in the front line of the campaign for political change.

However, the new situation was a huge professional challenge. This was so whether it involved journalists simultaneously struggling to understand for themselves – and then convey to their audiences – the mechanisms of capitalism and the vagaries of the transition; or whether it was getting rid of the censor inside one's head; or whether it was learning a new style of using language, opposed to the wooden wording of times past; or whether it was a question of learning to communicate events succinctly, not fogged with interminable speculation paid by the line. Conflicts between political generations also surfaced, with impatient younger media professionals chafing at the seeming spinelessness of older colleagues. Klíma (1996) has provided an absorbing fictional account of many of these processes from within the Czech context.

These five general comments concerning the available data and their focus need to be borne in mind throughout all three of the ensuing country studies. The published sources cited below have been helpful in interpreting the wild flux of mediatic events during these years, although inevitably all have been displaced at certain points by subsequent developments. The present analysis, although benefitting from a slightly longer period in which to assess developments, will ineluctably be subjected to the same re-evaluation.

The first such book-length source is the survey offered by Vatchnadze (1991) of media developments in the USSR immediately leading up to the attempted putsch of August 1991. Although technically preceding the period covered in this chapter, sociologically it is meaningless to absolutize the period between 18 and 22 August of that year. Androunas (1993) similarly focuses largely on the period immediately before the December 1991 collapse of the Soviet state, although her final chapter reviews developments since then up until January 1993. Goban-Klas (1994) primarily studies what he terms the 'orchestration' of the media in post-war Poland up to 1989, while noting events from then up to the middle of 1993 in the final section of his book. Splichal (1994) offers a comparative account of media developments in East-Central Europe from Poland to Bulgaria up to mid-1993. In the final chapters of their book Høyer, Epp and Vihalemm (1993) briefly address comparable developments in Estonia, Latvia and Lithuania up to 1992. The essays in Paletz, Jakubowicz and Novosel (1995) take the story as far as 1992 for one former Soviet republic (Belarus) and the former Soviet protectorates in East-Central Europe aside from Bulgaria. Giorgi (1995) reviews the Polish, Czech and Hungarian media scenarios up until early 1993. Most recently at the time of writing, Ganley (1996) has provided a quite comprehensive account of the spectrum of media, including computer communications, in the last days of the USSR. She focuses principally upon the years 1990–1, with especial attention (chapters 9–15) to the roles of media communication in the failed August 1991 coup. Price (1996: 83–149), on some levels akin to the present text, deploys empirical information on media performance during many of the Soviet bloc countries' transitions to wider issues, moving beyond the specific analysis of particular nations. In his case, he offers a series of reflections on the interacting roles of law and media in contemporary society in providing a sphere of public debate in which questions of national identity and globalism can be addressed. Boyle (forthcoming) offers an absorbing account of the mediatic process in the initial transition process in Eastern Germany up until the reimposition of Bonn's media model. A text by Sparks (forthcoming), addressing questions of broadcasting and democracy in post-transition Poland, Czechia, Slovakia and Hungary, also provides a valuable source and covers more recent developments.

These were far from the only published sources available at the time of writing. Others include major essays (see the Bibliography) by Condee and Padunov on everyday cultural flux in Russia, and by Jakubowicz (1990, 1992a, 1992b, 1993, 1994, 1995a, 1995b) on Polish and East-Central European media; research by Jakab and Gálik (1991), by Szekfü and Valko (1991), and by Kováts and others (1993, 1994, 1995), on Hungarian media; the *Post-Soviet Media Law and Policy Newsletter*; the *Soviet/East European Research Reports* and their successors the *RFE/RL Bulletins* and *Research Reports* up to 1994, and their successors in turn *OMRI Reports* and *Transition* from 1995; *Prism*, the Jamestown Foundation electronic news magazine on the CIS and the Baltic nations; collections of essays in the journals *MédiasPouvoirs* (26, 1992) and *Réseaux* (53, 1992); and anthologies edited by Autissier and others (1992; 1993). Still others are cited throughout this chapter.

Russia

Five Years of Rapid Changes: a Preliminary Overview

The landmark 'media moments' to grasp in the period leading up to the August 1991 attempted putsch, through to 1995, were as follows.

From late in 1990, Gorbachev, by then Soviet president, with formal powers greater than Stalin's, but with a radically different media situation and without the will or possibility to use Stalin's methods of repression, was faced with massive public discontent over economic hardship. He swung hard to the right as a tactic to try to contain the increasingly restive military, KGB and Party hierarchy, many of whom were at least as much infuriated by the collapse of the outer Soviet empire as by economic issues. This switch generated a period of much stricter control over the media, as in other realms of life. Leonid Kravchenko, formerly TASS director and a stern opponent of media freedom, was made director of state television in place of Mikhail Nenashev in order to bring it to heel. A number of adventurous TV news programs were shut down. The most violent repression of that period leading up to the putsch was the January 1991 assault on the television headquarters in Vilnius in order to try to control the determined Lithuanian independence movement: fourteen Lithuanians were killed by Soviet special forces.

During the three days of the putsch, most media[4] were closed, but not ultra-nationalist media, an important signal of the ideological provenance of the coup. Astonishing to say, foreign journalists were left alone, and CNN was able to function, neither of them errors likely to recur if there were ever another coup. A number of banned newspapers none the less combined forces to produce *Obshchaya Gazeta* (The General Newspaper) that circulated in Moscow, and *Izvestiia* published two issues on the same day, one reproducing the putschists' material, the second reversing itself and condemning the coup and reporting on widespread resistance throughout the Union. In Leningrad, most media continued to function as normal, and Mayor Sobchak was able to broadcast television appeals to hand local putsch collaborators over to the city authorities.

After the putsch, some domestic media that had complied with the putschists were in turn shut down for a month or so in an action that to many smacked of revenge by the victors, but could equally be interpreted as a sign of their nervousness. Kravchenko was replaced as head of broadcasting by Yegor Yakovlev, as we saw earlier one of the leading figures in the Gorbachev era through his appointment as editor of *Moscow News*. Yakovlev in turn would last until November 1992, only to be fired by Yeltsin for supposedly permitting unflattering news coverage of Russian troop actions in North Ossetia, in the Caucasus. His successor Vyacheslav Bragin, a Yeltsin loyalist, lasted until December 1993 when he in turn was fired, seemingly for permitting a hostile documentary on the ultra-nationalist politician Zhirinovsky to be aired the night before the national elections, when Zhirinovsky – despite it or even partly because of it – received a higher proportion of the vote than any other candidate.[5] Bragin was replaced by Aleksandr Yakovlev, Gorbachev's key Politburo ally on the domestic front in the *glasnost* years.

In the post-putsch years, a series of media laws were proposed in order to provide broadcasting with a legal framework, but none came to be passed into law. The exception, which took effect in February 1992, solely governed print media. Its initial version had actually represented a step backward from the 1990 law. However, its final version represented an advance on the 1990 Soviet law, that had already prohibited prior censorship and had banned arbitrary government interference with journalists' professional activities. The final version added de-funding of the censor's agencies (though not the KGB which, along with the censor in one's head, had always been a potent force). This reversal and re-reversal of direction is important to note as an index of the turbulence of the legislative process, and in turn, of the unstable situation within which many laws passed were compelled to operate – not least this press law. Foster (1993) provides a very detailed account of the saga, and specifically of the Russian parliament's struggle in 1991–2 to establish its control over the newspaper *Izvestiia*.

In the mean time, there was intense fluctuation in the newspaper sector, with new titles continuing to appear, and long-established titles going out of business or suffering colossal readership losses. Local newspapers were in particular jeopardy of closure on economic grounds, and died off in droves. New types of print media began to appear, including tabloid-style scandal-sheets and a thriving pornographic sector. Video and computer software piracy were endemic. Equally, there was fluctuation in broadcasting, with the repeated firing of state television directors serving as a key but not isolated example. Cinema continued to be produced, but the old state subvention system vanished, to be replaced by a very hit-or-miss, roller-coaster financial base, even at times involving money-laundering for one or other criminal interest. The 'everyday' media of the cultural flux that Condee and Padunov's essays analyse went through numerous phases.

What stayed constant throughout was the strength of the military, even though pared down in numbers, and especially of the KGB, the latter frequently re-titled and reconfigured, but still referred to under its old name by just about everyone. This continuity in power has already been noted, but it had its effect on broadcasting in particular. Yeltsin's debt to the military for – in the end – supporting him in his bloody October 1993 confrontation with the Russian majority parliamentary opposition, his use of them in suppressing or supporting revolts within and without Russian borders (Ingushetia, Chechnya, Abkhazia, Tajikistan), made this dependency predictable. His desire to keep tabs on his vociferous and sometimes malignant opposition across the political spectrum, and on labor unrest, accounted for his continued dependence upon the KGB. As it was, his political upbringing had already offered him a rather systematic prod in that direction.

Having sketched the general mediatic situation in this period, let us now focus in more detail on the economics of Russian media, including foreign media ownership, and on their relation to political power and political change.

Media and the Changing Political Economy

The economic issues for Russian media[6] following the putsch were virtually the same as those that had begun to confront Polish and Hungarian media two years previously. Totally dependent upon state subventions for, their operation, which in the case of print media included subsidized newsprint allocations and in the case of electronic media included subsidized signal distribution, the press and broadcasting agencies suddenly found themselves pushed into dependence on advertising revenues and faced with enormous bills for the material basics of their operations.

In the old system, the state monopoly *Soyuzpechat* (Unionprint, later *Rospechat*, Russprint, after the putsch) provided all the newsprint and publishing paper by stipulated quota to each newspaper or magazine, and also maintained a Union-wide network of distribution outlets. The main source of consumer revenue was, however, by annual subscription each autumn, organized through the local post offices. All prices were extensively subsidized, so that such annual subscriptions were very cheap and represented only a small fraction of production and distribution costs. The devastating impact of the January 1992 forty-fold price increase in newsprint needs no imagination to envisage.

The press certainly did not uniformly or gladly swing into the market mode. Some papers did: *Kommersant*, from its very inception in 1989, *Moscow News* from after the putsch, on the ground that only this would provide effective independence. Others continued to accept subsidies if they were available, such as *Komsomol'skaya Pravda* and *Trud*, which received nearly $20 million each in March and April of 1992 alone. The availability of the subsidies depended in part upon Yeltsin's preferences, and they were channeled through the Russian Press and Information Ministry whose prime activity this represented at the time. Mikhail Poltoranin was the first head of that ministry, and at that juncture was widely considered a key Yeltsin ally.[7]

The precise figures for these subsidies in any given instance were often hard to establish. For example *Izvestiiia* claimed it had received 55 million rubles in 1992, but *Rossiiskaya Gazeta* claimed the true amount was 858 million. Overall, in 1993, the Ministry of Finance distributed nearly 25 billion rubles to around 600 print outlets (to get a sense of proportion, this should be contrasted with the over 100 billion rubles that went to state television in the same year). In August 1994 about half the subsidy of 111 billion[8] rubles to the press went to two newspapers that belonged to the legislature (*Rossiiskiye Vesti* and *Rossiiskaya Gazeta*) and a single magazine, *Rodina* – a rather signal instance of political favoritism. (At the close of 1993 *Vesti* had voted to cut its ties with its founder, the Russian Council of Ministers, but was quickly brought to heel by the announcement it would immediately have to close until it had paid off its 130 million ruble debt to the state printing company.[9])

Broadcasting's economic problem as regarded subsidies was primarily generated by the enormous slice taken by transmitter and transponder costs, an activity under the control of the Ministry of Communication that represented 70–80 percent of the broadcasters' expenditures. For the Ministry the situation was also an unhappy one since the rates, however stiff they may have been for the broadcasters' budget, had not changed since 1981 but had also been previously covered by subsidies. With the withdrawal of the Ministry's own subsidies in 1992–3, it found itself bereft of finance. One consequence was that it could not pay its own employees. Along with many other staff in other sectors at the time, they were owed months of arrears in wages. In February 1994 the signal transmission workers struck for a day to try to force these arrears to be paid, blacking out a third of Russia's transmitters and most broadcasting outside Moscow itself, and putting still further pressure on the Ministry to collect revenue from the state broadcasters. And simultaneously with this crisis the Communication Ministry was advised by the Finance Ministry in early 1994 to prepare for 50 percent funding cuts – such was the chaotic situation of broadcasting finance at this period. In 1995, as of early October radio and television broadcasts had already gone off the air for this reason in forty different regions of the country at some juncture.[10]

Inevitably, this generated still further distortions as the media were caught up in the general movement of individuals and institutions trying to improve their own financial standing. Examples are legion. From Yeltsin on down, including Zhirinovsky, journalists were often charged for interviews. A number of journalists were known to have accepted bribes to write favorable copy from the donor's point of view.[11] Rental costs in

Moscow office-space were manipulated to keep their news media tenants pliant toward the owners, notably to the then Mayor of Moscow, Yuri Luzhkov. A number of critics charged that Sergei Mavrodi's notorious MMM investment fund scam, which had fleeced a mass of credulous and desperate investors, and in their pursuit had spent a reported 10 billion rubles a day on advertising at one point in 1994, had been effectively given a soft ride by the media. This was, they argue, because Mavrodi simply bank-rolled a compliant set of media that were only too glad of the revenue and thus were cautious about exposing him (Foster, 1994b).

The other economic aspect of media that requires comment is the move toward privatization, including the role of foreign ownership. The pioneer in this regard had been *Kommersant*, but others began to follow suit. *Nezavisimaya Gaseta* (The Independent Newspaper), *Yezhednyevnaya Gazeta* (The Daily Newspaper), *Obshchaya Gazeta* (The General Newspaper) – named after but different from the temporary anti-putsch paper – and *Segodnya* (Today), were some of the leading examples of new, independently financed newspapers. One of the more surprising developments was the bank-rolling of *Pravda* for a while by a foreigner, in this case a Greek Cypriot Communist millionaire. A new business press also emerged (Vatchnadze, 1991: 121–51; Zettner, 1995), some of it editorially revamped but still financed from state sources such as *Ekonomika I Zhizn'* (The Economy Today), and other examples being purely private. Two of the new press agencies formed, Interfax and PostFactum, managed to keep going. Together with these developments rapidly grew a far right ultra-nationalist press, again a mix between state-funded and private newspapers, from the old *Literaturnaya Rossiya* (Literary Russia) to the new *Den'*, (The Day), later changing its name after being banned to *Zavtra* (Tomorrow). As noted above, a privately owned pornographic press sector also made considerable inroads.

In the broadcast sphere, radio began the privatization process earlier than television, albeit only local radio. The best known was *Ekho Moskvy* (Moscow Echo). The most significant developments in this regard were, firstly, the 1993 start of the first private television channel, NTV, headed by the former deputy director of Ostankino Television, Igor Malashenko. Beginning in St Petersburg by renting time on St Petersburg TV, it received a Moscow license from Yeltsin on an 'experimental basis' (the decree's wording) in December 1993. Employing some of the best journalists from Ostankino and Russian TV, by the end of 1994 it was broadcasting fifty-eight hours a week. It quickly established a reputation for reliability in news. The channel was owned by the Most finance and construction consortium, which also owned the newspaper *Today* and part of *Moscow Echo*.

The second purely commercially owned TV channel in this early period was TV6, initially in 1993 a joint venture between the Moscow Independent Broadcasting System – headed by Eduard Sagalayev, a respected former senior television executive – and Turner Broadcasting. In 1994 the partners separated, with Sagalayev seeking domestic funding sources. Programming up to the split had been largely composed of unoriginal American product.

The third major case of privatization was a 51 percent public, 49 percent private joint stock corporation transformation of Ostankino Television announced in November 1994, taking effect from 1 January 1995, by one of Yeltsin's instant decrees – so sudden in this case that reportedly some of the scheduled investors discovered their potential involvement from the press! The new name was announced as ORT, Russian Public Television. The initial private stock-holders were twelve in number, including four banks and ITAR–TASS, successor to the former Soviet news agency TASS. Given the controlling interest secured by the Russian state in the decree, and the fragmentation of private investors into twelve entities, this barely qualified for the term 'privatization' in the sense of independent commercial control.[12]

However, the rather minimal private or foreign broadcast ownership in Russia during this period would be a poor guide to (1) the impact of advertising or (2) global media companies' program-content. Indeed, advertising took up a larger portion of airtime on Ostankino and Russian TV at that point than on the commercial NTV channel. Three-quarters of Ostankino's own programming was actually produced by independent companies, not in-house (see the discussion of the Listyev case below). Foreign films were a staple item both in television programming and in cinemas, not merely in the early months of TV6. The two most popular TV shows in 1992 were from Mexico's Televisa. Advertising (not only on TV) quite often used English as a signal of cachet, rather than Russian. Even when in Russian, the format of television commercials was generally heavily influenced by contemporary US advertising styles.

In May 1995, Reuters announced that it was planning a Russian and CIS financial information network. Its policy of offering relatively high salaries in Russian terms, and its connections with many of the leading Russian banks, were much in the news in Russia after the announcement. Commentators also noted the gradual expansion of Agence France-Presse.

These developments in foreign media activity led to quite widespread objections and protests, not simply by ultra-nationalist voices, but especially by them. In February 1994, Mikhail Poltoranin, by then State Duma Committee Chairman on Information Policy and Communications, denounced the broadcasting of low-grade foreign films for their negative impact on Russian morality, and simultaneously expressed his strong opposition to privatization of broadcasting as 'destruction of the common information space' in Russia. Solzhenitsyn, admittedly a Savonarola figure, but none the less voicing one strong current of opinion, even accused Radio Liberty of having become a US mouthpiece and of promoting Siberian separatism.[13]

In February 1995, the Moscow Mayor's office announced that all Moscow cable TV firms were to be nationalized, a step which clearly showed the bond between the official response to anxieties about cultural autonomy and the assertion of government control.[14] An article in *Obshchaya Gazeta* (25–31 May 1995) claimed that Reuters already owned half of Russia's 'information space' and that Russians could become 'slaves' of Reuters and 'foreign information empires'. The recently appointed Deputy Premier for media, Ignatenko, formerly ITAR–TASS director, promised to 'legally limit their presence in the Russian market'.[15] And in August 1995 Sergey Blagovolin, ORT director, publicly stated that 'the saturation of Russian television with Western programs has reached a critical point'.[16]

Summing up on the economics of Russian media during the period 1991–5, it is clear that those years presented all media with unprecedented financial crises for the various reasons noted. Many newspapers and magazines, particularly in the regions, simply folded. Even the government-financed *Rossiiskaya Gazeta*, a newspaper of record in so far as publishing government decrees and laws went, collapsed on financial grounds in December 1995. Broadcasting scraped by. Advertising had to be discovered *ab initio* as a revenue source, and this in a period of extremely fast inflation that sharply skewed the learning curve.

In turn, inevitably, this lent an air of tremendous insecurity to the work of media professionals and executives, clean counter to the rather dull security characteristic of the old regime. The dependence of media on continuing state subsidies and assistance to help them through the transition rendered them, arguably, politically vulnerable for different reasons, but at particular moments seemingly almost to the same degree, as they had been under the mechanisms of the old regime.[17] In June 1995, first *Nezavisimaya Gazeta* and then *Kuranty*, both of which had established themselves rather solidly as newspapers of the new era, were compelled to shut down for lack of finance. The former re-opened later in the year but experienced a dramatic internal struggle for editorial control that was resolved by its highly authoritarian editor seizing the premises with the aid of armed private security guards paid for by the newspaper's chief bankroller.

The most startling instance of the dynamics of Russian media economics in this period was the murder of the hugely popular TV journalist and talk-show host Vladimir Listyev, on 1 March 1995.[18] His funeral drew huge crowds, and he was buried next to the iconic guitar-poet Vysotskii. Professionally liquidated only a few days after his appointment as Director of Russian Public Television (ORT), public speculation in the first instance often presumed a political motivation. More informed insight suggested that the problem was of a quite different order. His prime task, it transpired, had been to reorganize the flow of advertising revenue to the TV channel. Previously, independent producers contracted to the channel had been creaming off (the term is a gross understatement) most of the advertising rubles that should have gone to the channel. Aleksandr Yakovlev reported that over a three-month period, 35 billion rubles had been generated by advertising, but only 5 billion had been received by the channel, with the result that amongst other problems it could not pay wages on schedule.

To get a grip on the situation, Listyev had set up a temporary ban on advertisements as of 20 February. It was clear there was going to be a major change, and that some people stood to lose a great deal of money on which they had no doubt been relying. It is also possible that Listyev himself may have been less than simon-pure, inasmuch as his agency, Inter-Vid, would be the only advertising agency shareholder in the new ORT, with 3 percent of the stock. Some commentators suggested that he would be in a prime position to channel advertising contracts to Inter-Vid rather than to Reklama, the previous agency, which had enjoyed a virtual monopoly.

Whatever the full story on this level, and however much this tragedy was principally a question of financial gain and media economics, there were inevitably also political consequences intertwined with it. Alexei Simonov, chairman of the Foundation for the Protection of Glasnost, commented:

> it means that if it is possible to kill one of the country's most popular journalists, if not the most popular, then in principle any journalist is not safe from such actions and no one can guarantee his security . . . it means that many today will face the question: should I take the risk or not? . . . I heard from his colleagues that they are ashamed, even more ashamed to be afraid now after what has happened. But what a person says publicly and what he says to himself can be entirely different. And without doubting anyone's declarations, I think that once the shock of what has happened passes, people will have to think of their own fates in the context of what happened.[19]

The Media and the State

The institutional relationship of media to the state, political forces and political movements was if anything even more turbulent than their economic plight. A different kind of survival was at stake, albeit often interlocking with economic survival.

There is a plethora of instances that could be cited to illustrate this turbulence, and shortly some selected ones will be examined. Underlying them, however, are certain constants: the *basso ostinato* of KGB dominance within the state and the question of state secrets; the closely connected post-colonial but not post-imperial state structure and ideology; the peculiarly intense currents (Laqueur, 1993) of extremist nationalism in Russia; the continuity of the ukase and instant dismissal as modes of government; and the fixation of the power structure, both tenants and challengers, on television as the most highly prized mass medium.

Let us begin with the KGB.[20] Its continued pre-eminence is quite stunning at first sight. Though many of its cadres originally were supportive of Gorbachev as Andropov's heir-apparent and as determined as Andropov to clean out the Augean stables of the late Brezhnev period, it was then deeply involved with the August 1991 putsch following widespread dis-illusionment with Gorbachev's seeming readiness to let the Soviet Empire 'go to hell in a handbasket'. Although apparently purged of 400 senior officials after the putsch, it quickly grew back to its former position of influence. On one level to say 'it' of such a large entity is unperceptive, since almost by definition there will be struggles for power and differential viewpoints to be found in an organization of that scale. And perhaps its pre-eminence only seems stunning against the backdrop of exaggerated expectations for the instantaneous democratization of Russia. Be all this as it may, no account of the media during this period makes sense without bearing the KGB in mind as a major actor in the drama. This was not least true of the provinces, where the original KGB structures survived virtually intact.

From half-way through 1990 and up to the putsch, the KGB itself organized a series of media exposés of abusive actions and repressive policies within its own ranks. The general public was struck at the time by the bravery of the journalists, not realizing that the initiative came, apparently, directly from Vladimir Kryuchkov, then KGB Director and in 1991 to be a leading putschist.[21] Evidently therefore his strategy in this regard was rather more complex than democratizing the position of the political police, or even correcting abuses by measured doses of *glasnost*. Yasmann (1993) cites an internal KGB source to the effect that the exposés were designed to create mutual suspicion and enmity between the relatively few reformers within the organization and the general run of officials, in order that the latter should be even more fearful and suspicious of Yeltsin and reform.

The main issue for our purpose is the close interest of the KGB in media during the period of attempted reforms, and their commitment to learning how to try to manipulate media coverage rather than simply censor it. There was apparently quite a noticeable immigration of younger operatives into the old Central Television, later Ostankino Television, during the later 1980s, 'cynical, educated, cunning young people who understand the laws of the market rather well' as a former moderator of the radical news magazine *Vzglyad* put it (cited in Yasmann, 1993). This interest did not abate after the putsch.

Albats (1994: 307) cites an example of three former officers drafted into the news reporters' desks at *Moscow News* in 1992, and other similar cases. This, however, was only one dimension of the situation, however disturbing. In February 1994 the system of presidential and governmental information *and* telecommunication lines was relocated back to the Federal Agency of Government Communications and Information, covering therefore both channels and information simultaneously. This represented the same lock on communication the KGB had originally had, and in what had formerly been a KGB department, but was now ostensibly a distinct agency. Links with the parent body were, however, probably not excessively complicated to resume. Or retain.

Another major issue was the question of state secrets, where the KGB effectively recuperated a great deal of control over its files. The 1993 Law

on Archives forbade any classified document in KGB files from being
opened earlier than fifty years after its date, and files concerning specific
individuals earlier than seventy-five years afterwards (Albats, 1994: 307).
This was retrospective as well as prospective, so that a file accumulated on
an individual in 1950 under Stalin would have to wait until 2025 before it
could be inspected. The mechanism of classification, as usual in these
situations, was conveniently vague – conveniently for the state, that is.
Yeltsin's February 1994 edict on the classification of state secrets author-
ized every government ministry to classify documents except the Ministries
of Culture and of Social Welfare.[22]

During this period of reviving state secrets legislation to repress communication in the public interest, there were six further notable instances of
the state–media relationship:

(a) the mediatic dimension of the continual attempts to bring Chechnya to
     heel;
(b) the Mirzayanov case;
(c) the Kholodov case;
(d) the mediatic-political situation in Primorskii Krai, the county around
     Vladivostok;
(e) tussles at the top to try to manipulate media coverage for political
     gain; and lastly
(f) the absurd case of *Kukly*, a satirical TV puppet-show.

Case 1: Chechnya

Yeltsin and his then Vice-President Aleksandr Rutskoi initially attempted
an invasion of Chechnya in late 1991, but were forced by public outcry to
cancel it. Military censorship was imposed on coverage of that campaign,
but leaks managed to alert the public. When Yeltsin resumed the endeavor
in 1994, it was with what he obviously thought was a much more carefully
designed set of tactics, including a media strategy. A covert war was
launched in the middle of 1994, a war repeatedly denied by Moscow up to
and including air attacks on Chechnya in early December 1994. When an
attempt was made even to deny responsibility for these, the implausibility
of other airforces penetrating Russian airspace undetected and unscathed
was much too large a lie to be sustained, and the Yeltsin administration
later admitted to the truth.

Before this period, traditional Russian hostility to the Chechens had been
carefully fostered, and lent partial plausibility in the public mind by the
role of some Chechens in organized crime (along with their many splendidly activist Russian colleagues[23]). After the October 1993 events, when
the Speaker of the Russian Parliament Ruslan Khasbulatov, a Chechen
brought up entirely in Russia but who had been repeatedly linked in his
opponents' propaganda to the Chechen mafia, was jailed, the police began
to round up Chechens on the street in Moscow and simply deport them
summarily to Chechnya. A number of thousands were so treated. By the

time of the 1994 invasion there had been a huge build-up of official government statements about Chechnya as a heartland of organized crime, supposedly harboring a thousand or more convicted criminals from Russian justice. The Chechens were consistently referred to as *bandity* – the word meaning 'thugs' rather than 'bandits' – just as Afghan guerrillas had been termed in Soviet media during the 1980s (Downing, 1988b). Yeltsin went so far as to proclaim that Chechnya was a major center of international crime.

During this later period of build-up to the December 1994 bloodbath, Russian media were almost universally hostile to the Chechen case, as Vladimir Molchanov, a respected Ostankino veteran of TV journalism, observed. So much so that in a tit-for-tat move Russian television was banned from Chechnya in August 1994, and Russian journalists in September. A 'holier-than-thou' Sergei Filatov, Yeltsin's chief of staff, opined thereupon that 'Every dictatorship seeks first of all to do away with objective coverage of its actions, but history teaches us that one cannot hide anything from the people.'[24] Inspiring words indeed: by early December Russian journalists' organizations were publicly protesting about Defense Minister Grachev's deceit concerning Russian involvement in fomenting strife within Chechnya, and announcing that 'Blatant lies have become the hallmark of the authorities' attitude to the press.'[25]

Thus when the invasion of Chechnya came, there was an attempt this second time around at a systematically orchestrated media campaign of spin control and deception, rather than simple silence, an empirical shift from the mediatic night of Stalinism to the mediatic twilight of capitalism.

However, the media campaign that the Yeltsin administration endeavored to launch was actually largely ineffective on a number of grounds. Firstly, public opinion was rather solidly against invasion, whether as reflected in polls or in the opposition expressed by all but the ultra-nationalist parties. It was one thing to despise Chechens, quite another to launch an invasion and thereby to risk Russian lads' lives in the military, as also the lives of the many Russians who lived in Chechnya. Secondly, it was impossible to conceal the opposition voiced by a great variety of very public figures, whether the Deputy Defense Minister Boris Gromov or the strongly nationalistic General Lebed, or a series of senior officers commanding invasion forces, or many of their troops, or former premier Yegor Gaidar. Their challenge was vocally echoed by the head of the Afghan veterans' organization, as by dyed-in-the-wool human rights campaigners such as Sergei Kovalyov, now head of Yeltsin's Human Rights Commission, and Yelena Bonner, widow of Andrei Sakharov.

Moreover, not only did journalists publicly protest about the government's deceptive stance, but one of the new privately owned television channels, NTV, owned by the Most financial group and politically very close to Moscow mayor Yuri Luzhkov, broadcast news bulletin after news bulletin with real war stories. It ran interviews with wounded soldiers, showed Russian officers halting their advance in the face of pleas from unarmed Chechen women and children, reported stories of Russian troops explaining to locals how to immobilize the tanks and then walking away out of sight, showed close-ups of bloody corpses. Yeltsin's coordinator of Chechnya policy publicly threatened to cancel NTV's license, a threat that sent a tremor through the ranks of independent-minded journalists.

To add to the brew, on 2 December 1994, the offices of the Most banking group were raided[26] and various staff beaten up by paramilitary troops in ski-masks who refused to identify themselves – who later turned out to be GUO officials. GUO was the Main Administration for the Protection of the Russian Federation, an elite group reporting directly to Yeltsin. KGB officers sent to make an emergency visit to investigate the clash were turned away by the GUO officials. The official claim in justification of this assault was that there were criminal connections that needed urgent investigation in Most. Immediately following this incident, the Moscow KGB head was dismissed by Yeltsin (reportedly on the ground that he was a supporter of Mayor Luzhkov).

These events coincided with the final build-up to the invasion of Chechnya (Deputy Defense Minister Gromov, after his protest, was relieved of his authority for the airforce on the same day). They also came on the heels of a larger Yeltsin administration campaign against the Most group. Yeltsin's Russian Security Council had singled out the Most group for blame for the previous October's catastrophic free-fall collapse of the ruble. Most had also been attacked in *Rossiiskaya Gazeta* (a daily under Yeltsin's aegis) for seconding staff to Luzhkov's election campaign office. In the same *RG* article, Most was further attacked for trying to build a huge media empire by allegedly attempting to gain control of St Petersburg TV, Ostankino TV and *Moskovskii Komsomolets*; for supporting Luzhkov's political ambitions; and in general for supporting the West against Russian 'national aspirations'.[27]

At the same juncture, Premier Chernomyrdin acknowledged that the government had been leaning very heavily indeed on Ostankino and Russian TV, warning them 'in the strongest possible terms' of the penalties for non-compliance with government directives on Chechnya coverage. He added his sneer, in a chilling reminder of how little had changed in government from sovietized days, that parliamentary deputies who were publicly opposing the invasion were approving of it in private telephone conversations. There was only one way he could have known this – through KGB bugging of the deputies and consequent reports to his office.[28]

As the merciless assault on Chechnya continued, targeting hospitals as well as apartment blocks in the capital Grozny, and as claims for imminent military victory drained away one after the other down the plumbing, directors of the Russian government's information center on the conflict changed almost weekly, beginning with State Press Committee Chairman Gryzunov. After his rapid resignation next came Valentin Sergeyev. He promptly vanished into a hospital with a heart attack, after being publicly denounced as having been sentenced to death by Chechen militants who circulated his address and phone number. He in turn was succeeded by Valery Grishin. All this was within three weeks.

The head of Russian TV, Oleg Poptsov, elected by the staff rather than appointed from above, none the less also came close to being fired because Yeltsin disapproved of the channel's war coverage.[29] Sergei Kovalyov, returning in early January 1995 from three weeks under fire in Grozny, publicly described the attack on Grozny as reminiscent of the Nazis' assault on Stalingrad, and the lies of the Yeltsin administration and the military as worse than those of 'the Communists and even Goebbels'. He also sharply attacked those media that had simply reproduced the government's line on its military successes.[30]

The policy war over media coverage of Chechnya continued throughout 1995. At a major public seminar in May that year, Alexei Simonov, Chairman of the independent Foundation for the Protection of Glasnost, detailed 105 Russian journalists reporting Chechnya who had been arrested, forty-six who had film or video equipment illegally confiscated, eight who were beaten up, six who were killed and two who were missing. In June two political party leaders on their way to address the European Parliament had a video on the Chechnya war impounded at Moscow airport. Moreover the Chairman of the Duma Chechnya Committee denounced NTV, *Moskovskii Komsomolets* and *Komsomol'skaya Pravda* for their coverage of an army massacre in the village of Samashki, Chechnya, in early April, claiming the coverage was a 'revolt' against the President, government, Parliament and the Russian people as a whole.[31]

This complex of military events and struggles for media power included ongoing conflicts at the top (Yeltsin/Luzhkov) with a media dimension, energetic efforts by some media organizations and many journalists to inform the Russian and international public, and also struggles by elements within the public to communicate their dissent from the Chechnya invasion. Along with energetic but ineffective efforts by the Yeltsin administration to control media coverage of its Chechnya invasion, they give a vivid sense of the massive importance of media in the minds of all concerned. They also clearly revealed the interconnections between public information strategies and policies, and the recomposition of the strong state in Russia.

Case 2: the Mirzayanov Affair[32]

This concerned a distinguished senior chemist who had found in his research that despite international claims to have discontinued binary chemical weapons production, Russia was continuing to produce them, was using Western money earmarked for defense industry conversion to do so, and in the process was generating extremely high levels of environmental pollution. The story had been published in the daily newspaper *Trud* in September 1991, in the alternative paper *Sovershenno Sekretno* (Absolutely Secret) six months later, but its publication in *Moscow News* in September

1992 came at a time when the KGB had reoriented itself after the putsch. Mirzayanov was jailed for eleven days, then charged with violating state secrets, an offense carrying an eight-year sentence. The offices of *Moscow News* were subjected to a police search. Following international outcry, he was released from jail pending trial, and eventually the case was dropped in February 1994. Mirzayanov did win damages against the state prosecutor and his former employer, but even then had to fight for a further six months to be given permission to travel abroad. The harassment did not end there: in December 1994 his former state institute sued him for defaming its public reputation.

Case 3: the Kholodov Murder [33]

Dmitrii Kholodov was a young journalist on the scandal-sheet newspaper *Moskovskii Komsomolets* (Moscow Young Communist), a daily that had definitively changed its contents though not its masthead. Kholodov was blown up on 17 October 1994 by a bomb concealed in a suitcase that he had brought to his newspaper office. He had been assured by the KGB source that passed it on to him that it contained important documentation on one of a number of his investigations into military corruption and secret defense programs. Another journalist was wounded in the same explosion. The KGB investigators described the device as a professional booby-trap.

Outrage was expressed by journalists' organizations and various leading political figures at a funeral three days later attended by between 7,000 and 10,000 people. The editor of the newspaper, Pavel Gusev, and one of its leading journalists, Aleksandr Minkin, openly put the blame on the Ministry of Defense, insisting that there was no interest evident in a serious investigation of the authors of the crime. Fingers were pointed at the Defense Minister, Grachev,[34] and the former C-in-C of Eastern Germany, Burlakov, whose corrupt dealings had already been exposed in print by Kholodov. Others suggested it was his research on the Chechnya situation, where the covert war had been in progress for many months, others again that the cause had been his discoveries concerning a secret training camp used by special military forces to train mafia hitmen, and still others that he had found out information on secret arms sales in CIS conflict zones such as Tajikistan or even Chechnya.

Any of these, clearly, could have been the reason for some powerful people to try to stop this young man once and for all. What was striking, in its quiescence, was the response of Bogdanov, then head of the Union of Russian Journalists and, echoing him, Yeltsin, who both drew the public conclusion from the murder that journalists should take to wearing special plastic identification cards. Yeltsin did not concur with Bogdanov's curious theory that it would protect journalists from harm, but he did add that journalists should work within a given ethical framework, and that the card could be removed from those who failed to stay within it. This official response from the top was extraordinarily revealing of the perspectives on media current at that level: a lethal attack on journalists and a serious threat to media freedom was effortlessly and instantaneously transformed into a proposal to subject journalists to stricter controls. (Up to the time of writing, however, the ID proposal had not been taken further.)

In early 1995, *Izvestiia* claimed that Kholodov's killer, a paratrooper by then serving in the Chechnya conflict, had been identified a month previously to Yeltsin's office, but that no action had been taken. The usual denials were forthcoming.

Case 4: the Primorskii Krai Saga

This story will be summarized very briefly, but it is included to emphasize how these media dramas at the national level might be replicated in the regions, though often without surfacing to public view outside them.[35] In this instance, though, the events were sufficiently extreme to begin to filter through to national awareness. In 1994 Nazdratenko, governor of the Primorskii Krai (Maritime County), in which Vladivostok was situated, and a cohort of his cronies in senior posts, took to the old Soviet tactic of denying newsprint to media that criticized his draconian and corrupt administration, firing critical journalists, and even banning a number of newspapers altogether. His bannings of newspapers, especially the Moscow press, at one point meant that virtually none was appearing at all. In the period leading up to registration to vote before an election, he first suddenly decreed that all his opponents had to have triple the number of signatures to qualify to stand. Then in the four days before registration electric power was cut off every evening from 7 to 11 pm, thus wiping out any political advertising on TV by his opposition. Yeltsin canceled the election, and Nazdratenko continued in office.

One radio journalist critical of him was abducted by unidentified men, tortured with a blowtorch and had his fingers crushed in a vice. Unidentified gunmen took shots at Russian TV's office windows. Two correspondents for Moscow newspapers received anonymous death threats. Action was eventually set in motion from the center to resolve the situation, but not until December of 1994 and even then very slowly and cautiously. The lack of speed was closely connected with Nazdratenko's fulsome public support for Yeltsin, as the latter's credibility and power shrank to almost zero. Such was the reality of democracy.

Case 5: Tussles in Moscow for Media Power

A different but significant example of the role of intense competition for power was the continuing struggle between the State Duma and President Yeltsin, both before and after the December 1993 elections, for authority over media, or between three government officials, Mironov, Gryzunov and Poltoranin (see below). The pitched battle outside Ostankino Television at the time of the military assault on the Parliament building was the most extreme case in point,[36] but far from the only one.

Battle was never joined in order for the public to have access to media, merely for the parliamentary forces to have 'their' media to balance the Yeltsin administration's media dominance. An example was the demand voiced in the State Duma in mid-December 1994 to restore broadcasting of parliamentary affairs on Ostankino and Russian TV. It was urged in many cases by precisely the same deputies who a mere fourteen months earlier in the previous parliament had voted to ban these broadcasts in the weeks before the October 1993 confrontation. At that time those self-same individuals were in full support of Yeltsin's policies and thus opposed to a majority of their fellow-deputies.[37]

The same dreary and dispiriting core assumptions about media were equally evident in the interminable battles, maneuvering and mutual accusations between Yeltsin and Parliament concerning potential media advantage in the run-up to the 1995 parliamentary elections, and the 1996 presidential elections. Examples are too numerous to list in their entirety, but practically any move in relation to media was interpreted by one or other side as a ploy to gain power. For instance the Duma and the Council of the Federation[38] voted overwhelmingly in May 1995 and again in December of that year to suspend the creation of ORT (Russian Public Television) out of Ostankino because its new structure was seen as a strong potential weapon for Yeltsin. Yeltsin, in turn, instantly vetoed their vote. *Izvestiia*, after October 1993 a highly independent newspaper, repeatedly drew attention to such moves by either side, such as parliament's move to close down the Judicial Chamber on Information Disputes which provided relatively impartial judgments on fair election coverage, and the Yeltsin administration's move to harness three state committees (Press, Film and Broadcasting) to the Central Electoral Commission's pre-election educational campaign.[39]

Numerous conflicts over media policy between high-ranking officials also illustrated this process. One such was Yeltsin's firing of the chairman of the State Press Committee, Mironov, ostensibly a blow for media freedom, but on closer inspection a good deal less encouraging. Another was a clash between Poltoranin, then Chairman of the State Duma (lower house) Committee on Information Policy and Communications, and Gryzunov, Mironov's successor as State Press Committee chairman. The detail in these cases means they should be read without undue haste. They closely reveal some of the endemic media issues of the period in Russia.

Let us take the Mironov case first, acknowledging as we do so that a detailed description of the official status of the high-sounding positions of the protagonists would be a waste of time given the confused circumstances of the period. It is pointless, unfortunately, to ask the – rationally speaking – obvious question as to whether State Press Committee chairman was a more authoritative position than that of chairman of the State Duma Committee on Information Policy and Communications, or what was their relative clout in the power structure *vis-à-vis* Aleksandr Yakovlev as head of Ostankino/Russian Public Television. At that point, most politicians were trying to carve out power for themselves, or hold on to it, or most often both at the same time, and to do so in a highly transitional situation subject to numerous shifting and conflicting vectors. At any given time, the formal attribution of power might enjoy a rather loose correlation to its reality.

Yeltsin summarily dismissed Boris Mironov[40] as chairman of the Federal Russian Press Committee at the beginning of September 1994. This followed a series of confrontations between Mironov and his deputy, Gryzunov, over the latter's reprimands to anti-semitic newspapers, and over Gryzunov's opposition to the allocation of subsidies to newspapers continuing a sovietist line such as *Pravda* and *Sovietskaya Rossiya*. Gryzunov's policy concerns, be it underlined, related to reprimands and subsidies, and fell well short of direct censorship or banning. Mironov, however, not only successfully defended the subsidies, but further publicly attacked Gryzunov for issuing the reprimands while he, Mironov, was on vacation. Throughout, even though Mironov's views were known to be close to some circles in the so-called 'Red-Brown' coalition, the Yeltsin administration left him free to pursue his line.

However, while a Council of Europe meeting on the very topic of media in Russia was under way in Moscow, Mironov chose to deliver himself of the public view to regional press editors that 'the media . . . should be managed more rigorously than our troops' (shades of Trotsky in 1919–20!). Upon public reports of his speech, he was then finally shown the door by Yeltsin.

The real question in the Mironov affair was surely that his policy positions could hardly have been a secret before Yeltsin's administration initially approved his appointment. His firing on the probable grounds of public embarrassment for the Russian government in its endeavors to portray itself internationally as committed to democracy does not answer the question of why a Mironov could have been appointed in the first place. It is a question which ultimately goes to the heart of the Yeltsin administration's policy on Russian nationalism, often portrayed outside Russia and even in it as locked in mortal combat with the extreme nationalists and old guard, but arguably more realistically perceived overall – not, clearly, in the case of every individual – as dancing closer and closer into their embrace while calling out ever more feebly its repugnance at the prospect.[41]

The struggle took a different form between Poltoranin – widely thought to have been Mironov's political patron and to share his views – and Gryzunov (now State Press Committee chairman), but it pivoted on rather similar considerations with respect to media issues.[42] Poltoranin argued vigorously for a law he drafted in 1994 on coverage of government bodies by state-owned media, that would actually have apportioned set times for news segments dealing with different branches of government. He also championed a set of amendments to the basic edict on news media, that were passed by the Duma but then rejected by the Council of the

Federation. These would have set up a national foundation for state media, ostensibly to put them on a secure financial footing. This latter proposal was fiercely attacked by many journalists as instituting a subsidy process that would inevitably reward those media organs favored by the administration of the day, and freeze out the others. Poltoranin was also hostile to the formation of media joint-stock companies, arguing that Russia was 'not yet mature enough'.[43]

Gryzunov publicly opposed Poltoranin's proposals as threatening media freedom. For his pains he was attacked by pro-Yeltsin newspapers as being a bridgehead of the Most group into the administration, and thus of being an arrant westernizer and *nouveau* capitalist. The purpose was to get ordinary Russians to write off his objections to Poltoranin's subsidy proposals as purely self-interested, and as representing the agenda of the newly rich, ruthless capitalist class. However, in view of these accusations, it is only fair to note that Gryzunov's proposal excluded subsidies only as a long-term solution, preferring tax breaks because they offered a more arm's length relationship between government and media. His proposal for the State Press Committee was for it to transform itself into a media policy formulation and review institute, and to give up any administrative functions or ambitions. If successful, this would hardly have enhanced his power as its chairman. He also expressed himself very clearly in favor of media that could promote dialogue between government and governed.[44]

Case 6: Kukly

Kukly (puppets) was a claymation political satire show on the commercial channel NTV during 1995. It drew its inspiration from the well-known British series *Spitting Image*, popular from the mid-1980s to the mid-1990s. Amongst its spoofs were sketches of Yeltsin and Korzhakov as mother and baby begging on a train, and Premier Chernomyrdin (well-known to have close links with the natural gas industry) selling parts of a gas boiler. In mid-July 1995 the Procurator General opened a criminal case against the series for insulting the honor and dignity of high government officials. Penalties if found guilty could include corrective labor for as much as two years, or a fine.

On one level, this showed the general proclivity of political leaders to be thin-skinned; the British show had similarly provoked howls of rage from Conservative Party officials. At the same time, the sanctions available to the Russian government were considerably more stringent. Furthermore, however, it seemed as though this was another round in the continuing war between the Yeltsin administration and NTV, inasmuch as the day before the Procurator General announced the case against *Kukly*, it also began an investigation of NTV journalist Yelena Masyuk for interviewing the leader of the Chechen raid on Budyonnovsk. If she refused to tell them his whereabouts, she could face five years in prison.[45] Yet she was only one of a number of journalists who had interviewed him.

Eventually, even though in August additional tax evasion and currency dealing charges were filed against the producer, carrying five- to ten-year terms, all charges were dropped in October. The producers of the show and NTV, to their great credit, continued to run it throughout these threats.[46]

Summary Observations on the Russian Situation

These cases together demonstrate the very considerable lengths to which the Russian state authorities would go in the media field in order to pursue their policies and edicts. They also illustrate the increasingly powerful role of nationalistic ideology at the time. At the same time, the energetic opposition of a number of journalists, media and of certain leading figures was a further and vital dynamic in the situation. Whatever Mayor Luzhkov's motivation, whatever the Most group's, they too represented an alternative power center. On one level, the issue is not to rank one power center as being somehow more democratic in inclination than another, or more honorable, but simply a matter of noting how the vicious competition for power may lead to an opening up of communication via media as the groups in contention seek to draw support for themselves, and to denounce their opponents, via media.

A similar point was made by political commentator Andrei Fadin in 1995[47] about the growing clout of (mostly highly authoritarian) provincial governors *vis-à-vis* Moscow, who represented a competitive pluralism of power rather than a strong democracy *per se*. In this connection it was interesting to note that provincial press subscriptions outpaced Moscow press subscriptions for the first time in 1994. Even though regional journalists were poorly paid and generally dependent both upon the favor of the provincial authorities, and the information in Moscow media, this perhaps represented a first, very faltering step toward the diffusion of media power away from the center.[48]

It is also true that sections of the Russian media were prepared to air any and all criticism of individuals, and unabashedly to rehearse pure speculation concerning trends and events. The development of a 'boulevard' press, such as the revamped *Moskovskii Komsomolets*, or – still further – the substantial growth of ultra-rightist media that knew no limits when it came to Jews or Muslims, or liberal democrats, were all cases in point. It is doubtful that this species of dissent marked a significant shift toward a responsibly critical and independent media system.

At the same time we need to exercise analytical caution on another level. Whereas Foster (1994a) argues that Russian media failed to promote confidence in the 'evolving norms, rules, institutions and procedures', it could be because these in turn were not evolving toward any clearly democratic goal-posts, but rather were turbulent and chaotic and often reflected the desire of the Yeltsin regime and other power centers to protect themselves against attack for political high-handedness or corruption. No doubt many media did not offer coherent alternatives, but it seems unduly harsh to focus the spotlight so intensely upon media rather than taking into equal account the situation they were covering and facing and sharing.

McNair (1994: 130–1) suggests a still further note of caution, albeit *en passant*, namely that the media may not have such a power 'to influence hearts and minds . . . in Russia or anywhere else', as presumed by political forces there during this period. He merely notes the point and moves on, but this is a standard note of methodological caution within media research circles. While the point has sometimes been taken to the extreme of virtually denying media impact at all (cf. Klapper, 1960), it is important to recall that – like their counterparts elsewhere in the world – Russian readers and audiences were not vacant pieces of blotting paper waiting to slurp up whatever inkblots were dropped on to them.

Lastly, and relatedly, it is essential to stand back from organized media and recognize the considerable importance of other media and cultural forms in the Russian cultural process. Few studies have emerged that thoroughly examine these dimensions of the situation in the period under discussion, but that does not rob them of their considerable significance. Condee and Padunov (1991a, 1991b, 1994, 1995) are, at the time of writing, among the few to do so. Their essays trace the cultural eddies and shifts over the years of this period in far more detail than can be addressed here, but let us note a few of their observations.

For example, they too draw attention to the 'mass production in Russia of Western and émigré-made cultural objects', but they argue that the impact of magazines such as *Reader's Digest, Omni, PC World*, was due less to their verbal content, and much more to their visual insights – via high-production-value color photographs – into images of Western life-styles. The accompanying text, often in English, German or even Japanese, functioned during this period not to communicate its literal content, therefore, but as a kind of guarantee of 'non-Russo-Soviet' authenticity. The authors go further to argue that Russian culture, traditionally richly logo-centric, was in the process of being transformed into an intensely visual social expressiveness. They further instance in this regard the rapid expansion of such everyday media as cheap comic-books, cheap erotic magazines, book dust-jacket design, plastic shopping-bag design.

Meanwhile conventional 'high' art – the object of virtually permanent veneration in Russia until this juncture – was struggling to find publishers, galleries, ballet school premises, readers, spectators. Many creative artists generated their own, very distinctly Russian formulations of themes that in the 'West' would be categorized as 'post-modern' – the collapse and evacuation of generally approved meaning, consensus, or stability, the pervasiveness of hybrid cultural perspectives, the fascination with the image, with the simulacrum. Yet in the Russian context, these were seemingly being played out with an existential intensity generally missing from the rarefied, arm's or pole's length atmosphere of such discussions in Western academic settings.

By way of illustration of this committedly post-modern disconnectedness, at the close of their 1995 essay Condee and Padunov describe a symbolically charged evening in May 1993 when the huge House of Literature in central Moscow hosted two major events. One was the launching of a titillating spy novel by a former KGB operative, attended by a mass of Soviet intelligence 'community' members. At the other end of the building was a counter-cultural 'event' with a rock band, energetically dancing crowds of young people, stands selling tapes and posters. In the street opposite the spy novel event was a very busy meat and poultry market, and on the other street outside the rock concert was an accordion player belting out old peasant songs. Certainly not the Moscow public sphere of yesteryear.

Poland

The Polish media situation was in certain specific respects akin to the Russian one at the same period. Continual conflict between President Walesa and successive parliamentary administrations was the order of the day, extending as much into questions concerning media as into other spheres of public life. Within the media, television took prime place as a site of dispute between these contending forces. The economic dimension of the media during the transition period was also very similar, with the huge system of subsidies characterizing the old regime being done away with, and threatening the survival of almost all existing newspapers. There was, simultaneously, an initial explosion of new print media, followed by the virtually immediate collapse of the majority of the new titles. Most media professionals none the less stayed within the profession, adjusting in various ways to the new and radically unfamiliar vectors that surrounded them.

At the same time, it is essential to note some of the key differences between the Polish and the Russian cases. The confrontations over media did not at any point in the period under review become part and parcel of an armed struggle for power, nor did Polish media find themselves pivoted around positions of national identity in the same way that Russian media did. The Polish security establishment was typically hunting for an agreed basis and established *modus operandi* during this period, and so could not perform the role of the KGB even had it wished to do so.[49] The other major difference was the role of the hierarchy of the Catholic Church in its quest for a secure and privileged place within Polish public and private life, including mediatic and cultural life. Lastly, however, it has proved harder to ascertain the currents and eddies of cultural change, except that very considerable disillusionment and cynicism seemed to gain ground rather rapidly within the public, especially among the young (cf. Drweski, 1995a).

Let us begin by noting the primary structural changes in media governance that took place, beginning with print media and then with broadcast media. The Polish equivalent to *Soyuzpechat* and *Rospechat* had been RSW

(*Robotnicza Spoldzienia Wydawnicza* or Workers' Publishing Cooperative). Like its Soviet analogue, RSW (Giorgi, 1995: 74–9; Kowalski, 1988; Sabbat-Swidlicka, 1992) controlled the supply of paper, of printers' ink, and other material components of the publishing process. It owned a dozen major printing plants. It further owned the national chain of kiosks which served as sales points for its newspapers and magazines, and the transport fleet that made the deliveries to the kiosks, employing almost 35,000 people over the entire operation.

Further still, it was owner of a series of national and local newspapers and 170 periodicals, including such well-known titles as the Warsaw daily *Zycie Warszawy* (Warsaw Viewpoint) and the somewhat independent weekly *Polityka*, which over the years, *ceteris paribus*, had filled the politico-cultural role played by *Literaturnaya Gazeta* in the USSR, or *Elet Es Irodalom* in Hungary. RSW was a virtual vertical monopoly, a monopsony, virtual only because of the existence of alternative publications and distribution sponsored by *Solidarnosc*, other oppositional groupings, and the Catholic Church. In fact its widespread ownership of print titles had put it in an even more advanced power position than *Soyuzpechat*, which was 'only' a network for materials supplies, distribution and sales.

When it was broken up, long a goal for *Solidarnosc*, the results were quite mixed. One hundred and forty-one of the periodicals were quickly auctioned off or transferred to worker cooperatives. Most of the national dailies went into private hands, including foreign private ownership, especially on the part of the French publishing corporation Hersant, whose most public coup was to achieve 51 percent ownership of *Rzeczpospolita*, the rough equivalent in function and prestige in Polish life of the new *Izvestiia* in Russia.[50] The local press frequently passed into the hands of the old local *nomenklaturas*, because many of the worker cooperatives to which local newspapers were sold patently did not have the money to continue publication, and thus were dependent upon private firms or credit institutions typically owned by the former governing class to supply the funds for that end. A further factor influencing this outcome was the pressure from trade unions to safeguard the jobs of media professionals, printers and other media staff.

Inevitably, that process maintained in post a high proportion of journalists and others professionally trained under the previous regime, typically without access to any new formal training and therefore con-stantly feeling their way. In so far as the local press was concerned, that often made for considerable caution on journalists' part, dependent as their newspaper frequently was on the good will of the continuing local power structure. As Sabbat-Swidlicka (1993: 29) noted, 'professional standards in the regional press are, on the whole, considered very low'.

Control over broadcasting was long and bitterly contested. The proposal offered by Karol Jakubowicz before and during his brief tenure as Director of Polish Television, that broadcasting should be organized approximately along the lines of the BBC, namely an independent corporation at arm's length from any branch of government, was never treated seriously either by President Walesa[51] or by any of the parliamentary administrations that came and went at regular intervals. Rather, the battle was joined between parliament, which wanted to have control, and the president, who clung to precisely the same ambition.

Neither side was able to prevail over the other. In the meantime, the old Radio and Television Committee, dating from the last broadcasting law of 1960, was the body still charged with administering broadcasting. Its directors were changed four times between 1989 and 1992, each time in response to a change of government or a change of political direction. Every time the chief executive was changed, the new director brought in a raft of new sub-executives, so that changes repeatedly rippled through the broadcasting organizations. Meanwhile, the queue for broadcast licenses grew bigger and bigger, and a number of pirate TV and radio stations went on the air, only half-heartedly harassed by the authorities (Sabbat-Swidlicka, 1992). There was even for a while a chain of twelve such radio stations with common core programming owned by Nicola Grauso, an Italian media entrepreneur who also held significant shares in TV stations in four major regional cities (Giorgi, 1995: 24).

Eventually, in March 1993, a compromise law was enacted. The National Broadcasting Council was set up with nine members, three nominated by the Sejm and three by the Senate (the lower and upper houses of parliament), and three, including the chairman, by the state president. Some commentators immediately noted (Sabbat-Swidlicka, 1993) that this division of authority simply institutionalized political party jockeying rather than dissipating it. The Council's powers were exceedingly wide, including the supervision of programming, the assignment of frequencies and licenses to broadcast, and the allocation of income from license fees. This gave state broadcasting interests control, amongst other things, over the access of would-be commercial broadcasters to the airwaves and a built-in advantage against them should the state authorities wish to use it.

Other features of the law included the establishment of state broadcasting ownership in the hands of a parastatal answering to the Treasury Department; the establishment of three sources of state broadcasting revenue, namely the Treasury itself, license fees and advertising; a 70 percent tax on any profits accrued; a 33 percent ceiling on foreign ownership of Polish broadcast media; and the requirement of respect in programming for 'the' (undefined) Christian value system.

The anticipation that the structure of the National Broadcasting Council, even though its members were required to resign from all other memberships in political or public bodies, would institutionalize party political conflict rather than lessen it, was amply fulfilled by events beginning within a year of its formation. The issue that confirmed the prediction was the NBC's assignment in January 1994 of the only national commercial broadcasting license to PolSat,[52] a company owned by expatriate Polish millionaire Zygmunt Solorz, that had broadcast to Poland since 1992 via a

Dutch satellite. Its programs were a mixture of Brazilian *telenovelas*, American and Italian serials and children's programs, all dubbed into Polish.

Walesa immediately fulminated in public against the decision, suggesting without offering any proof that Rupert Murdoch's News Corporation was using PolSat as a Trojan horse to enter Polish broadcasting. In March 1994, faced with a refusal by the National Broadcasting Council to back down from its decision, Walesa dismissed Marek Markiewicz, the NBC Chairman whom he himself had appointed, and then designated another of his own appointees to the Council, conservative politician Ryszard Bender, to the office of chairman. In May the Constitutional Tribunal ruled that the dismissal had been unlawful, but did not find itself able to rule that the subsequent appointment of Bender should therefore be nullified.

Walesa pursued the issue without ceasing, rejecting out of hand, for instance, the annual NBC Report. This, the law stipulated, must be approved by at least one entity out of the upper and lower houses of parliament and the presidency, otherwise the Council's members had to stand down and new ones be appointed. It was a close thing, because in July the Senate voted by a majority to reject the 1993–4 Report as well, seemingly because farmer deputies took issue with a TV comedy program, aired the night before the vote, that they felt had ridiculed farmers. The Sejm decisively voted to accept the report, however, notwithstanding strenuous criticisms of the recently appointed Director of Television by Sejm members from both the political left and right for – seemingly to them – favoring the other side.

In July Walesa appointed Janusz Zaorski, briefly a Director of Polish Television in the first years after the regime change, and widely defined as very closely allied with Walesa, to chair the NBC. Later, in September 1994, he dismissed Markiewicz from the Council altogether, and another of his own appointees, Maciej Ilawiecki, replacing them with two new members, one a retired general. Furthermore, he did so immediately following the announcement of the Supreme Administrative Court's decision that the original allocation of the license to PolSat had indeed been valid. He was also publicly furious that they had appointed Wieslaw Walendziak, hailing from Walesa's original stamping ground of Gdansk, but highly independent of both Walesa and the traditional broadcasting establishment, to chair Polish Television (Sabbat-Swidlicka, 1994: 43).

Consequently the Sejm voted to consider an amendment to the broadcasting law that would deprive the president of the right to appoint the NBC chairman. Then in October the Sejm voted 305 to eighteen, with only twenty-two abstaining, to urge Walesa not to destabilize the country by violating the independence of the NBC. These were just some of the many shots and counterstrikes between president and parliament over this issue in this period.

Walesa repeatedly asserted the need for the Polish presidency to have still more powers, including over the media. For example, during 1992 he toured a variety of media organizations. To television journalists in one such encounter in September that year, he articulated his view that they should either present the perspectives of the power structure or leave and set up their own newspapers, and that governmental and presidential news should be given priority in newscasts. In March that year he accused the assembled members of the Journalists' Center of 'provoking'[53] him, and a month earlier he charged other members of the profession of endangering Polish reconstruction by their irresponsibility (Kulakowska, 1992). He frequently attacked the independent daily *Gazeta Wyborcza*, edited by long-term opposition activist Adam Michnik, and sought successfully to have its *Solidarnosc* logo removed (Smolenski, 1991). To wrap up this list, it became widely known in 1993 that Walesa's Minister of State and his press spokesman had a telephone hotline to most of the TV management, and frequently invited such individuals for 'further talks' to the Belvedere, the presidential palace (Sabbat-Swidlicka, 1994: 42).

However, it should not be thought that his was the only voice in favor of tight media control. Premier Olszewski's record in this regard was notable. When the Olszewski administration took over, reputedly detesting the Mazowiecki broadcasting administrators even more than the former Communist leadership, they claimed they were restoring balance by firing the previous team. Yet they left all the sovietized regime's employees still in place . . . (Kulakowska, 1991). Olszewski tried – but failed – to take over *Rzeczpospolita*, on the ground that he had no media outlet to diffuse his views. His Chief of Staff, Wojciech Wlodarczuk, publicly referred to journalists as 'gangsters', and tried to freeze out from access to government sources those of whom he particularly disapproved (Kulakowska, 1992). He fired the non-political director of the Polish Press Agency (PAP) and replaced him with a political loyalist who in turn peopled the organization with journalistically inexperienced yea-sayers.

The second Pawlak administration had its own mediatic saga[54] as well. Relations between it and news media were poor at best, with Pawlak on one occasion crying 'censorship!' because TV news did not read out his statement on a strike word for word, yet later the same year, in December 1994, trying to prevent TV from even reporting on his talks with Russian leaders. The latter event prompted the Director of Television to complain publicly about politicians' desire to turn broadcasting into 'indoctrination'. In May 1994, having initially accredited journalists to a special two-day Cabinet 'retreat', he then abruptly canceled their press conference at it after they had arrived, leaving them standing in the open on the other side of the gates to the retreat center. He then grudgingly allowed just two to sit in on the discussions after they all vigorously protested at being shut out.

Furthermore, in July 1994 Pawlak suddenly fired the director of PAP yet again. The man had served in that capacity since September 1990 except for his brief period out of office under the Olszewski administration. During those four years, except for the interruption noted, PAP had maintained a good reputation as a professional wire-service, eschewing overt political adhesions. However, it transpired that an opposition party, the Freedom Union, had been drafting legislation to turn PAP into a joint-stock company rather than a government agency, and Pawlak's move against its director was widely interpreted as a defensive maneuver against potential loss of control. This was confirmed by the government's drafting of alternative legislation some months later to place PAP directly under the prime minister's office and funding, and with a mandate to 'popularize the positions [taken by] the parliament, the president, and the Council of Ministers'. In other words, a wire-service was being transformed into a prime ministerial press office (although the numerous conflicts between branches of government suggested that its tasks might be rather daunting).

A different problem in state–media relations, but one which exemplifed the same trends, was posed by the question of classified data. This is hardly peculiar as an issue to post-transition Poland, but in the countries of the former Soviet bloc it held a particular twist because of the enormous power of the secret police and their informer network in the previous system. The fierce conflicts in Germany over revelations from Stasi files, the continuing strength of the Securitate in Romania, the bitter rows in the Czech Republic over purging former Communists – and, by significant contrast, the degree of continuity of the KGB in Russia and the relative weakness of any movement in Russia to contest the sealing of KGB files – all in their respective ways underscored the extreme political sensitivity of the issue.

It was not simply a matter of struggling to avoid reproducing under the new regime the omnipresent state secrecy and lack of accountability to the public of the old one, but also of how far those who had once worked for the secret police in whatever capacity should be allowed to function in public life without being brought to book for any of their actions. And inevitably, as former Communist parties returned to government in a majority of Eastern European and Eurasian nations, their officials were likely to be especially alert to the risks that de-classifying files might present to them personally.

It was in this context that the topic of classified information presented itself in Poland during 1994,[55] with a government whose majority party was the core of the former Communist Party, and whose prime minister was leader of the Peasant Party, which until the later 1980s had been a dutiful ally of the Communist Party in the fictive multi-party system of the sovietized regime in Poland.

Student groups set the ball rolling in Warsaw and Krakow early in the year with a demand for the files to be released on the secret police murder of a KOR student activist in 1977, which at the time had galvanized student opposition.[56] An investigation commenced in 1991 and concluded in February 1994 proved he had been beaten to death and had not 'fallen down the stairs'. However, the Minister for Internal Affairs, Milczanowski, refused to disclose the names of the informants who had betrayed the student to the police. His decision was publicly criticized by the chairman of the Supreme Court as usurping the prerogative of the courts. The student groups accused him of shielding criminals.

However, at the end of June the Constitutional Tribunal ruled that the law on classified information covered only the intelligence and counterintelligence branches, not all security police employees, thus directly rendering Milczanowski's refusal illegal. Escalating the tension, simultaneously Milczanowski's own deputy minister in Internal Affairs suddenly found himself having to deny publicly that he had ever collaborated with the Stasi, even though newly divulged Stasi files appeared to indicate the contrary.

The ruling coalition then turned the heat up still further by drafting a bill to classify all intelligence and counterintelligence activities for eighty years, information relevant to national security for forty years, and economic secrets for thirty years. Details of security agents would remain classified for good. Further still, any journalists who published such material would be liable for prosecution, even if genuine abuses were disclosed or the common good could be proved to have been served. An amendment cancelling this liability for journalists was voted down by the former Communist party. Additionally it became known that the head of the National Security Bureau, Henryk Goriszewski, had written a formal note to the Sejm asking that they reject the amendment.

This last report fogged the situation still further, since Goriszewski was known to be very close to President Walesa, who at the same time was declaring that he would not sign the legislation in its current form. Walesa brushed the matter off as a misunderstanding, which did little to dispel the fog. In the constant jockeying between president and parliament, Walesa's own opposition to the bill could be interpreted as playing politics rather than being based upon principled adherence to the freedom of information. The Senate, however, when the bill came before them in October, decisively rejected it, only five voting for the measure. It then had to return to the Sejm, where it would need a two-thirds majority to survive. It did not return.

This reversal may have been prompted by the huge outcry against the bill from publishers, media professionals, writers and human rights activists. Media in a number of cities organized a public mockery of the bill, overtly withholding certain items from their news stories to demonstrate the likely effect of the legislation. As in Russia, this oppositional activism by media professionals and others was an important vector in the formation of media policy and practice. Finally, in November 1995, Milczanowski opened up a loophole by saying that he would disclose the names of the fourteen agents who had spied on Stanislaw Pyjas if so requested by a prosecutor or a judge, on the grounds of recent police law amendments that disclosure of security officials could take place if it would aid a murder investigation.[57]

An understanding of the relation between media and established power in Poland in this period cannot be complete without reference to the role of the Catholic hierarchy. Supported by President Walesa and several govern-ment administrations, the hierarchy also wished to imprint its stamp on media communication, the national culture and political debates. Especially prominent in this respect during the 1993–4 period were the issues of a ban on abortion and the approval of a Concordat with the Vatican, both of which the hierarchy, very actively backed by Walesa (Poland 'can only behave as a Christian nation, a nation of faith'[58]), supported energetically and at every opportunity.

The question of the Concordat was eventually postponed *sine die* because the Vatican did not wish to risk losing face by having the topic continually subjected to parliamentary rows. Toward the end of 1995, however, negotiations had reached the point where it appeared that some sym-bolically charged specifics were all that still stood in the way of its being legislated.[59] The attempt to reorient the abortion laws away from the draconian prohibitions legislated under the Suchocka administration was substantially passed by both houses, but then vetoed by Walesa. (He even hinted that if the necessary two-thirds majority were forthcoming to override his veto, he might consider abdicating from the presidency for a day in order to avoid having to sign it.[60]) It was, however, within those contexts of the Church hierarchy's aggressive involvement in public and private life that its interest in media needs to be understood, for instance its militant campaigning for broadcasting to be legally bound to respect Christian values.

The Church's access to broadcast media was not governed by the same restrictions or hiatuses that affected secular broadcasters. A 1989 law on Church–State relations was interpreted to exempt the Church from broad-cast licensing rules (Sabbat-Swidlicka, 1992), with the result that already by 1993 the Church was running 100 local radio stations. All it needed was for a diocesan bishop to write to the Minister of Telecommunications and a frequency would automatically and immediately be granted. However, the format of these stations during the period under review was essentially a standard commercial one, focusing on popular music and news flashes, and not pronouncedly religious. The religious aspects were the obligation to carry a Sunday mass, a short evening homily or discussion, strict avoidance of certain topics such as abortion rights or compulsory catechism in the schools, and a 'no-no' list of around a hundred individuals who could not be invited on the air because of their anti-Church positions.[61]

On one level, this was simply a mode of introducing commercial radio to Poland, even if adorned with some religious stipulations. On another level it represented a late attempt at *aggiornamento*[62] by the traditionalist Church hierarchy, targeting the younger generation in particular.

As regarded its presence in the press, however, the Church's position worsened after 1989, for several reasons (Sabbat-Swidlicka, 1992: 48). The newsprint and other press subsidies it received under the old regime vanished along with RSW. Journalists who had been banned by the former regime no longer needed to write for the Church press as their only outlet, with the result that the quality of Church publications drastically dropped. Some such journalists found themselves in active opposition to the hierarchy on the question of abortion or the Vatican Concordat, and so became unwelcome contributors anyway. Furthermore, some of the previously leading Church periodicals, especially the weekly *Tygodnik Powszechny* that had for many years been the main aboveground media opposition, identified themselves so wholeheartedly with the Mazowiecki administration that their credibility suffered in line with the huge unpopularity of the Balcerowicz plan.

Let us conclude this review of post-transition Polish media with some further summary observations on the spectrum of media available and simultaneously on the level of media professionalism within them, and with an overview of the impact of foreign ownership.[63]

We have already commented briefly on the programming of PolSat, on Catholic radio stations and newspapers, and on the generally mediocre to poor quality of the regional press. There were other voices, however, of which some of the most significant were the dailies *Gazeta Wyborcza* (Election Newspaper, from the days of its foundation early in 1989 when the title was equivalent to an in-your-face challenge to the old regime) – and its allied radio station, Radio Zet (from gaze*ta*) – *Rzeczpospolita* (Republic), *Gazeta Bankowa* (Finance Newspaper) and *Zycie Warszawy*, along with the weeklies *Polityka* and *Nowy Swiat* (New World) at the serious end, and the weeklies *Wprost* (Quite Right) and *Nie* (No) at the sensational-to-yellow end.

Gazeta Wyborcza and *Nie* were the two best-selling newspapers, with over half a million copies daily for the former and three-quarters of a million weekly for the latter. They occupied opposite ends of the spectrum, with *Gazeta Wyborcza* committed to continuing and developing the original vision of *Solidarnosc*, while *Nie* specialized in sensationalist muckraking. They were edited by two long-term political foes, Adam Michnik and the old regime's verbally adroit and supremely cynical press spokesman Jerzy Urban. *Gazeta Bankowa* offered in-depth financial analysis to its 20,000 weekly purchasers, whereas *Nowy Swiat*, with a similar number of readers, represented a nationalist and pro-clerical agenda. *Wprost*, based in Poznan, took the opposite tack, offering a strongly anti-clerical agenda. *Rzeczpospolita* and *Zycie Warszawy* provided very careful reporting of government activity (the former was the newspaper of record for the text of legislation) and in the latter case, of domestic politics. Along with *Gazeta Wyborcza* and *Gazeta Bankowa*, their standards of journalism were the highest in Poland in this period.

As will be seen from this list, the strength of the strictly conservative (i.e. nationalist, clerical) press was not very great. The spectrum mainly ran from political center to left of center. At the same time, with the best-selling title accounting for three-quarters of a million sales a week in a population of nearly 40 million, it was clear that television and to an unascertained degree radio were more widely used media at that point than the press.

Whether they were also more influential is a separate question, hard to answer in the absence of careful empirical research and equally careful definition of the paths of media influence.

There were many complaints concerning the level of journalism, with some *naïfs* arguing the totally impracticable, that the media should be almost entirely restocked with new blood, and, for their own ends, other interested parties such as Walesa, Olszewski, Wlodarczuk and Pawlak also making great play of media failings.

However, the critiques did not only come from those sources. Even those critical of the domineering predilections of the politicians acknowledged that drab and wooden word-production had often ceded overnight, it seemed, to rabid sensationalism and obsession with scandals, masquerading under the banner of investigative journalism. As Luczywo (1992) put it, before 1989 a clandestine letter from an opposition figure could make the system shake, but afterwards the most inflammatory and outrageous statements could be printed and circulated aboveground and legally, without any comeback. Kuron (cited by Kulakowska, 1992) argued that the problem was not the reporting of scandals, but the impression given that Polish political life was purely composed of such, thus risking the escalation of public cynicism about the political process to dangerous levels. Sabbat-Swidlicka (1993: 30) observed that 'insinuation and slander have become the norm . . . Overstatement and a tendency to discredit those who think differently, have all but replaced serious, reflective journalism.'

Foreign media ownership was, as we have noted, restricted to 33 percent in broadcast media by the 1993 law, and it was under that general heading that Walesa tried to block the allocation of the commercial TV channel to PolSat. However, there was a rather larger foreign presence in the press. Along with Hersant's 51 percent stake in *Rzeczpospolita*, through its affiliate company Socpresse, it claimed up until its divestments in 1994 to have a stake in eight other regional papers in Lodz, Gdansk, Krakow and Silesia. It was widely thought by media analysts, however, that it had a major stake in double that number through a number of banks in which it had a controlling interest (Kulakowska, 1994). German media capital was mostly involved in the magazine sector (Giorgi, 1995: 93–4). Eurexpansion was involved with *Gazeta Bankowy*, the *Wall Street Journal* with *Gazeta Wyborcza*, Radio France International at one point with Radio Zet. During the period under review, these foreign owners in Poland did not appear overly interventionist, although this could not securely presage their eventual stance.

The most obvious foreign intervention was of a different order, namely in television, whether broadcast or cable, where barter deals of various kinds had been struck for cheap packages of equally cheap Western programs. The result was that Polish TV screens were often saturated with Western European and American televisual dross, the cooperation and coproduction arrangements between neighboring countries that had been in force under the old regime (Downing, 1989) also having fallen by the wayside. Neither Polish ownership nor various stipulations about program origins seemed sufficient to halt that flood, equally visible as we have seen in post-transition Russia.

It would, naturally, be a considerable extra step to demonstrate that the flood in question was attractive to the majority of viewers to the point where Polish national culture would be under threat of anything so alarming as extinction, as some theorists of media imperialism might suggest, but none the less the plain absence of a large volume of well-produced Polish televisual material represented a process of de-nationalization of the airwaves, an avoidance of the appropriate mission of national broadcasters to develop a national cultural public realm on a great variety of levels, from the frivolous to the searching.

Hungary

Commentary on the post-transition media in Hungary has especially concentrated on the political battles between government and opposition parties over control of broadcasting policy, in this case both radio and television.[64] Such a focus is understandable in terms of standard political reporting, inasmuch as broadcasting policy was more bitterly and intensively contested in parliament even than economic policy, at least according to a spring 1994 observation by deputy Pozsgay Imre,[65] a former leader of the Communist reform wing under the old regime, by then co-chairman of a small parliamentary party. Rather soon into its term in office the main party in the first coalition government, Hungarian (Magyar) Democratic Forum (MDF), violently attacked broadcast media as agents of the opposition parties, and even worse. In the reported words of one government minister[66] the broadcast media were the most dangerous enemies of democracy and were guilty of disseminating a 'repertory of deceits'. The Alliance of Free Democrats, then the main opposition party, counter-attacked in like vein, for example comparing the March 1994 firing of 129 radio journalists to the Communist regime's policy in the aftermath of the 1956 revolution.[67]

Although the main elements of the so-called 'media wars' will be recapitulated below, it is also important to preserve a certain distance from the assumption that this was the only feature of Hungarian media in the period under review, or that the battle over broadcasting was precisely the same as the Russian or Polish confrontations, despite their apparently strong similarity. Furthermore, as Elemér Hankiss observed, 'It is better to have a war of words and political strategies around the Media than to have a war fought with tanks and guns' (1994: 293).

At the outset, many of the issues confronting Hungarian media were economic, as in Russia and Poland. The state's subsidies to a mass of print media were progressively reduced, forcing many out of business at the same time as another mass of hopeful start-up magazines and newspapers briefly flared into life. Ninety percent of average print media publication costs by 1992 were for newsprint and distribution (Oltay, 1992: 41). One senior print media executive even described the process of privatization at that juncture as primarily one of distributing losses.[68] Hundreds of millions of forints were still being expended in 1991 in order to subsidize the press.[69] In this situation, a number of foreign investors moved rather sharply into operation in the Hungarian media, perhaps swayed by Hungary's reputation of offering the most de-sovietized culture and economy of the former bloc.

The most striking of these forays was by Springer (Jakab and Gálik, 1991: 31–4). The story went as follows. Given that there had been no anticipation of any kind that a foreign private investor would either want or be permitted to own media under the former regime, there was no law in place forbidding it. Furthermore, in March 1990 the Communist Party had transferred ownership of regional dailies from itself to a limited private company, Servicing Ltd.

Two weeks after the spring 1990 elections were over Springer simply moved in and took over from Servicing Ltd. seven county daily newspapers, representing a readership of about a third of a million, and just over a third of the counties of the nation. At that juncture many print journalists who had faithfully served the old regime were extremely anxious about their professional futures, both because of the drastic political switchover that had taken place and because of the hazardous economic scenario in print media. Thus when Springer offered to hire everyone on these county newspapers for another one or two years, a number of newspaper staffs leapt at the offer, some agreeing in less than twenty-four hours. No editorial independence or rights to join professional journalists' bodies were conceded the staffs, merely 'protection' from the new coalition government, but to many the offer seemed too good to miss.

The Springer 'coup' caused considerable public outcry, but nothing could be done about it legally. Eventually Springer paid 200 million forints to the headquarters of the old Communist Party, but it was never officially established that there had been any obligation for it to do so.

This was the most dramatic incursion by foreign investors into the new Hungarian media market, but certainly not the only one (Jakab and Gálik, 1991: 21–31). Robert Maxwell's Mirror Holdings bought a large stake in *Magyar Hírlap*, beginning at 40 percent and rising subsequently to 51 percent. Bertelsmann bought a little over 40 percent of *Népszabadság*, and Hersant bought a similar amount of *Magyar Nemzet*. Rupert Murdoch's News Corporation started a daily, *Mai Nap*. Still other German and Austrian firms bought into other newspapers.

Simultaneous moves by the journalistic staffs of a number of papers to organize their own ownership and a consequent degree of internal autonomy were quite widespread and partially successful. Fifteen percent of *Magyar Nemzet* was thus owned, 32 percent of *Népszabadság*, 5 percent of *Magyar Hírlap*. In the remaining county dailies not snapped up by Springer, this share varied from 30 percent to 51 percent (Jakab and Gálik,

1991: 38). It is interesting to compare this partial success in Hungary, and the degree of foreign ownership there, with the much more radical experiments in self-management that characterized the media in Eastern Germany before they were swallowed up by the Western establishment (Boyle, forthcoming), and with the relatively high level of foreign press ownership in the Czech Republic, which by 1994 stood at over 50 percent.[70] In Hungary, as of late 1992, Western investment actually accounted for 80 percent of press capital assets (Oltay, 1992: 40). In 1994, however, Hersant sold its 92 percent of the national daily *Magyar Nemzet* back to the government (Giorgi, 1995: 17–18).

The origins of the so-called media wars were arguably threefold. One was, undoubtedly, the tradition of the media under the previous regime, where they were expected to be meticulous servants of the power structure. This was reflected in a 1974 media decree and a 1986 media law, which continued to hold sway through the period under review because insufficient agreement could be reached on an appropriate revision. This was despite the fact that in 1992 the Constitutional Court declared the 1974 decree unconstitutional and slated it to be abrogated by the end of 1992.

A second source of the media wars was the debate over Hungarian national identity referred to in Chapter 2 in which, clearly, the role of media was bound to be of paramount concern to the various protagonists. A third more proximate factor was the agreement worked out between the MDF and the AFD, then the two leading parties in parliament: (i) that key aspects of any media legislation, along with nineteen other contested zones of public life, needed to be passed by a two-thirds majority, which effectively gave the AFD veto power should it choose to use it; and (ii) that the AFD, in return for agreeing to reduce the total number of these zones to twenty, had the right to nominate the president of the republic. In the minds of many of those involved in hammering out these compromises, they would lead to a more consensual and less authoritarian style of government than might otherwise be the case. The 'tyranny of the majority' would be avoided.

Consensus was certainly not the outcome, unfortunately, and from the perspective of the AFD, the ensuing years constituted an ongoing struggle against consistent attempts by the MDF-led government to force its parliamentary majority's authority over broadcasting. From the MDF's typical angle of vision, by contrast, the broadcast media in particular – but also most of the press – did not simply criticize them unceasingly, but consistently amplified the specific critiques of the AFD. Kovats[71] has argued there was in addition a strong element of anti-Budapest sentiment involved, with the MDF leadership containing a number of individuals whose background was in the provinces, where the media practices in the latter years of the old regime had been quite unchanging, and with the AFD leadership being typically Budapest-based and with a tradition of challenging the power structure in and through media. As Giorgi (1995: 39) notes, a paradox of the latter period of the sovietized regime was that the Budapest press was actually less ironclad than the provincial media. Let us trace out the main elements in this saga.

Initially the two individuals placed at the head of television and radio, respectively Hankiss Elemér and Gombár Csaba, appeared to be on good terms with key figures in the government. Hankiss was personally friendly with Premier Antall, and Gombár was even publicly praised by the prominent ultra-rightist Csurka István during his confirmation hearing for having participated in the Lakitelek meetings in 1987. When Hankiss requested more funds to help with the transformation of television, the parliamentary Cultural Committee strongly supported him (Pataki, 1993: 17). All six parties in parliament agreed that he and Gombár should direct radio and television until a new media law was passed.

However, the honeymoon did not last very long. A number of events combined to persuade the government that broadcasters were conspiring with the opposition to defeat its policies. One concerned the government's effort to publicize its policy on compensating property owners who had been expropriated by the Communist regime, a policy opposed by the AFD. The director of the agency concerned did not receive a reply to his letter to Hankiss requesting airtime to explain the policy. Secondly, Gombár proposed reorganizing religious broadcasting, but an indirect effect would have been that Hungarian minorities in neighboring countries would no longer be able to receive such broadcasts. During this period there were repeated hostile demonstrations outside both the television and the radio headquarters by an assortment of neo-Nazis and other ultra-rightist factions, balanced by less frequent but far larger demonstrations in favor of democratizing media. All these served to intensify the more diffuse but tense climate of perpetual volleys of mutual accusations on the part of the governing coalition and media professionals against each other.

In May 1992, Premier Antall formally requested President Göncz to dismiss both Hankiss and Gombár, but the President declined on the ground that the proposed media law had not yet been legislated, so that such dismissals were premature. Following an appeal by Antall to the Constitutional Court, which decreed that the president should accede to such requests unless the democratic functioning of the institution in question were imperilled by the termination, Göncz for the second time refused to sign the dismissal letters, this time on the very ground cited by the Court.

The stage was now set for a further escalation of the strife, with the MDF loudly accusing the President of being loyal to his own party, the AFD, rather than to the office of the presidency. However, the situation was still further compounded by the fact that the Constitutional Court had, in declaring the 1974 media decree unconstitutional, simultaneously required that a media law be passed by the end of November 1992. In the event, it was put before parliament at the end of December, only to fail, and that without a single vote in its favor from any deputy.[72] In another debate in December 1992, this time over the 1993 national budget, a momentous vote as regards broadcasting was taken by the MDF majority, namely to include the 1993 radio and TV budgets in the budget of the prime minister's office, clearly another chapter in the war inasmuch as it gave the MDF a potential armlock on broadcasting finance.[73]

While this political situation was developing, there were further wars inside television itself. Hankiss had been directed to accept a vice-president of television, Nahlik Gabor, representing the MDF perspective. Hankiss refused to acknowledge Nahlik's appointment and indeed at one point suspended him for decisions made while he, Hankiss, was abroad. During the fall of 1992, Hankiss also dismissed two pro-MDF chief editors, because in his view their news and current affairs programs were highly unbalanced in favor of the nationalist right. The MDF-led government instituted disciplinary proceedings against Hankiss in November 1992 on the charge that he had mismanaged public funds by signing contracts with some private firms that did not proceed to deliver on their promises. Here again, there was evidence to suggest that the government had known about these contracts all along and was simply seeking a lever to force Hankiss out of office.

After the parliamentary debacle over the media law and the vote to put broadcasting funds in the prime minister's office for 1993, Hankiss and Gombár requested President Göncz (not Premier Antall) to dismiss them, on the ground they could no longer safeguard the independence of broadcasting. This strategic move backfired, because Antall promptly interpreted the letters as resignation letters and enthusiastically accepted them as such after the necessary fifteen days had elapsed during which public employees could withdraw a resignation. He then proceeded to put two aggressively rightist nationalists in charge of broadcasting, Nahlik in television and Csucs Lászlo in radio, both in an acting capacity. Hankiss and Gombár promptly denied they had resigned, and hence contested the legitimacy of these appointments. In this protest they were joined by many individual journalists and some journalists' organizations.

The tenor of the MDF's position on the new broadcasting heads was that television under Hankiss had slipped into 'alien' hands – a strange-sounding accusation until it is remembered that the ultra-nationalist 'Csurka' wing of public opinion was root and branch hostile to those it describred as aliens, cosmopolitans, liberals, Jews and Bolsheviks – and that as a result 'Hungarian national values' had been discounted under Hankiss' and Gombár's stewardship. Exactly what these values were was as muddily visible as the 'Christian values' insisted upon by some political forces in Poland. Two other conservative nationalist chief editors at TV, Palfy and Chrudinak, were reinstated (the latter in fact earlier, by a court decision), and they in turn appointed a slew of MDF supporters to jobs as chief editors and producers. These slots were vacated by internal transfers, for the most part, but also some firings.

Broadcast journalists by and large kept quiet on these happenings, largely because of job worries, but the same could not be said of the press, most of which attacked the moves as authoritarian and retrograde. Csucs and Nahlik insisted in response that they were simply trying to ensure the broadcast media could function free of party-political influence from any quarter – a hopelessly ambitious claim that by its very irrealism suggested propaganda rather than intent. (Not to mention the very clearly defined political ideologies of the two individuals and of many of their appointees.)

This was far from the end of the saga, however. In March 1994 Csucs announced that the following month 129 radio editors and journalists would be fired, the first batch of 320 in all due to be terminated (Pataki, 1994a). His public defense was that Hungarian radio was greatly over-staffed by comparison with some other European services (he instanced Switzerland and the Netherlands), and had to take this action to reduce its budget deficit.

His financial rationale, however initially plausible, none the less began to take on the air of convenient justification when the names of the 129 to be dismissed became known, and when he himself made statements such as 'my patience has lasted long enough' and that those fired had failed to meet journalistic and ethical standards. Many of the 129 were not only critics of the then government, but also had had a long and honorable career as critics of the old regime, when as we noted in Chapter 3, Hungarian radio had long been known as much more venturesome than television. In particular, the name of the chief editor of the program *168 Hours*, a program originating well before the transition and with a fine tradition of 'pushing the political envelope' under the previous regime, was among the 129. By contrast a number of those retained were widely recognized to be professionally less skilled than those let go.

Public reaction was swift and highly critical, especially in the light of the MDF's fast-sagging popularity in the polls and the imminence of national elections in May. After the announcement there were street demonstrations for two days running in Budapest to protest at the decision, including one demonstration of 30,000 people.[74] In the event, ironically, the announce-ment quite likely provided the *coup de grâce* to the MDF government, which went down to resounding defeat in the ensuing elections.

Even this was far from the final act in this tortuous epic. In July 1994, two months after the elections, President Göncz announced not only the dismissal of Gombár and Hankiss, without anyone's having consulted with them, and of Nahlik and Csucs, but also the appointment of two new chairmen for radio and television, and four deputy chairmen, all from inside the broadcasting organizations. It transpired that the dismissal of Nahlik and Csucs had been set up in a secret meeting between the outgoing MDF and the incoming Socialist Party administration. Each former acting chairman was given 3 million forints in severance pay, and was guaranteed that his tenure in that post would not be submitted to political scrutiny. Palvy István, chief editor of the TV news programs *Híradó* (News) and *Hét*

(Week), both well known for their conservative tilt, was fired yet again before Nahlik left office, as part of the deal.

However, the new government led by Horn Gyula and the Hungarian Socialist Party (effectively the reform wing of the former Communist Party), did not in the event consult with the other parties on the appointments although he had promised to do so. Nor were a variety of experienced candidates put forward by other parties selected, including some members of his own party. Horn claimed he had been told the parties were deadlocked and so had chosen to take prompt action to redress the long-irregular broadcasting situation. This sparked bitter denunciations from the other parties.

The new TV chairman Horvath Adam, having initially insisted he had no concrete plans and wanted to get to know his broadcasters better, especially those who worked on *Híradó*, proceeded on his second day in office to fire *Híradó*'s recently appointed chief editor. He followed this up by immediately sending home on full pay 174 of the 194 journalists working on the program.

The Hungarian media business, it seemed, was continuing as usual. All the issues had been swept under the rug in the deal between Horn and Göncz, including whether broadcasting answered to the president or the premier. In the absence of a law codifying the situation, media professionals were effectively dependent upon their sources of income ('he who pays the piper . . .'), and so somewhat intimidated, with the effect that investigative reporting and searching news analysis had died away to a trickle. Often salaries were paid two and three months late, which intensified the dependent situation of media professionals.

Broadcasting's sources of revenue in this period were threefold: a license fee (only collected from about 40 percent of viewers); a subsidy from the premier's office; and advertising, representing reportedly about 70 percent of income (but around two-thirds of that amount was in turn channeled through two government agencies). Thus one way or another the government held the strings, meanwhile not publishing figures that most observers thought reliable on broadcasting finance. Lastly, the core financial administration of broadcasting retained essentially all the personnel who had fulfilled that role from before the transition. From the perspective of a number of independent-minded media professionals the situation seemed to be locked on to the status quo, with no powerful agency, governmental or economic, appearing to wish to alter it.[75]

Later in the year the six parties reassembled for talks on the structure of broadcasting and this time seemed to reach agreement that radio, television, and the satellite service Duna (Danube) TV for Hungarians in neighboring countries, should all three be made into joint-stock companies. Later still, financial support was announced from Bonn and two *Länder* (Bayern and Baden-Württemberg) for broadcast privatization, among other infrastructural developments.[76] There could be little doubt that the overall economic plight of the country, given its huge budget deficit (72 percent of

GNP in 1995), was a further brake on change, inasmuch as neither private investment nor government subsidies were likely to flow at all freely in such circumstances.

Finally, in October 1995 the six major parliamentary parties agreed on a media law draft. Its provisions included the switch to public from state ownership of the main broadcasting channels, and allowed private investment, domestic or foreign, in broadcast stations. The second TV channel was put under concession for a ten-year period, and a (financially rather implausible) second satellite TV channel was legislated. The Smallholders Party subsequently withdrew its support, but the law was voted by a large majority in December and signed by President Göncz in January 1996.[77]

One bright spot on the horizon in some analysts' view was the development of local cable TV (cf. Fenton, 1994: 25–30). It did indeed show signs of rapid growth across the nation and was often proudly independent of government. However, its financing was akin to not-for-profit firms in the USA, inasmuch as it relied greatly on the energy and enthusiasm of local activists, but brought in rather little revenue, certainly too little to make it immediately attractive to commercial investors.

Conclusions

The issues raised in this chapter on post-sovietized media may be summarized as twofold. One is the empirical question of trends: in what direction are these media systems moving? Is it even possible to establish directions so soon after the major changes of 1989–91? The other is related to the ultimate objective of this book: what bearing do mediatic or political theories have on these developments, and what problems do these developments raise for mediatic and political theories? Here we will address the first issue, and will examine the second set of issues in the two succeeding chapters on mediatic theories.

A number of writers have addressed the question of media trends, in some cases for Russia, in other instances across East-Central Europe. Let us consider the positions of a select number, namely Foster (1994a), McNair (1994) and Tsabria (1993), for Russia; and Fabris (1995), Jakubowicz (1995b), Sparks and Reading (1994) and Splichal (1994), for East-Central Europe. In some cases, predictably, the writers' personal convictions concerning the desirability or danger of a given trend shape their analysis more than the data they cite in support of their interpretation. In fast-moving scenarios such as Russia, Poland and Hungary, and against the recent backdrop of sovietized systems of control and repression and the hope that they have been ditched for good, this blurring is understandable. Yet it will be very important for us to endeavor to winnow out what can be supported by evidence rather than by angst or passion.

Let us begin with Russia. In the immediate aftermath of the assault on the Parliament building in October 1993, Dmitrii Tsabria, then First

Deputy Press and Information Minister, articulated a threefold position concerning Russian media. Firstly, society needed to be protected by law against anti-social media practices; secondly, media needed legal protection from state persecution and harassment; and thirdly, due recognition should be given to the unanticipatedly great difficulty of the transition from sovietism to democracy. The rhetoric of his argument was largely prescriptive, but its analytical presumptions are worth reflection.

What he had in mind behind the terminology of legal protection was firstly that certain kinds of media activity ought to be able to be declared unlawful. The Russian instances he cited of media that ought to be able to be restrained legally, but were not able to be, were twofold. One was the failure of the court system to restrain in any way the poisonously chauvinistic and anti-semitic newspaper *Den'* (later to be re-named *Zavtra*, Tomorrow). The other was the encouragement he claimed had been given by large sections of the media to intensifying tensions leading up to the bloody 1993 assault on Parliament 'by feeding them the thought that violence was in order, that blood was in order'.

One of his examples of needed legal protection for the media was that journalists could be and had been physically ejected from firms they were investigating, in plain defiance of Criminal Code Article 140-1 that affirmed their right to conduct such investigations. Equally, they could be and were harassed and even badly beaten, as happened during the assault on Parliament, without any effective redress being available in the courts. In other words, enforcement mechanisms, especially prompt ones, were signally lacking to guarantee a free media system.

The main point he made concerning the difficulty of the transition process was the dilemma of state subsidies to Russian media. These inevitably compromised media independence but, in the immediate circumstances, to discontinue them would be to cancel out most if not all media communication altogether. This formulation rather bypassed the continuing reality of the Yeltsin administration's and other governmental instances' proclivities to steer media – by a combination of intimidation and financing mechanisms – toward unflinching support for their policies and disregard for their failures. It implied the problems were solely constitutional and revenue-based, not political (or criminal, as in the Listyev case). None the less, as we noted earlier in the chapter in the case of the 1995 closure of *Nezavisimaya Gazeta* and *Kuranty*, or the question of broadcast transmission costs, subsidies or tax relief were a life-and-death issue for print media in particular. In July 1995, *Segodnya* reported that more than 85 percent of Russian publications had not been able to acquire the necessary funds for printing or replacing obsolete machines, and were constantly threatened with collapse.[78]

In terms of its specifically Russian implications, Tsabria's commentary on the period under review demonstrated rather forcibly the fragility of media freedoms despite the Yeltsin administration's public rhetoric of democratic development. Tsabria's implied solutions lay in the realm of improving law enforcement and, presumably, waiting for the economy to improve so that media financing would not be a governmental responsibility. What he left out of account was the seeming vacuum of will at the apex of the Russian system to ensure that even existing legal codes regarding media were followed. He also failed to note the great importance of combativity on the part of media professionals in taking the lead to develop a functioning public sphere.

Foster's view of the last point, however, was rather less sanguine. She argued that the media in Russia had been a 'fundamental failure as a force for societal consolidation and moderation during a period of profound national crisis'. She specifically claimed that the media had encouraged public disunity, de-legitimized the new leadership, and had eroded public confidence in the inevitably checkered process of gradually establishing new democratic procedures. She concluded that the media had 'demystified and delegitimized the present as well as the past'. (The term 'demystified' is a little odd, seeming to imply that there needs to be a mystique of government or of national development.)

In drawing this conclusion, she contrasted Russian and US experience, noting that there was no culturally based commitment to democratic procedure yet in Russia, nor a commitment to a law-based, constitutional system. It is on this basis that she argued that media activities which would not be destabilizing in the USA, were so in Russia. She particularly emphasized that the media's 'unrelenting criticism and exposure of personal and systematic failings has eroded rather than fostered public confidence'.

There are some severe problems with this analysis. One is its romanticization of US media and political history, which is the pole against which Russia is judged and interpreted. She reads that history as one in which free media have offered a safety valve for discontent, and have persuaded the citizenry that political institutions are not completely closed off against change – a reading that fundamentally negates the contrary historical experience of US media, over a long historical period, by African Americans, Native Americans and Latinos, and by women.

Another problem is her assumption that media should act in favor of consolidation and moderation during a profound national crisis, that they should be a force for cohesion and integration. If she simply means that media should not encourage people to violence or the tolerance of violence, then she is hardly being controversial. But if she means that they should function as a secular equivalent of a consolidating and moderating religion, then that is a much larger claim, and one that is a little too close to pollyannaish in the face of the political thrust of the Yeltsin administration's and the Russian parliament's pronounced authoritarianism, phenomena that she elsewhere acknowledges.

Both she and Tsabria ultimately underline the same issue as key, namely the necessity of a democratic, constitutional state, a framework of functioning laws, for media to function democratically. Thus rather than open media being the lifeblood of democracy, to which Russia and other post-

Soviet nations should cleave in order to achieve democracy, they both propose that a law-based state may be a sociologically prior condition for such media.

Writing out of the heat of the battle for the White House in October 1993 and out of the fierce tussles for control of *Izvestiia* in the two years preceding that confrontation, and writing as professional legal scholars, this starkly bipolar diagnosis is understandable, but not especially helpful. It tends to render both legal-constitutional and mediatic institutions highly abstract and almost hypostatized, rather than the 'messy', 'leaky', ongoing and interconnected societal constructs that both actually are.

McNair's conclusions (1994: 133–4) introduce some needed additional complexity to the analysis. He certainly acknowledges the importance of a stable legal and constitutional framework for the future development of an open media system in Russia, but adds to that the need for economic stability and growth together with the emergence of a new cadre of media professionals untainted with sovietized professional instincts, and imbued with 'political courage' (p. 131).

It is perhaps hardly surprising that all three commentators emphasize so strongly the confused dynamic of law in Russia, with that nation's long history of authoritarian and anarchistic impulses, with its sometimes contradictory deep fear of disorder and deep hatred of repression. The transition of the first half of the 1990s was self-evidently much more crisis-ridden in Russia than in Poland and Hungary, for the reasons of size, history, empire, duration of the Soviet system, and the other factors already mentioned.

However, even McNair's more nuanced analysis arguably lacks perspective on the entirety of the dynamics in play. It is obvious that all three analysts are principally preoccupied with news media and the immediate – often chaotic – political process. In that sense, they omit consideration of the full range of media that continue to construct and reconstruct Russian culture, and thus implicitly are also trapped in the ratiocinative under-pinnings of Habermas' concept of *Öffentlichkeit*, criticized for this limitation in Chapter 1. The same limitation is salient, it must be confessed, in many of the illustrations of Russian media issues earlier in this chapter, which are drawn from the again rather similar focus of the *Post-Soviet Media Law and Policy Newsletter* or the *RFE/RL Research Reports*, admirable publications in every way but bounded by those same concerns. Yet as indicated by the discussion elsewhere in this book of the impact of youth and musical cultures on preparing the ground for the collapse of the Soviet system, the spectrum of media is far broader.

Furthermore, although McNair is right to draw our attention to the key questions of economy and professional socialization, his position seems overly schematic. Economic stability, he argues, will allow for the development of a strong consumer market and thereby avoid the colonization of Russian media by foreign media moguls. In fact, at least as of the time of writing, foreign media control of broadcasting and print media organizations was much less evident in Russia than in a number of other post-Soviet nations.

Media content, of course, especially highly visible material such as store advertising in English rather than Russian, gave a different impression to the general public. In turn this could easily feed into the central dynamic during the first half of the 1990s, namely the impact of an extremely troubled and sharply unequal economy on the intensification of extremist versions of Russian nationalism and hence on their expression and amplification in many Russian media. Within such a context, media imperialism could almost only succeed financially by attacking itself!

Additionally, McNair only briefly addresses (p. 126) the problematic specifics of media subsidy that Tsabria appropriately highlighted and that were explored earlier in this chapter.

Likewise, his call for 'a new generation of media professionals . . . [to] be reared and placed in positions of responsibility' (p. 134) with the aid of Western training programs is both strangely out of kilter with his worries about Western media imperialism, and somehow obliterates the reality that there was an existing corps of media professionals of varying talents and outlooks that would not simply bow out gracefully before Western-trained successors. Some members of this existing body were indeed relics of the past; others, as he pointed out earlier in the same article, fell into a variety of categories, from Soviet loyalists recycled into some new version of loyalist, or money-grubbers and scandalmongers, or tough-minded independent professionals. In turn, all are employed by media organizations of varying quality and financial security. It is thus tempting to ask, 'What is new here? In what significant way does this differ from the corps of media or other professionals in other lands? Is there not also a learning curve directly generated by experience of the new domestic Russian realities, which some professionals and some media will embrace to varying extents, in varying directions, and some will avoid – regardless of Western seminars on free media?'

Comparing these diagnoses of Russian media since 1991 with selected analyses of East-Central European media since 1989 produces the following parallels and contrasts.

Sparks and Reading (1994: 267), focusing specifically on television in four northern units of the old Soviet *cordon sanitaire* (Poland, the Czech and Slovak republics, Hungary), argue that 'the substantive continuity of the broadcasting structures and the continuation of a strong state element in the system' have been the order of the day. They further conclude that while market mechanisms in stable economies may easily co-exist with the norms of political democracy, the unstable conditions of this group of nations in the period under discussion illustrate the mutual functional independence of those norms and mechanisms. Such norms, they usefully point out, 'are at least flexible if not entirely dispensable' (p. 268).

Splichal (1994: 143–8) suggests that the most helpful framework within which to understand the general character of media systems in the region since 1989 is what he terms their 'Italianization'. By this he draws appropriate attention to the fact that 'Western' media systems have not themselves necessarily been the finest flowers of democratic rectitude. In Italy, for example, in the post-Second World War era, there was developed a broadcasting system which began with a complete political monopoly by the Christian Democratic Party. Toward the end of the 1960s, while the Christian Democrats retained major control, the Socialist Party was granted a subsidiary TV channel to propagate its line, and eventually a decade later the PCI, the Communist Party (always far larger than the Socialist Party) was in turn granted a minor channel only able to be received by certain areas of the country. But it was the PCI's to play *its* tunes through. With the advent of media magnate Berlusconi's hegemony over the newly permitted commercial channels in the 1980s, and his successful bid for the office of prime minister, the question of political control over media entered a new, still contested, but not qualitatively distinct phase.

Thus Splichal proposes East-Central European media are joining this variant of Western European media structures. Fabris (1995: 224–5) suggests by contrast that there are four possible directions of development: 'Westification'; 'Germanification'; the effective extirpation of the civil society developments that featured in the earliest phase of the transition; and the possibility, though he considers it unlikely, of a Europe-wide reconstruction of media from out of the commercial mold and into what he terms 'a repoliticization of the public sphere'. Fabris' categories are a little mixed, in the sense that by both 'Westification' and 'Germanification' he seems to have in mind primarily two types of media imperialism, the first demarcated by general culture-zone, the second by Europe's premier national economic power. He offers little or no sense for how either of these might play out politically in a given nation, given the differing corporate and political strategies of various media firms (for example Springer as opposed to Bertelsmann, or Hersant as opposed to Time-Warner or Turner). His suggestion that authoritarian regimes may simply reimpose themselves in the region is not so far from Sparks and Reading's prognosis.

However, he does briefly examine developments in Hungary, Eastern Germany and the Czech Republic to assess the validity of his four scenarios. In Hungary he found a mixed situation, depending on whether print or broadcast media were in focus, with 'Westification' in operation in print media, but a rise of authoritarianism in broadcast media. His analysis, however, only goes as far as the MDF's period in office up to 1994, so that it is easier on that basis to draw such a conclusion about Hungarian broadcast media. (Not surprisingly, he found 'Germanification' had been the dominant trend in Eastern Germany; his analysis of the Czech Republic, not our primary focus here, only covers the period up to 1991.)

Jakubowicz (1995b) offers a considerably subtler categorization into which to fit the mediatic panorama of Central and Eastern Europe. He proposed that media in the region be interpreted in terms of their position along a three-stage continuum, combining political, economic and mediatic dimensions. Stage 1 would include media de-monopolization and decentralization, and internationalization of television content; Stage 2 would include new media legislation, and signs of journalistic professionalization in new private media; Stage 3 would include the consolidation of media legislation, professionalization and democratization, but also the beginnings of media concentration and the influence of foreign media capital. He proceeded to assign the European CIS and East-Central European nations' media systems to provisional places in this grid.

Jakubowicz's suggestions for pointers to future trends were, however, in conflict with each other at one point. He strongly stated the non-equivalence of media de-monopolization with media autonomy, let alone with media democratization. He pointed out that links between the power structure and the media were still exceptionally close in the period under review, sometimes compelled to be so by the weak consumer market that made advertising insufficient as a revenue source to free media from government or political party subsidy, especially in conflict-ridden political periods where some patrons with influence became a practical necessity for institutional survival (pp. 83, 84). He also insisted that functioning democratic media require as their precondition stable governmental and party democracy, consensus on the economic and political system, and economic growth in market conditions (p. 83). Yet at the close of the article (p. 88) he asked whether the East-Central European nations whose success in achieving a democratic transition was most probable would actually find themselves having achieved very much worth having, given the testimony of critical media research in the West itself to the flawed character of Western media democracy.

It is a dilemma that Splichal, and Sparks and Reading, equally articulate in different ways. It is a dilemma partly pitched on hope – hope that there might not be a reversion to authoritarian media systems, hope too that the dissolution of the old Soviet system might just possibly enable a vault over the typical flaws of Western media to create something stronger, more energetically democratic. It is also a dilemma partly pitched on an emphasis on news and formal political structures, which is far from invalid, but is still partial in focus.

Thus the general conclusions which may be drawn from and about these essays reflect fairly closely the five caveats concerning the present state of research issued at the outset of this chapter, especially the tendential focus on news rather than entertainment media or other everyday cultural expression, on legal issues, and on television rather than other media. All these priorities are understandable and quite sensible, yet they may inadvertently distort our sense for the total picture. They give us a very state-centric, politically focused, rational-cognitive and capital-city perspective.

Their accounts of the travails and turmoil of changes in professional journalistic codes and the rather poor quality of many journalists certainly have the ring of truth to them at certain points, but often seem to homogenize journalists and media professionals and almost to judge the best by the worst. The sardonic British verse

You cannot hope to bribe or twist
– Thank God! – the British journalist
For seeing what, unbribed, he'll do
There really is no reason to

seems sometimes to be lurking in the background. Yet given the active participation of a number of journalists at the original forefront of opposition in all three nations, and given events such as the huge public turnouts in Moscow following the assassinations of Kholodov and Listyev, or the large Budapest demonstrations against the firing of radio journalists in spring 1994, or Polish parliamentary deputies' resistance to Walesa's attempts at corralling news media, or the stubborn stances of *Gazeta Wyborcza* or of Walendziak as Director of Polish TV, the true picture does not seem to emerge in its entirety from this concentration on the worst and most problematic. Any more than a blanket negative description of media in the West would produce an unobfuscated account.

From an audience/readership perspective, some data seemed to point in a similar direction, at least for Russia. A national survey conducted by the Open Media Research Institute in early 1995 of Russian public opinion concerning domestic and foreign media (Gigli and Warshaw, 1995), found that most Russians were simultaneously discerning in their evaluation of strengths and weaknesses in news reporting, and frustrated by failures they could perceive – such as Chechnya coverage – without being able to remedy them. As Wishnevsky (1993: 91) proposed concerning Russian media, after surveying their various flaws, 'While it is true that the media have a long way to go before they achieve the freedom and responsibility characteristic of a truly democratic society, no other institutions in Russia appear to be any closer to those goals than the media are.' On balance, a similar verdict could probably be pronounced on Polish and Hungarian media over the same period.

Thus the trends of media development in this initial period seemed neither to promise the media bliss seemingly envisaged by many who understandably hoped for something decisively better, perhaps even better than the West could offer; nor did they probably justify premature pessimism at the prospect of the return of renewed media repression. In the short term, they appeared rather to underscore the basic rule that strong democracy and open media are goals of continued effort and struggle, and never simple givens. In this perspective, the mediatic heritage of the three nations examined here, both Soviet and pre-Soviet, is a heritage that could never be expected to be sloughed off in a biennium, or even a generation.

Notes

1 Some of this discussion was very naive. Little attention was paid to the ways in which media freedom can also be compromised, threatened or canceled by corporate media ownership.

2 By 'non-events' is meant simply that years passed with no law being passed, or highly incomplete legislation. For those struggling to get laws on the statute books, and for those struggling to prevent them being legislated, these years were of course highly eventful.

3 In this sense, the dilemma Foster (1993: 739–47) poses, namely whether free media are a condition for a constitutional order, or vice versa, is indeed overly schematic and dualist. She herself, in responding to the dilemma as defined, briefly suggests that a key third factor in Russia was the absence of a constitutionalist culture, especially at the levels of language and symbols. This is not inappropriate as an observation, but is still insufficient inasmuch as it effectively omits the role of social movements of many kinds in the painful construction of a more participative political culture. Her hope that Russian media in and of themselves will assume the responsibility for initiating this process seems to betray an optimism about the role of media professionals in society that is hard to support empirically from most nations, let alone Russia at the period of her research. We will return to her arguments at the close of the section on Russian media.

4 *Soviet/East European Report*, VIII.44, 15 September 1991. See Bonnell and Freidin (1995) for a very intersting blow-by-blow account of television news during the putsch.

5 There were additional sources of hostility to Bragin. See Wishnevsky, 1994, esp. pp. 4–5.

6 For the detailed information in what follows on economic issues I am dependent for the most part on information in Vera Tolz, 'Russia', *RFE/RL Research Report*, 1.39, 2 October 1992, 4–9; Wishnevsky, 1993; Andrei Richter, 'Direct subsidies to the press: some background', *Post–Soviet Media Law and Policy Newsletter*, I.4, 27 January 1994, 2–3; Peter Krug, 'Pass the Advil: financial woes of Russia's state broadcasters', *Post–Soviet Media Law and Policy Newsletter*, I.5, 28 February 1994, 1–2.

7 Late in 1992 Poltoranin resurfaced as director of Yeltsin's newly created Federal Information Center in charge of the Ostankino and Rossiya (Russian) television channels, Radio Rossii, and the national news agencies ITAR–TASS and RIA (formerly Novosti). Then, in 1994, after Yeltsin abolished the Federal Information Center in an abrupt series of decrees concerning the media, he resurfaced again as chair of the State Duma Committee on Information Policy and Communications.

8 If the numbers seem suddenly to have soared into the stratosphere, the hyperinflation in Russia in those years needs bearing in mind.

9 Wishnevsky, 1994: 3.

10 *OMRI Daily Digest*, 196.I, 9 October 1995.

11 *Izvestiia*, 6 July 1994, cited in *RFE/RL Daily Report*, 129, 11 July 1994; cf. Wishnevsky, 1993: 87, 91.

12 In October 1995 Yeltsin signed a decree establishing the same basic 51/49 percent federal/private ownership for Russian TV, the newly national St Petersburg TV service, and three national radio stations.

13 *OMRI Daily Digest*, 53.I, 15 March 1995.

14 *OMRI Daily Digest*, 34.I, 16 February 1995.

15 *Monitor*, I.23, 1 June 1995; I.32, 12 June 1995; *OMRI Daily Digest*, 106.I, 1 June 1995.

16 Cited in *Post–Soviet Media Law and Policy Newsletter*, 21, 1995, 6.

17 Foster (1993: 722–4) offers a useful discussion of this issue in the Russian context.

18 'Murderous window: Listyev's death and Russian television', *Post–Soviet Media Law and Policy Newsletter*, 16, 1995, 1–3.

19 'Glasnost Defense Fund's Simonov assesses impact', *Post–Soviet Media Law and Policy Newsletter*, 16, 1995, 5–7.

20 In what follows on the KGB I am particularly indebted to Albats (1994), Rahr (1992, 1993), Waller (1994, chs. 7–8) and Yasmann (1992, 1993).

21 Kryuchkov had been appointed KGB head in 1988 by Gorbachev from the organization's foreign branch on the supposition that his perspectives on *perestroika* would have been less contaminated by the domestic branch's hierarchy.

22 Aleksei Simonov, 'Letter from Moscow', *Post–Soviet Media Law and Policy Newsletter*, 6, 31 February 1994, 9.

23 See Yasmann 1995a, 1995b, 1995c. Novikov (1996) argues that the trigger for the war

against Chechnya was a dispute over the profits from military-organized drug-smuggling, out of Tajikistan via Chechnya to Russia, between the Chechen leadership and some top military officials, including Defense Minister Grachev.

24 Molchanov cited in Steven Erlanger, 'Russians watch war on uncensored TV', *New York Times*, 20 December 1994, A7; Filatov cited in *Post-Soviet Media Law and Policy Newsletter*, 11 (15 October 1994), 9.

25 *RFE/RL Daily Report*, 230, 7 December 1994.

26 For an analysis of this event and its background, see David Remnick, 'The Tycoon and the Kremlin', the *New Yorker* (double issue), 20 and 27 February 1995, 118–39. Later in the year Yeltsin and Luzhkov publicly, at least, reconciled. See Victor Yasmann, who suggests that among other factors, Yeltsin needed a quiet Moscow in case the Chechnya war were to destabilize his position: 'Boris Yeltsin's favorite mayor', *Prism*, I.6, Pt 2, 2 June 1995. By March 1996, such was the panic in Moscow business circles at the renaissance of the Communist Party in the polls, that NTV's director, Malashenko, actually agreed to serve as Yeltsin's re-election campaign's top advisor – another index of the turbulence of Russian politics. Alessandra Stanley, 'Russia's press edits out a Communist', *New York Times*, 31 March 1996, Section 4, 1–4.

27 Erlanger, *New York Times*, 20 December 1994, A.7; Andrei Richter, 'NTV and the Most Bank media empire', *Post-Soviet Media Law and Policy Newsletter*, 12/13, 10 December 1994, 7; *RFE/RL Daily Report*, 229, 5 December 1994.

28 Erlanger, *New York Times*, 20 December 1994, A.7; *RFE/RL Daily Report*, 235, 14 December 1994.

29 *OMRI Daily Digest*, I.6, 9 January 1995. He was fired abruptly in February 1996, with many observers concluding his channel's independent stance on Chechnya to have been the reason. See *Post-Soviet Media Law and Policy Newsletter*, 26 (26 February) 1996, 1–10.

30 Alessandra Stanley, 'Bombing of rebel city lets up, but not the attacks on Yeltsin', *New York Times*, 6 January 1995, A1.

31 *OMRI Daily Digest*, 87.I, 4 May 1995; 110.I, 7 June 1995.

32 Albats, 1994: 325–8; *RFE/RL Daily Report*, 16, 25 January 1994; 18, 27 January 1994; 165, 31 August 1994.

33 Melissa Dawson, 'Death of a journalist', *Post-Soviet Media Law and Policy Newsletter*, 12/13, 10 December 1994, 12; *RFE/RL Daily Report*, 199, 19 October 1994; 200, 20 October 1994.

34 Grachev sued a *Moskovskii Komsomolets* journalist, Vadim Poegli, who had labeled him a thief. The court's decision a year later sentenced him to a year's corrective labor and the garnishing of 30 percent of his salary. Although the sentence was immediately abrogated by a Duma general amnesty, Poegli appealed the verdict, and the editorial board published a repeat of the offending assertion (*OMRI Daily Digest*, 211.I, 30 October 1995). The use of libel laws to intimidate journalists, common in Western countries, appeared to be on the rise in general in Russia (*OMRI Daily Digest*, 227.I, 21 November 1995).

35 *RFE/RL Daily Report*, 172, 26 September 1994; 'On the state of freedom of mass information in the Maritime Krai', article from *Rossiiskaia Gazeta*, 27 December 1994, in *Post-Soviet Media Law and Policy Newsletter*, 15, February 1995, 2–3; Wishnevsky, 1995: 37; Michael Specter, 'Old-time boss for Russia's showcase port', *New York Times*, 28 August 1995, A1, A2. Wishnevsky (1994: 2–3) gives other examples from the regions. At a December 1995 round table of regional newspaper editors in Moscow, participants observed that the survival of their newspapers often depended on supporting, or at least not criticizing, their local power structure (*OMRI Daily Digest*, 237.I, 7 December 1995). The deputy editor of the *Vologda Sever* newspaper was beaten up by unknown assailants shortly after publishing an article that queried where the provincial governor had obtained the funds to build a luxurious new dacha (*OMRI Daily Digest*, 229.I, 27 November 1995).

36 Steele (1994: 381) argues that Bragin's decision to cut off Ostankino Television a few minutes after the fighting began, and to resume from a distance away some hours later without live coverage, was not justified by the real level of threat to the building from the insurgents, but was rather a political communication designed to convey to the Russian public the

desperate nature of the struggle and the stop-at-nothing violence of the insurgents. His decision was certainly widely criticized by journalists (Wishnevsky, 1994: 5).

37 *RFE/RL Daily Report*, 237, 16 December 1994.

38 The Duma was the elected lower house; the Council of the Federation was the appointed upper house.

39 *OMRI Daily Digest*, 72.I, 11 April 1995; 81.I, 25 April 1995.

40 *Post-Soviet Media Law and Policy Newsletter*, 10, 10 September 1994, 1; *RFE/RL Daily Report*, 165, 31 August 1994; 167, 2 September 1994; 168, 5 September 1994; 170, 7 September 1994.

41 This is a topic already addressed earlier in the book (see Chapter 2, especially n.17), but general signals of the problem increased considerably during 1995. The extreme rightist Russian Officers Union was claiming organizations in 78 major military units, and much wider covert support (*Murmanskii Vestnik*, 5 April 1995, cited in *Monitor*, I.18, 24 May 1995. Alarmed articles in *Izvestiia*, 6 June 1995, and *Moskovskie Novosti*, 39, 1995 underscored the growing appeal of fascist groups because of Russians' intense desire for restoring law and order at any cost (cited in *Monitor*, I.28, 8 June 1995). Defense specialist Felgengauer (*Segodnya*, 26 May 1995, cited in *Monitor*, I.21, 30 May 1995) noted the uncharacteristic unity between Russian elite and public on the subject of NATO's eastward expansion, and also the failure of oppositionists to the Chechnya war to mount a single large-scale demonstration against it, suggesting most Russians were taking Russian territorial integrity and independence in their current form as absolutes. In May 1995 a distinguished public award, the Milestones Award, was given by the Duma to a deceased writer, Lev Gumilyov, who had vigorously propagated the view that Russian civilization was not only superior to the West's, but that intermarriage between Russians and other ethnic groups can lead to the degeneration of the Russian character (*Monitor*, I.17, 23 May 1995). Ultra-nationalist demagogue Zhirinovsky was made a reserve lieutenant-colonel on his fiftieth birthday by Defense Minister Grachev in recognition of his 'outstanding contribution to strengthening Russia's defense capability' (*OMRI Daily Digest*, 64.I, 30 March 1995). And human rights activist and deputy Sergei Kovalev, fresh from being dismissed as Duma Human Rights Committee chairman for his forthright stand on rights violations in Chechnya, publicly concluded that a rightist coup was no longer on the agenda for the simple reason that the extreme nationalists were 'already in power' around Yeltsin (quoted in *Monitor*, I.25, 5 June 1995). This received confirmation not only from the rapid ascendancy of Korzhakov, Yeltsin's *éminence grise*, and Grachev, Defense Minister, but also from extremely aggressive statements of Russian foreign policy inside and outside the CIS by Foreign Minister Kozyrev and his policy director Lukov (Vladimir Socor, 'Kozyrev signals harder line on CIS policy', *Prism*, 7 July 1995, Part 1; Paul A. Goble, 'Kozyrev advisor sees special path for Russia', *Prism*, 28 July 1995, Part 2). Mihalisko (1995) analyses the Yeltsin decree of September 1995 regarding Russian–CIS relations that codified much of this thinking. Lunev (1995) collates and analyses a number of less official signals in 1995 media reports and think-tank documents that strongly suggested a systematic reassertion by leading military circles of the priorities and methods of Soviet imperial policy.

42 'Poltoranin's dreams and hopes', *Post-Soviet Media Law and Policy Newsletter*, 11, 15 October 1994, 6–7; 'A press conference with Sergei Gryzunov', *Post-Soviet Media Law and Policy Newsletter*, 12/13, 10 December 1994, 10–11.

43 Poltoranin's crass discursive rhetoric was highly reminiscent of the old regime, especially of the 'villagist' current in Russian nationalism. His views as reproduced in the article cited above praised the honest quality of the regional media, where journalists apparently were not afraid to get cow-shit on their shoes through following up a story on farming life, as opposed to the high-decibel distance of Moscow's overly critical media from real life. He even suggested that on this account regional media were quickly overtaking national media in public esteem. His argument conveniently omitted the fact that many regional media had no significant local competitors by that time, and that they were often closer to being bulletins for the regional power structure than freely functioning media organs. Not that Moscow media should be thought to deserve immunity from searching criticism, but the countryside-versus-capital-city

thematic was too well-established a demagogic peg in the 'real Russia' versus the 'cosmopolitan urbanites' discourse to pass muster as more than bluster.

44 This seemingly innocuous generality was not to be taken for granted in the media policy climate of the time. In early October 1994, Yeltsin's chief of staff Sergei Filatov held a closed conference with Yeltsin's regional envoys. The topic was the failure of the media to 'convince the population of the correctness of presidential and governmental policies'. There was agreement that government newspapers should be subsidized, and that the finances should be transferred to the president's rather than the government's responsibilities. *RFE/RL*, 191, 7 October 1994. In the mean time, Gryzunov also attempted to investigate the finances of *Rossiiskaya Gazeta*, the most highly subsidized of the two government newspapers (25 billion rubles in 1994 as contrasted with 31 billion for all other print media combined), and was rewarded with being fired by Premier Chernomyrdin. Subsequently reinstated by Yeltsin after widespread protests from journalists, many of whom suspected he was also being punished for refusing to comply with official disinformation on Chechnya, he then met a barrage of invective in *Gazeta's* columns, including the accusation that he had mismanaged the State Press Committee and allotted press subsidies to his favorites. He took the paper to the Judicial Chamber on Information Disputes, which found in his favor (*OMRI Daily Digest*, 43.I, 1 March 1995; 56.I, 20 March 1995; 83.I, 27 April 1995).

45 *OMRI Daily Digest*, 137.I, 17 July 1995; 138.I, 18 July 1995; 147.I, 31 July 1995.

46 *OMRI Daily Digest*, 162.I, 21 August 1995; 200.I, 13 October 1995.

47 In *Obshchaya Gazeta*, 20, cited in *Monitor*, I.15, 19 May 1995.

48 Victor Yasmann, 'The fate of the second oldest profession in Russia' (*Prism*, I.2, 12 May 1995).

49 This did not mean it played no role at all. Jacek Kuron and Karol Modzielewski, two war-horses of the dissident intelligentsia during the Soviet era who between them served the best part of 20 years' prison sentences for their efforts, publicly accused certain top security officials from the 1980s of having simply switched their allegiance to Walesa (Jane Perlez, 'Dissidents say secret police still make trouble in Poland', *New York Times*, 23 January 1996, A5). The reason for their charge was the smarting Walesa's bitter accusation, when he lost the presidential election at the close of 1995, that Premier Jozef Oleksy, who like incoming president Kwasniewski had been a leading Communist official in the 1980s, had been a direct Soviet agent and pawn of the KGB. The photographs and documents that ostensibly underpinned Walesa's allegation had been supplied by these same security officials.

50 In 1994, frustrated by its failure to buy into the audio-visual sector, Hersant sold virtually all media it had a stake in except *Rzeczpospolita* to a comparatively small German media firm, Passau Neue Presse (Giorgi, 1995: 93).

51 To give a little of the flavor of Walesa's style, and the legal tools at his command, he was perfectly at ease using Article 270 (1) of the pre-transition penal code, still in force, that provided for six months' to eight years' imprisonment, and various fines, for insulting the president. In 1993, for example, an inebriated night watchman overheard insulting the worthy Walesa in a bus-stop conversation was given a fine equivalent to a month's wages, and a year's suspended sentence; two students were fined about the same amount each in a separate incident; August 1993 Helsinki Watch report, cited in *Labour Focus On Eastern Europe*, 46, 1993, p. 38.

52 *RFE/RL Daily Report*, 19, 28 January 1994; 40, 28 February 1994; 91, 13 May 1994; 126, 6 July 1994; 182–6, 26–9 September 1994; 195, 13 October 1994; and especially Anna Sabbat-Swidlicka, 'The travails of independent broadcasting in Poland', *RFE/RL Research Report*, 3.10, 11 March 1994, 40–50, esp. 46–9.

53 In the tradition of official Soviet-speak, to accuse someone of a 'provocation' was much more confrontational than to accuse them of being insulting. A 'provocation' signified that not to crush the provoker instantaneously was an act of heroic self-restraint that could not be relied upon to be repeated.

54 *RFE/RL Daily Report*, 83, 2 May 1994; 89, 10 May 1994; 136, 20 July 1994; 190, 6 October 1994; 237, 16 December 1994.

55 *RFE/RL Daily Report*, 41, 1 March 1994; 118, 23 June 1994; 163, 29 August 1994; 182, 23 September 1994; 191, 9 October 1994; 192, 10 October 1994.

56 Stanislaw Pyjas. See Lipski (1985: 142–58) for an account of Pyjas' murder and the shock-waves it generated.

57 *OMRI Daily Digest*, 214.II, 2 November 1995.

58 *RFE/RL Daily Report*, 96, 20 May 1994. It is perhaps worth emphasizing that a Concordat with the Vatican statelet is a distinctly different animal from a state policy in favor of religious freedom of expression, as it locks the signatory state into a tight embrace with the *verkhushka* of the Catholic hierarchy, not with ordinary Catholic believers worldwide. The Polish hierarchy's abortion policy was directly contrary to the clearly expressed majority position in endless public opinion polls. The hierarchy's view was perfectly expressed in the church of St Mary in Krakow in summer 1988, a medieval mausoleum encrusted with altars and shrines and entombed in darkness except for flickering sanctuary lamps, a Counter-Reformation crypt in all respects but one. One chapel at the back had been cleared for a dramatic invasion of late twentieth-century information culture: a photo exhibit, in glorious Kodachrome, of top quality fetuses . . .

59 E.g. the burial of non-believers in church cemeteries, religious instruction in kindergartens, government financing of the Papal Theological Academy in Krakow (*OMRI Daily Digest*, 198.II, 11 October 1995).

60 *RFE/RL Daily Report*, 125, 5 July 1994.

61 'La radio privée en Pologne', *Le Monde Diplomatique*, 486, September 1994, 24.

62 The term ('updating') used of the reforms introduced over thirty years before in the early 1960s by Pope John XXIII via the Second Vatican Council.

63 On these themes I have drawn especially on 'Bref aperçu de la presse polonaise', *La Nouvelle Alternative*, 28, December 1992, 39–40; Kulakowska, 1992; Chantal Deltenre, 'À l'Est, l'audiovisuel happé par les lois de la concurrence: déjà les deçus de la démocratie médiatique?', *Le Monde Diplomatique*, 486, September 1994, 24–5, and on the other references cited in the text.

64 Edith Oltay, 'Hungary', *RFE/RL Research Report*, 1.39, 2 October 1992, 39–43; Pataki, 1993; Edith Oltay, 'Hungarian radio and television under fire', *RFE/RL Research Report*, 2.38, 24 September 1993, 40–4; Pataki, 1994a, 1994b.

65 Cited in Pataki, 1994a: 38.

66 Horvath Balasz, addressing the MDF's youth wing, reported by Budapest's Radio Kossuth on 3 March 1992, cited in Foreign Broadcast Information Service: East European Reports EER-92-031 (23B). An official of the youth wing immediately denied the remarks had been made (23A). Furmann Imre, MDF Vice-President, said the party had been living 'in a fortress under siege' since it formed the government (*Kritika*, 11/91, 27–8, cited in EER-92-005 (1)). Even more ferocious attacks were repeatedly spearheaded by Csurka Istvan, who eventually formed his own party, but for some years was an MDF member of the parliamentary Culture Committee, which had formal responsibility to review media issues. Csurka led a demonstration outside the TV building, replete with bodyguards in paramilitary uniforms, and attacked the heads of radio and TV as the 'two red bishops on the chessboard' (*Magyar Forum*, 4 June 1992, cited in EER-92-099 (28)).

67 Pataki, 1994a: 42.

68 Németh Jenö, president of the Pallas publishing company that specialized in magazines rather than newspapers, cited in *Nepszabadsag*, 14 June 1990, p. 4.

69 *Tallozo*, 12, 22 March 1991, 547–8, cited in FBIS EER-91-068 (39).

70 *RFE/RL Daily Report*, 119, 24 June 1994.

71 Kováts Ildikó, 'Difficulties in the process of the democratization of the media in Hungary', paper presented to the 19th Conference of the International Association for Mass Communication Research, Seoul, Korea, July 1994.

72 The AFD objected because, among other things, the bill stipulated that political parties would get airtime in proportion to the percentage of votes cast for it at the previous general election, thus in its view unduly favoring the MDF or any governing party. The AFD also wanted all the law's provisions to receive a two-thirds majority, not just the issues originally

agreed upon in the six-party pact. When the opposition parties refused to vote, there was nothing much of substance left for pro-government deputies to vote on, hence the absence of any vote in favor.

73 Hankiss, 1994: 303.

74 Jane Perlez, 'Thousands in Hungary denounce dismissal of broadcast journalists', *New York Times*, 16 March 1994, A2.

75 For a number of the observations in these final paragraphs on the Hungarian situation in 1995, I am grateful to a round table of Hungarian journalists that took place at the University of Texas at Austin in late August 1995, consisting of Falussy Orsolya, Fazekas Zsolt, Gera Gabriella, Kurucz Peter, Lendvai Szabolcs and Orosz Jozsef. No one of them should be identified necessarily with any conclusion drawn here.

76 *RFE/RL Daily Report*, 217, 15 November 1994; 239, 20 December 1994.

77 *OMRI Daily Digest*, 206.II, 23 October 1995 4.II, 5 January 1996; 8.II, 11 January 1996.

78 *Segodnya*, 11 July 1995, cited in *Monitor*, 12 July 1995, Jamestown Foundation.

7

Mainstream Media Theory and Change in Eastern Europe

In the first chapter we examined a number of political science discourses that are essential to understanding media communication processes in the three nations under consideration and, we argue, in many if not most other nations as well. At the same time, we noted the curious failure to engage with communication in most contributions to those conceptual and empirical discourses. The moment has now arrived to review media communication discourses with the same critical eye. Are they typically limited in applicability to one or a very few nations? If communication research is generally absent from political science discourses, how far are questions of political and economic power dealt with, or dealt with adequately, in communication research?

As already noted, media communication theories may be divided into three categories, namely **segmented**, **fragmented** and **totalist**. By 'segmented', I refer to approaches, typically US-based, which theorize media as discrete entities in society, and correspondingly suffer from a frequent failure to integrate their findings with research on communication in educational institutions, family processes, religious bodies, organized 'leisure' activities, or everyday interpersonal communication. Examples would include agenda-setting (Protess and McCombs, 1991); cultivation theory (Melischek, 1984; Signorielli and Morgan, 1990); 'uses-and-gratifications' theory (Rosengren et al., 1985); media system dependency theory (DeFleur and Ball-Rokeach, 1990).

By 'fragmented', I refer to people writing from a great variety of perspectives, much of their work long pre-dating the post-modernist wave of celebration of fragmentation, such as Benjamin, Barthes, Bakhtin, Enzensberger, and much current cultural studies research. Their work offers a plethora of insights, but is couched more in the form of highly suggestive but often disconnected *aperçus* – the carnivalesque, the aura, the possibilities of the photocopier, bureaucratic language – than it addresses interlocking factors across the entire society.

By 'totalist', I mean marxist approaches, such as Gramsci, Williams, Althusser, Hall, Schiller, but also non-marxist systematists such as Habermas, and functionalists such as Parsons. Neither this last category nor the middle one includes people who restrict themselves, as do theorists in the 'segmented' group, to media as such, but this capacity to analyse interlocking factors strengthens their theoretical positions rather than somehow invalidating them from consideration.

We will now proceed to review a series of these theoretical positions in terms of their coherence and of their capacity to illuminate the mediatic and political transitions in Russia, Poland and Hungary. The term 'illuminate' is deliberately chosen in preference to 'explain', which tends to convey a level of total certainty characteristic of elementary propositions in the natural sciences – boil some copper sulphate and the water turns blue – that are on an infinitely more simplistic level than what is being investigated here.

This chapter and the next, however, organize the treatment of communication theories along a different axis from the one just enunciated. This chapter will examine theories conventionally described as 'mainstream', and the succeeding chapter those termed 'critical'. In other words the treatment that follows pivots on a politico-sociological taxonomy current within the communication research profession in the final decade of the twentieth century, rather than the more purely logical categorization above of segmented, fragmented and totalist. The latter, however, needs bearing in mind throughout, since even though the argument here will be that concepts in the 'critical' zone are generally more helpful than 'mainstream' ones, the questions at issue are not simply professional or political ones.

Indeed the key problem with 'mainstream' theorists really is that – with exceptions on some levels – they are overly media- or communication-centric, 'segmented' as described above, seemingly almost uninterested in societal change, the economic and political structure, or political resistance to the status quo. It might be argued that these theories only set themselves the task of accounting for media operations, not for societal realities, but this would be a lame and flimsy defense. Media are only interesting because they are integral to culture and society, not because like the infant Macduff they may be from their *societal* 'womb untimely ripped'.[1]

Thus we are confronted with the mirror-paradox of the political science approaches addressed in the first chapter that typically omit or refer only tangentially to communication processes and media. Such mutual insulation has not served social research well.

Let us then examine some leading mainstream media theories, namely agenda-setting, cultivation analysis, diffusion theory, gatekeeper theory, de Sola Pool's 'soft technological determinism', 'press' theory (i.e. the Four Theories approach), and uses and gratifications theory. I will leave till last media system dependency, since it does make a more serious attempt than the others to address societal dimensions of media, and Parsons' approach to media. We will investigate how far any of these approaches shed light on the communication processes in any of the following: the build-up to the 1989–91 biennium; the crisis years themselves (the 'transition' in political science terminology); and/or the liminal period that followed up to the end of 1995 (the 'consolidation' period in political science terms). Let it be noted once more, however, that although those particular empirical foci are selected in this argument, they are chosen because they represent a much wider gamut of societal examples generally left unaddressed by media communication research.

Agenda-Setting

Agenda-setting theory (Protess and McCombs, 1991) focuses overwhelmingly on the news genre. It claims that the media rank-order news issues, which the public then takes to be significant as a result of this highlighting. It does not claim to predict how the audience will respond to specific content, only that there will be wide consensus that the issues underscored are indeed important. It is 'a theoretical concept about the transmission of salience' (McCombs, 1991: 43). It began life also as an early attempt to claw back some significance for media research in the aftermath of the Yale studies and other research summarized by Klapper (1960), which seemed to indicate the media were so impotent in social life that they were hardly worth studying.

As Protess and McCombs themselves acknowledge (1991: 45), however, the evidence in support of the agenda-setting approach is primarily correlative rather than sequential in character. More recent studies have refined the agenda-setting process in various directions, including duration of exposure to the media agenda, national versus local agenda-issues, prior audience orientations, and the impact of differing media technologies, amongst other issues (Protess and McCombs, 1991: Parts III and IV).

It is not an approach, evidently, which greatly illuminates the communicative dimensions of the Eastern European situation, past or current. It strongly implies a level of legitimacy which was not enjoyed by most East European media before the changes: indeed, we noted earlier that in the Brezhnev era East European media had helped to keep discussion of economic stagnation and the need for radical economic reform out of the public arena, even though the public experienced stagnation in numerous practical ways. In the former situation in the USSR and elsewhere in the region, public reactions to official media-set agendas often varied by topic, with foreign news generally enjoying somewhat more credibility than domestic news. Although the issue of media credibility does not hold center-stage in the agenda-setting approach, it is a precondition of successful agenda-setting. Foreign radio broadcasts could probably be argued to have helped set the agenda for those who received them, but hardly to have set the general or governmental agenda (except, in the latter instance, in the area of counter-propaganda).

Nor does the approach give us very much insight into the post-Soviet phase in East European development, given that economic and ethnic issues are widely dominant, and no one needs a news bulletin to enable them to foreground these topics. Perhaps the growth of nationalist feeling in Hungary and the excoriation of the 1920 Trianon settlement in which Hungary's borders were substantially shrunk, would represent a viable case study in the development of an irredentist agenda by media, except that far from all Hungarian media joined in this chorus. Some political commentators and especially some politicians bemoaned what they perceived as the endemic cynicism of journalistic reporting in the post-Soviet period, suggesting that news media were effectively setting a public agenda of automatic distrust of political leaders. Similar angst was commonly expressed in Western Europe and the United States during the same period. Even if true, however, it would be a weak instance of agenda-setting because the evidence would be constituted only by that single item on the public agenda, rather than a hierarchy of items.

In his survey of mass communication theory, McQuail (1994: 356–7) has suggested that the evidence for the agenda-setting hypothesis is in any event rather inconclusive. Ettema et al. (1991) have proposed, along with Molotch et al. (1987), that the attempt to posit a causal-sequential linkage between media agendas, government policy-setting and public agendas, is foredoomed to failure, and that only an analysis which focuses on concatenated effects and ricochet effects of actions and interpretations on all three levels can capture the full dynamics of the process by which public issues get assigned an effective ranking (1991: 96–7). At the same time, the news issue Ettema et al. chose to demonstrate their point – child abduction by an estranged foreign parent who removes the child to their own country of birth, and then is shielded by their government – was of great specificity and high emotive content, with few implications for core national agendas, and so not the best type of issue with which to test out their own or the more classical version of the agenda-setting approach.

To this writer, the agenda-setting notion seems plausible, but only under rather specific conditions. Where the public or a segment of the public, correctly or incorrectly, considers that it has reason to know better than the media agenda, then the hypothesis falls. To that extent, agenda-setting fails to draw attention to the sources of resistance to having one's agenda set in the first place. It is like a theory of pack-journalism, or of fashion, but with no space in it for the boy in the crowd who first shouts out 'He's naked!'

It could be argued, to the contrary, that the whole *glasnost* era was a classic case of media agenda-setting, inasmuch as the mounting excitement generated with each new millimetre the information door was opened in the media, whether in news or in literature, in turn gave birth to a quite extraordinary spiral of expectations of change. That spiral of loquacity was certainly a reality. However, it is also clear that in the USSR, in post-martial law Poland, and in Kádár's Hungary, these piecemeal door-openings were primarily dictated from the *verkhushka*, or at least some of its members, and not by media editors, until the trickles cumulatively interacted and at long last became a flood that could not be stemmed. Only in interaction with *verkhushka* strategies, economic decline and all the often mutually contradictory factors noted in earlier chapters could the media be said to have had an agenda-setting function in the *glasnost* process.

Cultivation Analysis

The cultivation analysis approach seeks to define the long-term role of television in contemporary society, proposing that heavy television exposure blends attitudes in the direction of mainstream cultural values, and bends them in line with the somewhat conservative political agenda of media owners and the power structure in general (Gerbner, 1984: 343). Its strongest empirical support to date comes from US data (contrast Bouwman and Stappers, 1984 and Bouwman 1984, for the Netherlands; Wober, 1984 and 1990, for Britain; and Bock, 1984, for the German Federal Republic). It may indeed be that television has played to date a stronger integrative role in the USA than in other nations – Gerbner has drawn analogies between TV in the USA and religion in preindustrial societies, as well as with gravitational pull (Gerbner, 1986: 260–1) – and this in turn may derive from the fragmented character of US culture in which more conventional sources of solidarity are weaker than in longer established nations.[2]

The strength of the approach lies primarily in its attempt to pin down the long-term impact of media taken in the broadcloth, as opposed to the more typical 'one-shot/one-topic' analysis of media use by an audience. It presents an interesting comparison with the agenda-setting approach in that both seek to establish long-range media effects. Cultivation analysis, however, makes a strong claim regarding content-specific effects, in this respect going further than the agenda-setters' resolution merely to focus on what people think about. (Whether that caution is always appropriate is another matter again.)

In fact, although neither discourse seems familiar to him, Shlapentokh (1986: 39–40) produces an interesting amalgam of elements in both positions *vis-à-vis* sovietized media. He argues both that

> this monotony of ritualistic slogans . . . [and] their continuous repetition . . . [signal] to all that the . . . system remains intact, and that the authorities will act to block those who seek to change the system

and that by

> sheer repetition, Soviet ideology has managed to persuade many citizens that the Soviet system of economic planning is more efficient than capitalist market economics, that the 'national question' has been solved in the USSR but remains perplexing in Western societies, that a one-party system is the most effective way of meeting the needs of the population, and that political pluralism would be counterproductive.

In other words, a cultivation hypothesis, complete with empirical indicators. The agenda-setting dimension in this example is not really so much based on news as on the communication of political hegemony, so does not strictly speaking draw upon the core agenda-setting approach. None the less, the example does illustrate the tendency to complementarity of these two positions on media effects.

The most problematic issue in cultivation analysis is the assumption of political and social stability. In general, this may be claimed of the USA since the Second World War, in that the main conflict issues have generally been relatively short-lived and often regionally or even locally focused. The civil rights movement was at the center of conflict in the decade 1955–65, but overwhelmingly in the South-East; major demonstrations against the war in South-East Asia ran from 1965 to 1975; major social outbursts in African American communities were prominent from 1964 to 1972, but almost never simultaneously, with the exception of response to Dr King's assassination in 1968. The issues raised by these social explosions admittedly went to the very heart of US society, both in its domestic and in its global dimensions, but the explosions themselves did not dissolve the society or the negative forces against which they were directed. Still less did the assassination of one president, and the forced abdication of another. African Americans are still concentrated at the foot of the social hierarchy, and foreign intervention has not ceased despite its taking more cautious forms. Stability – a socially costly stability – has persisted.

However, as this book insists, this degree of continuity cannot be presumed for all societies. Levendel and Terestenyi (1984) have noted specifically the difficulty in applying cultivation analysis to Hungary, even a number of years before the regime transition. The point at which cultivation analysis might be of most help in analysing the East European situation could be in examining the degree to which sovietized media did set up certain frameworks that have endured in the public mind past the transition – for example, on the relative merits of job security in the East as opposed to economic dynamism in the West. (In Russia, unlike Poland or Hungary, the military threat of the West would constitute another such perduring framework.)

There is no necessity, after all, for elements of the mainstream culture toward which television and other media may be said to bend us, to be logically consistent with each other. The 'commercial populism' that Gerbner identifies in one essay (1984) as typically the product of heavy TV viewing in the USA – namely a simultaneous enthusiasm for more government spending and for lower taxes – is clearly internally contradictory. In this sense, we should perhaps avoid a maximalist expectation of how sovietized media needed to perform in order successfully to cultivate certain mind-sets that worked in favor of regime stability, even while others co-existed with them that pulled in opposite directions. Being proud of Soviet space achievements while simultaneously being ready to steal from the state might be an example.

The question of media audiences in Eastern Europe is a very complex one, particularly but not exclusively before the transition, since our data for that period are necessarily fragmentary. I have already indicated what I consider to be the strengths of Shlapentokh's analysis of Soviet public opinion, but his analysis would not necessarily apply to Polish or Hungarian audiences in the same degree. The degree of electoral support given in the post-Soviet period to 'reformed' Communist parties in the three nations – the Russian party being much the least reformed of the three – would certainly suggest the potency of certain key pre-transition media propositions concerning job security and welfare provision, especially in the face of deepening economic insecurity.

However, Ellen Propper Mickiewicz's (1981) summary of a number of empirical audience studies carried out in the former Soviet Union during the 1970s showed that many of them implied Soviet media had little impact on political consciousness. This judgment may be based, though, on more exacting standards of political consciousness than simply the economic security issue, and probably does not penetrate to the dimension of political consciousness addressed above by Shlapentokh.

Zimmerman (1987: tables 11.6–10) summarized some audience data from the 1983 Soviet émigré survey cited in Chapter 5, including *samizdat* media and foreign broadcast listening. Set at the close of the Brezhnev era, they suggested more intensive use of unofficial news media by both intending émigrés and the highly placed, and most dependence on the press rather than broadcast media. At the same time, Sinyavsky (1990) has argued that Soviet ideology has had a very long-term impact on patterns of thinking, at least in the former Soviet Union. This, like Shlapentokh's analysis, addresses a different order of reality to the question of adherence to particular political propositions.

And finally, to complicate the question still further, there is the question of the younger generation and their perspectives, as reviewed in Chapter 4. Official media cultivation seemed to have had much less impact on them than their parents, but at the same time maybe rock music should be acknowledged as a mediatic cultivation agent. To date cultivation analysis has only addressed mainstream television, but rock videos and music television in Eastern Europe were one of the media success stories of the early 1990s.

As indicated, the great strength of the cultivation analysis approach lies in its longitudinal method and in its implicit involvement of social memory in the media communication process. At the same time, it is at its strongest when faced with a relatively unchanging societal and mediatic reality, and with a rather strong level of public trust in media (more arguably present, perhaps, among the Russian population in the former USSR than among Poles or Hungarians). The situation in Eastern Europe is further complicated by our knowledge that the parallel lecture-communication system – required attendance at political lectures organized on a monthly and even weekly basis in the workplace (Remington, 1988: chs. 2–3) – and the educational system, were overwhelmingly pulling in the same direction as the media system, whereas in the United States there has never been an analogue to the lecture-system, and extensive homogeneity between media and school messages cannot be presumed.

Diffusion Theory

Diffusion theory (Brown, 1991; Rogers, 1962) effectively links media with consequent (or existing) interpersonal networks, and is primarily concerned with news, technical innovations or campaigns, and how these 'travel', sociologically speaking. To the extent that it links media with interpersonal communication, it has a strength that many media theories do not. Its roots, as Katz (1960) early pointed out, are in the preoccupation of US rural sociologists with how to help promote technical innovations in agriculture, a concern which rather naturally extended itself into the study of development communication projects in the 'Third World'. The presumption is of a straightforward, positive and helpful message which will be clearly understood in principle immediately, but which may meet with misguided resistance to its diffusion. Hence the typical concerns of diffusion theorists with the complexity of the message, its observability, its reversibility as a practice, its impact on social relations, its relative advantage (e.g. cost-effectiveness, increased comfort or security), and – naturally – with community opinion leaders, peer pressure and categorizing people into shades of good (= yielding) and bad (= recalcitrant).

It is then the kind of definition of media communication with which, ironically, many pro-system cadres and media personnel would have gladly concurred in the former Soviet bloc. It evokes the famous agit-trains of the early Bolshevik republic, the enthusiastic but tragically misguided collectivization volunteers of the first Five-Year Plan, and later the army of instructors in the parallel lecture-communication system. The notion of more or less informed audience resistance would need to be replaced with one of an obduracy which needed to be shoved in the right direction to have it yield, rather than manipulated – and which until long into the Gorbachev period ran the constant risk of being defined as invincible ignorance of a subversive stripe, and thus as sanctionable.

There is, however, little room in diffusion theory to conceptualize the potentially system-buckling communication of *Solidarnosc* messages. Nor does diffusion analysis lend itself easily to the review of oppositional readings of the official press, or of the key role of word-of-mouth communication in sovietized societies (Bauer and Gleicher, 1953). Its agenda is very different. Least of all, perhaps, is it equipped to deal with the post-Soviet situation of a press system falling apart, a broadcasting system under the very anxious eye of new, unstable governments, and a telecommunications system that belongs for the most part to a pre-Second World War era. Its preoccupations are with benign planned local change in a generally benign environment.

Gatekeeper Theory

Gatekeeper theory originally focused only on news. It identified media executives as making patterned decisions as to what news items to select out of the total flow of information reaching the newsroom (Snider, 1967; White, 1949). The difference between applying this approach in a Western capitalist society, and in the former Soviet bloc, is that in the former it normally takes a sociologist's research to discover and analyse the patterns and processes behind these decisions (Gans, 1979; Schlesinger, 1987; Tuchman, 1978). In Communist societies, the core news criteria were formally stated in Party documents and pronouncements, and updated by very regular briefings and phone-calls.

The merit of the approach is that it does directly address the question of power in media, rather than seeing them as spontaneous flowers of democratic communication. In neither setting, however, is it really credible that media executives themselves should wield so much untrammeled power, seemingly independent of the *nomenklatura*, or of the corporate owner and major advertisers, depending upon the social system. There is an inappropriate fixation on one level of power in gatekeeper theory.

More recently, Gitlin (1983) and Herman and Chomsky (1988) have in passing and in principle given a certain new impetus to the gatekeeper approach, Gitlin by identifying the multiple, often conflicting gatekeepers at work in prime time entertainment TV in the USA, Herman and Chomsky by coining the notion of 'filter', which is not so distant from that of gatekeeper, and especially by drawing attention to the influence of advertisers and proprietorial filters/gatekeepers in the economic power structure. We might compare Gandy's (1991) redirection of focus of the agenda-setting model on to how the corporate media agenda is set (rather than the public's), as an effort in similar vein. As none of the four would be happy to be included under the 'mainstream' heading, it may be rather indelicate, if not actually inappropriate, to consider them here. None the less, conceptually speaking, their focus on the ultimate controls over media – different as it is between Gitlin or Herman/Chomsky or Gandy – represents a very useful recomposition of the original rather flat recognition of the basic realities of selection that was the basis of the original 'Mr Gates' study.[3]

Hough (1977: ch. 8), employing 'gatekeeper' in the more general sense in which it is used in Eastonian political science (Easton, 1965) – not a discourse with which conventional gatekeeper-analysis seems familiar – asks an interesting question concerning the implied power of the gatekeeper in a political system. He questions whether the gatekeeper is seen simply as someone who sifts (like the copy-taster sitting at the wire-service terminal in a media structure), or as someone who transforms generalized societal inputs into specific demands directed to the political system. Clearly the latter is much the more influential role, and in the context of Eastern Europe directs our attention to at least one very interesting question.

In the latter days of sovietism and since the transition in both the USSR's republics and in Hungary, one might for example ask how media executives and those above them to whom they owed their allegiance processed nationalist or ethnic sentiments. It is a particularly interesting question because within the Soviet bloc, the expression of long-suppressed nationalist sentiment first emerged from toward the end of the Brezhnev era in smaller literary publications. They typically focused on issues of language-survival and details of pre-Soviet and even ancient history, seemingly abstract from contemporary concerns, but in practice almost always charged with immense symbolic significance. Since the regime change, these more delphic manifestations of nationalism have given way to often strident, extremely chauvinist and even militaristic calls to action. The media gatekeeper-role (more widely defined than by its originators) potentially becomes of great relevance at this point, not least since mostly the ordinary foot-soldiers of journalism and the media were the same individuals as before the change in regime.

Uses-and-Gratifications

The 'uses-and-gratifications' approach to media tries to establish which aspects of media output are utilized by which audience segments in the light of their existing desires and preferences. In its inception, the model was implicitly psychologistic and static (cf. Elliott, 1975), as Weibull (in Rosengren et al., 1985: 125) acknowledged in a major symposium on the approach:

> A certain media system with certain inherent properties was taken as given, and the question asked was what use the individual made of this system and what needs he or she gratified through media use.

The Rosengren et al. symposium certainly offered a series of critiques of this model (see the contributions by McQuail, Weibull and Lull). The concluding essay by Blumler, Gurevitch and Katz acknowledged a series of hitherto unresolved issues in the approach, such as the constraining features of texts, cross-national comparisons, and generally the need to relate uses-and-gratifications research to the communication process as a whole.

However, the dominant model in the symposium was what might be termed the 'public opinion' vision of society. This conceives of society as an accumulation of individual viewpoints which may or may not alter over time, which may be internally stratified (e.g. by life-cycle position), but which constitute the tranquil or heaving sea of the general mood. It is a mass-psychological version of Max Weber's methodological individualism. Unfortunately this version lacks Weber's sense for history or structure, aside from media structure, and even then presents us only with an abstract choice between 'responsive' and 'unresponsive' (i.e. insufficiently market-driven) media structures (Palmgreen et al., in Rosengren et al., 1985: 35).

Attention is scant in the symposium to power, the state, conflict, economic forces, structural relations between social classes, societal change or historical development. Change is said rather vapidly to be the 'norm' (p. 35), yet it is not posited or conceptualized in any specific manner, and turns up under the sub-heading 'Challenges for the Future' (p. 33), rather than being listed under achievements already attained through the benefit and under the rubric of the uses-and-gratifications model.

In general, a number of the essays in the volume exhibit a poverty of understanding of sociological theory, with Palmgreen et al. confusing functionalist approaches with static approaches, instead of recognizing that functionalism can incorporate dynamic equilibrium and even conflict (see also the discussion of media system dependency theory below). There is also a poverty in understanding of the basic economics of media, with Palmgreen and Rayburn defining the decline of newspapers or failure of TV shows simply in relation to audience popularity (p. 71). Would that it were so.

Wenner's chapter in the same volume links together demographic variables, dispositions (i.e. political views), habitual media exposure, 'consequent' beliefs, and what he terms the 'media reference foreground' of gratifications sought and obtained from media. He then identifies this commercial audience researcher's operationalization of contractual tasks as the heart of media research. He makes no wider reference to societal structures, and by not doing so limits his grasp to that of a simple social cartographer, rather than assigning himself the task of a comprehensive account of the media–society relationship. Levy and Windahl's essay (1985) similarly privileges the immediate in media research – why this program, that channel, this medium – rather than longer term impact, providing in so doing a kind of snapshot sociology.

Faced with the transitions in Eastern Europe, adherents of this position would seem likely to ask the following questions (at best). What did Eastern Europeans derive from their media system before, during and after the transition? Not an unreasonable question in and of itself, but one senses they would need to be prompted to refine the question in order to differentiate between nations, or between elites and the more general public's responses, and that they would be obtuse in recognizing the roles of either marginal or underground media, since their focus is always on mainstream media provision. They might be adept at acknowledging a null-hypothesis case of media gratification in the instance of boring or frontally propagandistic sovietized media output, but one imagines they would be less successful in tracing the distinction Shlapentokh explores between the ideological and the pragmatic audience responses to media, or, still less, in tracking the declining excitement of *glasnost* or the cumulative impact of economic stagnation, global decline and the other array of factors in media and political transition outlined earlier. Each one of these topics is progressively further removed from the uses-and-gratifications lens.

In particular, the relation between media and the public sphere, or that between media and political movements, are completely out of frame, since their mass-psychologistic focus drives them only to examine a direct relation between given media output and its atomized, at best stratified, consumers-cum-opinion-holders. Finally, the role of owners, directors or – in the case of the Soviet system – Party or KGB authorities, is invisible, a non-problem, in this tradition of media research. Quirky in the Western context, to say the least; but such an omission would be positively perverse in the Eastern one.

de Sola Pool and 'Soft Technological Determinism'

A very different perspective on the media is taken by de Sola Pool (1983). His theory is difficult to pin down with precision, inasmuch as it is more developed in the empirical details of his argument than in any formal presentation of it. Indeed even his term 'soft technological determinism' (1983: 5) conveys rather the air of an attempt to deflect accusations of technological determinism, than of a conceptual assertion in and of itself. He does note on the same page that he is referring specifically to the interaction between free speech and changing communication technologies over the period since 1800 CE, and that his basic position is that the diffusion of instruments for communication at a distance favors, whereas their concentration, scarcity or monopolization disfavor, freedom of communication.

He further qualifies his position by asserting that 'institutions that evolve in response to one technological environment persist and to some degree are later imposed on what may be a changed technology' (p. 5). This qualification is central to his book's argument, inasmuch as de Sola Pool was primarily concerned to argue that legal restrictions on digital telecommunications and multi-channel cable television, deriving in his view from the 1920s definition of broadcast channels as scarce, represented an outmoded and unconstructive public policy. More appropriate rather for the present electronic communication era was the communication policy model derived from an earlier phase still, namely that of a plethora of print communication outlets (as during the epoch during which the First Amendment was drafted to the US Constitution).

Having said that, it is only fair to note that his formulations are often slipshod, as where he claims that social institutions 'evolve in response to one technological environment'. That certainly sounds like simple technological determinism. However, the ultimately important thing is the argument he intended, which seems to have been to assert some, but not a supremely determinative role for technology in interaction with other factors, whose mutual impact is neither 'simple . . . unidirectional, nor . . . immediate' (p. 5).

The argument of the book, effectively for massive (though not total) deregulation, has been immensely influential in both scholarly and policy-making circles within and beyond the United States. It is almost an arithmetical one: more means of communication equal the heady automatic potential for less centralized domination over communication, good legislation permitting. It is as though the politico-cultural *Geist* of the First Amendment had miraculously incarnated itself in electronic pulses for 'self-expression, human intercourse and the recording of knowledge' (p. 226).

Indeed, de Sola Pool envisages a splendid 'win–win' situation both for the individual and for the corporation:

> Companies with information services and carrier billings in the millions will invest in their own networks, leased circuits, compression devices, and other marvelous gadgets designed to help them operate efficiently or cut costs. (p. 228)

It is hard to carp at such visions of bliss. The rosy glow is something we all rather badly need. None the less, we also need a measure of sobriety, a concern in US terms for the Fourth Amendment's protections against arbitrary search as well as for the First's of free speech.

This is provided by those analysts who stress the role of digital communication technologies in enabling vastly expanded and more efficient business and governmental surveillance and control, and the urgent need for privacy mechanisms as a defense against those inroads.[4] Whether it is Habermas warning against the contemporary colonization of the lifeworld by the corporate sector and the state, or Foucault depicting the strategies of control over daily behavior developed in the modern era, or Giddens noting the massive expansion of technological surveillance capacity now available to the contemporary state, the demand is compelling for a much more balanced, less pollyannaish evaluation of the cultural and political applications of communication technologies.[5] These 'marvelous gadgets' may indeed 'efficiently' invade and loot our personal computer memories and may indeed enable a firm to 'cut costs' with the effect of unemploying one family member and making another work a gruelling schedule.

What bearing might de Sola Pool's study have on our understanding of Russia, Poland and Hungary during the transition era? His basic claim as to the quasi-exponential potential for freedom supplied by new communication technologies very much underlies the argument of S. Frederick Starr (1990), namely that they enabled the emergence of a new 'civil society' in the USSR, a 'technotronic glasnost' (p. 50). Starr produces the most detailed case in support of this quite widely propounded contention (cf. Shane, 1994), which indeed has some solid elements standing in its support in that context but, as was argued in Chapter 4, often breaks down in terms of the specifics as well. It is a mixed case in that sense, which is indeed what might be expected. It is not necessary to dispute all de Sola Pool's positive claims for these technologies in order to acknowledge the negative dimensions he entirely neglects.

As regards the consolidation phase in post-Soviet nations, it was hard at the time of writing to know how far new electronic surveillance techniques – beyond the long-favored bug and high-performance distant microphone – were being used by the KGB and other political police forces in the former bloc. In Russia, at least, given the rather solid budgets allocated such forces as against even the military in the early 1990s, it would be consonant with other data to presume that these marvelous gadgets were indeed in the process of being deployed.

The strength of de Sola Pool's arguments lies in his address of technological issues, particularly of new developments. These are too easily left out of the equation both by mainstream and critical theorists (with some exceptions, such as Martín-Barbero). To some degree the fault may lie with McLuhan, inasmuch as his scattershot utterances on the subject of communication technology may have served in part to make that concern seem overly speculative and crassly materialistic to a number of media researchers. The problem for de Sola Pool is the problem of much mainstream work, however, namely the failure to get a grip on the various dimensions of power in the communication complex. All he could see was the single axis of multiplicity/freedom.

Four Theories of the Press

The 'four theories' of the media (Siebert et al., 1956) have for some time been a target of criticism in media studies, often for their strongly normative aspects. They have also been supplemented with other categories (McQuail, 1994: 127–33). The elements within them which have a bearing on this essay are of course the categories of 'authoritarian' and 'Soviet' media theory, which effectively recapitulate many of the distinctions drawn by Kirkpatrick (1982) between authoritarian and totalitarian regimes. The underlying assumptions are that authoritarian media systems may operate some of the same mechanisms of control, such as pre-publication censorship, as do totalitarian systems, but that both the explicit objectives (e.g. sovereignty of the proletariat) and the systematic depth of surveillance were peculiar to the Soviet system.

The problems in this view have already been addressed. There is a presumption of homogeneity between the units of the Soviet bloc, and between stages of development in the USSR itself (e.g. between the later Brezhnev and the later Stalin periods), which it is hard to sustain empirically. There is a presumption that Soviet regime rhetoric (e.g. about 'class') always functioned purely on the level it asserted, whether in the minds of the *nomenklatura* or of the general public. This too would be hard to justify from the evidence available. Finally, there is an equation of Hitlerism with Francoism with Stalinism, which has a more invective than analytical appeal. Taken together, these indicate that the media categorization proposed is far too broad a brush with which to operate in the portrayal and explication of Soviet media realities.

Media System Dependency

The accusation of media-centrism cannot be laid at the door of media system dependency theory, which explicitly addresses the relationship between media and other social institutions as an effort to explain the role of the former. In the fifth edition of their text *Theories of Mass Communication*, DeFleur and Ball-Rokeach identify a series of 'systems' – politics, economics, religion, family, education, the military, recreation, the law (1990: 305) – with which the media 'system' interacts. The list is reminiscent in some ways of Talcott Parsons' (1951) quadripartite conceptualization of society into economic, political, cultural and personality subsystems, and in other ways (with the exception of labor unions) of Althusser's (1971) listing of 'ideological State apparatuses'. The adoption of the term 'system' is not argued for, so it is unclear whether the term is intended to be more or less equivalent to 'social institution', or whether it is designed to ascribe an internally systemic, equilibrated character to media and the other complexes listed, as per Parsonian uses of the terms 'system' and 'subsystem'.

The media system dependency approach is certainly functionalist in general terms, or to be more exact, an uneasy combination of phenomenological, evolutionist and functionalist strands.

The core reason they offer as to why media create dependency upon their operation is a phenomenological one, namely because 'the social world is held together by fragile subjective understandings of reality',[6] and media function to 'resolve' the chronic contemporary problem of 'ambiguity, threat and social change' (DeFleur and Ball-Rokeach, 1990: 315–16).

The evolutionist component of their concept of media system dependency is to be found in their claim that there are inherent expansionist tendencies in all such 'systems':

> the media, like all other systems, seek opportunities to maximize their resources control and minimize their dependency, that is to create asymmetric relations in which they are more powerful. (p. 321)

There is a kind of personification or species-being projection at work here, with the media system implicitly conceived of as a single actor and identified as a successfully adapting aggressive species, as opposed to some unspecified 'spotted owl' system. The particular system they flag as ceding ground to the media system is the political system, by which in turn they only seem to have in mind the electoral process and possibly the authority of the (US) presidency, rather than the entire power structure (p. 322). This evolutionary dimension of their theoretical construct seems designed above all to try to account for the growth to societal prominence of mass media over the past century in the USA.

DeFleur and Ball-Rokeach flatly deny they are functionalists, claiming incorrectly that 'classical structural functionalists' (pp. 320–1) regard conflict as aberrant or non-existent, as opposed to their own view of conflict as normal and as promoting change.[7] 'Conflict theorists' (read Marxists), on the other hand, they accuse of seeing media simply as 'a tool employed by ruling elites to further their interests' (p. 320).[8]

The relation between media and the power structure is given no more shrift than this, except to note that the media system's 'primary goal' in capitalist society 'is to make a profit' (p. 305). How this meshes with the system's other primary function that they identify, namely to socialize and inform (pp. 316, 321), is not addressed in the chapter, nor is how the key dynamic of making a profit might just conceivably have some working relationship with ruling elites.

The total construct, even though this fifth edition version represents some advance over its earlier renditions, is distinctly ramshackle. The problems noted above – imprecision in the adoption of 'system' as a concept, personification of 'system', vagueness about the power structure, and the determinedly functionalist (*malgré eux*) adaptive-integrative-evolutionist role assigned to media as information-purveyors – certainly do not assist media system dependency theory to address the issues raised by the transitions in Eastern Europe.

Unfair, it may be said: it was not developed to do so. Very good; but in that case why was their text not entitled *Theories of US Mass Communication*? To be fair, in the fourth edition DeFleur and Ball-Rokeach did explicitly allude to 'the peculiar media-political system relation in America' which provided political information that would be unavailable in 'other societies (such as the USSR)' (1982, 4th edn: p. 240). None the less, their statement in the earlier version was celebrating US exceptionalism, not an acknowledgement of the constraints of multiple societal patterns of media use on the construction of an adequate theory of media communication.

Thus despite its laudable proposal to integrate a theory of media communication with a theory of society, or at least of the relations between media and other major social institutions, media system dependency theory has very severe internal flaws.

It certainly comes nowhere near offering a satisfactory conceptualization of the former sovietized media system, even aside from the latter's admittedly *sui generis* official dual information circuit. Nor can the theory begin to handle the tremendous fluctuations in East European media which accumulated through the later 1980s. Media professionals in Eastern Europe were as confused and divided about what was going on as was the general public, and, not least, the *nomenklatura* itself. How could media possibly 'resolve the problem of ambiguity' when a resolution was unavailable? If we turn to *samizdat* media, then the theory also offers silence, focused as it is on mainstream media. Only in the case of Western broadcasting stations was there an alternative mediatic mode of 'resolving ambiguity' made available within the Soviet bloc. And even the tussles in the post-Soviet period between presidents and parliaments over media control and policy that were covered in Chapter 6 were not a battle for ground between a media system and a political system, but a ferocious struggle among different instances within the political system.

Talcott Parsons

The only point at which this classical exponent of functionalist theory directly addressed questions of media was in an article entitled 'The mass media and the structure of American society' originally written in 1960 with Winston White and then republished in Parsons' 1969 book of essays *Politics and Social Structure*.[9] In it, they address in part a review-essay on the sociology of mass media published in the same year (Bauer and Bauer, 1960), but do so in order to launch an attack on C. Wright Mills' analysis of media and culture in his *The Power Elite* (Mills, 1956) in particular, and against views generally analogous to his on the subject of 'mass' society.

Unlike DeFleur and Ball-Rokeach, Parsons and White are very specific
in emphasizing that their analysis is only of media in the United States.
They propose (1969: 245–50) that within the US context it is fruitful to
draw analogies between three 'systems', namely the economic, the political
and the mediatic. In doing so, they aim to counter the notion that the
United States is suffering from an increasingly degenerating culture, with
the general public being fed communications constructed along the lowest
common denominator that simultaneously ratchet up corporate wealth in
the media industries, and excise the sting of critical thought. They do not
go beyond the parallels they propose to suggest precise sociological
interconnections except in the general inference that all three systems are
representative of a highly differentiated post-traditional society.

Their analysis of each of the three 'systems' focuses on four points, all
supportive of the notion that freedom is more characteristic of US society
than the increasing restraint claimed by mass society theorists. In the case
of the US economy, the individual may choose (a) the supplier with
whom to spend money, (b) the configuration of items desired, (c) the price
that is acceptable, and (d) when the purchase will be made. In the case of
the US political system, the voter may choose (a) between parties,
(b) policies, (c) the trade-off between policy-implementation and its costs
(i.e. taxes), and (d), along with political leaders, 'may enjoy greater
flexibility with respect to time' (this last assertion is extremely obscure,
and is not clarified further in the text). In the case of the US mediatic
system, the reader/viewer/listener may choose (a) between a great variety
of media and programs, (b) between different contents and levels of program, (c) the payment, amount of time and level of receptivity furnished,
and (d) the points in time to use particular media. (It must be said that
the differences between assertions (a), (b) and (d) for the media are
particularly gossamery.)

They proceed in each case to acknowledge shortfalls raised by critics
such as Mills – again, four of each. In the case of the economic system they
instance a certain trend to monopoly ownership, a deterioriation in the
quality of goods, a reduction in real wage-levels, and inflation. In the case
of the political system, the shortfalls identified are an increasing concentration of political power, the increasing predominance of highly placed
special interests, the corresponding weakening of the public interest, and
the general lack of responsiveness of the political system. Having listed
them, however, they then cite the stability of the USA through two world
wars and the Depression as indices that there must be 'countervailing
factors' (pp. 247, 248) that effectively neutralize the negative impact of any
of these economic or political trends in so far as they may indeed be at
work. They do not offer any more detailed empirical refutation of the
critics' assault, merely this general assertion of self-evident functionalist
equilibrium.

For media, they claim the same kind of division of labor and power
between producers and consumers as exists in the economy and polity, and

'the same order' of specialization in different kinds of 'communication output' (p. 248). Concentration of media ownership among larger producers is also evident, as are institutionalized mechanisms of control, both formal and informal. None the less, they urge that harping on media concentration plays down the 'very wide variety' (p. 249) of media available, instancing the then-recent explosion of cheap paperbound titles. They proceed to note certain standard critiques: the preponderance of *kitsch* media products; the manipulation of the irrational, as in violence programming; and the steady erosion of the public's taste standards. Against these claims, however, they simply cite the Bauers' survey article as evidence that 'institutionalized standards and favorable "market" conditions do in fact prevail to a significant degree' (p. 250).

In their summing up, they underscore the much greater accessibility of media to the public in the USA than in traditional top-heavy societies, the considerable differentiation of media rather than their 'mass' character, and in general the upgrading of taste in many media. They exempt television from this latter process, defining it as an immigrant to the cultural system that enabled earlier media on the scene, such as film and radio, to enhance their previous status and character. Their fundamental point of attack, however, is on the claim that the United States is an 'atomized' rather than a 'pluralist' society with 'an increasingly ramified network of criss-crossing solidarities' (p. 251). They do not seek, they insist, to deny the 'many inadequacies' of US society or its cultural system, only to contest the ability of critics such as Mills to explain or confront them.

Like DeFleur and Ball-Rokeach, so too Parsons and White offer a 'totalist' approach. On one level, their argument neatly escapes the kind of critique presented in this book in so far as it explicitly limits itself to one nation and therefore cannot in all fairness be accused of offering anything more comprehensive, either by implication or along the lines of development proposed in this book. Inasmuch as it can be criticized, it will be in the Conclusions chapter as a classic example of the failure of most US-based media analysis to take into account the full dynamics of the US system (though the critique will not be from a 'mass society' perspective). Their explicit comparisons of the US media system are basically with feudal (p. 245), barter (p. 246), traditional (p. 249) and – once – totalitarian (p. 249) societies. These constitute the benchmarks against which the US media and cultural system are evaluated, and in comparison to which they are judged clearly superior, patently more evolved.

The point at which it is entirely appropriate here to query their model is its simplistic parallelism between economy, polity and media. They base this on a Durkheimian premise, namely that as society becomes more populous so the division of labor grows, and as the division of labor grows so it extends itself into all fields of social activity, including the three 'systems' they address, with the effect of splitting producers from recipients. No longer are there direct ties between lord and serf, producer and consumer. For media, they claim this means that there is a direct analogy between the anonymity of car advertising, electoral campaigns and broad-casting soap operas or symphony concerts.

By selecting these very three examples, they make the parallelism seem more plausible, since all are in fact examples of communication. Yet how these parallel 'systems' actually interact with each other in terms of their core specific operation in society, why drawing parallels between them illuminates media – the notably gossamery quality of the mediatic specifics in their argument has already been noted – and how far it is useful to posit a *Zeitgeist* demi-urge of 'differentiation' constantly at work generating more choice and more freedom, all these issues are left distinctly murky in the exposition. In the end the essay seems a roundabout way of asserting that things are not nearly as awful as C. Wright Mills proposed, while never endeavoring to address a series of the particular empirical problems he raised. A *plaidoyer* against anti-American negativism.

Conclusions

European commentators on earlier versions of this chapter frequently queried why one would bother at all to confront most of the theoretical positions addressed in it with the macroscopic media issues involved in the period 1980–95 in Russia, Poland and Hungary. The implication was that these theories constituted a series of overly easy and not particularly productive targets for critique.[10]

It is indeed fair to say that mostly they are framed with certain particularities of the United States in mind, and that they do not take into account the issues of change, power, conflict and the rest that are so sharply raised by the three nations studied here, which also stand in for many others across the globe that do not evince the Anglo-American pattern of development. An exception is cultivation analysis, which does indeed offer a series of propositions that may hold in some nations and not in others, and thus is structured to encourage comparative research.

At the same time, whatever the shortcomings of these theories, it is extremely important that we engage in and develop conceptual discourses that address the specifics of media operations on all levels and then interrelate those with broader societal analysis. The problem with critical media theory is often, as will be argued in the next chapter, that it has barely begun to address the specifics of media, any more than most political science research – aside from psephology – has engaged with communi-cation research in any systematic form.

The basic issue is this: most mainstream approaches are not so much completely off the wall as underdeveloped, empiricist and unreflective. For example, the wave of often subtle and perceptive qualitative and ethno-graphic audience studies of the 1980s and 1990s showed that the limitations of 'uses-and-gratifications' research did not nullify the basic insight from which it began, namely that audiences process media texts and are not simply putty in the hands of their authors. Similarly, the 'gatekeeper' model was founded on the observation of a very elementary reality of media and social life in general, namely that selection of information is inherent in the communication process. As suggested above, however, if gatekeeper research is to become more than a statement of the obvious, it needs developing much further in terms of the political economy and sociology of media organizations as well as in cultural terms.

Even acknowledging these elemental cores, however, risks being too rosily eirenic. It is important to acknowledge that some theoretical positions are so poorly framed that to continue to work with them would be like attaching a ball-and-chain to one's foot. Such, frankly, are the four theories of the press and media system dependency approaches.

The first, although its revision at the time of writing by Christians, Nordenstreng and White will hopefully succeed in rescuing and redirecting it, is an ancient monument to ideologies of the free market, the Cold War and (implicitly) US exceptionalism. Its recognition of the importance of comparative media research does not exculpate it. Furthermore, there are inbuilt problems with normative theories in so far as their analytical and normative components often become inextricably intertwined. There is nothing wrong with normative positions *per se*, but where they fail to connect the ethical 'ought' with the sociological 'can', or interpret media in the light of official pronouncements rather than actual performance, then the result is confusion and pontification rather than light.

Media system dependency theory is a different kind of monument, this time to the vacuity and tautology of functionalism and evolutionism and, let it be said in sorrow, to a series of enfeebled echoes of even those constructs (along with the others harnessed or critiqued).

Thus when it comes to specific analysis of media, mainstream theory leaves us mostly adrift. Some of the 'fragmented' media theories that will not be addressed here – Walter Benjamin on the storyteller, Mikhail Bakhtin on *raznorechie*/heteroglossia, Roland Barthes on aspects of 'myth' and the pleasurable appeal of the text, Hans-Magnus Enzensberger on subversive applications of media technology – are much more suggestive.[11] But now let us see whether critical theories serve us any better.

Notes

1 Shakespeare, *Macbeth*, V, viii. 44–5.

2 See the argument on this issue between the writer and Rod Hart (Hart and Downing, 1992).

3 We will take up the Herman and Chomsky position again in the following chapter. Gitlin's analysis, though very valuable, tends to present all the 'players' in the process as more or less evenly weighted, a series of endless but equivalent hurdles from the point of view of the production company trying to get a TV series made. It is hard to suppose that those with financial power have the same clout as the obscenity or copyright lawyers. There is a significant difference between the power to finance, and the power to hold up.

4 Gandy (1993), following Foucault, proposes the image of the panopticon, the starfish-

pattern jail architecture devised in the nineteenth century so that prisoners could cheaply be under effective surveillance from the center. He also offers a very detailed empirical survey of commercial electronic surveillance practices in the USA (ch. 3). See too Bamford (1982), Burnham (1983) and Donner (1980).

5 For Habermas' position, see Chapter 1; for Foucault's, see his work, *passim*; for Giddens' analysis of the generic and now expanding surveillance operation of the state, see his *A Contemporary Critique of Historical Materialism* (1981: 169–76), and his *The Constitution of Society* (1984: 183ff.).

6 This is very much a phenomenological assertion, characteristic of Alfred Schutz's work (cf. Schutz, 1962: 207–356), rather than of symbolic interactionism.

7 In 1956 Lewis Coser published the widely diffused *The Functions of Social Conflict*, which specifically argued for the compatibility of conflict and functionalist theory; in 1966 Yale sociologist Cynthia Russett published *The Concept of Equilibrium in American Social Thought*, in which among other things she pointed out very clearly how the concept of equilibrium in social theory could equally well draw on Pareto, for whom it had an engineering derivation in which it was produced by the balance of contending forces, rather than the organic and implicitly harmonious organic model proposed by Durkheim. Their rendition of the functionalist tradition in sociological analysis is very superficial.

8 Something of a straw man version of Marxist media research, as segments of the next chapter will indicate. They are apparently unaware of the work of Stuart Hall, Raymond Williams, the earlier work of Roland Barthes, Vincent Mosco and a number of others.

9 In other writings he sometimes discussed what he called the 'cultural system', but focused almost entirely on questions of value-systems and what he saw as the typical constellation of core values dominating modern societies as distinct from more traditional ones (for example, the contemporary prestige of personal achievement as opposed to the prestige once assigned family background). He also deployed the term 'media' in a radically different sense to the one used here, to refer to both money and political power as mechanisms of societal exchange of inputs and outputs.

10 Sometimes there seemed to be an added prejudicial spin of 'what would you expect intellectually from the United States?' European intellectual snobbery is a comforting ethnocentric fad; those as astonishingly gifted as its exponents should know that a theory is judged by its quality, not its provenance.

11 Walter Benjamin, 'The storyteller', *Illuminations*, 1973, 83–109; Mikhail Bakhtin, 'Discourse in the novel', *The Dialogic Imagination*, 1981, 259–422; Roland Barthes, 'Myth Today', excerpt from 'The Pleasure of the Text', Inaugural Lecture at the Collège de France, in Susan Sontag, ed., *A Barthes Reader*, 1982, 93–149, 404–14, 457–78; Hans-Magnus Enzensberger, 'Constituents of a theory of media', in his *The Consciousness Industry*, 1974, 95–128.

8

Critical Media Theory and Change in Eastern Europe

This chapter offers an appraisal of some 'critical' media and cultural theory in the light of the issues of power, conflict, change and allied themes raised by the transitions in Russia, Poland and Hungary. The approaches reviewed will be those of Gramsci; Althusser and Poulantzas; Adorno and Horkheimer; cultural studies perspectives; perspectives from Raymond Williams and Jesús Martín-Barbero; Herman and Chomsky; and the concepts of cultural and media imperialism, and globalization. These approaches have certain traits in common. They mostly owe some parentage to the marxist analytical tradition; they consequently put issues of power, conflict, change and ideology center-stage, and when they refer to media, place them within those vectors; and are usually ultimately pivoted upon the aim to understand social reality in order to enable its oppressive dimensions – or some of them – to be overcome.

In those respects they generally differ from the approaches reviewed in the previous chapter. Thus they are, typically, what were labeled earlier in the book as 'totalist' theories, where media communication is principally defined in relation to other power-institutions. In many instances this loses something of central importance to understanding media, precisely their textual and audience dimensions. This is not inevitable, and indeed various approaches within cultural studies have been in part an attempt to fill in this crucial blank, as have the writings of Williams and Martín-Barbero. At the same time, this critical tradition has the signal merit of asking awkward questions of the status quo and of ripping apart flatulent and merely celebratory research. Its analysts also incorporate the dynamic of societal change into the very center of their models, a frequent crucial blank in mainstream approaches.

Gramsci

In many Western intellectual circles, Gramsci has virtually become, as W.H. Auden said of Freud, 'no more a person Now, but a whole climate of opinion' (*In Memory of Sigmund Freud*, 1939). And just as this diffusion, as well as raising stimulating issues, also arguably flattened Freud out into a number of half-digested clichés, so too with Gramsci.

Gramsci wrote relatively little about media, despite his years working on *L'Ordine Nuovo*.[1] None the less, he has been widely perceived as offering a general framework for the analysis of culture and power within which the roles of media can readily be slotted and understood. It is a framework which focuses rather closely on the questions typically omitted by US media communication theories, especially on the state, though scarcely at all on the economy, Gramsci's disquisitions on Fordism notwithstanding. (The assumption that every marxist analyst is an economic reductionist is particularly ill-founded in his case.)

The critical core of Gramsci's theory[2] of hegemony – which I am going to refer to as *egemonia*, since the term 'hegemony' has become overly diffuse through intensive use – consists of (a) the recognition, hardly original to him, that the stability of a given politico-economic order's domination depends upon mass consent as well as simultaneously upon coercion; (b) the assertion that an alliance of dominant social classes is an integral component of this *egemonia*; (c) the insistence that since the dominated classes' political consciousness is divided, not simply providing 'legitimacy' *à la* Weber, this consensus, this stability, are not permanent but shifting and therefore potentially open to decay, crisis and disruption; (d) the focus on 'organic intellectuals'[3] as key players in the process of *egemonia*; whether for or against the status quo; and (e) the consequent importance in Western Europe of the cultural and ideological dimension – and hence, logically, of media communication – as a terrain of struggle for organized political forces representing the majority social classes in their attempt to claim control over the direction of society's development.

It is more than a little historically ironic that we should be asking how useful this theoretical position can be in illuminating events in Eastern European transitions or comparable situations elsewhere, given that Gramsci developed it precisely to account for the fact that the Bolshevik revolution happened in 'gelatinous' Russia, as against the failure of marxist revolutionary upsurges elsewhere in culturally 'bulwarked' Europe.[4] (In fact, with the perpetual advantage of hindsight, his emphasis on class alliances as a key component of *egemonia*, based on the strategy of union (*smychka*) between proletariat and peasantry in the early USSR, stands as a tragic monument to hope, given the crushing state terrorism practiced against the peasants and the total liquidation of anything beyond a pretence to such an alliance in the Soviet Union from 1928 onwards.)

On the other hand, it is very possible that the theory of *egemonia* was conceived by Gramsci as relevant to Mussolinian fascism as well as to liberal democracy. If so, if he was in part concerned to account for the ideological appeal of Mussolini's fascism across classes, then his approach to power and culture may have a great deal more resonance with the realities of political life in the last decade of the Soviet bloc than might have been supposed. The issue is very large and can only be touched upon here, but it needs recalling that despite the gross and violent[5] aspects of the first decade of Mussolini's rule, his version of fascism in the second decade, beginning from the mid-1930s, was much closer to Hitlerism or

Stalinism than in the first. (We noted in Chapter 1 how Arendt identified 1938 as the point at which Italian fascism became totalitarian by her definition.)

Furthermore, there are many indications that to begin with the Mussolini regime carried support within all social classes. Denis Mack Smith's (1982) biography of Mussolini clearly shows what perhaps might have been anticipated, namely the effective absence of serious opposition within governing circles, all the way to the king. Marcia Landy's study (1986: 7 *et passim*) of Italian fascist cinema strongly suggests that there were many conjoined themes in the ordinary films of the period (as opposed to news propaganda bulletins) that effectively intertwined both popular and regime messages and concerns. Passerini's oral history (1987) of the Turin working class under Fascism – a sector of the working class particularly resistant to Fascism – also shows that even there, alongside a frequently found visceral hatred of Mussolini and Fascism, there were those who either stayed neutral or were actually energetic supporters, even three decades after his execution and the regime's collapse. Her analysis is much more nuanced than this, or than there is space to explore here, but suffice it to say that Gramsci's theory of *egemonia* does not, arguably, imply a radical break between pre- and post-Mussolini. The very exercise of state violence by the latter can be interpreted within Gramsci's schema as the normal response of a regime under threat, not of a regime that has given up on trying to communicate effectively with as much of the nation as possible, and is wedded to pure force to maintain itself. The 1929 Vatican Concordat shows the folly of the latter assumption.

However, a key issue here is how far Gramsci's approach can actually get us past generalities of hegemony and counter-hegemony, and into a more exact understanding of media, political power and transition, in or out of the former Soviet bloc. Although he endlessly discusses the state, he does so in notoriously 'gelatinous' terms. The extraordinary detail of his historical and cultural analysis is rarely matched by the same conceptual exactitude in the use of key terms.[6]

Where he is more precise – let us take the instances of class alliance, or organic intellectuals – then we immediately run into rather heavy weather. What would we make of these concepts in the transitions in Eastern Europe, or in the aftermaths?

We could jump into an analysis of 'the emergent historic bloc' of a class alliance of workers, intellectuals and perhaps farmers in *Solidarnosc* in 1980 – but would instantly be faced with its dissolution thirteen years later, seemingly sealed not by martial law but by the electoral return of reformed Communist parties to government in Poland in September 1993. Which hardly makes it very historic.

Furthermore, what do we conceivably mean when we talk of intellectuals, even in Gramsci's particular sense of the term, as part of an alliance of classes?[7] Gramsci was a Leninist, class was a core concept in his thinking, he did urge a *smychka*, Italian-style, yet 'organic intellectuals' were not themselves a social class in his view, rather a part of whichever class they represented. What kind of organic intellectuals, if it comes to that, were the *samizdat* media communicators, or the often *acharnés* exiles of Radio Liberty and Radio Free Europe who amplified *samizdat*? Organic to what? What kind of organic intellectuals, too, were regime communicators such as Poland's Jerzy Urban[8] or the 1960s Khrushchev generation *gorbachevtsy* such as Fyodr Burlatsky or Yegor Yakovlev or Aleksandr Bovin?

If it comes to that, was the *nomenklatura* a social class? Did it exercise *egemonia* in conjunction with other classes? There is no point second-guessing how Gramsci himself might have analysed the later Soviet system, but unless we eviscerate his concepts of their marxist specifics and reduce him to a general analyst of culture and conflict, as Jackson Lears (1985) has argued we usefully may, then these questions cannot be hedged.

For the purpose of attacking the oversimplifications of the 'totalitarianists', one dimension of *egemonia* does have some purchase on the later sovietized system. As argued earlier, sovietized societies, at least since the latter 1950s, were mostly not held together simply by fear – in other words, when that noxious political glue began to dissolve, the system did not promptly fall apart. At the most minimal, there was a certain understood social contract, expressed cynically as 'they pretend to pay us, and we pretend to work', or defined more moralistically *à la* Vaclav Havel in terms of classical existentialism, frowning at the readiness of *das Man* to succumb to the self-abuse of compliance.[9]

In reality, the full flavor of *egemonia* in the sense of the public's daily acknowledgment, management and manipulation of domination in post-Stalinist Eastern Europe was far more complex than either of these positions.[10] Its interpretation needs the skills of film-makers and authors such as Andrzej Wajda, George Konrád, Kira Muratova, Andrei Amalrik, Meszaros Marta, Tadeusz Konwicki, Alexander Zinoviev[11] at least as much if not more so than the concepts of cultural analysts. Some of the discussion of youth cultures and music earlier in the book acts as another pointer to the complexity of these issues, especially during the 1980s.

Thus Gramsci's insistence on the operation of a cultural *egemonia* rather than terror 'in normal times', as equally his insistence that not all times were normal, that *egemonia* was not a permanent given, that it could dissolve in favor of other, more rebellious public reactions which otherwise evinced themselves only in occasional flashes – this insistence perhaps captures rather well, if only phenomenally, the realities of late sovietized societies and the extraordinary ruptures of 1989 and 1991.

But at this point, have not Gramsci's concepts lost any particular originality? Did not his notion of a divided subaltern consciousness always seem subtle and advanced simply because Western leftist analysts stood it up against the absurd Lukacsian emphasis on 'false consciousness'?[12] Did not his discussions of 'common sense', 'good sense' and 'philosophy' simply seem less offensive, more democratically digestible, than Lenin's 'Better

Fewer, But Better'[13] elitism? This picking and choosing pieces from the theory of *egemonia*, by those who sometimes rather fancied themselves as organic intellectuals attached to the morally admirable, if not the winning side, was easy but imprecise.

If we turn to the present, to the uneasy flux between sovietism and capitalism, does either Gramsci-as-generalist or Gramsci-as-Gramsci have anything much to say to the question of media? In particular, does he have anything to contribute to three key mediatic questions: the role of government in relation to media, of foreign ownership of media, or of media professionals' ingrained occupational practices inherited from the previous situation?

It would be consonant with his approach to recognize how in a period of flux neither education nor religion have the immediacy needed to sustain a given political order on a monthly, even daily basis. Battles over media, as we have seen, have generally been at the center of political conflict in Eastern Europe. The struggle for hegemony – in the diffuse sense – has predictably targeted its main daily institution. Pitched battles around the radio headquarters in Budapest in 1956, at the TV headquarters in Bucharest in 1989, in Vilnius and Riga in 1991, and in October 1993 around Ostankino, were only the most extreme expression of this struggle. In *Solidarnosc*'s confrontations with the Kania regime in 1980–1, one of the most strongly resisted demands was for access to television. When negotiations recommenced over the Round Table, this was once again one of the most difficult issues.[14]

But does Gramsci enable us to see any more clearly than we can without him the place of media, especially of television, given the anxiety of many of the new regimes – all too conscious of the recency of their arrival in power, knowing rather well the turbulence of the public mood in a period of harsh economic changes as people perceive the authorities' own threadbare, ad hoc strategies for economic recovery? Is the regimes' consensual enthronement of television as the most penetrative medium of mass communication a phenomenon restricted to Eastern Europe? Is it conceptually to be apprehended lucidly only via Gramsci?

I would suggest not, unless his concepts are so eviscerated of their specifics that they cannot really be described as Gramsci's own any more. The 'enriched' Gramscianism of which some have written would seem to be flying the bend sinister (cf. Harris, 1992: 27–8). Arguably the best use of Gramsci in our context, as in others, is to hew to his overall method and problematic, a method of great historical and cultural precision that cleaves to the basic problematic of tracking the warp and weft of the exercise of cultural power. In this respect we pay more respect to his original contribution than by wrenching his specific concepts out of their mold. His supple liberation of marxist analysis from its Stalinist straitjacket is not honored by simultaneously flash-freezing and yet bending his terminology, itself sometimes written for the Fascist prison censor rather than for us.

Thus in the same way as earlier the term 'public sphere' was offered in preference to Habermas' original term *Öffentlichkeit*, so the terms 'hegemony' and even 'counter-hegemony' are preferable, once defined carefully by their users in contradistinction to Gramsci's sense, to the covert imposition of post-Gramscian content on to his concept of *egemonia*. Given this, it has to be said that Gramsci's orientation constitutes a very helpful push in the direction of puzzling over and teasing out the interrelation between media and the power structure, media and societal change and the other major issues that mainstream theory generally leaves on one side. We need to acknowledge his heritage – and move onwards.

Althusser and Poulantzas

Writing in 1995, a discussion of these two writers has faintly the feel of talking about sadly traduced rock-idols of a bygone era, especially – for some – given the tragic anecdotal information that the former, in the grip of acute depression, killed his beloved spouse of many years and also later renounced all the writings that had made him internationally famous, and that the latter threw himself to an early death from a high-rise apartment block. The logical, if not also ethical, flaw in our dismissing them on the basis of these personal circumstances, even on Althusser's disavowal of his own work, lies in our unthought insistence on the moral integration of the thinker's personality with their texts and the further presumption that the author is the final authority on her or his own work. Hence their consignment, with an easy and superior smirk, to the trash can of dead marxist concepts.

The fact remains that many students continue to find Althusser's essay 'Ideology and ideological state apparatuses' (Althusser, 1971), written originally in early 1969 in the aftermath of the immense student and worker turbulence in France in May and June 1968, a very illuminating text for media research. Whether they are correct in doing so will be examined in a moment, but it is also the case that Poulantzas (1974: 195–6; 299–356), basing himself on an often critical reading of Althusser's concept of 'ideological State apparatus' (and writing in the year after that essay first circulated), produced a very interesting analysis for our present purposes of the interlocking roles of ideological and repressive institutions within German and Italian fascisms. His analysis of media communication in totalitarian regimes, brief as it is, is the nearest we have to an attempt to define the topic conceptually within this or any other body of research.

Not that, in the end, either Althusser or Poulantzas have very much to say that is specific about media. Both claim Gramsci as their ultimate source, and as we have seen, he had little to say specifically about media either. Their focus is on the panoply of 'ideological state apparatuses', as they term them, by which they mean education, media, the family, labor unions, the churches and similar intermediate social institutions. In addition, Althusser sought to expand the term 'ideology' beyond its cognitive, idealist, externalized referents in everyday use and to recast it as something deeply internalized both in these institutions' daily functioning and in the individual's sense of self – in other words, as a highly material force in societal life. He uses the image of someone who is addressed formally in a court setting and who readily acknowledges the fundamental rightness of their being pinpointed and addressed in that way, in order to illustrate the apparent directness and obviousness of the communication of ideological perspectives to an individual. He does not, however, engage in the kind of split consciousness analysis that Gramsci offered, and to that extent is far stronger in portraying the impact of ideological communication on those who swallow it whole than on those who feel queasy or worse.

What Althusser's essay offers in principle is a grid, a framework within which to place media communication in relation to other communication institutions. His particular slant is to suggest a connectedness between their communicative operations that he never specifies beyond the extremely abstract propositions that (a) there is a dominant ideology in capitalist society, and (b) that the capitalist state unifies power around itself. Having said that, he then proposes that these 'ideological apparatuses' are 'relatively autonomous'[15] from the state, that is to say that they are not simply puppet-institutions dancing to the orders of whomsoever; but at the same time, by selecting the term 'apparatus' he underscores that they are not independent social institutions either, that they can be substantially restructured from above.

It is Poulantzas (1974: 314–15) who proceeds to dot the i's and cross the t's by emphasizing that this position is very contrary to the notion of 'civil society'. Rather than seeing the institutions of civil society, including the media, as the independent bulwarks of a democratic order, both Althusser and Poulantzas attack this as an obfuscation of their real operation of maintaining a capitalist social order (in Gramsci's terms, their role within the process of *egemonia*). The attractiveness of this position is that it is less dewy-eyed about civil society's institutions than civil society theorists tend to manage to be, especially those US analysts who turn instantly misty at the mention of de Tocqueville's account of the American proclivity for civic associations. It is a position, however, that at least in Poulantzas' case does not simply turn civil society theory upside down, but rather claims that within the confines of these apparatuses' state-defined boundaries there may still be sites of contestation and opposition, even within fascist regimes.

Whereas Althusser's formulation, however, as he partly acknowledges in his postscript, never really leaves behind the sense that he envisaged a smoothly functioning system of control – a place for everyone and everybody in their place with 'the dominant ideology' as glue[16] – Poulantzas offered a much more dynamic and conflictual interpretation. Admittedly, this has to struggle for expression within his typically over-schematized argument – he seems to have had an almost Linnaean passion for classification – but it is interesting that in dissecting the most draconian form of power where everything might be expected to be nailed into place, he none the less achieves a much less functionalist presentation than Althusser's.

His core positions are twofold. Firstly, that a fascist state is still a capitalist state, albeit with '*key differences*' (p. 315), and not a *sui generis* entity (thus taking a view directly contrary to both the Third International's, which claimed they were no different, and Arendt's). Fascism is a particular version of what he terms the 'exceptional' state, other instances being a military dictatorship or a Bonapartist[17] regime. Secondly, that within German and Italian fascisms the relation between the state's repressive dimension and the communicative dimension – he uses the term 'apparatuses' rather than 'dimension', and 'ideological' or 'propaganda' interchangeably with 'communication' – was different from their typical interrelation in the standard capitalist framework.

In this latter, more familiar structure, Poulantzas argues, the different apparatuses frequently generate their own internal ideologies, 'perceptibly different from the dominant ideology'[18] (p. 317), as is customary inside the civil service, the army, education, the churches. The 'exceptional' state (i.e. fascism), by contrast, comes into being in the first place because of a major crisis in the dominant ideology – a Weberian might say because of a breakdown in legitimacy – and this crisis needs very active ideological intervention by a centralized force to restore the situation. Furthermore, extensive repressive intervention is also demanded to resolve the crisis situation, and this too needs sustained public justification of a kind rarely to be expected from more autonomous 'apparatuses'. Hence, under fascism, the expunging of independent public debate and commentary and the harnessing of public communication to a vast propaganda apparatus governed and led by the political police. Any professional ideology such as 'freedom of the press' or 'objective reporting' is dispelled from practical application, and the relative autonomy of the media is canceled.

The assertion here is very clearly that ideology, propaganda and media communication are of central importance to a fascist regime and thus are prime targets for drastic reorganization under the aegis of the political police.[19] In addition, fascism always has a major social base, unlike a *coup d'état*. To that extent, ideology and its communication within that base are also key components of fascism's political structure, whereas a military coup typically relies on surprise and fear in the initial transition to power. Finally, the position of the fascist 'leader' who has ultimate control over the state means that various apparatuses, whether the party, the political police, the military, or special sectors or units of these, can be commandeered very quickly for a new ideological drive if this is thought necessary to assert renewed control. Quite often they operate in a kind of competition with each other, or even different sections of the same entity do, as 'parallel power networks' (p. 329).

Poulantzas did not analyse Stalinist or post-Stalinist regimes, so a sense for his position regarding them would have to be based on guesswork. None the less, a number of his observations above could be applied to Stalinist regimes in so far as they share certain features with fascism. Perhaps the most important of his insights concerned the dominant role of the political police and the continuing importance of ideology and propaganda to these regimes, that they did not and could not simply rely upon terror to communicate their demands to the public. By implication, as that ideology increasingly failed to communicate itself at all levels, including within the political police and the Communist Party, the seeds of the regime's dissolution would be sown with greater and greater abandon. This is indeed what we saw to have been the case, and yet at the same time the persistence of the Russian political police's dominance represents one of the most disquieting features of the post-transition era.

Thus what Althusser's and Poulantzas' work has in common of value is its skepticism concerning naive approaches to the notion of civil society; its determination to explore the interfaces between various 'ideological' institutions, including media; its acknowledgment of their often changing relation to political power and each other; its refusal to acknowledge an absolute division between the operation of power in liberal capitalist democracies and authoritarian, even totalitarian regimes, whilst retaining a clear recognition of the significant differences between them, as indeed between different fascist regimes. Neither, in the works cited, addressed sovietism, except in so far as Althusser for most of his career endeavored to stay a loyal reformist firmly within its carapace, and Poulantzas critiqued standard Third International definitions of fascism – again from a loyalist reformist position. This does not mean that there are no fertile implications for the analysis of sovietism, post-sovietism and media communication within their writings. None the less, the word is 'implications': as with Gramsci, we are presented with a conceptual schema but not a specific research agenda.

Adorno and Horkheimer

Some of the best-known work of these two key members of the Frankfurt School addressed very directly the question of communication, culture and domination (Adorno, 1981; Horkheimer, 1986; Horkheimer and Adorno, 1987a, 1987b), focusing both on culture and the Nazi state and on culture and the US mega-economy in the 1940s. As is rather well known, they perceived chilling analogies between the two systems, not at the level of concentration camps or militarism, but rather at the level of the evacuation of independent thinking by advertising and mass culture in the US system. In their analysis, this expunging of critical faculties represented the same essential process in both the United States and in pre-fascist Germany, a process which left the way clear for authoritarian rule to emerge without significant opposition. Thus their primary focus was not on the mechanisms, communicative or otherwise, of the strong state, but on the cultural conditions for its emergence, asserting that 'today the order of life allows no room for the ego to draw spiritual or intellectual conclusions . . . so that self-examination of the mind which works against paranoia is defeated', for people 'are already deadened by the culture industry' (Horkheimer and Adorno, 1987b: 197–8).

As Adorno wrote in his critique of Spengler (1981: 69):

> Culture . . . arises in men's struggle to acquire the means to reproduce themselves. Culture thus contains an element of resistance to blind necessity – the will to determine oneself on the basis of knowledge.

A little later on the same page he added that Spengler seemed to want to wipe out 'what is antithetical and rebellious in man, consciousness' from his account of modern society.

Buck-Morss (1977: 183) cites a similarly idealist passage on the reverse problem, mass political ignorance, from Adorno's jointly authored text *The Authoritarian Personality* (1950):

> The ultimate reason for this ignorance might well be the opaqueness of the social, economic and political situation to all those who are not in full command of all the resources of stored knowledge and theoretical thinking. In its present phase our social system tends objectively and automatically to produce 'curtains' which make it impossible for the naive person to see what it is all about.

Horkheimer (1986: 277–8), similarly, identified as disastrous

> the transformation of personal life into leisure and of leisure into routines supervised to the last detail, into the pleasures of the ball park and the movie, the best seller and the radio . . . Long before culture was replaced by these manipulated pleasures . . . men had fled into a private conceptual world and rearranged their thoughts when the time was ripe for rearranging reality . . . But . . . man has lost his power to conceive a world different from that in which he lives. This other world was that of art.

Thus they argue that propaganda – whether political as in Nazi Germany or Stalinist Russia, or analogically economic, in the minutely calibrated advertising strategies in the USA tied in to mass leisure culture[20] – had replaced art, the one social 'space' where human beings could allow themselves to be stimulated into a reflective, transversal, even oppositional stance to contemporary society. That had been the single setting in which conformism, naivete and political ignorance might be challenged.

However, how people might then activate their challenge was always left to one's imagination in these writers' work. There often seems to be an implicit individualistic existentialism lurking behind their text rather than any thought of social or political movements that might emerge to counter domination.[21] Since they primarily addressed the pre-fascist situation in Germany, it seems odd they did not include, for example, the immensely damaging split between the German Social Democratic and

Communist parties into their discussion of the draining away of critical consciousness.

Thus both Adorno's and Horkheimer's critical dissection of power and culture, for all its eloquence, was, like C. Wright Mills' beautifully written Americanization of their argument in his *The Power Elite* (1956: ch. 13), infinitely stronger in its characterization of the mechanisms of attempted and even real domination than in its understanding of what other options existed for the dominated. Interestingly, it resonates much better with some of the depictions of the 'tightest' versions of late sovietism, especially with some of the accounts of Czechoslovak cultural conditions after the Prague Spring had been crushed and the Brezhnev–Husak 'normalization' policy had been clamped down on to the society (cf. Simecka), than it does with the increasingly assertive currents in Russia, Poland and Hungary in the build-up to the transition biennium.

In view of the many attacks leveled against Adorno for elitism, which is a valid observation but is not sufficient cause simply to dismiss his work or Horkheimer's, it is important to emphasize that he was an extremely subtle thinker, perpetually inverting and juxtaposing contradictory realities in the approach he termed 'negative dialectics'. As Buck-Morss (1977: 186) put it,

> he addressed the ontological issues of anthropology in terms of historical change. He defined social atomization by social conformism, alienation by collectivization [soviet-style, J.D.]. The purpose of what in Adorno's case could be called 'anti-theories' was to avoid such conformism at all costs. This lends to negative dialectics the quality of quicksilver . . .

It would be inappropriate, therefore, to hang all his formulations around his neck as though they were ponderous social-scientific conclusions, aimed at canceling debate rather than provoking it. This is notably true of his and Horkheimer's best-known essay on the US culture industry, which fifty years later retains its power to infuriate readers into critical reflection.

Thus in the analysis of culture, communication and power in Eastern Europe or in other fast-moving historical developments, it is his method rather than his seemingly finished judgments that will be the best stimulus to thought and perception. So while his conflation of the genesis of cultural domination in Nazi Germany (and by implication, Stalinist Russia as well) and in the 1940s USA does not stand up to detailed scrutiny, and while indeed he omits many aspects of those nations' life, he does none the less provoke a searching reflection on the character of *US* culture. In that sense his approach anticipates and underscores a major argument in the Conclusions chapter to this book, namely that in the process of focusing media research mostly on Britain and the United States, not only have communicative processes more characteristic of human society in general been left out of account, but also significant communicative dimensions of both those nations.

In considering the actual dynamics of communication and power in Germany during the fascist period, it is instructive to examine Kershaw's

(1983) study of Bavaria during it. Drawing on a variety of sources, from secret police reports to accounts assembled by covert Social Democratic agents and shipped to the SPD's headquarters in exile, the picture he reconstructed was considerably more complex on some levels than the blanket, generic analysis produced by Horkheimer and Adorno that often reads like a mass psychology.

Several points are worthy of note from Kershaw's account. One is that despite the repression, people were still ready to grumble, surprisingly often out loud, and especially about economic discontents, though generally not to organize opposition. Those who did not grumble out loud were often in jobs where there was ready and universal surveillance, such as the civil service, rather than farmers or even in some instances factory workers. Another is that some forms of organized resistance did take place, notably by Catholics against Nazi attempts to ban Catholic school education. A third is that physical persecution of Jews was widely discountenanced, although the crucial next step – organizing against their assets being seized, or their being physically removed from their homes, including to outside the country – never took place, unlike the opposition of Catholics to attacks on their religious institutions.

A fourth is that dissent really did have to be repressed, as opposed to the sheeplike readiness to conform at all points that Horkheimer and Adorno, perhaps only polemically, asserted to have been in force (and so to have made repression unnecessary, rather as in Huxley's *Brave New World*). Fifthly, there was a longer-term effect over the Nazi period, Kershaw suggests, of certain general elements in the propaganda concerning such issues as Germany's need for great power status, or the validity of a Germany for the ethnically pure Germans. Lastly, there was an echo of the tragically absurd attitude of many Russians to their tsars and to Stalin, namely that abuses that everyone was aware of, especially conspicuous corruption among the Nazi elite, were not the responsibility of Hitler, and there existed genuine hope that he would find out about them and strike them down.

Thus although Kershaw offers no conceptual commentary upon the communication issues that preoccupy us here, the situation as he describes it helpfully complicates the abstractions of Horkheimer's and Adorno's dissection of pre-fascist and fascist culture and communication. How do subjected publics in authoritarian or totalitarian regimes process communication from the top, and how do they themselves communicate, either laterally or vertically? What roles do racism and ethnicity play? Are there specific issues, such as the religious issue in Bavaria, where the regime's writ cannot really run? What is the relation between abstract questions, such as the legitimacy of Germany's need for international power, and support for specific policies officially designed to achieve that goal? Is there an important difference in terms of conclusions that can be drawn from the data between the twelve-year period of direct Nazi rule, and the much longer period of Stalinist rule?

Cultural Studies

The intellectual character of cultural studies varies according to a consider-able variety of factors. There are to some degree different national approaches in Britain, the USA and Latin America (Rêgo, 1993).[22] In turn, the Gramscian priorities of a Stuart Hall in Hall et al. (1980) are distinct from the more cultural-populist, some have said neo-consumerist, focus of a John Fiske (1987). And many contemporary studies within this mold spend such time exploring cultural detail – 'everyday life construed as a rich domain of the unfathomable' as Bennett (1989: 11) has put it – that rather little time is left for elaborating conceptual issues. Thus it becomes hard to pick a fully representative statement of conceptual priority or an empirical study to critique.

David Harris (1992) and Jim McGuigan (1992) have critically assessed the corpus of the British literature. Harris attacks much of Hall's and the Birmingham Centre's work for a lack of interest in actual audiences, and specifically Hall for a tendency to reduce theory to a handservant of party-political commitments, in Hall's case a commitment to the anti-Stalinist British Communist Party of the 1980s. McGuigan, targeting his critique more toward Fiske's approach, identifies a strongly populist vein in the discourse, inflating the public's immediate perspectives and reactions into fully adequate explanations of societal process, combined with a common refusal to deal with economic and structural forces in the determination of cultural expression – a critique very close to the one voiced in this book.

The cultural studies literature is no more primarily interested in media than the other approaches surveyed in this chapter. That, let me reiterate, is an advantage over strictly mediatic angles of vision. Yet as we saw earlier in our review of cultural movements in Russia, Poland and Hungary in the build-up to the Crisis, cultural studies usefully directed our attention to certain issues, but without necessarily being able to account for them in a major way. There is little that is original to it conceptually, being often a more-or-less considered blend of Gramsci, Barthes, Bakhtin, Foucault, feminism, and often relying on such vague notions as 'articulation' as a substitute for saying 'there is a connection here and let me now specify it'.[23]

As regards the liminal post-transition period, the continuing cultural – and economic – disaffection of young people was also a potent force in the determination of the media future in all three nations, perhaps all the more so for often being relegated to the margins in the 'high politics' of broad-casting policy. Thus issues such as youth cultures, fashion, advertising, punk rock, heavy metal, rap, images of the USA and of Germany, inter-connections with neo-Nazi groups, 'No Future' subcultures, and the ways media refract, amplify or dismiss these trends, are the stuff of cultural studies. The MTV phenomenon in Eastern Europe is a point at which a number of these issues currently intersect, heir to the longer tradition of popular music as a vehicle for youth dissent examined earlier, whether in the Russian ballad form, or in rock music, or in jazz.

Thus the cultural studies approach validates attention to these issues, rather than defining them as epiphenomenal and marginal. However, with the exception of the studies cited there is so far as I know very little written in this realm in the region, with the exception of Condee and Padunov's series of essays on cultural transitions in Russia discussed earlier in the book. The cultural studies approach marks out a territory and draws on a quiver of fragmented theoretical *aperçus*. It is, as Bennett (1992: 33) put it, 'a gravitational field in which a number of intellectual traditions have found a provisional *rendez-vous*'. 'It' does not set out to provide too many connections, with the single exception of the intermittent use of the term 'articulation'.

Articulation: a *mot clef* for Cultural Studies

Let me offer a critique of the term 'articulation' as used by a number of contemporary cultural studies writers. On the face of it, its frequent use belies the claim that this analytical tradition tends to separate out popular cultural activity from other societal forces. It is the only concept used in recent years within the cultural studies literature that might, on the face of it, have some explanatory force to bring to bear on multiple interconnected factors in socio-cultural analysis (Grossberg, 1992: chs. 1–4; Hall and Grossberg, 1986; Jameson, 1993), including media communication.

Jameson has indeed asserted that articulation 'stands as the central theoretical problem or conceptual core of cultural studies' (1993: 32). He offers a brief history of its use, but effectively its use within cultural studies discourse began with Hall. Admittedly the latter acknowledges a debt to Laclau (Hall and Grossberg, 1986: 53), but the Laclau text cited uses the term without especial definition as equivalent to linkage, and does not even refer to it in the index (Laclau, 1979: 7–13, 34, 38, 42–3, 78, 164, 194–5). Laclau's concern was to explore Althusser's and Poulantzas' statements of the 'relative[24] autonomy' of political and ideological 'instances' from the economic 'instance', whether in relation to rural Latin American economies' linkage with global capitalism, or in relation to fascist and populist ideologies' linkage with class relations.[25]

Hall claims his own use combines the notion of articulation as expression, and articulation as connection or link (as in the tractor-trailer/articulated lorry). He does not explore the truck metaphor further, although it seems implicitly as though it is only the hitching of one unit to another which he has in mind, rather than the fact that the truck pulls the trailer hitched up to it.

In this combining of meanings he slides conceptually a step beyond Laclau, who described neither populism nor fascism as articulations in the sense of 'expression'. For Hall it seems to be in particular the linkages between ideology and political action that interest him, for instance in his summary remarks on the Rastafarian ideology and movement in Jamaica

(Hall and Grossberg, 1986: 54–5). Thus aside from positing a dual sense to the term, he does not explain how the two senses actually – if I too may use the word – articulate with each other. He fudges the two meanings – 'a theory of articulation is both a way of understanding how ideological elements come . . . to cohere together within a discourse, and a way of asking how they do or do not become articulated . . . to certain political subjects' (1986: 53) – but does not explain the two meanings' mutual imbrication. Calling them 'absolutely dialectical' (p. 55) increases the resonance in the air, but not much else. In the rest of the interview with Grossberg he effectively only uses the metaphor in its primary sense of joint or linkage.

This is worrying. Any functionalist sociologist knows that elements of social life are interconnected, and the fact that these writers, all strongly influenced by the marxist tradition and by absorption with the flux of multiple ideological currents, would dismiss the functionalist tendency of seeing social integration and stability everywhere, does not give them the excuse to posit linkage, reinvent it as articulation, and leave it at that.

Grossberg (1992) does not leave it at that, but it could be concluded it might have been better if he had. It is difficult at times to pin down his fast-flowing use of terms: even he, having defined cultural studies as politicized, conjuncturalist, contextualist and interdisciplinary (1992: 18–22), forthwith castigates his definition as 'so obviously too romanticized' (p. 22). However, let us examine further what he endeavors to bring to the notion of articulation.

Fairly early on in his argument, articulation retains its primary sense of joint or link:

> The concept of articulation provides a useful starting point for describing the process of forging connections between practices and effects . . . Articulation links this process to that effect, this text to that meaning, this meaning to that reality, this experience to those politics. And these links are themselves articulated into larger structures, etc. (p. 54)

From there he develops the point that articulation forces us to pay attention to context. It 'offers a theory of contexts. It dictates that one can only deal with, and from within, specific contexts' (p. 55). He then proceeds to underscore that simply asserting linkage is insufficient: 'Pointing out that two practices are articulated together, that the pieces "fit" together, is not the same as defining the mode of that articulation, the nature of that fit' (p. 56).

At this point it feels as though we are on the verge of a forward movement, but unfortunately Grossberg immediately dives into a highly indeterminate set of assertions about articulation and causality:

> articulation can be understood as a more active version of the concept of deter-mination; unlike notions of interaction or symbiosis, determination describes specific cause-and-effect relations. But unlike notions of causality and simple

> notions of determination, articulation is always complex: not only does the cause
> have effects, but the effects themselves affect the cause, and both are themselves
> determined by a host of other relations. (p. 56)

This formulation regrettably provides the flavor of much of the argument, which ultimately seems to be designed to freeze Proteus rather than
explain him. No statement is provided which is not usually immediately
thrown back into a set of unpredictably whirling conceptual dervishes,
seemingly to ensure that no reader may assume the analytical game is over.
That objective is laudable, but could be achieved satisfactorily whilst still
standing still to define terms thoroughly.

A little later, Grossberg comes back to articulation and causality,
ascribing substantial causal power to linkages.

> One can conceive of such articulations as lines or vectors, projecting their effects
> across the field. Each vector has its own quality (effectivity), quantity and
> directionality . . . Articulations may have different vectors, different forces and
> different spatial reaches in different contexts. And they may also have different
> temporal reaches, cutting across the boundaries of our attempts at historical
> periodization. (pp. 60–1)

At this point the term 'articulation' is perilously close to being hypostatized, rather in the way that Hall in the reference already cited[26]
sometimes tends to hypostatize the term 'ideology'. It is a common vice of
theorists to personify the concepts they most love. But is it the joints
themselves that move the arm and the hand? Do they not simply enable
movement?

Or is Grossberg feeling, not for the elbow, but for the notion of
combination, almost of overdetermination, rather than linkage as such? He
does not say so, but it might be a way out of what at times seems a
conceptual morass.

The project Grossberg set himself, the dissection of contemporary
political conservatism, is interesting and important, and he offers numerous
penetrating insights along the way, both conceptual and empirical. The fact
that I have attacked some of his and Hall's formulations rather sharply is
not meant to distract from that achievement. Indeed, both the book by
Hall and others (1978) on media images of 'mugging' and Britain's 1970s
crisis, and this work by Grossberg, do attempt on a certain level the
integrated analysis that this book argues should be undertaken in order to
understand changes in Eastern Europe. The problem is that the term
articulation is either relatively banal, or bears such a gigantic weight that it
cracks under the strain. And both books actually fail to link together their
constituent parts, Hall's mediatic analysis of 'mugging', for example, sitting
rather uncomfortably next to his and his colleagues' macroscopic analysis
of the British conjuncture of the time.

One more example may serve to drive home my point about the
impossible burden Grossberg places on the term articulation. After having
reiterated yet again his continuing caveats against overly tidy ascriptions of

causality – 'There are no simple or necessary correlations between, for example, cultural identities and subject-positions . . . and economic or political sites of agent-hood' – Grossberg then writes: 'Individuals must be *won or articulated* into these positions' (p. 127, emphasis added).

Seduced or stapled? What *does* this mean?

Conversely, when Jameson (1993: 31–2) offers a formulation of the term articulation, it is in terms which suggest it means conjuncture:

> It implies a kind of turning structure, an ion-exchange between various entities, in which the ideological drives associated with one pass over and interfuse the other – but only provisionally, for a 'historically specific moment,' before entering into new combinations, being systematically worked over into something else, decaying over time in interminable half-life, or being blasted apart by the convulsions of a new social crisis. The articulation is thus a punctual and sometimes even ephemeral totalization, in which the planes of race, gender, class, ethnicity and sexuality intersect to form an operative structure. [Why only these 'planes'?]

Thus although the importance of a cultural studies perspective is beyond dispute for communication research – to take from this book but one example, for an understanding of the dynamics of the build-up period to the transition in the three nations surveyed – cultural studies discourses still often fail to connect conceptually with any other processes outside their popular culture focus, except when *egemonia*, or a version of it, is deployed. Thus cultural studies may be argued to offer a very important corrective to traditional kremlinological, *verkhushka*-heavy research, whether before or even after the transition, but at the same time to be radically insufficient as a research discourse on its own.

Williams and Martín-Barbero

One of the difficulties in producing a brief characterization of Williams' contributions to media and cultural theory[27] is that they are so attractively written, and in such a flowing style, that it can be quite hard to pick out specific concentrated propositions. His work is literary, at the opposite end of the room from theory-speak in the Althusserian, Parsonian, Habermasian or post-modernist formats. Furthermore, his greatest skill was his ability to link together, in a credible political synthesis, abiding structural questions with the evanescent, the emergent, the tendential – and without doing violence to either level of analysis.

Much of his basic inspiration, like the inspiration for Hall and some other cultural studies analysts, came from Antonio Gramsci, along with Walter Benjamin, Lucien Goldmann, the Frankfurt School. (The same can be said of Martín-Barbero.) However, what he did with these influences was to meld them creatively with his research into English social history, drama and literature. Given that national focus, his work might seem rather tangential to the argument of this book concerning the need to take change, conflict, crisis, as normal features of international society, and untroubled hegemony as exceptional. Yet in fact his analysis incorporated those issues into its very heart, in the manner that in the Conclusions chapter it will be argued mainstream media theory has typically failed to do, even in considering its home ground of Britain and the USA.

Here the main emphasis of discussion will be the point already mentioned, Williams' ability to link together core structural questions with issues of process and becoming in the cultural and mediatic spheres. His most interesting elucidations in this regard are on tradition, the residual, formations, structures of feeling, and generally the oppositional process, and on their relation to culture and society as a whole. In these reflections he spans the gap that few others whom we have reviewed have succeeded in addressing.

His observations on tradition and the residual focus on their powerful role within the constitution of a dominant social and cultural order. He argues that cultural tradition is never simply a dead piece of archaism, but rather something clearly selective, offering 'a historical and cultural ratification of a contemporary order . . . tied, though often in complex and hidden ways, to explicit contemporary pressures and limits' (1977: 116, 117). The cultural 'residual', similarly, is not the archaic, but 'certain experiences, meanings and values which cannot be expressed or substantially verified in terms of the dominant culture, [but which] are nevertheless lived and practised . . . because they represent areas of human experience, aspiration, and achievement which the dominant culture neglects, undervalues, opposes, represses, or even cannot recognize' (pp. 123, 124). All these represent foci of conflict between contending social forces.

Applied to earlier discussions of the growing role of sanctioned nationalist discourse in the declining years of sovietism, and equally of the persistence of egalitarian discourse in the years of emerging capitalist culture after the transition, these observations are illuminating. They illustrate the ways in which dissimilar and conflicting cultural currents co-exist within a polity and the various types of legitimacy which may be drawn from one or the other in pursuit of particular social goals, whether the shoring up of the previous regimes or popular challenges to the new regimes.

Williams' use of the term 'formations' (1977: 118–20; 1982: 57–86) was to designate 'conscious' cultural movements and tendencies that fall short of becoming fully institutionalized but none the less play an increasingly important role in contemporary societies. His own instances are drawn from the sphere of 'high' culture, namely the Bloomsbury Set and the Futurists, but there is a plethora of potential examples that could be cited, from the Russian guitar-poets' and jazz musicians' formations of the 1960s and 1970s, to the Nagymoros dam activists' formation in Hungary in the 1980s, to the Orange Alternative formation in Poland in the same decade. Also, such formations may not all necessarily be alternative or oppositional, but may simply be variants within the dominant order 'which resist any simple reduction to some generalized hegemonic function' (1977: 119).

According to the 'totalitarian' analysis, all such formations would have been an impossibility in sovietized structures, and indeed it is hard to imagine such in Russia before the Khrushchev thaws, although sometimes there were possibilities in the more distant regions.[28] During the 1980s, especially in the case of *Solidarnosc*, a completely different reality began to emerge, but even in the very early thaw era, the Petöfi Circle's formation and role in preparing the ground for insurrection in Hungary in 1956 despite its being formally banned, or the Crooked Circle Club forum in Warsaw from 1956 to 1962, or from 1964 to 1968 the Czech Writers' Union, are further and not exclusive examples,[29] and as we have seen, this growth in cultural formations eventually had an increasingly disruptive impact on sovietized power.

Williams' pages (1977: 128–35) on his concept 'structures of feeling' are amongst his very best known and yet, because of their consistent attempt to capture the fleeting and turbulent elements in cultural processes without crushing them under ferro-concrete jargon, the hardest of all to reduce to core propositions. As he wrote, with doctrinaire versions of marxism particularly in view, 'the ideological systems of fixed social generality, of categorical products, of absolute formations, are relatively powerless' to handle changing reality, especially in the realm of experience and consciousness: 'Marx often said this, and some Marxists quote him, in fixed ways, before returning to fixed forms' (p. 129).

He proceeds to offer the most extraordinarily nuanced account of the eddies and shifts characteristic of cultural consciousness, giving the full attention due to emotional as well as rational-cognitive forces and processes:

> We are talking about characteristic elements of impulse, restraint and tone; specifically affective elements of consciousness and relationships: not feeling against thought, but thought as felt and feeling as thought: practical consciousness of a present kind, in a living and interrelated community. (p. 132)

Williams deliberately eschews alternative terms such as 'world-view', or even structures of 'experience', on the ground that they both donate much too much in the way of fixity to what he is endeavoring to capture analytically. These pages could be read and re-read to great advantage by analysts of the political, cultural and mediatic changes in Russia, Poland and Hungary reviewed here.[30] They are tuned to a level of social reality all too often totally obscured in the master-narratives of those events. They especially draw attention to emergent formations that express a particular structure of feeling, but which it is impossible to define with clarity until time has passed for their implications and interconnections to be properly perceived. This offers a classic insight into the way in which *glasnost* and young people's musical formations, for example, led beyond themselves in ways unimagined by almost anyone, except perhaps those for whom the slightest deviation automatically had to be crushed anyway. But even those doing the crushing were generally acting on a knee-jerk reaction rather than a connected forecast of doom.

Thus Williams presents not only a vocabulary and a framework, but most particularly the definition of a series of dynamics in cultural processes, that offer a rich lode for any researcher concerned with the interrelation between media, culture, power, conflict and change. His work is far from being any final word, but it penetrates much further to the interconnected levels of cultural reality than many of the theorists assessed so far.

Martín-Barbero (1993) proposes a major synthesis of concepts and approaches drawn from Latin American media and cultural research, and from Gramsci, Williams, and European cultural studies discourses. His book is laden with conceptual and empirical insight, so no attempt will be made to summarize its richness here. Instead, certain key elements will be singled out for comment. They are his core concepts of *mestizaje* and mediations; his refusal to accept the bifurcation of culture into 'popular' and 'mass'; and his analytical ability to focus on the specifics of a given medium without losing any of its connections to wider societal processes.

Mestizaje could roughly be translated 'hybridity' in the general sense in which that term came to be used during the 1990s in post-modernist discourse, in order to indicate the fluidity and mixture of social identities and categories in the contemporary world. What it would lose in such a translation is one of its specific referents within a Latin American context, one namely where in differing degrees in every nation there is a blending – both cultural and physiognomic – of Native, European and African histories. A *mestizo*, literally, is a person of mixed European and American descent, the majority in most Latin American nations, but the abstract noun denotes a more general process (and one which regionally speaking embraces Lebanese, Jewish, Japanese, Chinese and still other histories as well).

Martín-Barbero centers his discussion on this concept in part to anchor his research in Latin American rather than European or US realities (although from the 1990s, in particular, it would fit both those regions). In his text he conducts a running argument with Latin American analysts of the political right and left who have refused to engage with those specifics, seemingly more at ease with an abstract imposition of what he terms 'one-dimensional' (p. 188) categories drawn from European or US sociologists' definitions of reality. He stresses that *mestizaje* 'is not simply a racial fact, but the explanation of our [Latin American] existence, the web of times and places, memories and imagination which, until now, have been adequately expressed only at a literary[31] level' (p. 188), '. . . the interweaving of modernity and the residues of various cultural periods, the mixture of social structures and sentiments' (p. 2).

To that degree it is closely tied to his other core concept, that of 'mediation' (1993: 33–8, 46–53, 163–78, 216–18). This does not appear to be drawn from the work of Lucien Goldmann, but to be Martín-Barbero's term of choice to dislodge attention from a narrow focus on media to a much wider focus on media's roles within cultural and political processes. As he writes:

To introduce the analysis of the cultural sphere does not mean, however, that we add a new and separate theme, but that we focus on those aspects of the social process that articulate the meaning of the economic and the political. This would mean writing the history of the mass media from the perspective of cultural processes as articulators of the communication practices – hegemonic and subaltern – of social movements.[32] (p. 164)

This anti-mediacentric approach is reminiscent of Williams, as cited in the Introduction, but in this text is very specifically related to a variety of institutions and processes, ranging from TV viewing within the daily life of the family, to media in the processes of nation-formation, to those of transnationalization and media. Only, Martín-Barbero insists, through considering the enormous cross-cutting maze of these and other mutually interpenetrating forces is it possible to comprehend the roles of media at all. The alternatives are either a barren focus on the power of media technology, or simply on the corporations that endeavor to aggrandize their market position through media products.

His refusal of the popular/mass bifurcation and his linkage of media technology specifics with hegemony are the remaining points which will concern us.

When Adorno later revisited his and Horkheimer's famous essay on the culture industry, he sought to make it clear that they chose the term 'mass' culture to differentiate it, as commercially and industrially generated, from culture that actually arose from the public itself, or 'popular'[33] culture. This attempt to avoid some of the stronger accusations of elitism leveled against the original essay is bypassed by Martín-Barbero, who is both concerned to address the uses to which people put mass media, and to demystify the romantic notion of pure folk expression. For these reasons, and for historical reasons, the commercial-industrial origin of a TV program is not for him the last word on the subject. He vigorously attacks

a reading that considers this industry purely and simply an instrument of domination. This is a reading which does not really know or understand the system of representations and images used by the popular classes to decodify the symbols produced in the mass media . . . within mass culture there are quite heterogeneous products, some consistent with the logic of the dominant cultural judgements and others following the logic of symbolic expectations coming from the dominated classes. (1993: 230–1)

He engages in a careful historical analysis of the development of serial novels, their original genesis within 'popular' culture, their adoption into the commercial nexus, their parentage of the radio and TV soap opera, but not least their ongoing engagement with the public's fantasies and fears. He does the same for sensationalist crime reporting, tracing it back to 'the tradition of sensationalism and terror that goes back to the gothic stories in England, the Spanish *cordel* and the French *canards*' (p. 143), and for the feeder-traditions of melodrama, circus and music hall that helped shape cinema.

In so doing he is neither celebrating nor denouncing mass culture, rather endeavoring to analyse its role in national development and as a transnational force within Latin America. His historical sweep and coordination of evidence bring a fresh breath of air and perspective to tired and clichéd debates concerning culture and domination.

Finally, his commentary on different media technologies and their varying roles is also refreshing, moving away from both the homogenization of contemporary media – 'the' media – and the fetishization of technology *per se*. Whether he is discussing the emergence of print, the explosion of computer communications, the different roles at different times of radio and television, or the particular historical role of cinema, Martín-Barbero consistently succeeds in acknowledging their specificity in concert with their societal and historical locations, both general and national. He also gives appropriate space to their alternative forms of deployment, eschewing the notion of technology as automatically a mechanism of domination.

Looking back at the transitions in Russia, Poland and Hungary, these two writers' principal contributions may be said to be a stress upon the powerful flux of cross-cutting and contradictory cultural forces (both authors), the location of media within those vectors rather than as discrete entities (both authors), transnational, national and regional specificities (Martín-Barbero), the roles of tradition and the 'residual', and thus of historical process (both authors), the oppositional process (Williams). Contrasted with the sheer, strong propositions of Adorno and Horkheimer, or of Althusser and Poulantzas, they have notable abilities to bring the analytical focus much closer to the ebb and flow of everyday existence while never losing sight of the power structure. In all these ways, they bring some of the very best writing to the cultural studies approach.

In this way, they exemplify both the achievements and the difficulties of a thorough-going media studies analysis, which perhaps more than any other single focus in social analysis requires that levels are pulled together in relation to each other, from the international and the *verkhushka* to the rock concert and the billboard, from the sedimentation of traditional symbols to high-speed, high-capacity telecommunications, from visual and aural aesthetics to democratization processes.

Herman and Chomsky

The 'propaganda model' put forward by these authors (Herman and Chomsky, 1988: 1–35) in a book whose international impact has been considerable, represents a pleasantly mixed case in terms of the categories proposed earlier, whether conceptual or politico-professional. On the one hand it applies primarily to the United States and to news, inasmuch as its empirical application in the book concerns US news media and US foreign relations.[34] On the other, it is a theory of the relation between the media, the state and the capitalist class, and so falls outside the 'segmented' category. Lastly, it engages in very specific, sometimes even quantitative, analysis of actual media content.

The use of the term 'propaganda' is justified in their Preface (p. xi) by reference to Walter Lippmann's assertion earlier in the twentieth century that propaganda was growing in size and sophistication as a US government operation. They offer no further definition of the term, but it is hard to resist the notion that it was deliberately chosen for its rhetorical, 'in-your-face' challenge to the standard claim of US ideologues, namely that 'our' media are free and honest, and only other nations' media engage in propaganda. (Rather as in the irregular verb '*I* am right, *you* have an opinion, *he/she/it* is victim of an ideology'.) In other words, they claim that news media foreign coverage is not just sometimes in error, but systematically and organizationally in error whenever US policies are seriously at stake.

By 'organizationally' (my term) Herman and Chomsky's argument does not mean 'conspiratorially'. They identify five interacting and mutually reinforcing 'filters' that enable 'money and power' to bring it about that overwhelmingly in major media the news is 'fit to print',[35] dissent is marginalized, and 'the government and dominant private interests . . . get their messages across to the public' (p. 2). The system works so smoothly, so 'naturally', they propose, that the very journalists who administer it 'frequently . . . with complete integrity and good will' consider themselves as purveyors of objectivity and a professional service (p. 2): 'alternative bases of news choices are hardly imaginable'.

The five filters which 'fix the premises of discourse and interpretation, and the definition of what is newsworthy in the first place' are: the concentrated ownership of media; advertising, the primary revenue source for media; reliance on approved sources, whether from government, business, or a stable of politically kosher 'experts'; organized anti-media campaigns directed at actual or potential lapses from political propriety ('flak'); and the US 'national religion' of anti-Communism.

In a later essay summarizing and recapitulating the case, Herman suggests that the fifth filter always had the benefit of a rather fuzzy definition of what 'Communism' actually was, stretched often to cover any form of labor or public protest, and effectively was a particular vehicle for the more general process of demonizing opponents (Herman, 1995: 89; cf. Rogin, 1987: 272–300). Thus the collapse of the Soviet system did not mean that the effective function of the fifth filter would be lost, even if some of its specific referents would be.

While their very detailed review of a series of appalling chapters in US foreign relations and their serious distortion in major US news media is both impressive and valuable, the propaganda model does rather tail off into space at two important junctures. The authors do not address entertainment media,[36] or domestic political issues (or their interrelation). This is not necessarily to claim that the propaganda model could not be applied in those contexts, but its tremendous stress on imperial foreign relations in the initial formulation gives little clue to how that might be done. On the other hand, if the model is to work, it needs to be done, inasmuch as it is hard to visualize two mutually insulated media tiers.

Furthermore, their phenomenology of news professionals is caught awkwardly between the concession of ethical integrity to journalists and the latters' reliable operation within the process of producing the 'cleansed residue' of news politically fit to print. There seems to be an almost Althusserian concept of ideology at work here, rather than a more Gramscian acknowledgment of the possibility of fragmented consciousness.

On the other hand, the model does not only take seriously the interconnections between media and concentrated economic and political power, often presumed to be rather tangential to their operation (cf. Parsons[37]), but actually goes so far as to specify them in terms which virtually compel the recognition of their influence. It does so, too, with a recognition of the manipulated populism (the fourth filter), which takes the issue of politics and media beyond the upper reaches of power, the American *verkhushka*, and poses it in terms of wider processes of politicized communication.

Perhaps inevitably, given its focus, the model is more likely to offer insight into the post-sovietized situation in Russia, Poland and Hungary, although once again its particular emphasis on foreign relations may restrict its utility mostly to the first of those three nations. The near-fusion of economic and political power in the sovietized media situation was so patent that the application of the model at the points of media concentration and the supply of politically acceptable sources is hardly controversial, even though advertising was institutionally absent (and unnecessary as a source of finance). Public campaigns, such as waves of press letters from the outraged – such 'flak' against media was especially visible during the middle years of the *glasnost* era – were also well-known features of the sovietized system. Last but not least, they had their own political demon, though not it must be said usually Americans or Germans (though often Israelis) *per se*, rather the militaristic nuclear-tipped menace of the Western ruling classes against which the Soviet system was reluctantly but determinedly defending itself. Journalists in many cases did not share the integrated consciousness Herman and Chomsky attribute to US journalists.

As a propaganda model, some would perhaps have an instinctive prior expectation that it would fit many aspects of the Soviet system. What it in fact does is to direct our attention to the aspects of the so-called free market media situation that do not ring in any way true to the claims of that ideology. In that sense it echoes Adorno and Horkheimer's urging that the investigation of media and cultural power be not restricted to nations that most commentators can agree are structurally autocratic, even totalitarian. The implication, again, is that media in the post-Soviet nations have emerged from something resembling night into something resembling twilight, not into a supposedly dazzling daylight.

Cultural Imperialism and Globalization

Cultural imperialism is a perspective that has largely been identified with leftist analysts such as Schiller (1969, 1989), and is therefore often dismissed, especially in Schiller's case, as a kind of generalized *Medienschmerz* that blots out any capacity of the world's citizens to resist or appropriate in their own fashion the messages of global advertising or US television, and additionally presumes that worries about cultural survival are uniquely provoked by the policies of the major powers, and not equally by nation-states against ethnic minorities within their own frontiers.

Yet it is interesting that while the mode of posing the problem is often attacked, some form of the problem continues to be acknowledged. Garnham (1993b: 265) for instance, having relegated Schiller's position more or less to the margin of concern, still concludes a recent essay by worrying how, in view of media internationalization and the erosion of state sovereignty, we should 'envisage the construction of a new international public sphere and parallel system of democratic accountability?'

Tomlinson (1992) is one who vigorously attacks cultural imperialism's discourse for its imputation of complete mental plasticity to citizens of the Third World. He also makes great play, this time rather less credibly, of the absence of a centralized, purposive imperial policy in the post-colonial era, which in his view evacuates any valid meaning from the term 'cultural imperialism': 'the problem of explaining how a cultural practice can be imposed in a context which is no longer actually coercive' (p. 173).[38] He himself prefers to see the current global conjuncture as one of the extension of the simultaneous advantages and demerits of 'modernity' across the face of the planet, to powerful and impoverished nations alike (p. 175). Yet he too concludes by worrying about the extraordinary power and unaccountability of transnational corporations (p. 176), and calls in his final pages (pp. 178–9) for identity and community, to be fostered among other means through our own, rather than others', television images.[39]

Up until 1989–91, if cultural imperialism were to be spotted in the East, it would have been by official representatives of the previous regimes who – as we saw in Chapter 4 – were prepared for reasons which were always in pitifully bad faith to denounce everything from the BBC World Service to rock music to *Solidarnosc* in this vein. Schiller (1989: 125), in his own usual vein, was quick to spot this dread virus[40] in its early stages, noting how in 1988 the former Polish regime was contracting to receive Italian television in southern Poland (the relentless critic seemingly insouciant of the fact it would still be in Italian). This is a good example of how the discourse of cultural imperialism has managed at times to make its concerns look ridiculous. Radio Danubius, the commercial German-language station opened in Budapest in 1986 to service the needs of German-speaking tourists, was much more significant in its impact on Hungarian media policy because of its commercial character than because of its alien cultural content (Gabor, 1993).

Yet, far more significantly, Jakab and Gálik (1991) are amongst those in Eastern Europe who have drawn attention to the contemporary issues raised in the region by the advent of foreign investment in media, no doubt in their case in part because of the extraordinarily rapid acquisition of Hungarian media by British and German firms, a process unparalleled in speed or extent elsewhere in Eastern Europe at that time. Without having to tie oneself to many of the doom-laden prophecies of cultural homogenization intoned by typical exponents of the cultural imperialism thesis, the realities of accountability – or rather, of its loss – become potentially even more troubled if major control of media is vested outside national frontiers. The USA, for example, with all its media and economic power, imposes a maximum 25 percent rule on foreign ownership of any broadcast station.

There are many other practical dimensions to this question, including the urgent need experienced by East European film-makers to acquire co-production finance, the functional differences between television, radio, the daily press, the magazine press, advertising, public opinion research, the music business, and not least software and telecommunications, as aspects of the communication complex. No country is an island, as the theorists of global society like to remind us (Featherstone, 1990; Robertson, 1992), and as the British cheerfully deny. Yet the process of cultural adaptation and change is one thing, the problems of democratic accountability are another, and the issues of investment in a post-sovietized information-based economy are a third. We need a de-theologized discourse of cultural imperialism to grapple with these questions, and in the mean time it is important that East European analysts should draw attention to the issues adumbrated but also obscured in that discourse.

With one important addition, already registered: that inequality of right to freely willed cultural expression is as valid an issue inside East European societies as it is in that society's relations with more economically powerful cultures. Thus Romanies and other minority social groupings deserve as much in terms of their rights to communicate and to be understood as do nations within the global public sphere.

The more diffuse discourse of globalization does not present the same targets for attack as cultural or media imperialism. It is primarily concerned, it seems, to refocus attention on human society as a global rather than merely national phenomenon, without putting forward anything equivalent to the – inconveniently! – testable claims of cultural imperialism discourse (e.g. Robertson, 1992 and many of the contributors to Featherstone, 1992). Appadurai (1992) has come closest to offering a taxonomy of globalizing processes that could in turn generate a series of specific analyses, but even in his essay the predominant message seems to be that flux is king in the flows of international human traffic. In Eastern Europe flux of many kinds was certainly evident during the fifteen-year span of this study, and a motor of this flux was undoubtedly the array of non-national flows and influences already examined. It was far from the only motor, however, either before or since the biennium of 1989–91. Its relative novelty since then may give the impression of massive and preponderant influence by way of contrast with the previous era, but in the light of a longer view, the story of Eastern Europe may prove to be one that suggests culture rather than economy is the true social infrastructure.

Conclusions

The theoretical approaches considered in this chapter are distinguished more by their capacity to point us in certain fruitful directions for further study and reflection than by their capacity to illuminate the mediatic processes that have taken place in Eastern Europe, specifically Russia, Poland and Hungary, in the period under review. This is not particularly their fault, inasmuch as most of them have not directly been concerned with media *per se*, rather with processes of power, change and culture, a part of which is formed by media.

Once again, however, we see the curious tendency to insulation between theoretical discourses that was already the topic of the book's initial discussion of communication research and political science, but this time at work within these major writers with great influence on the study of media communication itself. The mainstream analysts tend to focus strictly on media *per se*, the critical analysts strictly on their relation to other powerful social forces. Is this insulation accidental or inevitable? This will be addressed in the final chapter.

Notes

1 *The New Order*, a socialist newspaper produced in the industrial center of Turin, especially important during the two years of factory occupations in Turin that followed on the end of the First World War.

2 See his *Selections from the Prison Notebooks*, 1971; Femia, 1981; Forgacs, 1988; Hall, 1986; T.J. Jackson Lears, 1985; Portelli, 1974; Showstack Sassoon, 1987; Williams, 1977.

3 The term 'organic intellectuals' could, without much violence, be re-translated as 'communicator/organizers' in so far as Gramsci had in mind people in almost any walk of life whose role included the active articulation, in words and in action, of positions and strategies related to a social class (not necessarily the one into which they had been born). Thus priests, journalists, political activists, philosophers, economists, artists, engineers, might all fit within the category. 'Intellectual' in the narrower sense of an ivory tower logic-chopper was not what he had in mind.

4 He described Tsarist Russia as gelatinous in the sense that it had no institutional system of cultural domination such as a mass educational system, a mass media system – the relative weakness of literacy, despite its rapid advance in the decades before the revolution (Brooks, 1985), was the common factor here – or even a religious institution with intensive connections between clergy and laity. By contrast, these and many other institutions represented bulwarks of the established order in Western Europe by the early twentieth century. In Russia, therefore, there was an institutional vacuum between the Tsarist regime and the public, meaning that once the reins of supreme power were seized there were no other institutions of power to frustrate the Bolsheviks' control. Gramsci exaggerated, perhaps with his eye principally upon the 80 percent or so of denizens of the Russian Empire who then lived in small and often

farflung villages, rather than on the much more complex situation in the largest cities. However, this contrast was a major consideration in his theory of *egemonia*.

5 Ranging from the forced drinking of large amounts of castor oil in front of groups of jeering fascists, after which the victims involuntarily soiled themselves to the delight of the onlookers, and then had to struggle home in that condition, all the way through to planned, cold-blooded murders, including of parliamentary deputies. At the same time these practices fell far short of colonialist war, undertaken against Ethiopia in 1935, or the gulag or extermination camps.

6 Unlike most theorists, he had the acceptable excuse of writing in secrecy in prison, of being unable to edit his work, which had to be smuggled out, and of prolonged bouts of agonizing sickness.

7 Konrád and Szelényi (1978), in their analysis of the East European intelligentsia in late sovietism, defined them as marching steadily toward 'class power', but used the term as provocative rhetoric rather than as measured concept.

8 Urban (Goban-Klas, 1994, *passim*; Rosenberg, 1995: 226–7), notorious for his acid tongue, was the chief press spokesman for the Jaruzelski regime during and after martial law; after the transition he ran a sensationalist, slanderous weekly, *Nie* [No]. *Gorbachevtsy* looks odd, but 'gorbachevites' even odder: Burlatsky, Yakovlev and Bovin were editors respectively of the cultural-political weekly *Literaturnaya Gazeta*, the '*glasnost* flagship' weekly *Moscow News*, and the government daily *Izvestiia* (Cohen and vanden Heuvel, 1989: 174–229), all three actively supportive of Gorbachev's reform attempts. See Chapter 3, n.3.

9 Cf. Jirina Smejkalová-Strickland, 1994, especially pp. 202–3.

10 Interestingly, the classic text on totalitarianism by Friedrich and Brzezinski (1966: Part IV) has a much more nuanced discussion of the role of terror, even in the utter nadir points of sovietism or fascism, than the crass reductionist identification of pure fear as those regimes' cement.

11 Wajda's two films *Man of Marble* and *Man of Iron*; Konrád's novels *The Loser, The Caseworker, The Citybuilder*; Kira Muratova's films *Brief Encounters, Change of Fortune, The Asthenic Syndrome*; Andrei Amalrik's memoirs *Involuntary Journey to Siberia* and *Notes of a Revolutionary*; Meszaros Marta's film trilogy *Diary for My Children, Diary for My Love, Diary for My Mother and Father*; Tadeusz Konwicki's novel *The Polish Complex*; Alexander Zinoviev's novel *The Radiant Future*.

12 Lukács, 1971.

13 V.I. Lenin, *Collected Works*, vol. 33. London, Lawrence and Wishart, 1974, 487–502: perhaps the last article Lenin wrote, expressing concern for a better quality of leadership in the new Soviet republic. Although some of his stated objectives were laudable, he relapsed back into his customary reliance on a small dedicated group to achieve them. Contrast Gramsci in Forgacs, 1988, sections XI and XII.

14 Goban-Klas, 1994: 174–7; 206–10. Before 1989 the story used to be told in Eastern Europe that a short, stout gentleman with a flowing white beard, a very familiar face, and speaking a very nineteenth-century German, turned up at the huge new TV headquarters in East Berlin one day and demanded to be allowed to speak to the working class over the screen. He announced that his name was Marx, Karl Marx. He was met with combined skepticism and fear from the doorman on upwards, the fear being based principally on the possibility he really was Marx and on what he might say that would upset the applecart. After being met with refusals from the TV bureaucrats – 'You've resurrected, how will we square that with our teaching of scientific atheism?' – and counter-arguments from him ('Where would you all be without me anyway?'), they settled that he could have just five seconds live. He grumbled loudly and bitterly but then as the camera rolled took a deep, deep breath and said looking directly into it: 'Workers of all lands: forgive me!'

15 See note 12 below.

16 For an analysis of Althusser's affinities with classical functionalism, see Bryan S. Turner (1986: 194–6).

17 The standard term in marxist terminology for an authoritarian regime, named from

Marx's analysis (in his *The Eighteenth Brumaire of Louis Bonaparte*) of the seizure of power in France by Louis Bonaparte in 1851.

18 The dominant ideology is defined as commodity fetishism, although curiously it has to be hunted down in a footnote long into the argument (Poulantzas, 1974: 306, n.8): a critique of this assertion, one of the weakest in the marxist lexicon, is beyond the remit of the present discussion.

19 In fact Poulantzas places them third, after the fascist party which becomes the means to coordinate ideology, and the redefinition of the family – i.e. the authority of the father, the subordination of women (1974: 333). On the previous page he argues that the political police dominates overall and has 'the key ideological role'.

20 'The defiant reserve or elegant appearance of the individual [in the media] is mass-produced like Yale locks, whose only difference can be measured in fractions of millimeters' (Horkheimer and Adorno, 1987a: 154; cf. pp. 122–6).

21 It is perhaps symptomatic that right up to 1938 Adorno continued to visit his family and fiancée in Germany, with 'no political objection [to staying] . . . except that every possibility for effectiveness would have been cut off from me' (Buck-Morss, 1977: 137). By 'effectiveness' he appears to have meant the opportunity for continued scholarly activity. Truly the intellectual's intellectual.

22 A further instance is the Australian – or at least Griffith University – variant of cultural studies proposed by Bennett and his colleagues at their Institute for Cultural Policy Studies (Bennett, 1992: 32), which argues that cultural studies research should have direct implications for public policy, that it should 'concretely influence the agendas, calculations and procedures' of cultural agencies and movements.

23 See below for a more extended critique of this term's use in cultural studies.

24 Laclau (1979: 65) insisted the English translation as 'relative' is misleading, signifying 'partial' rather than 'relational'.

25 Laclau and Mouffe's (1985) 'Long tortuous march out of Marxism' also deploys the term 'articulation' (e.g. 58, 65, 104–13, 136, 140) but not in ways that transcend Hall's or Grossberg's uses (see below). Sadly the term is, conceptually speaking, a naked emperor . . .

26 He says of Rastafarian ideology that 'it functioned so as to harness or draw to it sectors of the population', and a little later 'One has to see the way in which a variety of social groups enter into and constitute for a time a kind of political and social force, in part by seeing themselves reflected as a unified force in *the ideology which constitutes them*' (p. 55, emphasis added). The fact he then immediately calls this a dialectical process does not help, because the word 'dialectical' still implies, in this setting, a process between two actors or consciously operating forces. To be fair, he also applies the term 'emerges' once to ideology, but this tends to contribute to the confusion, as does his veering back and forth between describing Rastafarian ideology as the product of different 'sectors' and 'other determinations' and yet as unified, the product of a 'shared collective situation'.

27 *Television: Technology and Cultural Form*, 1974; *Marxism and Literature*, 1977; 'Means of communication as means of production', in *Problems in Materialism and Culture*, 1980; *The Sociology of Culture*, 1982; *The Year 2000*, 1983, 145–50.

28 As Bakhtin's experience indicates. See Holquist, 1981: xxi–xxvi.

29 Lomax, 1976: 32–44, 47, 51, 81, 83, 109, 111; Ost, 1990: 47–8; Downing, 1984/1996: 312–13.

30 Svetlana Boym's *Common Places* (1994) is a fine example of what has too often been missing.

31 In the novels of such authors as Gabriel García Márquez, Alejo Carpentier, Mario de Andrade and many others.

32 By 'social movements' he means all movements for social change from any quarter, not simply oppositional movements.

33 In English the word 'popular' only means 'temporarily fashionable' of a thing or 'well-liked' of a person. Absent is the other and equally strong sense it also has in Latin languages of 'belonging to the people' (albeit with a whiff of hauteur in French!), or similarly in German

of 'national trait' or 'folk characteristic' (*volkstümlich*). Russian imported *popularniy* for the English sense, but has its own *narodniy* for the second.

34 Its analysis could in principle be applied to the other G7 nations' media–foreign relations nexus.

35 Another sly but cheerful dig at the pretensions of the US media, this time at the claim 'All the News that's Fit to Print' on the masthead of the *New York Times*. The original sense was that the newspaper would always avoid the gutter sensationalism of the yellow press; Herman and Chomsky twist this around into a concealed assertion that political issues questioning the very foundation of US policies will generally be filtered out from even the 'quality' press.

36 For one of the few studies that endeavors to link the two in relation to political issues, see Schlesinger et al. (1983).

37 One wonders how he would have responded to the dramatic increase in media concentration since his original essay with White in 1960.

38 Is economic pressure absolutely distinct from coercion, and was cultural policy purely based on coercion in the heyday of colonialism?

39 Schiller himself (1989), in his final chapter, wittingly or unwittingly joins Habermas in calling for a bypassing of media in favor of face-to-face public meetings and interaction, the only speech situation he seems able to contemplate with confidence.

40 The term Schiller himself uses: 'it is not only US television programming that carries the virus of transnational corporate culture. Politics, sports, tourism, language, and business data flows transmit it and reinforce it as well' (1989: 134). Elsewhere he opts for the imagery of sexual conquest: 'Eastern Europe and the Soviet Union . . . were relatively virgin areas to the advertising folk' (p. 121) '. . . Italy's principal state TV network – a structure itself deeply penetrated by US programming' (p. 125). Oddly, the US public itself is not portrayed as subject to a virus or sexual aggression, but to be 'encapsulated in a corporate-message cocoon' (p. 168). Should we read an implicit theory out of the difference between these metaphors?

9

Conclusions

I

Thus far, the argument has conducted a rather major ground-clearing and map-making exercise of the terrain of media communication theory. The metaphor of ground-clearing is intended to cover the critical appraisal and 'winnowing' of existing approaches to media and power. The metaphor of mapping (cf. Wood, 1992) is intended to cover the realignment and reconfiguration of priorities in media communication theorizing that I have argued for on both conceptual and empirical grounds.

Firstly I have argued that stark modern era issues of overweening state power, societal change and conflict, draconian economic forces, social movements, cultural processes, international vectors, of the kind patently visible in Russia, Poland and Hungary from 1980 to 1995, have an irreducible, core dimension – itself multiply refracted – that is communico-mediatic.

Secondly I have argued that despite the specificities that characterize sovietized and post-Soviet nations, and despite the specificities that always distinguished Soviet bloc nations from each other, this fierce conflictual brew of state power, communication, social movements, cultural change, economic dislocation and all the rest, is far more characteristic of planetary society than is the relative stability of Britain or the United States (the predominant sources of empirical illustration in media theory).

Thirdly I have argued that the best in both communication research and political science need each other badly, even though to date these approaches to understanding have each usually tried to operate as though the other were off the map.

There has also been a nexus of subsidiary arguments, some of them concerned with the specifics of the three nations considered, others calculated to explore the intrinsic assumptions and weaknesses of a variety of theories, political and mediatic, mainstream and critical.

The net result, hopefully, is that the pointless and mediocre features of current media theory and research have been identified as such and may now be relegated with some sense of relief to the circular file. Whole chunks of both 'segmented' and 'totalist' theorizing stand to be disposed of in this manner. That was the ground-clearing exercise, but one also applied in the winnowing of the more relevant political science approaches.

The more vigorous aspects of media theory, especially in close combination with a certain number of partially refined political science concepts, will serve as the basis for future development of media communication theory – along with some approaches from the 'fragmented' category that have been mentioned but not explored in the book. The ground-clearing was not a total razing, more an exercise in landscape architecture. Below there will be outlined some summary concluding positions in this regard. Before doing so, however, let us return to a particular point of some importance.

II

Reference is made above, and was in the Preface, to Britain and the USA as, historically speaking, the heartland nations of media research. However, a further advantage of this book's argument is that it not only enables us to address media communication processes in the forms in which they most often present themselves across the planet, but also permits us to acknowledge and address some endemic faults in the conceptual treatment of media *within* those heartland nations, and in somewhat comparable nations.

As observed earlier in the book, existing mainstream theories generally presuppose certain levels of societal stability and consensus. Equally, critical media theories generated within the heartland nations tend to set themselves the task of trying to explain how media feed such a large degree of acceptance of the status quo, and thus why social divisions do not erupt into more powerful confrontations. Why do people not rebel more often than they do?

Examples of the ways this issue is posed are numerous. Parsons and White (1969), on the mainstream side, readily acknowledged there are problems in US society, including cultural and mediatic problems, but insisted they are manageable and not disruptive of the societal order, and this basically because of the degree of flexibility and choice available to the public.

On the critical side, Gramsci and neo-Gramscians dissect the hegemonic cultural processes of modern capitalist nations, which also presume a generally rather settled societal order, although they define them in terms that leave more room for intermittent disruptive crises than such analysts as Parsons and White.

Some other critical writers still, such as Radway (1984) and Fiske (1987), using the later work of Roland Barthes on the pleasures of the text/communication and the complementary 'death' of the author/communicator, and also seeking to establish contestatory readings of media texts on the part-basis of literary reception analysis, try to redefine the situation from a quite different angle, that of the restive audience.

These latter writers urge that life in developed bourgeois society is one of far less quiescence than researchers have concluded from the absence of explicit organized challenge to the status quo. They propose that one of the audience's pleasures is precisely a spontaneous, sometimes conversationally shared and sometimes personal fantasy-based redefinition of media texts, in the direction of challenging the hegemonic process that those texts ostensibly only serve to endorse. They deny that audience use of and pleasure from media texts is necessarily an affirmation of their often class-based, racist or sexist implications – indeed that the audience may rather be engaging in oppositional guerrilla-readings. Textual 'poachers' is a term that has been coined in this connection (Jenkins, 1992).

The research of this second group offers rich and often absorbing evidence of dissonant interpretations of mainstream media texts that circulate among media audiences in Britain or the USA. The fact, however, persists that the societal order does remain stable. Unlike Galileo's planet earth, *non si muove*.

Underlying these varied conclusions and consequent research agendas concerning media in Anglo-American society is in large part a shared and generally unexamined sociological presumption. This presumption is that because a societal order is stable it must also be generally morally acceptable to the public – at least in the absence of totalitarian terror stifling all dissident expression. The more conservative will take this acceptability as axiomatic: no overt dissent means there is no significant problem in society. The more radical, keenly aware of such problems, will find quiescence a paradox to be explained, even explained away, perhaps as a product of hegemony (the Gramscians), or as a research failure to delve beneath the surface into the dynamism of everyday cultural resistance, into the weapons of the weak (Scott, 1985).

But the heart of the unexamined common presumption is that where there is oppression, there is resistance of some kind. This postulate contains a fatal flaw. That flaw is the failure to take into account the divisibility of oppression. Therefore, moreover, it discounts the corresponding fragmentation of resistance and additionally discounts the often easy mobilization of members of one extruded group against another. In such situations, truculent resistance often appears doomed, perhaps even to threaten a worse situation than the present.

None the less, whether we are considering the vulnerability and isolation into separate domestic units – or deserted places – of women of all ages faced with those males morally capable of attacking them physically; or whether we are considering the lack of autonomous public voice of women, as the mute objects featuring in countless advertisements; or whether we are considering the near-extermination of Native Americans and their forced relocation to remote and harsh locations; or whether we are considering the system of racist terror that pervaded the rural South East of the USA for centuries, and that still retains considerable vitality through the police, courts and prisons; or whether we are considering the abject peonage to which Chicano farmworkers have repeatedly been subjected in the South West; or whether we are examining the societal humiliation and extrusion of people of color in Britain: *in any and all of these instances we are considering a situation that at the receiving end feels close to totalitarian* even though it does not affect a clear majority of the society.

This is akin to what Raboy (1992), referring to the position of women, refers to as 'the invisible crisis of everyday life'. The invisibility in Raboy's use is ironic, signifying the blindness of those out of the line of fire with regard to the situation of those who are in it. The title of Ralph Ellison's novel *The Invisible Man* drew on the same metaphor with reference to African Americans, only literally visible in a majority White nation.

These situations are not, however, instances of asymmetrical power merely. They are also instances in which in recent decades political up-surges and movements have succeeded in transitionally redefining the rights and public definition of the groups in question. In both these respects, in respect of overwhelming force and in respect of political challenge to that force, and the ensuing transitions that have painfully slowly begun to take place, *these* dimensions of stable nations have a profound kinship with the planet at large.

Such realities have generally been absent from the research agendas of media analysts. The result is that it has been possible to produce analyses of media communication which may well have had some validity for some 'included' sectors of the public, but those sectors have been allowed to be stand-in's for the whole society, a privileged synecdoche. Of course media communication has been present within all these sectors of the nations in question – they have not been totally insulated from each other – but its signification and weighting have often been radically different for different sectors. Questions of overweening state power in the shape of legislation, police, courts and prisons, social movements such as Civil Rights and Black Power, cultural formations *à la* Raymond Williams (e.g. in music), draconian economic changes, have all been among the central experiences of the groups mentioned.

Albeit differing the one from the other (with certain overlaps on the planes of gender and age), and sometimes at odds with each other as within their own ranks, these groupings demographically constitute a very large proportion of the US and British population. Where are *their* experiences with media, mainstream or alternative or international, in the theorizing about media communication that has taken place, which was reviewed in Chapters 7 and 8?

Virtually nowhere. They are not 'normal', not at the center of social concern. They are *women-'n'-minorities*, a strange hybrid that researchers seemingly unconcerned with the 'real' mainstream of social communication sometimes specialize in studying, earning brownie points as they do so for social conscience or just plain idiosyncracy.

The experiences of these sectors are, however, integral to US or British national identity, and closer in experience to the planet as a whole than the relatively included sectors that may generally be more content to reaffirm the hegemonic order. Not that the processes of hegemony fail to operate in these wider, less protected sectors, as witness for example the enthusiasm and personal dedication to service in the US military that can easily be encountered in representatives of all four of the sectors named. Or the readiness of many British Asians to reject their definition as Black.

Yet also this hegemony, as Gramsci, Williams, Martín-Barbero and others working within that discourse have insisted, is rarely a flat 'legitimacy, yes-or-no' in the Weberian tradition. It is very often fragmented, temporary, sectoral. For example, Black soldiers who fought with passion and dedication in the Second World War simultaneously protested against racism in the segregated military and were leaders in the earliest phase of the Civil Rights movement.

It is the intersection between media communication and sharply asymmetrical power, between media communication and huge economic changes, between media communication and ethnic ideologies of race or nationality, between media communication and international forces, that is the planetary mainstream for media research and theorizing. Thus the focus of this book, although away from the United States and Britain, also leads directly back into them, into the very central issues often left unexamined or marginalized in research to date.

III

In what follows, namely the summary of a proposed new topography of media communication theory, I hope to steer a path between three, to my mind, entirely inadequate theoretical stances concerning media communication: the intemperate excesses of Jean Baudrillard's (1983) dissolution of societal reality into mediatic representation; the sere reserve of the otherwise energetic Elihu Katz concerning any claim of strong social impact of media; and the invertebrate zone that merely contents itself with standing 'somewhere between' these two extremes.

There is a further large problem in wading straight into a theoretical construction concerning media communication, namely what exactly is meant to be covered by 'media communication'. Although evidently many writers on the subject share a working consensus as to what is meant and what is excluded, and although the foregoing chapters argued for an inclusive, and interconnected, definition of media communication – see particularly the six summary points flagged toward the close of the Introduction – that does not mean that framing theoretical issues applies in precisely the same way to all media, whether defined by technical means or by format or by cultural content.

Furthermore, there are sharp differences between – let us say – US researchers shaped by the empiricist study of 'mass communication' and researchers framing their work in the cultural studies tradition. They would hardly agree on whether for instance dress or commodity packaging or architecture constitute media.

Interestingly Lucien Sfez (1993: ix–x), in his monumental critical dictionary of communication, explicitly refuses to offer readers a single definition of the word, but rather guides them toward several hundred pages of text that collectively address questions of communication from a variety of angles. His explicit acknowledgment of the dangers of over-tidiness and premature summarization is a warning well taken, and his two volumes' definition of the field are absorbingly different in emphasis from the standard Anglo-American framework.

None of these issues can be settled here. What follows is, then, intended as a beginning, as the preliminary redefinition of a set of significant and often interconnected issues in media communication theory that have quite often been marginalized, or not addressed at all, or inadequately conceptualized. It is a long way short of a comprehensive statement. In particular, it does not address questions of communication technology, newer or older.

Media, Political Power and Conflict

Seemingly endless treatments of media and electoral politics, and of strategies by governing parties for media management in their short-run favor ('spin-control'), have wrested research attention away from the more perduring issues of media and the power structure, which were especially sharply raised by the consideration of media in Russia, Poland and Hungary in a period when power structures were initially seemingly unchallengeable, then in enormous flux, and then being reconstituted.[1] We need to prioritize the seriously neglected topic of how media operate *over time and during major societal change* in their relationship to and imbrication with the power structure. In the book's earlier discussion, the focus was on the dissolution of an authoritarian power structure and its reconfiguration, but it might equally be on the dissolution of a democratic power structure and its reconfiguration into an authoritarian regime.

As we saw, for some writers and commentators, such as Habermas, this mediatic issue is restricted to the intense moments of the actual collapse of a regime. Clearly those moments are part of the issue. Its core they are not. A key question, rather, is the *cumulative* impact of media daring and disclosures on both the confidence of the public in speaking freely, and on sapping the self-confidence of the regime. A further key question is the role of political patronage, by a reform wing of the established order, in the genesis and protection of dissonant media voices, and consequently too the role of these dissonant – not underground – media as symbolic targets in intra-elite struggles for ascendancy.

In a transition from democracy, the corresponding issue is the *cumulative* impact of media timidity and obsequiousness. Not of all media – which tend to evince these qualities anyway in relation to power structures – but of those that in the public mind enjoy a reputation for a certain degree of independence and forthrightness. Similarly, what are the roles of media that become colonized by anti-democratic forces?

What, in particular, is the phenomenology of media professionals of all types and ranks during these processes?

One of the most complex problems in media communication analysis is the phenomenology of professional communicators. On one level they are simply employees, subject to dictates and subcultural codes, to economic necessities, to habit, and thus their phenomenology could be argued to be no more – and no less – complicated to understand than a bank clerk's or an auto worker's.

At the same time, they are constantly called upon to handle change, cultural and structural. Media institutions are perpetually being set the task of interpreting and reinterpreting the world's flux. In so far as they address the challenge by insisting on reiterating certain enduring truths and tropes, political or religious, their task becomes very easy in practical terms, in terms of a day's work. All they have to do is recycle the shibboleths. Yet even in this limiting case, precisely because of the professionals' involvement in shibboleth-processing, its very juxtaposition with the greater and greater complexities all around them forces many into a dual consciousness.

We saw this phenomenon over and over in the later Soviet bloc situation, for example in the exaggerated discrepancy between public and private affirmations by senior officials, or in the prominence precisely of journalists and other media professionals among the voices for change as it gathered momentum.

We noted too, however, that neither terror, at that point in Soviet history, nor rather infrequent interventions from the censor's office, could explain the readiness of many other journalists to conform. The instance was cited of a Polish journalist's pride and interest in being a member of the Polish regime's equivalent to TASS, namely the institution providing accurate information to restricted high government officials, and her sense of privilege through having access to data unavailable to the general public. The instance was also cited of the sense of privilege enjoyed by foreign correspondents. Instances might equally be cited of contented and unimaginative hacks, freely dispensing the brutalism of the elite against its foes and malcontents;[2] so might the readiness by the ambitious to participate in the Party's national political lecture program as a means of social ascent.

These varied situations and responses, amongst others, resonate rather clearly with the situations of journalists, or media entertainment artists, in nations that are less radically asymmetrical in power terms. The awareness in these latter of what is, and is not, possible to communicate, of the boundaries drawn by advertisers and editors and broadcast executives, is generally very clear. The staffs do not have to be blue-pencilled all the time. They typically try to model their work on the current high-fliers in their profession, those who are evidently best regarded from on high.

Yet at the same time, there is a spectrum of attitudes among media professionals in this latter group of nations, from the true believers and hacks through to the alienated and oppositional. There is a continuous demand that they all have to meet, namely to reinvent and re-express the conventional wisdom of their authorities, but in terms and images that have an ongoing purchase upon the public's minds. Their greater 'space' in these nations, as compared to more authoritarian regimes, is very far short of full freedom. Perhaps advertising copywriters face this issue as acutely as anyone. In that mental mobility, agility and suppleness lies the ongoing contradiction of imagination at the service of power.

It could be said then that we need a much closer appreciation of the links in the chain between political authorities, media owners and the processes of mediating products and texts. Part of the problem, however, is precisely the image of links in a chain, which nicely mirrors the Leninist transmission-belt theory of the media, but which aggressively oversimplifies the actual process of control. A much better metaphor would be that we need more sophisticated models in order to search out the multiple refractile overlaps and reinforcements in the processes that effectively combine to steer the public's professional communicators, yet which also at times open up spaces to the refractory.

It is also vitally important to evaluate how significantly genuinely refractory media operate, clandestinely or semi-clandestinely, in relation to the power structure, and what their relations are with cultural movements for autonomy, be these youth-based, religious, ethnic, racist, regional, or a mixture. These small-scale media have often been defined simply in glowing terms as heroic exemplars of the human spirit's craving for freedom, or alternatively snickered at as curios of the quixotic temperament. What, once separated out from these ideological perceptual grids, are their actual roles, especially in relation to social movements?

Lastly, in the period of consolidation of a less authoritarian regime, what are the roles played by media? Do they destabilize it by flexing their newly gained muscles? Do they begin to generate a culture of civic engagement? Do they address ethnic and other social divisions in ways that encourage them to be negotiated rather than become the source of bloodshed? Do they simply switch allegiance from one power center to another (whatever its designation on a democratic spectrum)? Do they move to pander to the raw sensationalism and sexist exploitation that are safe commercial bets for media?

All these are possibilities. All have been seen, in or out of the three nations surveyed, within the transitional era in the region. What is really interesting, from the perspective of generating better media communication theory, is the analysis and evaluation of the mixture as it affects the formation, performance and stability of the new power structure. However, to repeat, perhaps needlessly, the observation made at the outset of this subsection, what is meant by the stability of the power structure here is not particularly the survival in government of a given political party, although in a given conjuncture that can have its impact on stability more generally conceived. The question is rather one of a new regime, a new politico-economic order, struggling toward hegemony *à la* Gramsci.

Media, Cultural Change and Cultural Coagulation

Much more has been involved in East European transitions, and transitions elsewhere in the world, than just the direct configuration of political power. Cultural issues have consistently driven the agenda as well. One of the problems with the standard usage of the term 'culture' is its implicit fixity, which is why it always needs to be intimately coupled with the term 'communication' in order to signify the flux that actually characterizes cultural process.

A conceptually interesting case is precisely that of the later sovietized regimes, especially in most of the Soviet republics, where at least on the official plane culture seemed indeed to have coagulated and clogged to the point of total stasis. As we have seen, official culture was consequently a King Canute, screaming vainly at the waves to retreat and not to swallow it up. Molecularly, from rock music to ecological circles, from Jewish refuseniks to nationalist resurgence, from innovative theater to restive labor movements, the incoming tide was increasingly insistent.[3]

Two sets of issues are of particular interest here as regards media communication theory. One is the question of certain concepts: civil society, public sphere, social movements, hegemony and counter-hegemonic currents. The other is the question of political and social memory.

Some of these discourses and concepts, as we have seen, have a certain utility but urgently need refinement and further definition. Especially the terms civil society, public sphere/*Öffentlichkeit*, hegemony/*egemonia*, have been seen to be subject to several, sometimes mutually contradictory dangers: of claiming a univocal meaning, or a direct parentage they did not possess, or of acting like vacuum cleaners that sucked up into their maw whatever the writer wished to throw in there. Some discourses concerning social movements, like the New Social Movement literature, may offer certain helpful insights while suffering from their limitation to very specific phenomena such as environmentalism or feminism in a 'First World' context.

What they all do, to one degree or another, is focus attention on the processes of public discussion, debate, cultural renewal and ferment, that operate in all but totalitarian societies. Some are headily – and naively – democratic in their usage, implying that in normal human society, untainted by political repression, the free and open and rational expression of opinion and a similar exchange of information will lead to the sensible balancing of societal needs and concerns. This is then a kind of yardstick held up against actuality, which is consequently revealed in all its harshness and bureaucratic absurdity and then acts as a spur toward a more constructive political order. 'Civil society' in this usage became a kind of mantra rather than a concept in some East European circles in the latter 1980s.

Notions of hegemony, with their acknowledgment of the multifarious forms of politico-cultural intervention in daily life, long-term and short-term, and consistently tilting the process away from any ideal, can be one important corrective to this incipiently moralistic and idealized discourse.[4] The actual processes of public debate, as we have seen, are much messier and untidier than the nirvanic-ratiocinative vision, with sometimes violent antagonisms convulsing the very ranks of those excluded from power, not to mention the nigh-universal presence of emotion and symbol in communicative exchange. None the less, these processes of debate do exist everywhere in society, do have numerous short-run and long-term effects, often unanticipated, and are sparked, sustained, diffused and amplified by media (in the broadest sense). Social and cultural movements live off and through such discussion within and around such media.

Without then having to be tied to either a particular definition of the concepts and terms listed above, or to persisting in their frequent woolliness in usage, an adequate theory of media communication *must* address the realities to which they point. Social and cultural movements and the public discussions that swirl around them need to be foregrounded analytically in media communication research, not treated as curious and fleeting epiphenomena. Cultural coagulation in the official public sphere seems to generate particular pressure for such movements of cultural change. But care is also needed not to assume that every movement of cultural change is constructive, as some of the remarks on memory and media just below will remind us.

The other important, very important conclusion that these concepts of civil society, public sphere, social movements and hegemony press on our thinking is the conceptual absurdity of the media/non-media division in communication research. As noted already in note 15 to the Introduction, this arbitrary divide is sustained by the heavily empiricist character of most interpersonal communication research, which makes it conceptually and methodologically almost unable to be integrated into media and cultural studies research. Moreover, and almost equally perversely, the concepts just listed above are often unsullied in the research literature by any systematic consideration of the roles of media.

There is no rational reason to prolong this mutual insulation given the mutual porousness that actually characterizes societal discourse.

Memory and media, the second point under our sub-heading of media and cultural change, is potentially an enormous topic. In the empirical materials surveyed in the book, questions of memory surfaced in a series of ways. The most obvious was memory in the sense of history, namely the recovery of the largely buried past of almost unimaginable Stalinist horrors (that recovery being a much more complex phenomenon in Russia, though not in Poland and Hungary,[5] than it first seemed in the West in the heady rush of *glasnost*).

The second most obvious? Probably the recycling of inherited ideological codes and media tropes from the sovietized past while simply switching explicit content, for instance substituting fiercely moralistic denunciation of those who had collaborated with the sovietized regimes, for savage diatribes against imperialism, or naively celebrating the bliss of 'the market' and the US political system instead of, as previously, listing the world-shaking successes of Soviet state planning. The opponent sat on the same chair as its predecessor.

The third could be argued to be the emotive rediscovery of tradition, especially the revised and refreshed discourse of nationhood and ethnic identity, resurfacing – with sometimes deadly effect – atavistic stereotypes and seemingly dusty grudges that previously had circulated in private conversation and in relatively under-the-counter ways. One of the very first visible effects of *glasnost* in Russia was the public resurgence of dismayingly vicious expressions of anti-Semitism.

In other words, what might be termed the recovery of social memory had multiple consequences, some of immense benefit, a number extremely negative. None the less, negative or positive or a mixture, media and cultural memory experienced a very forceful interaction.

Such an interaction worked rather differently in Western capitalist countries, where the relation between cinema and historiography, for instance, sometimes spun itself out in a continuing rather than a politically deaf mode. The Hollywood Western film's normal overview of the nations of Native America, for example, or French cinema's treatment of France's colonial and neo-colonial relationships, did not block out memory or history altogether, but rather sought to build up one particular construction of memory to the detriment of others (Buscombe, 1991; Sherzer, 1996). Inflection, rather than complete burial, was the strategy. (The same could be said of Soviet films about the Second World War.)

The interesting question is what impact these differing patterns of media-induced memory may have exerted. Perhaps the closest parallels with the sovietized case would be with the communication of either African history in the New World, or women's history. For example the two *Roots* mini-series represented a real revelation of the horrors of slavery to at least a number of viewers, even of African descent, in both the USA and Britain. Women's history was equally ignored by textbooks and other media alike until the closing decades of the twentieth century.

Part of the issue, necessarily, is the degree of continuity involved. Certainly not all, but none the less most Soviet labor camps had been emptied of their surviving population by the end of 1956. By 1986, when for the first time since the limited exposés under Khrushchev the realities of the camps came to be acknowledged in public by the reform wing of the Soviet regime, a whole generation and a half had come into existence. The degree of continuity with people's immediate experience was rather minimal, and the exposés consequently politically rather safe.

By contrast, the overall degradation of social existence for most African Americans and for most women may have changed many of its mechanisms over the past two centuries, but not its ultimate impact, their assignment to specific, unattractive places and roles. Memory, once revived or reconstructed by media, turns up the flame of current experience.

In terms of the application to new targets of long-memorized media tropes and codes, there has been no transition in Britain or the USA of the kind visible in Eastern Europe. Most of African Americans' representation in film and television still restricts them to the genres of comedy entertainment, violent gang life, music, or sport. Women continue to dominate advertising copy even as they are rendered totally voiceless in it. Latinos barely exist, Native Americans still less so, except as, respectively, gangmembers and figures from past centuries.

The continuous mediatic interpretation of social change, discussed already just above, thus draws on or reconstructs or neglects memory in many different ways. By 1995 in Russia, to take yet a different example, intense nostalgia was widespread for the known and seemingly secure social order of the later Soviet era. At this juncture then, a highly selective memory was able to be mobilized, actively encouraged by a considerable number of Russian media voices, albeit primarily as a form of protest against the endemic confusion, economic and political, that characterized the first five years of post-Soviet Russian life. Poles and Hungarians could easily be found who would concur. This powerful undertow was one factor in the return of former Communist parties to government in all three nations.[6]

Without its ever being stated as such, it was also effectively a protest against what had been the unremarked re-enactment of yet another well-memorized Soviet trope, namely the possibility of instantaneous societal achievement of desired goals. Under Stalin, this might have signified damming a giant river or collectivizing agriculture; in 1990–1, for a substantial number of Russians, it meant junking the old order and switching to instant consumer gratification via a flash-leap into 'democracy' and 'the market' (often conflated in the public mind within the region). As we saw, not only Russians initially bought into this utopia. Many Poles initially did too.[7]

Thus memory and media interact in multiple fashions to assist both cultural change and coagulation. There is a great deal more that could be said about memory and media than this, and the subject warrants a much more detailed treatment (cf. Zelizer, 1995). It is a major area for media research to embrace, but perhaps gets blotted out somewhat by the tendency toward contemporaneity in media research, itself a too-easy reflex of the constantly evolving media communication zone and industries at the present time.

The International Dimension

Both the USA and Britain have a curious history of cultural insularity conjoined with huge imperial power. By and large it has been researchers in the critical tradition who have explored the international dimension of media, precisely in order to puncture the pretensions of either power to be automatically a global force for good. Or the similar public pretensions of transnational corporations based in the leading economies. Combined with the insular, not to say isolationist tradition in the USA in particular, this has left the field of international communication research as rather a marginal topic for mainstream researchers.

Naive and know-nothing for Britain in the extreme, naive and know-nothing even for the rather more self-sufficient USA, this definition of international communication as a kind of research condiment of choice has been shown to be extremely misleading if ever it were to be slapped on to the situation in Russia, Poland or Hungary over the period examined. South Africa, South Korea, South American nations, these are only some of the numerous comparable instances. Moreover, media communication flows simply cannot be halted at national borders and redefined as extraneous for convenient analytical purposes. They are intrinsic to the contemporary media communication process at innumerable junctures. To neglect them is seriously to skew analysis.

In the previous chapter, the fuzziness of much 'globalization' writing and the overkill of much 'cultural imperialism' writing were attacked. There is much to be done to achieve better levels of precision in global media research, and better specifications in comparative media research. One of the key themes of the argument of this book, however, remains the decisive advantage of media communication research that engages with and incorporates these dimensions.

Economic Relations and Media Communication

This topic has been explored rather little in this book, given its importance. Part of the problem is to get beyond strong simple statements of the sledgehammer impact of economic forces at certain junctures – state subsidy or advertising as enablers of media production, for example. On that level, as noted in the first chapter, there is very little dispute concerning the role of economic factors. What remains remarkably unexplored is what goes on aside from the sledgehammer.

In the Eastern European context, for instance, there has been an unparalleled opportunity to contrast the impact of state subsidy and advertising on media activities. The discussion has often been pre-empted by ideologues who have equated advertising-based media with freedom of information and expression, *tout court*. A more sober appraisal over time would be very informative, taking into account, for example, the problems of developing regional cable television in Hungary. On one level cable TV could have been a major opportunity for diversity of content, but was effectively hog-tied in the mid-1990s for want of advertisers who thought it worth their while to promote their wares through it.

A different example for research would be the development of the financial consortium that was awarded various slices of Ostankino Public Television, or the Most banking group that owned a series of media outlets. What in their cases was the interaction between conventional financial processes and goals, and political objectives? How far were their various objectives achieved? The same could be asked of Solorz or Grauso in Poland, or of Hersant, which entered the Polish and Hungarian media markets only to withdraw for the most part a few years later.

A different research opening again would be the expansion of consumerist appetites via advertising. This latter should not be attributed solely to the power of advertising. Consumerist appetites were already whipped up to a near-frenzy among many Russians and Poles well before 1989, as was shown in a way even by the example of the believing Communist couple from Leningrad, wandering and wondering in the Budapest supermarket (cited in Chapter 1). Pirated Western video-cassettes, and travellers' tales, inflaming the frustrations born of the anti-consumer bias of sovietized economies, fertilized the ground long before the first TV ad.

What would be more to the point would be to analyse the character of anticipatory consumerist socialization, given that effective demand lay only with the ex-*nomenklatura* and the small layer of early business entrepreneurs in the initial changeover years. Its interaction in Russia with earlier envy of somewhat higher living standards in East-Central Europe and some of the outer republics, and its coinherence with patriotic and neo-imperial ideology, would make a particularly interesting study.

Audiences and Social Consciousness

This is a topic that can hardly be said to have been under-researched, given the market research and audience research industry, and also the explosion of academic qualitative studies from the 1980s onwards. In addition, a number of observations above have already addressed this dimension of media communication.[8]

Audiences in heavily authoritarian regimes and unstable nations do, however, represent a very different, and interesting, case – as do the more extruded sectors' audiences in stable democracies – from the typically researched favored sectors in the latter nations. The faithful regime loyalists, the absolute cynics, increasingly alienated youth, the generally exhausted with no energy to be an active audience, women with less time to use media than men because of their double shift, the retired with all the time in the world, guerrilla readers between the lines, the alternative media activists and dissidents, the heady roller-coaster transition from fear in the accelerating dispersal of taboos, the disillusionment with consolidating regimes and the roles of media during that vexed process, rightist nationalist movements and media critique: there is enough and to spare here that can lift audience analysis right out of its currently well-worn grooves.

IV

In the end, one of the most productive basic statements of how these major vectors interact in the sphere of media is still probably the long citation from Williams in the Introduction, where he underscores the ultimate inseparability of societal and mediatic analysis, using the metaphors of 'solution' and of the key turning twice. I would add to it some final thoughts derived in part from current conceptual developments in fractal geometry, fuzzy logic, chaos theory and complex systems (Hayles, 1991; Kosko, 1993; Shlain, 1991; Stewart, 1989; Waldrop, 1992). The remarks that follow are especially tentative, but may hopefully help to spark further and deeper reflection.

The merit of these newer approaches to scientific and mathematical analysis for our present purposes lies firstly in their attempt to acknowledge the key importance of interrelation, rather than the separation out of factors from each other and the consequent spurious simplification of reality. The ostensibly reasonable temporary strategy of making research manageable by such selection has too often failed to return to base upon mission completion, and has instead permanently imposed its provisional straight lines and 90-degree angles on data that are overtly refractory to such confinement.

Secondly, these approaches encourage intellectual involvement with the turbulent embrace of constant, swirling change, rather than the artificial imposition of stasis. At the same time, the forms that change takes – however complex, however misshapen by the standards of simplified science – are fully acknowledged. Change is not perceived simply as a foggy blur.

Thirdly, the significance of the minimal in relation to major processes is given full weight. The standard summary image of this point, perhaps overworked, is of the putative ultimate influence of the movement of a butterfly's wings in Brazil on a subsequent howling hurricane off the Texas Gulf coast. The social and political researchers who neglect the movements and eddies of popular culture should take note here.

Some writers have virtually proposed chaos analysis as a new master-metaphor for understanding science, the arts, and human society in general.[9] This, however, as Knoespel (1991) has pointed out in a splendidly incisive essay contrasting deconstructive practice with chaos theory, is to take the point far too far to be useful. Mathematical chaos theorists are concerned to develop a more effective, more realistic, approach to mathematics, not to provide a Heraclitean *Urtheologie* of life. This is equally true of complexity theorists, even given their interest in phase transitions and 'the edge of chaos', and their readiness for conceptual bricolage on a grand scale.

Moreover, the decisive difference between active cultural subjects and unthinking chemical or astronomical processes absolutely cannot be overlooked. Against Weber, on the one hand, not everything in human society is to be explained by the conscious thought processes of its members. In their very different ways, Marx, Durkheim, Freud, all rightly emphasized the powerful impact of factors beyond our explicit awareness. At the same time, on the other, Weber's emphasis on the distinctiveness of the purposive action dimension of human society cannot be sloughed off in its study except at the cost of extreme distortion.

All this acknowledged, the very bending of the supposedly absolute rules and canons of good science in the interest of attending much more closely than before to the full dimensions of what is being measured, is a direct encouragement to media communication researchers to engage with the major vectors flagged by this book both in principle and by example. Indeed, to the more hidebound, their brains molded by their high school physics texts of decades past, this trend in science ought to constitute a direct challenge to so engage. The very great complexity of the mediatic and other social processes we have examined here during their period of intense change – in many respects echoing, we argued, the experience of numerous other nations – is a far more suitable task for media communication analysis than the safe little boxes of frozen peas that constitute the research question across much of the literature.

What this study has shown, amongst other things, is that the Baudrillard–Katz antithesis is completely fake. Developing from Williams' metaphors of solution and the key, we might consider that the point is not whether media are powerful or not, but how their power operates in conjunction *and* dissonance with other forces, within themselves, and within numerous processes of change. Isolating them out and freezing them is the same tactic deployed by the simplicity approach in natural science.

Yet as was noted just above, taking 'media' as a single, discrete object of study, along with education as another, religion as another, government as another, economic processes as another, is already to try to cram the contents of Pandora's box back inside it. There is perhaps a little more purchase in conducting such a discrete exercise with economic processes. But media communication, of all the so-called social institutions listed, is precisely and absolutely the most relational. The question therefore of the unique social effect of media as distinct from that of other 'institutions' is exactly absurd. Their dismissal as consequently largely impotent in society parallels that absurdity with a little final flourish of its own.

Metaphors cautiously to explore as heuristic tools for understanding key aspects of the societal roles of media might rather be those of iteration and refraction and synapse.

'Iteration' has acquired a very particular sense in chaos theory language. It signifies the way that series of repetitions in nature or replicated by a computer model will sometimes produce quite extraordinary variations and new patterns with but the tiniest alteration of a single small variable (hence the butterfly–hurricane image). Geometrically and visually, these may be expressed by Julia or Mandelbrot fractal sets, that in video translation appear somewhat like the constantly unfolding surprise patterns of a kaleidoscope, repeating and yet not indefinitely repeating.

Again, it must be underscored that the component of human agency, as opposed to observable patterns in mathematics or nature, is not an element within the concept of iteration. It is none the less stimulating to query – since if media do nothing else, they iterate throughout our lifespans – whether and how human agency might be introduced into a revised and expanded notion of media iteration; particularly if the circulation and development of culture via media from a variety of corners of society (some much more than others) is taken into account.

'Refraction' refers literally to the bending of lightwaves or energy waves as they pass from one medium to another (e.g. from air to glass). Again, not a concept addressing human agency, but at the same time, perhaps it could be developed to involve the numerous, but not endless, processes of redefinition of reality that may take place in and through media communication.

'Synapse' literally refers to the bonding of one nerve with another, except that many synapses in the human body are very long, connecting distant points. The same caveat applies as in the other two examples, but the recognition of the irrelevance of distance, in certain senses, is one which could greatly help to sensitize our research to the impacts of international media communication flows.

What all three metaphors lack is the key dimension of power relations, whether political, economic or cultural, whether hegemonic or oppositional. This book has especially argued – and here we may conclude – that without constant attention to that dimension, media studies might as well shut up shop. Whatever the shortcomings of political science as currently practiced, power relations are the primary energy source, organized along a variety of axes, but mediatically through processes of iteration and refraction, and through synaptic connections, all of them in conjunction and/or dissonance with other societal forces.

There is, then, no armoury or quiver from which perfectly minted conceptual weapons may be drawn in order to pin down the restless, quivering hulk of Media for sterilized dissection and analysis. There are only more, or less, adequate conceptual instruments for illuminating a protean cultural phenomenon as penetrative and universal as the ether. Their adequacy can only be argued for or against, delicately or clumsily, but can never ultimately be proved. But to have a chance of understanding the amazing phenomenon of Gulliver, we must at least move beyond Lilliput, beyond the foreshortened perspectives redolent of US or British media systems as the latter are experienced from relatively favored social circumstances.

Notes

1 This framing of the issue depends on the prior framing presented in Chapters 1–5, where the character of the late sovietized state was differentiated from its Stalinist predecessor more strongly than from non-sovietized authoritarian states around the globe or, in the argument immediately above, from the authoritarian faces of the power structure in developed capitalist nations toward certain social sectors. The argument has also been made in Chapter 6 that the post-soviet power structure does not signify dazzling daylight either.

2 One such Hungarian journalist, noted for his thuggish professional behavior, was found preening himself at one point in the mid-1980s at his description in print by one of his enemies as someone who wrote in concrete, stupidly assuming that he had been described as fulfilling the Leninist precept to focus on the concrete . . .

3 In Poland, once the regime had changed, the Catholic hierarchy that had placed such weight on obdurate refusal to change, began increasingly to feel itself under similar pressures too.

4 Calling it 'moralistic' is not a cheap way of downgrading the significance of political ethics, nor is it to underrate the enormous impact of the assertion of ethical integrity within a corrupt and abusive situation (e.g. especially Martin Luther King, but also Andrei Sakharov or Vaclav Havel in Eastern Europe). It is to acknowledge the fact that ethical considerations alone cannot bear the full weight of social analysis.

5 The 1990 confirmation that KGB officers had systematically massacred at least 15,000 Polish Army officers in the forest of Katyn after the Soviet–Nazi partition of Poland in 1939, came almost as an anti-climax after two decades of persistent affirmation in the underground press that this had happened. In Hungary, the redefinition of the 1956 revolution as a national uprising rather than a counter-revolutionary action by pro-Western malcontents, similarly confirmed and vindicated a memory. Reclaiming that memory in Russia was much more complicated (White, 1995), partly because Russians had wrought devastation on Russians (indeed one attempt from the extreme right was to cope with this by blaming much of the Bolshevik Revolution and its aftermath on Jews and their supposed Russophobia, even hunting out distant Jewish connections in Lenin's family for example). Partly also because despite the strict controls of the regime, and the low levels of personal consumption, people also had memories of getting by and living their lives, and of having experienced the everyday mores and rituals of the Soviet regime together. This indisputable part of their past, especially during the acute turmoil of 1990–95, was the subject of a great wave of nostalgia for the clarities of yore.

6 The differences between the policies and styles of these reinvigorated Communist parties should not be neglected, however; see Chapter 2.

7 Utopianism is perhaps an unlikely vice for Hungarians to embrace.

8 Stevenson (1995: 75–113) has recently produced a very incisive and fair critique of the recent academic work. His commentary says most of what I would wish to say on the subject at the present time. See also the thoughtful article by Carragee (1993).

9 Waldrop (1992: 9) actually begins his book on complexity systems with the collapse of the Soviet system as his first example of 'the constantly shifting zone between stagnation and anarchy' (p. 12), along with the sudden disappearance of species, the genesis of the first living cell, and a number of other paradoxes. Although he himself does not do so, such a presentation runs the risk of homogenizing qualitatively disparate processes, and especially – see the next paragraph – of blotting out human society's distinctive qualities of thought, intention and (very complex) language.

Bibliography

Adamson, Walter L. (1987) 'Gramsci and the politics of civil society', *Praxis International*, 7(3–4): 320–39.

Adirim, I. (1991) 'Current development and dissemination of computer technology in the Soviet economy', *Soviet Studies*, 43(4): 651–67.

Adorno, Theodor W. (1981) 'Spengler after the decline', in *Prisms*. Cambridge, MA: MIT Press. pp. 51–72.

Albats, Yevgenia (1994) *The State within a State: The KGB and Its Hold on Russia – Past, Present, and Future*. New York: Farrar, Straus, Giroux.

Alberoni, Francesco (1984) *Movement and Institution*. New York: Columbia University Press.

Alexeyeva, Liudmila (1985) *Soviet Dissent: Contemporary Movements for National, Religious and Human Rights*. Middletown, CT: Wesleyan University Press.

Alexeyeva, Liudmila (1987) *US Broadcasting to the Soviet Union*. New York: Helsinki Watch.

Althusser, Louis (1971) 'Ideology and ideological State apparatuses (Notes towards an investigation)', in *Louis Althusser: Lenin and Philosophy and Other Essays*. London: New Left Books. pp. 123–73.

Álvarez, Sonia (1990) *Engendering Democracy in Brazil: Women's Movements in Transition Politics*. Princeton, NJ: Princeton University Press.

Amalrik, Andrei (1982) *Notes of a Revolutionary*. New York: Knopf.

Andor, László (1994) 'The Hungarian Socialist Party', *Labour Focus on Eastern Europe*, 48: 58–82.

Androunas, Elena (1993) *Soviet Media in Transition: Structural and Economic Alternatives*. New York: Praeger.

Antonkin, Alexei (1983) *Les Chiens de faïence*. Paris: Éditions de l'Équinoxe.

Appadurai, Arjun (1992) 'Disjuncture and difference in the global cultural economy', in Mike Featherstone (ed.), *Global Culture: Nationalism, Globalization and Modernity*. London: Sage Publications. pp. 295–310.

Arato, Andrew and Cohen, Jean (1992) *Civil Society and Political Theory*. Cambridge, MA: MIT Press.

Arendt, Hannah (1958) *The Origins of Totalitarianism*, 2nd enlarged edn. New York: Meridian Books.

Arendt, Hannah (1994) *Essays in Understanding, 1930–1954*. New York: Harcourt Brace Jovanovich.

Ash, Timothy Garton (1990) *We the People: The Revolutions of '89*. London: Penguin.

Ash, Timothy Garton (1993) *In Europe's Name: Germany and the Divided Continent*. London: Jonathan Cape.

Asselain, Jean-Charles (1981) *Plan et profit en économie socialiste*. Paris: Presses Universitaires Françaises.

Autissier, Anne-Marie, Feigelson, Kristian, Lange, André, Mattelart, Tristan and Razlogov, Kirill (eds) (1992) *Guide du cinéma et de l'audiovisuel en Europe Centrale et Orientale*. Paris: Eurocréation et L'Institut D'Études Slaves.

Autissier, Anne-Marie and Mattelart, Tristan (eds) (1993) *Entre état et marché: Audiovisuel et cinéma en Europe Centrale et Orientale*. Paris: Eurocréation.

Avdeenko, T. et al (1990) 'The attitude of the population toward the development of cooperatives', *Soviet Review*, 31(6): 20–9.

Babkhina M.A. (ed.) (1991) *New Political Parties and Movements in the Soviet Union.* Commack, NY: Nova Science.

Bachkatov, Nina and Wilson, Andrew (1988) *Les Enfants de Gorbatchev.* Paris: Calmann-Lévy.

Bahro, Rudolf (1978) *The Alternative in Eastern Europe.* London: New Left Books.

Bakhtin, Mikhail (1981) *The Dialogic Imagination.* Austin, TX: University of Texas Press.

Bamford, James (1982) *The Puzzle Palace: A Report on America's Most Secret Agency.* Boston, MA: Houghton Mifflin.

Barany, Zoltan (1992) 'East European armed forces in transition and beyond', *East European Quarterly*, 26(1): 1–30.

Baudrillard, Jean (1983) 'The precession of simulacra', in *Simulations.* New York: Autonomedia. pp. 1–79.

Bauer, Raymond A. and Bauer, Alice H. (1960) 'America, "mass society" and mass media', *Journal of Social Issues*, 16(2): 3–66.

Bauer, Raymond A. and Gleicher, David B. (1953) 'Word-of-mouth communication in the Soviet Union', *Public Opinion Quarterly*, 17(3): 297–310.

Benjamin, Walter (1973) *Illuminations.* London: Fontana Books.

Benn, David Wedgwood (1989) *Persuasion and Soviet Politics.* Oxford: Basil Blackwell.

Bennett, Tony (1989) 'Culture: Theory and policy', *Media Information Australia*, 53 (August): 9–11.

Bennett, Tony (1992) 'Putting policy into cultural studies', in Lawrence Grossberg et al. (eds), *Cultural Studies.* New York: Routledge. pp. 23–37.

Berger, Christa (1990) 'Movimientos sociales y comunicación en Brasil', *Comunicación y Sociedad [México]*, 9: 9–27.

Bernhard, Michael H. (1991) 'Reinterpreting Solidarity', *Studies in Comparative Communism*, 24: 313–30.

Bernhard, Michael H. (1993) *The Origins of Democratization in Poland: Workers, Intellectuals, and Oppositional Politics, 1976–1980.* New York: Columbia University Press.

Beschloss, Michael and Talbott, Strobe (1993) *At the Highest Levels: The Inside Story of the End of the Cold War.* Boston, MA: Little, Brown.

Bettelheim, Charles (1983) *Les Luttes de classes en URSS, 3ème période 1930–1941*, vol. 2. Paris: Seuil/Maspéro.

Blumsztajn, Seweryn (1988) *Une Pologne hors censure.* Paris: Solidarité France-Pologne.

Bobbio, Norberto (1988) 'Gramsci and the concept of civil society', in John Keane (ed.), *Civil Society and the State: New European Perspectives.* London: Verso.

Bock, Gabriele (1984) 'Not every shoe fits every foot: Some perspectives on international cultural indicators research', in Melischek et al. pp. 129–36.

Bognár, Robert (1992) 'Lettre de mon village', *La Nouvelle Alternative*, 26: 18–19.

Bonnell, Victoria E. and Freidin, Gregory (1995) 'Televorot: The role of television coverage in Russia's August 1991 coup', in Condee (ed.) (1995), pp. 22–51.

Boorstin, Daniel (1963) *The Image, or What Happened to the American Dream.* London: Pelican.

Bordyugov, Gennadii (1995) 'The policy and regime of extraordinary measures under Lenin and Stalin', *Europe-Asia Studies*, 47: 615–32.

Bouwman, Harry (1984) 'Cultivation analysis: The Dutch case', in Melischek et al. (1984), pp. 407–22.

Bouwman, Harry and Stappers, James (1984) 'The Dutch violence profile: A replication of Gerbner's message indicators research', in Melischek et al. (1984), pp. 113–28.

Bova, Russell (1991a) 'Political dynamics of the post-Communist transition: A comparative perspective', *World Politics*, 44: 113–38.

Bova, Russell (1991b) 'Worker activism: The role of the state', in Sedaitis and Butterfield (1991), pp. 29–42.

Boyd, Douglas (1989) 'The videocassette recorder in the USSR and Soviet Bloc countries', in Mark Levy (ed.), *The VCR Age, Home Video, and Mass Communication.* Newbury Park, CA: Sage.

Boyle, Mary Ellen (forthcoming) *Capturing the East German Mind: Press and Politics in East Germany 1945–91*. Chapel Hill, NC: University of North Carolina Press.

Boym, Svetlana (1994) *Common Places: Mythologies of Everyday Life in Russia*. Cambridge, MA: Harvard University Press.

Bozoki, András and Sükösd, János (1993) 'Civil society and populism in the Eastern European democratic transitions', *Praxis International*, 13: 224–41.

Breslauer, George W. (1984) 'The adaptability of Soviet welfare-state authoritarianism', in Erik P. Hoffmann and Robbin F. Laird (eds), *The Soviet Polity in the Modern Era*. New York: Aldine. pp. 219–45.

Brinton, William (1990) 'The role of media in a telerevolution', in William M. Brinton and Alan Rinzler (eds), *Without Force or Lies: Voices from the Revolution of Central Europe in 1989–90*. San Francisco, Murray House. pp. 459–70.

Brooks, Jeffrey (1985) *When Russia Learned to Read: Literacy and Popular Culture, 1861–1917*. Princeton, NJ: Princeton University Press.

Brown, J.F. (1991) *Surge to Freedom: The End of Communist Rule in Eastern Europe*. Durham, NC: Duke University Press.

Brown, Marilyn A. (1991) 'Diffusion', *International Encyclopedia of Communication*, vol. 2. New York: Oxford University Press. pp. 31–6.

Brudny, Itzhak (1991) 'The heralds of opposition to perestroyka', in A. Hewett and Victor H. Winston (eds), *Milestones in Glasnost and Perestroyka: Politics and People*. Washington, DC: Brookings Institute. pp. 153–89.

Brzezinski, Zbigniew K. (1989) *The Grand Failure*. New York: Scribner.

Buck-Morss, Susan (1977) *The Origin of Negative Dialectics: Theodor W. Adorno, Walter Benjamin and the Frankfurt Institute*. New York: The Free Press.

Burdick, John (1992) 'Rethinking the study of social movements: The case of Christian base communities in urban Brazil', in Éscobar and Álvarez (1992), pp. 171–84.

Burnham, David (1983) *The Rise of the Computer State*. New York: Random House.

Buscombe, Edward (ed.) (1991) *The Hollywood Western*. London: British Film Institute.

Bushnell, John (1990) *Moscow Graffiti*. Evanston, IL: Northwestern University Press.

Butterfield, Jim and Weigle, Marina (1991) 'Unofficial groups and regime responses in the Soviet Union', in Sedaitis and Butterfield (1991), pp. 175–95.

Calhoun, Craig (1991) 'Tiananmen, television and the public sphere: Internationalization of culture and the Beijing Spring of 1989', *Public Culture*, 2(1): 54–71.

Calhoun, Craig (ed.) (1993) *Habermas and the Public Sphere*. Cambridge, MA: MIT Press.

Carey, James (1975) 'A cultural approach to communication', *Communication*, 2: 1–22.

Carr, E.H. (1952) *The Bolshevik Revolution 1917–1923*, vol. 2. London: Macmillan.

Carragee, Kevin M. (1993) 'A critical evaluation of debates exmining the media hegemony thesis', *Western Journal of Communication*, 57: 330–48.

Cerf, Christopher and Albee, Marina (eds) (1990) *Small Fires: Letters from the Soviet People to Ogonyok Magazine*, 1987–1990. New York: Summit Books.

Cheng, Tun-jen (1989) 'Democratizing the quasi-Leninist regime in Taiwan', *World Politics*, 41: 471–99.

Chirot, Daniel (ed.) (1991a) *The Crisis of Leninism and the Decline of the Left: The Revolutions of 1989*. Seattle: University of Washington Press.

Chirot, Daniel (1991b) 'What happened in Eastern Europe in 1989?', in Chirot (1991a), pp. 3–32.

Cockburn, Andrew (1983) *The Threat*. New York: Random House.

Cohen, Stephen F. (1971) *Bukharin and the Bolshevik Revolution*. New York: Vintage.

Cohen, Stephen F. and vanden Heuvel, Katrina (1989) *Voices of Glasnost: Interviews with Gorbachev's Reformers*. New York: W.W. Norton.

Condee, Nancy (ed.) (1995) *Soviet Hieroglyphics: Visual Culture in Late Twentieth Century Russia*. Bloomington, IN: Indiana University Press.

Condee, Nancy and Padunov, Vladimir (1984–6) *Newsletters*. Institute of Contemporary World Affairs, Dartmouth, New Hampshire.

Condee, Nancy and Padunov, Vladimir (1987) 'The outposts of official art: Recharting Soviet cultural history', *Framework*, 34: 59–106.

Condee, Nancy and Padunov, Vladimir (1991a) 'Makulakul'tura: Reprocessing culture', *October*, 57: 79–103.

Condee, Nancy and Padunov, Vladimir (1991b) 'Perestroika suicide: Not by bred alone', *New Left Review*, 189: 69–91.

Condee, Nancy and Padunov, Vladimir (1994) 'Pair-a-dice lost: The socialist gamble, market determinism, and compulsory postmodernism', *New Formations*, 22: 72–94.

Condee, Nancy and Padunov, Vladimir (1995) 'The ABC of Russian consumer culture: Readings, ratings and real estate', in Condee (ed.) (1995), pp. 130–69.

Corradi, Juan E., Fagen, Patricia Weiss and Garretón, Manuel Antonio (eds) (1992) *Fear at the Edge: State Terror and Resistance in Latin America*. Berkeley, CA: University of California Press.

Coser, Lewis (1956) *The Functions of Social Conflict*. Glencoe, IL: The Free Press.

Crowley, Stephen (1994) 'Barriers to collective action: Steelworkers and mutual dependence in the former Soviet Union', *World Politics*, 46: 589–615.

Csepeli, György (1991) 'Competing patterns of national identity in post-communist Hungary', *Media, Culture & Society*, 13: 325–39.

Cumings, Bruce (1992) *War and Television*. London: Verso.

Curry, Jane Leftwich (1990) *Poland's Journalists: Professionalism and Politics*. New York: Cambridge University Press.

Curry, Jane Leftwich (1993) 'Pluralism in Eastern Europe: Not will it last, but what is it?', *Communist and Post-Communist Studies*, 26: 446–61.

Curtis, Liz (1984) *Ireland: The Propaganda War*. London: Pluto Press.

Dallin, Alexander (1992) 'Causes of the collapse of the USSR', *Post-Soviet Affairs*, 8(4): 279–302.

Dalton, Russell L. and Kuechler, Manfred (eds) (1990) *Challenging the Political Order: New Social and Political Movements in Western Democracies*. New York: Cambridge University Press.

Davies, R. W. (1989) *Soviet History in the Gorbachev Revolution*. Bloomington, IN: Indiana University Press.

DeFleur, Melvin and Ball-Rokeach, Sandra (1982) *Theories of Mass Communication*, 4th edn. New York: Longman.

DeFleur, Melvin and Ball-Rokeach, Sandra (1990) *Theories of Mass Communication*, 5th edn. New York: Longman.

Delpeuch, Thierry (1995) 'Les aspects institutionnels de la transition vers la démocratie en Europe centrale et orientale', *La Nouvelle Alternative*, 40: 51–3.

Demac, Donna (1990) *Liberty Denied: The Current Rise of Censorship in America*. New Brunswick, NJ: Rutgers University Press.

Demszky, Gabor (1988) 'Un éditeur de samizdat: nous intéressons plus', *La Nouvelle Alternative*, 9: 6–7.

Di Leo, Rita (ed.) (1973) *Operai e fabbrica in Unione Sovietica*. Bari, Italy: De Donato.

Di Palma, Giuseppe (1990) *To Craft Democracies: An Essay on Democratic Transitions*. Berkeley, CA: University of California Press.

Di Palma, Giuseppe (1991) 'Legitimation from the top to civil society: Politico-cultural change in Eastern Europe', *World Politics*, 44: 49–80.

Doder, Dusko (1986) *Shadows and Whispers: Power Politics Inside the Kremlin from Brezhnev to Gorbachev*. New York: Penguin.

Donner, Frank J. (1980) *The Age of Surveillance: Aims and Methods of America's Political Intelligence System*. New York: Knopf.

Dowmunt, Tony (ed.) (1993) *Channels of Resistance: Global Television and Local Empowerment*. London: British Film Institute Press.

Downing, John (1984/1996) *Radical Media: The Political Experience of Alternative Communication*. Boston, MA: South End Press. (Revised edition forthcoming 1996, titled *Alternative Media and Political Movements*, Thousand Oaks, CA: Sage.)

Downing, John (1985) 'The Intersputnik system and Soviet television', *Soviet Studies*, XXXVII(4): 465–83.

Downing, John (1986) 'Government secrecy and the media in the United States and Britain', in Peter Golding, Graham Murdock and Philip Schlesinger (eds), *Communicating Politics: Mass Communication and the Political Process*. New York: Holmes and Meier. pp. 153–76.

Downing, John (1988a) 'An alternative public sphere: The organization of the 1980s antinuclear press in West Germany and Britain', *Media, Culture & Society*, 10(2): 163–81.

Downing, John (1988b) 'Trouble in the backyard: Soviet media reporting on the Afghanistan conflict', *Journal of Communication*, 38(2): 5–32.

Downing, John (1989) 'International communications and the Second World: Developments in communication strategies', *European Journal of Communication*, 4(1): 117–37.

Drweski, Bruno (1992) 'Un nouveau souffle?', *La Nouvelle Alternative*, 25: 22–3.

Drweski, Bruno (1995a) 'Chanter sur tout ce qui bouge', *La Nouvelle Alternative*, 37: 59–62.

Drweski, Bruno (1995b) 'Que sont les communistes devenus? Le cas polonais', *La Nouvelle Alternative*, 38: 7–11.

Dunham, Vera S. (1976) *In Stalin's Time*. New York: Oxford University Press.

Dunlop, John (1992) 'KGB subversion of Russian Orthodox Church', *RFE/RL Research Report*, 1.12, 20 March, 51–3.

Dzirkals, Lilita, Gustafson, Thane and Johnson, A. Ross (1982) *The Media and Intra-Elite Communication in the Soviet Union*. Santa Monica, CA: Rand.

Easton, David (1965) *A Systems Analysis of Political Life*. New York: Wiley.

Easton, Paul (1989) 'The rock music community', in Riordan (1989), pp. 45–82.

Eisen, Jonathan (ed.) (1990) *The Glasnost Reader*. New York: Plume.

Elliott, Philip (1972) *The Framework of Television Production*. London: Constable.

Elliott, Philip (1975) 'Uses and gratifications research: A critique and a sociological alternative', in Jay Blumler and Elihu Katz (eds), *The Uses of Mass Communication: Current Perspectives on Gratifications Research*. Newbury Park, CA: Sage. pp. 249–68.

Enzensberger, Hans-Magnus (1974) *The Consciousness Industry*. New York: Seabury Press.

Éscobar, Arturo and Álvarez, Sonia E. (eds) (1992) *The Making of Social Movements in Latin America: Identity, Strategy, and Democracy*. Boulder, CO: Westview Press.

Ettema, James S., Protess, David C. and Leff, Donna R. (1991) 'Agenda-setting as politics: A case-study of the Press–Public Policy connection', *Communication*, 12: 75–98.

Evans, Peter, Rueschemeyer, Dietrich and Skocpol, Theda (eds) (1985) *Bringing the State Back In*. Cambridge: Cambridge University Press.

Eyal, Jonathan (1992) 'Military relations', *Pravda* (1992a) 35–72.

Fabris, Hans Heinz (1995) 'Westification?', in Paletz, Jakubowicz and Novosel (1995), pp. 221–31.

Featherstone, Mike (ed.) (1990) *Global Culture: Nationalism, Globalization and Modernity*. London: Sage.

Feffer, John (1992) *Shock Waves: Eastern Europe after the Revolutions*. Boston, MA: South End Press.

Femia, Joseph (1981) *Gramsci's Political Thought: Hegemony, Consciousness, and the Revolutionary Process*. Oxford: Clarendon Press.

Fenton, Tom (1994) *Quiet Revolution: Cable Television Comes to Central Europe*. New York: Freedom Forum Media Studies Center, Special Report Series.

Ferguson, Marjorie (1992) 'The mythology about globalisation', *European Journal of Communication*, 7: 69–93.

Ferguson, M. and Golding, P. (eds) (forthcoming) *Beyond Cultural Studies*. London: Sage.

Feshbach, Murray and Friendly, Alfred (1992) *Ecocide in the USSR: Health and Nature under Siege*. New York: Basic Books.

Fireside, Harvey (1979) *Soviet Psychoprisons*. New York: W.W. Norton.

Fiske, John (1987) *Television Culture*. New York: Routledge.

Forgacs, David (1988) *An Antonio Gramsci Reader: Selected Writings 1916–1935*. London: Lawrence and Wishart.

Foster, Frances (1993) 'Izvestiia as a mirror of Russian legal reform: Press, law, and crisis in the post-Soviet era', *Vanderbilt Journal of Transnational Law*, 26(4): 675–747.

Foster, Frances (1994a) 'Free press: Some cautionary notes', *Post-Soviet Media Law and Policy Newsletter*, I(5): 12.

Foster, Frances (1994b) 'The MMM case: Implications for the Russian media', *Post-Soviet Media Law and Policy Newsletter*, 10: 2–3.

Fox, Elizabeth, (ed.) (1988) *Media and Politics in Latin America: The Struggle for Democracy*. Thousand Oaks, CA: Sage.

Fraser, Nancy (1993) 'Rethinking the public sphere: A contribution to the critique of actually existing democracy', in Calhoun (1993), pp. 109–42.

Frentzel-Zagorska, Janina (1990) 'Civil society in Poland and Hungary', *Soviet Studies*, 42(4): 759–77.

Friedrich, Carl J. and Brzezinski, Zbigniew (1966) *Totalitarian Dictatorship and Autocracy*, 2nd edn. New York: Praeger.

Frybes, Marcin (1992) 'Les médias d'Europe centrale dans la transition vers une économie de marché', *MédiasPouvoirs*, 26: 120–6.

Gabor, György, (1993) 'Bref historique de la naissance de la première radio commerciale en Europe de l'Est', in Autissier and Mattelart (1993), pp. 108–11.

Gandy, Oscar H. Jr (1991) 'Beyond agenda-setting', in Protess and McCombs (1991), pp. 263–75.

Gandy, Oscar H. Jr (1993) *The Panoptic Sort: A Political Economy of Personal Information*. Boulder, CO: Westview Press.

Ganley, Gladys (1996) *Unglued Empire: The Soviet Experience with Communications Technologies*. Norwood, NJ: Ablex Publishing.

Gans, Herbert (1979) *Deciding What's News*. New York: Vintage.

Gardawski, Juliusz and Zukowski, Tomasz (1993) 'What the Polish workers think', *Labour Focus on Eastern Europe*, 46: 35–8.

Garnham, Nicholas (1993a) 'The media and the public sphere', in Calhoun (1993), pp. 359–76.

Garnham, Nicholas (1993b) 'The mass media, cultural identity, and the public sphere in the modern world', *Public Culture*, 5(2): 251–65.

Gerbner, George (1984) 'Political functions of television viewing: A cultivation analysis', in Melischek (1984), pp. 329–43.

Gerbner, George (1986) 'The symbolic context of action and communication', in Ralph L. Rosnow and Marianthi Georgoudi (eds), *Contextualism and Understanding in Behavioral Science: Implications for Theory and Research*. New York: Praeger. pp. 251–68.

Giddens, Anthony (1981) *A Contemporary Critique of Historical Materialism*. Berkeley, CA: The University of California Press.

Giddens, Anthony (1984) *The Constitution of Society: An Outline of the Theory of Structuration*. Berkeley, CA: The University of California Press.

Gigli, Susan and Warshaw, Matthew (1995) 'Wary trust in Russia's media', *Transition* (28 July 1995), 51–3.

Giorgi, Liana (1995) *The Post-Socialist Media: What Power the West?* Brookfield: Ashgate.

Gitlin, Todd (1981) *The Whole World is Watching: Mass Media in the Making and Un-Making of the New Left*. Berkeley, CA: University of California Press.

Gitlin, Todd (1983) *Inside Prime Time*. New York: Pantheon.

Goban-Klas, Tomasz (1994) *The Orchestration of the Media: The Politics of Mass Communications in Communist Poland and the Aftermath*. Boulder, CO: Westview Press.

Goble, Paul A. (1991) 'Nationalisms, movement groups and party formation', in Sedaitis and Butterfield (1991), pp. 165–74.

Goldfarb, Jeffrey (1981) *The Persistence of Freedom: The Sociological Implications of Polish Student Theater*. Boulder, CO: Westview Press.

Goldfarb, Jeffrey (1989) *Beyond Glasnost: The Post-Totalitarian Mind*. Chicago: University of Chicago Press.

Goodwyn, Lawrence (1991) *Breaking the Barrier: The Rise of Solidarity in Poland*. New York: Oxford University Press.

Gradvohl, Paul (1990) 'Cela vaut-il la peine d'oser se dire de gauche?', *La Nouvelle Alternative*, 19: 17.

Gradvohl, Paul (1995) 'Le complot nomenklatouriste: Un miroir aux alouettes', *La Nouvelle Alternative*, 38: 5–7.

Gramsci, Antonio (1971) *Selections from the Prison Notebooks*, edited by Quintin Hoare and Geoffrey Nowell-Smith. London: Lawrence and Wishart.

Graziano, Luigi (1993) 'Pluralism in comparative perspective: Notes on the European and American traditions', *Communist and Post-Communist Studies*, 26: 341–51.

Gregory, Paul (1987) 'Productivity, slack and time theft in the Soviet economy', in James Millar (1987), pp. 141–75.

Gregory, Paul (1991) 'The impact of perestroika on the Soviet planned economy: Results of a survey of Moscow economic officials', *Soviet Studies*, 43: 859–73.

Gregory, Paul and Dietz, Barbara (1991) 'Soviet perceptions of economic conditions during the period of stagnation: Evidence from two diverse emigrant surveys', *Soviet Studies*, 43: 535–51.

Grigorenko, Petro (1982) *Memoirs*. New York: W.W. Norton.

Grilli Di Cortona, Pietro (1991) 'From communism to democracy: Rethinking regime change in Hungary and Czechoslovakia', *International Social Science Journal*, 128: 315–30.

Gross, Natalie (1990) 'Youth and the Army in the USSR in the 1980s', *Soviet Studies*, 42: 481–98.

Grossberg, Lawrence (1992) *We Gotta Get Out of This Place: Popular Conservatism and Postmodern Culture*. New York: Routledge.

Grossberg, Lawrence, Nelson, Cary and Treichler, Paula (eds) (1992) *Cultural Studies*. New York: Routledge.

Guetta, Bernard (1995) 'Anciens et nouveaux communistes à l'Est', *La Nouvelle Alternative*, 38: 11–14.

Habermas, Jürgen (1984, 1987) *The Theory of Communicative Action*, vols 1 and 2. Boston, MA: Beacon Press.

Habermas, Jürgen (1962/1989) *Strukturwandel der Öffentlichkeit*. Neuwied, Luchterhand/*The Structural Transformation of the Public Realm*. Boston, MA: Beacon Press.

Habermas, Jürgen (1993) 'Further reflections on the public sphere', in Calhoun (1993), pp. 421–61.

Halamska, Maria (1992) 'Ville-campagnes: Regards croisés', *La Nouvelle Alternative*, 25: 25–6.

Hall, Stuart (1986) 'Gramsci's relevance for the study of race and ethnicity', *Journal of Communication Inquiry*, 10(2): 5–27.

Hall, Stuart and Grossberg, Lawrence (1986) 'On postmodernism and articulation: An interview with Stuart Hall', *Journal of Communication Inquiry*, 10(2): 45–60.

Hall, Stuart, Hobson, Dorothy, Lowe, Andrew and Willis, Paul (eds) (1980) *Culture, Media, Language*. London: Hutchinson.

Hall, Stuart, Clarke, J., Critcher, C., Jefferson, T. and Roberts, B. (1978) *Policing the Crisis*. London: Macmillan.

Halperin, Charles J. (1985) *Russia and the Golden Horde: The Mongol Impact on Medieval Russian History*. Bloomington, IN: Indiana University Press.

Hanchard, Michael (1994) *Orpheus and Power: The Movimento Negro of Rio de Janeiro and São Paulo, Brazil, 1945–1988*. Princeton, NJ: Princeton University Press.

Hanchard, Michael (1995) 'Black Cinderella? Race and the public sphere in Brazil', *Public Culture*, 15: 165–85.

Hankiss, Elemér (1994) 'The Hungarian media's war of independence: A Stevenson Lecture, 1992', *Media, Culture and Society*, 16: 293–312.

Hansen, Miriam (1993) 'Unstable mixtures, dilated spheres', *Public Culture*, 5(2): 179–212.

Hárászti, Miklos (1979) *Opposition = 0.1%: extraits du samizdat Hongrois*. Paris: Éditions du Seuil.

Hárászti, Miklos (1987) *The Velvet Prison*. New York: Basic Books.

Harris, David (1992) *From Class Struggle to the Politics of Pleasure: The Effects of Gramscianism on Cultural Studies*. London: Routledge.

Hart, Roderick and Downing, John (1992) 'Is there an American public?', *Critical Studies in Mass Communication*, 9(2): 201–15.

Hayles, N. Katherine (ed.) (1991) *Chaos and Order: Complex Dynamics in Literature and Science*. Chicago: University of Chicago Press.

Held, Joseph (ed.) (1992) *The Columbia History of Eastern Europe in the Twentieth Century*. New York: Columbia University Press.

Held, Joseph and Hanák, Péter (1992) 'Hungary on a fixed course: An outline of Hungarian history', in Held (1992), pp. 164–228.

Heller, Mikhail and Nekrich, Aleksandr M. (1986) *Utopia in Power: The History of the Soviet Union from 1917 to the Present*. New York: Summit Books.

Helsinki Watch (1986) *Reinventing Civil Society: Poland's Quiet Revolution, 1981–86*. New York: Helsinki Watch Committee.

Helsinki Watch (1987) *From Below: Independent Peace and Environmental Movements in Eastern Europe and the USSR*. New York: Helsinki Watch Committee.

Helsinki Watch (1990) *Nyeformaly: Civil Society in the USSR*. New York: Helsinki Watch Committee.

Herman, Edward (1995) 'Media in the US political economy', in John Downing, Ali Mohammadi, Annabelle Sreberny-Mohammadi (eds), *Questioning the Media: A Critical Introduction*. Thousand Oaks, CA: Sage. pp. 77–93.

Herman, Edward and Chomsky, Noam (1988) *The Manufacture of Consent: The Political Economy of the Mass Media*. New York: Pantheon.

Hewitt, Ed A. and Winston, Victor H. (eds) (1991) *Milestones in Glasnost and Perestroyka: Politics and People*. Washington, DC: The Brookings Institute.

Hockenos, Paul (1993) *Free to Hate: The Rise of the Right in Post-Communist Eastern Europe*. New York: Routledge.

Hoffman, Eva (1993) *Exit into History: A Journey Through the New Eastern Europe*. New York: Viking.

Hollander, Gayle Durham (1972) *Soviet Political Indoctrination: Developments in Mass Media and Propaganda since Stalin*. New York: Praeger.

Holquist, Michael (1981) 'Introduction', Mikhail M. Bakhtin, *The Dialogic Imagination: Four Essays*. Austin, TX: The Univerrsity of Texas Press, pp. xv–xxxiii.

Hopkins, Mark W. (1970) *Mass Media in the Soviet Union*. New York: Pegasus.

Hopkins, Mark W. (1983) *Russia's Underground Press*. New York: Praeger.

Horkheimer, Max (1986) 'Art and mass culture', in *Critical Theory: Selected Essays*. New York: Continuum. pp. 273–90.

Horkheimer, Max and Adorno, Theodor W. (1987a) 'The Culture Industry: Enlightenment as mass deception', in *Dialectic of Enlightenment*. New York: Continuum. pp. 120–67.

Horkheimer, Max and Adorno, Theodor W. (1987b) 'Elements of anti-semitism: The limits of enlightenment', in *Dialectic of Enlightenment*. New York: Continuum. pp. 168–208.

Hosking, Geoffrey (1985) *The First Socialist Society: A History of the Soviet Union from Within*. Cambridge, MA: Harvard University Press.

Hough, Jerry (1977) *The Soviet Union and Social Science Theory*. Cambridge, MA: Harvard University Press.

Høyer, Svennik, Lauk, Epp and Vihalemm, Peeter (eds) (1993) *Towards a Civil Society: The Baltic Media's Long Road to Freedom – Perspectives on History, Ethnicity and Journalism*. Tartu, Estonia: Baltic Association for Media Research/Nota Baltica.

Huelle, Pavel (1992) 'Un vide sociologique à combler', *La Nouvelle Alternative*, 27: 17–19.

Hughes, James (1994) 'Regionalism in Russia: The rise and fall of Siberian Agreement', *Europe-Asia Studies*, 46(7): 33–61.

Jakab, Zoltan and Gálik, Mihaly (1991) *Survival, Efficiency and Independence: The Presence of Foreign Capital in the Hungarian Media Market*. Manchester: European Institute for the Media.

Jakubowicz, Karol (1990) 'Musical chairs? The three public spheres of Poland', *Media, Culture and Society*, 12: 195–212.

Jakubowicz, Karol (1992a) 'Media and the terminal crisis of communism in Poland', in Raboy and Dagenais (1992), pp. 79–93.

Jakubowicz, Karol (1992b) 'From Party propaganda to corporate speech? Polish journalism in search of a new identity', *Journal of Communication*, 42(3): 64–73.

Jakubowicz, Karol (1993) 'Les programmes de la télévision polonaise: sources, structures et financements', in Autissier and Mattelart (1993), pp. 131–39.

Jakubowicz, Karol (1994) 'Equality for the downtrodden, freedom for the free: Changing perspectives on social communication in Central and Eastern Europe', *Media, Culture and Society*, 16: 271–92.

Jakubowicz, Karol (1995a) 'Poland', in Paletz, Jakubowicz and Novosel (1995), pp. 129–48.

Jakubowicz, Karol (1995b) 'Lovebirds? The media, the state and politics in Central and Eastern Europe', *Javnost/The Public*, II(1): 75–91.

Jameson, Frederic (1993) 'On "Cultural Studies"', *Social Text*, 34: 17–52.

Jancar, Barbara Wolfe (1975) 'Religious dissent in the Soviet Union', in Tökes (1975), pp. 191–230.

Jansen, Sue Curry (1988) *Censorship: The Knot that Binds Power and Knowledge*. New York: Oxford University Press.

Jenkins, Henry (1992) *Textual Poachers: Television Fans and Participatory Culture*. New York: Routledge.

Johnson, Priscilla (1965) *Khrushchev and the Arts: The Politics of Soviet Culture, 1962–1964*. Cambridge, MA: MIT Press.

Kagarlitsky, Boris (1988) *The Thinking Reed: Intellectuals and the Soviet State from 1917 to the Present*. London: Verso.

Kaiser, Robert G. (1991) *Why Gorbachev Happened: His Triumphs and His Failure*. New York: Simon and Schuster.

Kaiser, Susana M. (1993) 'The Madwomen Memory Mothers of the Plaza de Mayo', MA Thesis, Communications Department, Hunter College, City University of New York.

Kaminski, Bartlomiej (1991) 'Systemic underpinnings of the transition in Poland: The shadow of the Round-Table agreement', *Studies in Comparative Communism*, 24: 173–90.

Karklins, Rasma (1994) 'Explaining regime change in the Soviet bloc', *Europe-Asia Studies*, 45(1): 29–45.

Karl, Terry Lynn and Schmitter, Philippe C. (1991) 'Modes of transition in Latin America, Southern and Eastern Europe', *International Social Science Journal*, 128: 269–84.

Karlinsky, Basile (1992) 'Succès commercial de la presse érotique', *MédiasPouvoirs*, 26: 104–9.

Katz, Elihu (1960) 'Communication research and the image of society: Convergence of two research traditions', *American Journal of Sociology*, 65(5): 435–40.

Katznelson, Ira (1990) 'Does the end of totalitarianism signify the end of ideology?', *Social Research*, 57(3): 557–69.

Kellner, Douglas (1992) *The Persian Gulf TV War*. Boulder, CO: Westview Press.

Kende, Pierre (1985) 'Censorship in Hungary', in Zdenek Mlynar (ed.), *Crisis in Soviet-Type Societies 9*. Cologne, Germany. Self-published. pp. 43–54.

Kende, Pierre (1988) 'Le renouveau du paysage politique hongrois', *La Nouvelle Alternative*, 12: 57–9.

Kende, Pierre (1991a) 'L'épuration à la hongroise: un "compromis historique" toujours présent?', *La Nouvelle Alternative*, 21: 14–15.

Kende, Pierre (1991b) '"Embourgeoisement" et avenir hongrois', *Cahiers d'Études Hongroises*, 3: 22–9.

Kenedi, János and Mihancsik, Zsófia (1993) 'The mass media war in Hungary', Unpublished paper.

Kenez, Peter (1985) *The Birth of the Propaganda State: Soviet Methods of Mass Mobilization, 1917–1929*. New York: Cambridge University Press.

Kennedy, Michael P. (1991) *Professional Power and Solidarity in Poland: A Critical Sociology of Soviet-Type Society*. New York: Cambridge University Press.

Kershaw, Ian (1983) *Popular Opinion and Political Dissent in the Third Reich: Bavaria 1933–1945*. Oxford: Clarendon Press.

Keynes, John Maynard (1964) *A General Theory of Employment, Interest and Money*. New York: Harcourt Brace Jovanovich.

Kim, Chie-woon and Lee, Jae-won (eds) (1994) *Elite Media Amidst Mass Culture: A Critical Look at Mass Communication in Korea*. Seoul: NANAM Publishing House.

Kirkpatrick, Jeane (1982) *Dictatorship and Double Standards: Rationalism and Reason in Politics*. New York: Simon and Schuster.

Kis, János (1986) 'Limites et possibilités de l'opposition', *La Nouvelle Alternative*, 1: 37–9.

Klapper, Joseph (1960) *The Effects of Mass Communication*. New York: The Free Press.

Klíma, Ivan (1996) *Waiting for the Dark, Waiting for the Light*. New York: Picador USA.

Knight, Amy (1993) 'Russian security services under Yeltsin', *Post-Soviet Affairs*, 9: 40–65.

Knoespel, Kenneth J. (1991) 'The emplotment of chaos: Instability and narrative order', in Hayles (1991), pp. 100–22.

Kobylinski, Anatol (1989) *Szesc Lat Podziemnej Poczty W Polsce (1982–1988)*. Rapposwil, Switzerland: Muzeum Polskiego (in 5 languages).

Konrád, George (1984) *Antipolitics*. New York: Harcourt Brace Jovanovich.

Konrád, George and Szelényi, Iván (1978) *Intellectuals on the Road to Class Power*. New York: Harcourt Brace Jovanovich.

Köpeczi, Béla (1993) 'Les débats suscités en France par *L'Histoire de la Transylvanie*', *Cahiers d'Études Hongroises*, 5: 191–201.

Kopelev, Lev (1980) *No Jail for Thought*. London: Penguin Books.

Korbonski, Andrzej (1992) 'Poland: 1918–1990', in Held (1992), pp. 229–76.

Kosko, Bart (1993) *Fuzzy Thinking: The New Science of Fuzzy Logic*. New York: Hyperion.

Kováts, Ildikó (1994) 'Difficulties in the process of the democratization of the media in Hungary', Paper presented at the IAMCR Convention in Seoul, Korea.

Kováts, Ildikó and Tölgyesi, Janos (1993) 'On the background of the Hungarian media changes', in Splichal and Kováts (1993), pp. 35–47.

Kováts, Ildikó and Whiting, Gordon (1995) 'Hungary', in Paletz, Jakubowicz and Novosel (1995), pp. 97–127.

Köves, Andras (1992) *Central and East European Economies in Transition*. Boulder, CO: Westview Press.

Kowalski, Tadeusz (1988) 'Evolution after revolution: The Polish press system in transition', *Media, Culture and Society*, 10(2): 183–96.

Król, Marcin (1990) in 'Post-Communist Europe': A survey of opinion. *East European Politics and Society*, 4(2): 153–207.

Kubik, Jan (1994) *The Power of Symbols Against the Symbols of Power*. University Park, PA: State University of Pennsylvania Press.

Kulakowska, Elisabeth (1991) 'Les Polonais paient le prix fort des réformes économiques radicales', *La Nouvelle Alternative*, 23: 4.

Kulakowska, Elisabeth (1992) 'Politique et médias en Pologne', *La Nouvelle Alternative*, 28: 35–6.

Kulakowska, Elisabeth (1994) 'Une presse écrite de moins en moins diversifiée', *Le Monde Diplomatique*, 486: 25.

Kuron, Jacek (1991) 'Aider ceux qui en ont vraiment besoin', *La Nouvelle Alternative*, 23: 5–11.

Kuron, Timur (1991) 'Now out of never: The element of surprise in the East European revolution of 1989', *World Politics*, 44: 7–48.

Laba, Roman (1991) *The Roots of Solidarity: A Political Sociology of Poland's Working Class Democratization*. Princeton, NJ: Princeton University Press.

Laclau, Ernesto (1979) *Politics and Ideology in Marxist Theory: Capitalism-Fascism-Populism*. London: Verso.

Laclau, Ernesto and Mouffe, Chantal (1985) *Hegemony and Socialist Strategy: Towards a Radical Democratic Politics*. London: Verso.

Lampert, Nicholas (1985) *Whistle-Blowing in the Soviet Union: Complaints and Abuses under State Socialism*. London: Macmillan.

Landes, Joan (1988) *Women and the Public Sphere in the Age of the French Revolution.* Ithaca, NY: Cornell University Press.

Landy, Marcia (1986) *Fascism in Film: The Italian Commercial Cinema, 1931–1943.* Princeton, NJ: Princeton University Press.

Laqueur, Walter (1993) *Black Hundred: The Rise of the Extreme Right in Russia.* New York: HarperCollins.

Lawton, Anna (1992) *Kinoglasnost: Soviet Cinema in Our Time.* Cambridge: Cambridge University Press.

Lears, T.J. Jackson (1985) 'The concept of cultural hegemony: Problems and possibilities', *American Historical Review,* 90(3): 567–93.

Lee, Aie-Ree (1993) 'Culture shift and popular protest in South Korea', *Comparative Political Studies,* 26(1): 63–80.

Lee, Benjamin (1993) 'Textuality, mediation, and public discourse', in Calhoun (1993), pp. 402–18.

Lefort, Claude (1986) *The Political Forms of Modern Society: Bureaucracy, Democracy, Totalitarianism.* Cambridge: Polity Press.

Lerner, Daniel (1959) *The Passing of Traditional Society.* New York: The Free Press.

Letowska, Ewa (1992) 'Un amateurisme généralisé', *La Nouvelle Alternative,* 27: 15–18.

Levendel, Adam and Terestenyi, Tamas (1984) 'Some aspects of the relation between politico-social changes and culture: The case of Hungary', in Melischek et al. (1984), pp. 453–60.

Levy, Mark and Windahl, Sven (1985) 'The concept of audience activity', in Rosengren et al. (1985), pp. 109–22.

Lewicka, Ewa (1992) 'Il n'y a plus de politique sociale', *La Nouvelle Alternative,* 24: 46–7.

Lewin, Moshe (1988) *The Gorbachev Phenomenon: An Historical Interpretation.* Berkeley, CA: University of California Press.

Lidtke, Vernon (1985) *The Alternative Culture.* New York: Oxford University Press.

Lipset, Seymour Martin and Bence, György (1994) 'Anticipations of the failure of communism', *Theory and Society,* 23(2): 169–210.

Lipski, Jan Jozef (1985) *KOR: A History of the Workers' Defense Committee.* Berkeley, CA: University of California Press.

Lloréns, José A. (1994) 'Popular radio in Peru: Mass media and collective identity', PhD dissertation, Department of Radio–Television–Film, University of Texas at Austin.

Lochon, Pierre-Yves (1992) 'Fallait-il vraiment se ruer vers l'Est?', *MédiasPouvoirs,* 26: 127–41.

Lomax, Bill (1976) *Hungary 1956.* London: Allison and Busby.

Louw, P. Eric (ed.) (1993a) *South African Media Policy: Debates of the 1990s.* Bellville, South Africa: Anthropos.

Louw, P. Eric (1993b) 'Language and media policy: Exploring the options', *Ecquid Novi,* 14(2): 127–52.

Louw, P. Eric (1994) 'Shifting patterns on political discourse in the New South Africa', *Critical Studies in Mass Communication,* 11: 22–53.

Luczywo, Helena (1992) 'Le journaliste apprend en même temps que le lecteur', *La Nouvelle Alternative,* 28: 37–8.

Lukács, György (1971) 'Class consciousness', in *History and Class Consciousness: Studies in Marxist Dialectics.* London: Merlin Press. pp. 46–82.

Lukács, John (1988) *Budapest: A Historical Portrait of a City and its Culture.* New York: Grove Weidenfeld.

Lunev, Stanislav (1995) 'Russia's new military doctrine', *Prism,* 25, Part I (1 December 1995).

Lynn, Terry Karl and Schmitter, Philippe C. (1991) 'Modes of transition in Latin America, Southern and Eastern Europe', *International Social Science Journal,* 128: 269–84.

Lyu, Han-ho (1994a) 'Internal democratization of media and the Press Union movement: A Korean case since June 1987', Presented to the Political Economy section, IAMCR Conference, Seoul, July 1994.

Lyu, Han-ho (1994b) 'Journalists' participation in media organization for the democratization of communication', Presented to the Working Group on Participatory Communication Research, IAMCR Conference, Seoul, July 1994.

Máckow, Jerzy (1994) 'Der Totalitarismus-Ansatz und der Zusammenbruch des Sowjetsozialismus', *Osteuropa*, 44(4): 320–9.

Magas, Istvan (1990) 'Reforms under pressure: Hungary', *East European Quarterly*, 24(1): 65–100.

Mainwaring, Scott, O'Donnell, Guillermo and Valenzuela, J. Samuel (eds) (1992) *Issues in Democratic Consolidation: The New South American Democracies in Comparative Perspective*. Notre Dame, IN: Notre Dame University Press.

Markwick, Roger D. (1994) 'Catalyst of historiography, Marxism and dissidence: The Sector of Methodology of the Institute of History, Soviet Academy of Sciences, 1964–68', *Europe-Asia Studies*, 46: 579–96.

Martín-Barbero, Jesús (1993) *Communication, Culture and Hegemony: From the Media to Mediations*. Thousand Oaks, CA: Sage.

Mason, David S. (1992) *Revolution in East-Central Europe: The Rise and Fall of Communism and the Cold War*. Boulder, CO: Westview Press.

Mattelart, Armand and Mattelart, Michèle (1974) *Mass média, idéologies et mouvement révolutionnaire: Chili 1970–73*. Paris: Éditions Anthropos.

Mattelart, Armand and Siegelaub, Seth (eds) (1983) *Communication and Class Struggle*, vol. 2, *Liberation, Socialism*. New York and Bagnolet: IMMRC.

Mattelart, Tristan (1992a) 'Vidéo Est–Ouest avant 1989: divertissement sans frontières', *Réseaux*, 53: 25–40.

Mattelart, Tristan (1992b) 'Télévision Est–Ouest: le temps du divertissement?', *MédiasPouvoirs*, 26: 150–5.

McCombs, Maxwell (1991) 'Agenda-setting', *International Encyclopedia of Communication*, vol. I. New York: Oxford University Press.

McCombs, Maxwell and Shaw, Donald (1972) 'The agenda-setting function of mass media', *Public Opinion Quarterly*, 36: 176–85.

McGregor, James P. (1991) 'Socialism and youth in People's Poland', *East European Quarterly*, 25(2): 207–22.

McGuigan, Jim (1992) *Cultural Populism*. London: Routledge.

McHenry, William K. (1988) 'Computer networks and the Soviet style information society', in Richard F. Staar (ed.), *The Future Information Revolution in the USSR*. New York: Crane Research. pp. 85–113.

McNair, Brian (1991) *Glasnost, Perestroika and the Soviet Media*. London: Routledge.

McNair, Brian (1994) 'Media in post-Soviet Russia: An overview', *European Journal of Communication*, 9: 115–35.

McQuail, Denis (1994) *Mass Communication Theory: An Introduction*, 3rd edn. Newbury Park, CA: Sage.

McReynolds, Louise (1991) *The News under Russia's Old Regime: The Development of a Mass-Circulation Press*. Princeton, NJ: Princeton University Press.

Melischek, Gabriele, Rosengren, Karl Erik and Stappers, James (eds) (1984) *Cultural Indicators: An International Symposium*. Veröffentlichungen des Instituts für Publikumsforschung 8. Vienna: Verlag der Österreichischen Akademie der Wissenschaften.

Melucci, Alberto (1989) *Nomads of the Present: Social Movements and Individual Needs in Contemporary Society*. London: Hutchinson Radius.

Melville, Andrei and Lapidus, Gail (1990) *The Glasnost Papers*. Boulder, CO: Westview Press.

Merrett, Christopher and Gravil, Roger (1991) 'Comparing human rights: South Africa and Argentina, 1976–1989', *Comparative Studies in Society and History*, 33: 255–87.

Mickiewicz, Ellen Propper (1981) *Media and the Russian Public*. New York: Praeger.

Mickiewicz, Ellen Propper (1988) *Split Signals: Television and Politics in the Soviet Union*. New York: Oxford University Press.

Migranyan, Andronik (1991) 'Gorbachev's leadership: A Soviet view', in Hewitt and Winston (1991), pp. 460–4.

Mihalisko, Kathleen (1995) 'Yeltsin outlines strategy for a renewed superpower', *Prism*, 21, Part I (6 October 1995).

Millar, James (ed.) (1987) *Politics, Work and Daily Life in the USSR: A Survey of Former Soviet Citizens.* New York: Cambridge University Press.

Millar, James (1988) 'The Little Deal: Brezhnev's contribution to acquisitive socialism', in Terry L. Thompson and Richard Sheldon (eds), *Soviet Society and Culture: Essays in Honor of Vera S. Dunham.* Boulder CO: Westview Press.

Millar, James and Clayton, Elizabeth (1987) 'Quality of life: Subjective measures of relative satisfaction', in James Millar (1987), pp. 31–57.

Mills, C. Wright (1956) *The Power Elite.* New York: Oxford University Press.

Mische, Ann (1993) 'Post-Communism's "lost treasure": Subjectivity and gender in a shifting public sphere', *Praxis International*, 13: 242–67.

Misztal, Bronislaw (1992) 'Between the state and Solidarity: One movement, two interpretations – the Orange Alternative movement in Poland', *British Journal of Sociology*, 43: 55–78.

Mitchell, Timothy (1991) 'The limits of the state: Beyond statist approaches and their critics', *American Political Science Review*, 85: 77–96.

Molnár, Miklós (1990) *La Démocratie se lève à l'Est: société civile et communisme en Europe de l'Est: Pologne et Hongrie.* Paris: Presses Universitaires Françaises.

Molotch, Harvey L., Protess, D.L. and Gordon, M.T. (1987) 'The media-policy connection: Ecologies of news', in David L. Paletz (ed.), *Political Communication Research.* Norwood, NJ: Ablex. pp. 26–48.

Mond, Georges (1992) 'L'évolution des cadres législatifs', *MédiasPouvoirs*, 26: 72–83.

Moore, Wilbert and Tumin, Melvin (1949) 'Some social functions of ignorance', *American Sociological Review*, 14: 787–95.

Morgan, Michael (1990) 'International cultivation analysis', in Signorielli and Morgan (1990), pp. 225–48.

Motyl, Alexander J. (ed.) (1992) *Thinking Theoretically about Soviet Nationalities: History and Comparison in the Study of the USSR.* New York: Columbia University Press.

Naskowska, Krystyna (1992) 'Les plus pauvres doivent changer de métier', *La Nouvelle Alternative*, 25: 23–5.

Negt, Oskar and Kluge, Alexander (1972) *Öffentlichkeit und Erfahrung.* Frankfurt-am-Maine: Suhrkamp Verlag.

Nove, Alec (1987) *An Economic History of the USSR*, 2nd edn. New York: Penguin.

Nove, Alec (1989) *Glasnost in Action.* Boston, MA: Unwin Hyman.

Novikov, Evgueni (1996) 'Drugs from Afghanistan and Central Asia and the war in Chechnya', *Prism*, Part 3, 26 January 1996.

O'Donnell, Guillermo (1992a) 'Transitions, continuities, and paradoxes', in Mainwaring et al. (1992), pp. 17–56.

O'Donnell, Guillermo (1992b) 'Delegative democracy?', Working Paper 172, Kellogg Institute. Bloomington, IN: University of Notre Dame.

O'Donnell, Guillermo (1993) 'On the state, democratization and some conceptual problems', Working Paper 192, Kellogg Institute. Bloomington, IN: University of Notre Dame.

O'Donnell, Guillermo, Schmitter, Philippe C. and Whitehead, Lawrence (eds) (1986) *Transitions from Authoritarian Rule: Comparative Perspectives.* Baltimore, MD: Johns Hopkins University Press.

Ogarkov, Dmitri (1982) 'Toujours prêt à défendre la patrie', *Stratégique*, 30: 7–75.

Oltay, Edith (1992) 'Hungary', *RFE/RL Research Report*, 1.39, 2 October 1992, 39–43.

Orechkine, Dmitri (1993) 'L'écologie, reflet du pouvoir', *La Nouvelle Alternative*, 29: 13–15.

Ost, David (1990) *Solidarity and the Politics of Anti-Politics: Opposition and Reform in Poland since 1968.* Philadelphia, PA: Temple University Press.

Paletz, David, Jakubowicz, Karol and Novosel, Pavao (eds) (1995) *Glasnost and After: Media and Change in Central and Eastern Europe.* Cresskill, NJ: Hampton Press.

Palmgreen, Philip (1985) 'Uses and gratifications research: The past ten years', in Rosengren et al. (1985), pp. 11–37.

Palmgreen, Philip and Rayburn, J.D, II (1985) 'An expectancy-value approach to media gratifications', in Rosengren et al. (1985), pp. 61–72.

Parsons, Talcott (1951) *The Social System*. Glencoe, IL: The Free Press.

Parsons, Talcott and White, Winston (1969) 'The mass media and the structure of American society', in Talcott Parsons, *Politics and Social Structure*. New York: The Free Press. pp. 241–51.

Partos, Gabriel (1992) 'Hungarian-Soviet relations', in Pravda (1992a), pp. 120–50.

Passerini, Luisa (1987) *Fascism in Popular Memory: The Cultural Experience of the Turin Working Class*. Cambridge: Cambridge University Press.

Pataki, Judith (1993) 'Power struggle over broadcasting in Hungary', *RFE/RL Research Report*, 2.11, 12 March 1993, 16–20.

Pataki, Judith (1994a) 'Hungarian radio staff cuts cause uproar', *RFE/RL Research Report*, 3.19, 13 May 1994, 38–43.

Pataki, Judith (1994b) 'Controversy over Hungary's new media heads', *RFE/RL Research Report*, 3.31, 12 August 1994, 14–17.

Patynski, Wladyslaw (1991) 'Une tentative de mobilisation sociale autonome en Pologne: le comité de défense des chômeurs', *La Nouvelle Alternative*, 23: 16–18.

Pilkington, Hilary (1994) *Russia's Youth and its Culture: A Nation's Constructors and Constructed*. London: Routledge.

Pittman, Riita H. (1990) 'Perestroika and Soviet cultural politics: The case of the major literary journals', *Soviet Studies*, 42: 111–32.

Plyushch, Leonid (1979) *History's Carnival: A Dissident's Autobiography*. New York: Harcourt Brace Jovanovich.

Portelli, Hugues (1974) *Gramsci et la question religieuse*. Paris: Éditions Anthropos.

Postone, Moishe (1993) 'Political theory and historical analysis', in Calhoun (1993), pp. 164–77.

Poulantzas, Nicos (1974) *Fascism and Dictatorship: The Third International and the Problem of Fascism*. London: New Left Books.

Pravda, Alex (ed.) (1992a) *The End of the Outer Empire: Soviet-East European Relations in Transition, 1985–90*. London: Royal Institute for International Affairs/Sage.

Pravda, Alex (1992b) 'Soviet policy towards Eastern Europe in transition: The means justify the ends', in Pravda (1992a), pp. 1–34.

Price, Monroe, E. (1996) *Television, the Public Sphere, and National Identity*. New York: Oxford University Press.

Protess, David and McCombs, Maxwell (eds) (1991) *Agenda-Setting: Readings on Media, Public Opinion and Policy-Making*. Hillsdale, NJ: Lawrence Erlbaum.

Przeworski, Adam (1992) 'The games of transition', in Mainwaring et al. (1992), pp. 105–52.

Putnam, Robert D. (1993) *Making Democracy Work: Civic Traditions in Modern Italy*. Princeton, NJ: Princeton University Press.

Raboy, Marc (1984) *Movements and Messages: Media and Radical Politics in Québec*. Toronto: Between The Lines.

Raboy, Marc (1992) 'Media and the invisible crisis of everyday life', in Raboy and Dagenais (1992), pp. 133–43.

Raboy, Marc and Dagenais, Bernard (eds) (1992) *Media, Crisis and Democracy: Mass Communication and the Disruption of Social Order*. London: Sage.

Radvanyi, Jean (1982) *Le Géant aux paradoxes: fondements géographiques de la puissance soviétique*. Paris: Messidor/Éditions Sociales.

Radway, Clarice A. (1984) *Reading the Romance: Women, Patriarchy and Popular Literature*. Chapel Hill, NC: University of North Carolina Press.

Rahr, Alexander (1992) 'The KGB survives under Yeltsin's wing', *RFE/RL Research Report*, 1.13, 27 March 1992, 1–4.

Rahr, Alexander (1993) 'Kryuchkov, the KGB, and the 1991 putsch', *RFE/RL Research Report*, 2.31, 30 July 1993, 16–23.

Rahr, Alexander (1994) 'Reform of Russia's State security apparatus', *RFE/RL Research Report*, 3.8, 25 February 1994, 19–30.

Rakowska-Harmstone, Teresa (ed.) (1984) *Communism in Eastern Europe*, 2nd edn. Bloomington, IN: Indiana University Press.

Ramet, Sabrina P. (1991) *Social Currents in Eastern Europe*. Durham, NC: Duke University Press.

Rau, Zbigniew (ed.) (1991) *The Reemergence of Civil Society in Eastern Europe and the Soviet Union*. Boulder, CO: Westview Press.

Ray, Larry J. (1993) *Rethinking Critical Theory: Emancipation in the Age of Global Social Movements*. London: Sage.

Rêgo, Cacilda (1993) 'On readers and texts: Tracking the routes of cultural studies', in José Marques de Melo (ed.), *Communication for a New World: Brazilian Perspectives*. São Paulo: School of Communication and Fine Arts, Universidade de São Paulo. pp. 87–108.

Reidy, David A. Jr (1992) 'Eastern Europe, civil society and the real revolution', *Praxis International*, 12: 168–80.

Remington, Thomas F. (1988) *The Truth of Authority*. Pittsburgh, PA: University of Pittsburgh Press.

Remington, Thomas F. (1990) 'Regime transition in Communist systems: The Soviet case', *Soviet Economy*, 6(2): 160–90.

Remmer, Alexander (1989) 'A note on post-publication censorship in Poland 1980–87', *Soviet Studies*, 41(3): 415–25.

Remnick, David (1993) *Lenin's Tomb: The Last Days of the Soviet Empire*. New York: Random House.

Remnick, David (1995) 'The tycoon and the Kremlin', *The New Yorker*, 20–27 February, 118–39.

Revuz, Christine (ed.) (1980) *Ivan Ivanovitch écrit à la Pravda*. Paris: Éditions Sociales.

Riordan, James (ed.) (1989) *Soviet Youth Culture*. Bloomington, IN: Indiana University Press.

Robertson, Roland (1992) *Globalization: Social Theory and Global Culture*. London: Sage.

Rochon, Thomas (1990) 'The West European peace movement and the theory of new social movements', in Dalton and Kuechler (1990), pp. 105–21.

Roe, Sarah (1995) 'IMF approves package to help stabilize Hungary', *Central European Business Week*, 24–30 March, p. 8.

Rogers, Everett M. (1962) *Diffusion of Innovations*. Glencoe, IL: The Free Press.

Rogin, Michael Paul (1987) *Ronald Reagan, the Movie and Other Episodes in Political Demonology*. Berkeley, CA: University of California Press.

Rosenberg, Tina (1995) *The Haunted Land: Facing Europe's Ghosts after Communism*. New York: Random House.

Rosengren, Karl Erik, Wenner, Lawrence A. and Palmgreen, Philip (eds) (1985) *Media Gratifications Research: Current Perspectives*. Newbury Park, CA: Sage.

Rothschild, Joseph (1977) *East Central Europe between the Two World Wars*. Seattle: University of Washington Press.

Ruble, Blair (1983) 'Soviet trade unions and labor relations after "Solidarity"', in Joint Economic Committee of Congress, *Soviet Economy in the 1980s: Problems And Prospects*. Washington, DC: US Government Printing Office. pp. 549–66.

Ruble, Blair (1984) 'Muddling through', in Erik P. Hoffmann and Robbin F. Laird (eds), *The Soviet Polity in the Modern Era*. New York: Aldine. pp. 903–14.

Russett, Cynthia E. (1966) *The Concept of Equilibrium in American Social Thought*. New Haven, CT: Yale University Press.

Rutland, Peter (1991) 'Labor unrest and movements in 1989 and 1990', in Hewitt and Winston (1991), pp. 287–325.

Ryback, Timothy (1989) *Rock Around the Bloc*. New York: Oxford University Press.

Rychard, Andrzej (1992) 'La société civile polonaise se construit là où on ne l'attendait pas', *La Nouvelle Alternative*, 27: 12–15.

Rywkin, Michael (1982) *Moscow's Muslim Challenge: Soviet Central Asia*. Armonk, NY: M.E. Sharpe.

Sabbat-Swidlicka, Anna (1992) 'Poland', *RFE/RL Research Report*, 1.39, 2 October 1992, 47–52.

Sabbat-Swidlicka, Anna (1993) 'Poland', *RFE/RL Research Report*, 2.19, 7 May 1993, 29–30.

Sabbat-Swidlicka, Anna (1994) 'The travails of independent broadcasting in Poland', *RFE/RL Research Report*, 3.10, 11 March 1994, 40–50.

Sanford, George (1992) 'Polish-Soviet relations', in Pravda (1992a), pp. 94–119.

Sapir, Jacques (1990) *L'Économie mobilisée*. Paris: La Découverte.

Scammell, Michael (1984) *Solzhenitsyn: A Biography*. New York: W.W. Norton.

Schell, Orville (1988) *Discos and Democracy: China in the Throes of Reform*. New York: Pantheon.

Schell, Orville (1994) *Mandate of Heaven: A New Generation of Entrepreneurs, Dissidents, Bohemians, and Technocrats Lays Claim to China's Future*. New York: Simon and Schuster.

Schiller, Herbert (1969) *Mass Communications and American Empire*. Chicago: Augustus Kelley.

Schiller, Herbert (1989) *Culture Inc.: The Corporate Takeover of Public Expression*. New York: Oxford University Press.

Schlesinger, Philip (1987) *Putting 'Reality' Together*, 2nd edn. London: Routledge.

Schlesinger, Philip, Elliott, Philip and Murdock, Graham (1983) *Televising 'Terrorism': Political Violence in Popular Culture*. London: Marion Boyars. Comedia Series 16.

Schroeder, Gertrude (1979) 'The Soviet economy on a treadmill of "reforms"', in Joint Economic Committee of Congress, *Soviet Economy in a Time of Change*, vol. 1. Washington, DC: US Government Printing Office. pp. 312–40.

Schroeder, Gertrude (1982) 'Soviet economic "reform" decrees: More steps on the treadmill', in Joint Economic Committee of Congress, *Soviet Economy in the 1980s: Problems and Prospects*, vol. 1. Washington, DC: US Government Printing Office. pp. 65–88.

Schudson, Michael (1993) 'Was there ever a public sphere? If so, when? Reflections on the American case', in Calhoun (1993), pp. 143–63.

Schutz, Alfred (1962) *Collected Papers I*. Amsterdam: Nijhoff.

Schweizer, Peter (1994) *Victory: The Reagan Administration's Secret Strategy that Hastened the Collapse of the Soviet Union*. New York: Atlantic Monthly Press.

Scott, James (1985) *Weapons of the Weak*. New Haven, CT: Yale University Press.

Sedaitis, Judith (1991) 'Worker activism: Politics at the grass roots', in Sedaitis and Butterfield (1991), pp. 13–27.

Sedaitis, Judith and Butterfield, Jim (1991) *Perestroika from Below: Social Movements in the Soviet Union*. Boulder, CO: Westview Press.

Seleny, Anna (1994) 'Constructing the discourse of transformation: Hungary, 1979–82', *East European Politics and Society*, 8(3): 439–66.

Sfez, Lucien (ed.) (1993) *Dictionnaire critique de la communication*. Paris: Presses Universitaires Françaises, 2 volumes.

Shane, Scott (1994) *Dismantling Utopia: How Information Ended the Soviet Union*. Chicago: Ivan R. Dee.

Shanor, Donald (1985) *Behind the Lines*. New York: St Martin's Press.

Sherzer, Dina (ed.) (1996) *Cinema, Colonialism, Post-Colonialism*. Austin, TX: University of Texas Press.

Shlain, Leonard (1991) *Art and Physics: Parallel Visions in Space, Time and Light*. New York: William Morrow.

Shlapentokh, Vladimir (1986) *Soviet Public Opinion and Ideology: Mythology and Pragmatism in Interaction*. New York: Praeger.

Shohat, Ella and Stam, Robert (1994) *Unthinking Eurocentrism: Multiculturalism and the Media*. New York: Routledge.

Showstack Sassoon, Anne (1987) *Gramsci's Politics*, 2nd edn. Minneapolis, MN: University of Minnesota Press.

Siebert, F., Peterson, T. and Schramm, W. (1956) *Four Theories of the Press*. Urbana, IL: University of Illinois Press.

Signorielli, Nancy and Morgan, Michael (eds) (1990) *Cultivation Analysis: New Directions in Media Effects Research*. Newbury Park, CA: Sage.

Silver, Brian D. (1987) 'Political beliefs of the Soviet citizen: Sources of support for regime norms', in Millar (1987), pp. 100–14.

Simpson, Christopher (1994) *Science of Coercion: Communication Research and Psychological Warfare 1945–1960*. New York: Oxford University Press.

Sinyavsky, Andrei (1990) *Soviet Civilization: A Cultural History*. New York: Arcade.

Skidmore, Thomas J. (ed.) (1993) *Television, Politics, and the Transition to Democracy in Latin America*. Baltimore, MD: Johns Hopkins University Press.

Skilling, H. Gordon (1989) *Samizdat and an Independent Society in Central and Eastern Europe*. Columbus, OH: Ohio State University Press.

Slider, Darrell (1991) 'Embattled entrepreneurs: Soviet cooperatives in an unreformed economy', *Soviet Studies*, 43: 797–821.

Smejkalová-Strickland, Jirina (1994) 'Censoring canons: Transitions and prospects of literary institutions in Czechoslovakia', in Richard Burt (ed.), *The Administration of Aesthetics: Censorship, Political Criticism, and the Public Sphere*. Minneapolis, MN: University of Minnesota Press. pp. 195–215.

Smith, Alan (1992) 'Economic relations', in Pravda (1992a), pp. 73–93.

Smith, Denis Mack (1982) *Mussolini: A Biography*. New York: Vintage.

Smith, Gerald Stanton (1984) *Songs to Seven Strings*. Bloomington, IN: Indiana University Press.

Smith, Hedrick (1976) *The Russians*. New York: Quadrangle/New York Times Book Company.

Smolenski, Pawel (1991) *Gazeta Wyborcza: Miroir d'une Démocratie Naissante*. Montirichier, Switzerland: Les Éditions Noir Sur Blanc.

Snider, Paul (1967) 'Mr Gates revisited: A 1966 version of the 1949 case-study', *Journalism Quarterly*, 44: 419–27.

de Sola Pool, Ithiel (1983) *Technologies of Freedom*. Cambridge, MA: Bellknap Press.

Sontag, Susan (ed.) (1982) *A Barthes Reader*. New York: Noonday Press.

Sparks, Colin (forthcoming) *Television and Democracy in Eastern Europe*. London: Sage.

Sparks, Colin and Reading, Anna (1994) 'Understanding media change in East Central Europe', *Media, Culture and Society*, 16: 243–70.

Spechler, Dina (1982) *Permitted Dissent in the USSR: Novy Mir and the Soviet regime*. New York: Praeger.

Splichal, Slavko (1992) 'Le transfert de l'économie de l'information vers l'Europe de l'Est: rêve ou cauchemar?', *Réseaux*, 53: 75–88.

Splichal, Slavko (1994) *Media Beyond Socialism: Theory and Practice in East-Central Europe*. Boulder, CO: Westview Press.

Splichal, Slavko and Kováts, Ildikó (eds) (1993) *Media in Transition: An East–West Dialogue*. Budapest: Ljubljana University and Hungarian Academy of Sciences.

Sreberny-Mohammadi, Annabelle and Mohammadi, Ali (1994) *Small Media, Big Revolution: Communication, Culture, and the Iranian Revolution*. Minneapolis, MN: University of Minnesota Press.

Staniszkis, Jadwiga (1984) *Poland's Self-Limiting Revolution*. Princeton, NJ: Princeton University Press.

Starr, S. Frederick (1983) *Red and Hot: The Fate of Jazz in the Soviet Union 1917–1980*. New York: Oxford University Press.

Starr, S. Frederick (1990) 'New communication technologies and civil society', in Loren R. Graham (ed.), *Science and the Soviet Social Order*. Cambridge, MA: Harvard University Press.

Steele, Jonathan (1994) *Eternal Russia: Yeltsin, Gorbachev, and the Mirage of Democracy*. London: Faber.

Stepan, Alfred (1988) *Rethinking Military Politics: Brazil and the Southern Cone*. Princeton, NJ: Princeton University Press.

Stepan, Alfred (ed.) (1989) *Democratizing Brazil: Problems of Transition and Consolidation*. New York: Oxford University Press.

Stevenson, Nick (1995) *Understanding Media Cultures: Social Theory and Mass Communication*. London: Sage.

Stewart, Ian (1989) *Does God Play Dice? The Mathematics of Chaos*. Cambridge, MA: Blackwells.

Stites, Richard (1992) *Soviet/Russian Popular Culture: Entertainment and Society Since 1900*. New York: Cambridge University Press.

Straubhaar, Joseph (1989) 'Television and video in the transition from military to civilian rule in Brazil', *Latin American Research Review*, 24(1): 140–53.

Sugar, Peter F., Hanák, Péter and Frank, Tibor (1990) *A History of Hungary*. Bloomington, IN: Indiana University Press.

Szabó, Ildikó and Wald, Paul (1992) 'Hongrie: antisémitisme ou anti-assimilationisme?', *La Nouvelle Alternative*, 26: 50–1.

Szekfü, András (1989) 'Intruders welcome? The beginnings of satellite television in Hungary', *European Journal of Communication*, 4: 161–71.

Szekfü, András and Valko, E. (1991) 'Die ungarische Film-, Fernseh- und Videoindustrie im Überblick', *Media Perspektiven*, 2: 111–19.

Tamás, Gaspár Miklós (1991) 'Crise de confiance, minorités et racisme en Hongrie', *La Nouvelle Alternative*, 22: 17.

Tamborini, Ron and Choi, Jeonghwa (1990) 'The role of cultural diversity in cultivation research', in Signorielli and Morgan (1990), pp. 157–80.

Tarrow, Sidney (1989) *Democracy and Disorder: Protest and Politics in Italy, 1965–1975*. Oxford: Clarendon Press.

Teague, Elizabeth (1988) 'Perestroika – the Polish influence', *Survey*, 30(3): 39–58.

Tischner, Jozef (1989) 'La situation de la foi polonaise', *La Nouvelle Alternative*, 15: 7–11.

Tismaneanu, Vladimir (1992) *Reinventing Politics: Eastern Europe from Stalin to Havel*. New York: The Free Press.

Tökés, Rudolf (ed.) (1975) *Dissent in the USSR*. Baltimore, MD: Johns Hopkins University Press.

Tolz, Vera (1990) *The USSR's Emerging Multi-Party System*. New York: Praeger.

Tomaselli, Keyan G. and Louw, P. Eric (1991) *The Alternative Press in South Africa*. Bellville, South Africa: Anthropos.

Tomlinson, John (1992) *Cultural Imperialism*. Baltimore, MD: Johns Hopkins University Press.

Toranska, Teresa (1987) *'Them': Stalin's Polish Puppets*. New York: Harper and Row.

Toth, István János (1991) 'L'entreprise: privée ou publique? Les préférences des Hongrois, selon les sondages', *La Nouvelle Alternative*, 22: 39.

Touraine, Alain (1981) *The Voice and the Eye: An Analysis of Social Movements*. New York: Cambridge University Press.

Tsabria, Dmitrii (1993) 'Free press: Romantic dream?', *Post-Soviet Media Law and Policy Newsletter*, I(2): 12.

Tuchman, Gaye (1978) *Making News: A Study in the Construction of Reality*. New York: The Free Press.

Turner, Bryan S. (1986) 'Parsons and his critics: On the ubiquity of functionalism', in Robert J. Holton and Bryan S. Turner (eds.), *Talcott Parsons on Economy and Society*. London: Routledge and Kegan Paul. pp. 179–206.

Turnley, David and Turnley, Peter (1990) *Moments of Revolution*. New York: Stewart, Tabori and Chang.

Urnov, M.Iu (1991) 'How ready are we for democracy?', *Soviet Review*, 32(4): 3–22.

Vainshtein, Grigory (1994) 'Totalitarian public consciousness in a post-totalitarian society: The Russian case in the general context of post-communist developments', *Communist and Post-Communist Studies*, 27: 247–59.

Van Atta, Don (1989) 'The USSR as a "weak state": Agrarian origins of resistance to perestroika', *World Politics*, 42: 129–49.

Van Zoonen, Liesbet (1994) *Feminist Media Studies*. London: Sage.

Varró, István (1989) 'Hongrie: un tournant décisif ou une amorce de changement?', *La Nouvelle Alternative*, 14: 4–7.

Vatchnadze, Guéorgui (1991) *Les Médias sous Gorbatchev*. Colombes Garenne: Éditions de l'Espace Européen.

Vavrousek, J. (1989) 'Gabcikovo-Nagymaros: l'abandon du projet', *La Nouvelle Alternative*, 15: 53–5.

Viatteau, Michel (1992) 'Pologne: vers une agence moderne et indépendante', *MédiasPouvoirs*, 26: 84–90.

Waisbord, Silvio (1995) 'Leviathan dreams: State and broadcasting in South America', *The Communication Review*, 1(2): 201–26.

Walder, Andrew G. (1994) 'The decline of communist power: Elements of a theory of institutional change', *Theory and Society*, 23(2): 297–323.

Waldrop, M. Mitchell (1992) *Complexity: The Emerging Science at the Edge of Order and Chaos*. New York: Simon and Schuster.

Walker, Martin (1986) *The Waking Giant*. London: Penguin.

Waller, J. Michael (1994) *Secret Empire: The KGB in Russia Today*. Boulder, CO: Westview Press.

Wandycz, Piotr S. (1992) *The Price of Freedom: A History of East Central Europe from the Middle Ages to the Present*. New York: Routledge.

Warner, Michael (1993) 'The mass public and the mass subject', in Calhoun (1993), pp. 377–401.

Warszawski, David (Konstanty Gebert) (1989) 'Une période difficile de transition', *La Nouvelle Alternative*, 14: 7–12.

Warszawski, David (Konstanty Gebert) (1991) 'Élections en Pologne: le risque d'un parlement et d'un gouvernement assez fragiles', *La Nouvelle Alternative*, 23: 53–4.

Weibull, Lennart (1985) 'Structural factors in gratifications research', in Rosengren et al. (1985), pp. 123–47.

Wenner, Lawrence (1985) 'Transaction and media gratifications research', in Rosengren et al. (1985), pp. 73–94.

White, Anne (1990) *De-Stalinization and the House of Culture: Declining State Control over Leisure in the USSR, Poland and Hungary*. London: Routledge.

White, Anne (1995) 'The Memorial Society in the Russian provinces', *Europe–Asia Studies*, 48(8): 1343–66.

White, David Manning (1949) 'The gatekeeper: A case-study in the selection of news', *Journalism Quarterly*, 27: 383–90.

White, Stephen (1979) *Political Culture and Soviet Politics*. London: Macmillan.

Willerton, John (1979) 'Clientilism in the Soviet Union', *Studies in Comparative Communism*, 12: 177–211.

Willerton, John (1987) 'Patronage networks and coalition-building in the Soviet Union', *Soviet Studies*, 39: 175–204.

Williams, Gwyn A. (1960) 'The concept of "Egemonia" in the thought of Antonio Gramsci: Some notes on interpretation', *Journal of the History of Ideas*, 21: 586–99.

Williams, Raymond (1974) *Television: Technology and Cultural Form*. London: Fontana.

Williams, Raymond (1977) *Marxism and Literature*. New York: Oxford University Press.

Williams, Raymond (1980) 'Means of communication as means of production', in *Problems in Materialism and Culture*. London: Verso. pp. 50–63.

Williams, Raymond (1982) *The Sociology of Culture*. New York: Schocken Books.

Williams, Raymond (1983) *The Year 2000*. New York: Schocken Books.

Wishnevsky, Julia (1993) 'Media still far from free', *RFE/RL Research Report*, 2.20: 86–91.

Wishnevsky, Julia (1994) 'The Russian media after the State of Emergency', *RFE/RL Research Report*, 3.6: 1–6.

Wishnevsky, Julia (1995) 'Manipulation, mayhem and murder', *Transition* (15 February): 37–40.

Wober, J. Mallory (1984) 'Prophecy and prophylaxis: Predicted harms and their absence in a regulated television system', in Melischek et al. (1984), pp. 423–39.

Wober, J. Mallory (1990) 'Does television cultivate the British? Late 80s evidence', in Signorielli and Morgan (1990), pp. 207–24.

Wood, Denis (1992) *The Power of Maps*. New York: Guilford Press.

Woodward, Bob (1987) *Veil: The Secret Wars of the CIA*. New York: Simon and Schuster.

X.Y. (Varsovie) (1986) 'La télévision à voix humaine', *La Nouvelle Alternative*, 7: 37–40.

Yasmann, Victor (1992) 'The KGB and internal security', *RFE/RL Research Report*, 1.1: 19–21.

Yasmann, Victor (1993) 'Where has the KGB gone?', *RFE/RL Research Report*, 2.2: 17–20.

Yasmann, Victor (1995a) 'The Russian mafia and the Chechen war', *Prism*, Part 2, 24 June (Jamestown Foundation).

Yasmann, Victor (1995b) 'Does Russia need death squads?', *Prism*, Part 2, 14 July (Jamestown Foundation).

Yasmann, Victor (1995c) 'Murder incorporated, Russian style', *Prism*, Part 1, 11 August (Jamestown Foundation).

Young, Iris Marion (1990) *Justice and the Politics of Difference*. Princeton, NJ: Princeton University Press.

Zawadzki, Paul (1991) 'Entre histoire et politique: la constitution du 3 mai et la construction étatique en Pologne', *La Nouvelle Alternative*, 23: 56–61.

Zelizer, Barbie (1995) 'Reading the past against the grain: The shape of memory studies', *Critical Studies in Mass Communication*, 12(2): 214–40.

Zettner, Steven (1995) 'The Russian Business Press', MA Thesis, Department of Journalism, The University of Texas at Austin.

Zha, Jianying (1995) *China Pop: How Soap Operas, Tabloids and Best Sellers are Transforming a Culture*. New York: The New Press.

Zimmerman, William (1987) 'Mobilized participation and the nature of the Soviet leadership', in James Millar (1987), pp. 332–53.

Zubek, Voytek (1991) 'The Polish Communist elite and the petty entrepreneurs', *East European Quarterly*, 25(3): 339–62.

Index